PORCELAIN

PORCELAIN

MOBY

PENGUIN PRESS | NEW YORK | 2016

CONTENTS

PARKING LOT, 1976

THE FUTURE

All the stores at the Dock mall in Stratford, Connecticut were closed for the night, except for the Fresh-n-Kleen Laundromat. My mom was inside the Laundromat, wearing blue jeans and a brown winter jacket that she'd bought at the Salvation Army for five dollars. She stood at a cracked linoleum counter underneath flickering fluorescent lights, smoking a Winston cigarette and folding clothes. Some of the clothes were ours, and some belonged to our neighbors, who sometimes would pay us to wash and fold their laundry. On this March night the storefronts were dark; the parking lot was empty except for our silver Chevy Vega and one other car. The cold was wet and heavy, and the piles of snow in the corners of the parking lot had turned gray and were melting in the rain.

Every two weeks I'd find myself at the Dock, doing laundry with my mom. I would help her, or just sit on the fiberglass shell chairs in the Laundromat and watch the giant dryers spinning in their fast, lopsided way. My mom had been unemployed for over a year, and her last relationship had ended when her boyfriend tried to stab her to death. Sometimes I would find her crying while she folded the neighbors' clothes. She would be folding furiously, a cigarette lodged in her mouth, tears falling onto the neighbors' T-shirts. I was ten years old.

After helping her sort laundry I would usually go outside and walk around the empty parking lot. I would wander behind the mall, past the loading docks and the rusting Dumpsters, and walk down to the ruined dock that gave the mall its name. The dock was black and burned; at some point it had a purpose, but now it just sat stoic and resigned in the dark Housatonic River. Sometimes, if I was lucky, I'd see giant river rats scurrying in and out of holes in the mud.

This night in March 1976 it was too cold and rainy to go exploring, and the Laundromat was choked with cigarette smoke. And sitting next to the washing machines on the cold fiberglass seats, watching my mom smoke and fold and cry, made our poverty seem even more vicious. So I spent the evening in the car, huddled in my wet thrift-store down jacket, playing with the radio. The rain made a steady drumbeat on the roof of the Vega, and I kept spinning the dial back and forth on the AM radio.

I was indiscriminate when it came to music: if it was played on the radio, I loved it. I assumed that the people playing music on the radio knew exactly what they were doing and wouldn't, under any circumstances, play music that wasn't perfect. Every week I listened to Casey Kasem's *American Top 40* countdown and memorized the songs that he played. I didn't have favorites—I loved them all equally and religiously, from the Eagles to ABBA to Bob Seger to Barry White to Paul McCartney and Wings. I just accepted that all music played on the radio was worthy of my complete and undivided worship.

My damp Wrangler blue jeans were sticking to the vinyl seat of our cold car, but I listened happily to whatever was on the radio. It was the age of disco and rock and country rock and prog rock and yacht rock and ballads. Led Zeppelin coexisted benignly with Donna Summer, and Aerosmith lived peacefully with Elton John. Then I heard something new: "Love Hangover," by Diana Ross. I knew disco music, although I didn't think of it as being particularly different from the other types of music played on AM radio. But "Love Hangover" was different. The opening was languid—otherworldly and seductive—and it scared me.

Anything related to sex or sensuality terrified me and made me want to go watch Looney Tunes cartoons. Whenever I watched TV with my mom and the characters on *Maude* or *The Love Boat* hinted at sex or intimacy I froze and waited silently for the moment to end.

But "Love Hangover" was different. First of all, it was on the radio, so it had to be good. Second of all, it sounded futuristic. I was obsessed with *Star Trek* and *Space: 1999*, and had decided that I loved all things futuristic. The future was clean and interesting, and didn't involve sad parents smoking Winstons in Laundromats. So even though I knew it was about sex, I listened to "Love Hangover" all the way through. It was a futuristic song on the radio, and neither the radio nor the future had ever betrayed me.

I sat watching the blurred lights of the Laundromat through the rain-streaked windshield, gradually accepting that the song made me uncomfortable but that I loved it. It represented a world I didn't know, the opposite of where I was—and I hated where I was. I hated the poverty, the cigarette smoke, the drug use, the embarrassment, the loneliness. And Diana Ross was promising me that there was a world that wasn't stained with sadness and resignation. Somewhere there was a world that was sensual and robotic and hypnotic. And clean.

Sitting in my mother's Chevy Vega, I imagined a gleaming city a lifetime away from the parking lot. I could see people moving confidently through this gleaming city, striding through tall buildings with giant glass windows that looked onto discos and spaceports. As the frenetic disco outro of "Love Hangover" played, I imagined people dancing, all wearing white and looking like robot angels.

The song ended. I turned off the radio. I stepped out of the car into the rain and looked at the parking lot stretching all the way to the river, empty except for melting snow and puddles. Through a plate-glass window, I watched my mom smoking and folding, and somehow I could stand it. There was more to life than this cold, defeated shopping mall. The seed had been planted and was gently encoded somewhere in my DNA. A disco song on AM radio had given me a glimmer of hope:

Someday I would leave these dead suburbs and I would find a city where I could enter a womb. A disco womb where people would let me in and let me listen to their futuristic music. I imagined opening the doors to a disco at the top of the tallest building in the world and seeing a thousand people smiling at me and welcoming me inside.

DIRTY MECCA, 1989–1990

ONE HUNDRED SQUARE FEET

The roosters finally shut up at seven a.m.

There were four recurring sounds around the abandoned factory where I lived, a mile south of the Stamford train station.

1. Gunshots. The crack dealers would regularly shoot at each other, usually starting after the sun went down.
2. Amplified gospel. Every weekend there were big revival tents set up by the nearby storefront Dominican and Jamaican churches, trying to get the crack dealers to leave the neighborhood.
3. Public Enemy. Or EPMD. Or Rob Base and DJ E-Z Rock. Every fifteen minutes, a car would drive by playing "Fight the Power" or "It Takes Two" at toaster-oven-rattling levels.
4. Roosters. Everyone on the street opposite the abandoned factory kept roosters in their backyards. The roosters would start roostering around four thirty a.m., exactly when I was trying to go to bed. I kept an old radio next to my bed and tuned it to a non-station when I needed to sleep. The static just barely masked the dawn staccato stylings of the testosterone-fueled roosters across the street.

I had moved into this abandoned factory two years ago, and I loved it. In the nineteenth century it had been a huge lock factory, comprising twenty or thirty giant brick buildings. Now, in 1989, it was a dark and hulking mass in a neighborhood famous for having the highest murder rate in New England. A decade earlier a real estate developer had bought the whole complex, put up a fence, and hired some security guards to look after it.

A few of the guards made extra money by charging squatters and other random people $50 a month to illicitly live or work in the abandoned factory. I was making about $5,000 a year, so $50 a month for "squatter's rent" was within my budget. My space was small and sandwiched between a gay porn production studio and an artist's loft, but it was all mine: one hundred square feet of abandoned factory where I could live and work as long as the security guards took their $50 and looked the other way.

My walls were built out of discarded plywood that my friend Paul and I found in a Dumpster. Paul and I had gone to Darien High School together, where we had bonded over loving science fiction and being the only poor kids in Darien, Connecticut. The walls of my one-hundred-square-foot loft looked like a brown wooden quilt, and in the summer heat the plywood would smell like the Dumpster where we had found it. My space had a solid, beautiful door that we had rescued from an abandoned house near Route 7 in Norwalk, and the entire floor was covered with thick, beautiful ivory carpeting that I had taken from the garage of a friend's parents. I hadn't gotten permission to take the rug, but I told myself that it was fine because I would give it back if they ever noticed it was missing. I had never cleaned the rug, but it remained improbably pristine.

I had a small, brown school desk for my Casio keyboard, my Alesis drum machine and sequencer, my TASCAM four-track mixer, and a terrible Yamaha sampler. I couldn't afford speakers, so I listened to everything through a pair of Radio Shack headphones. I cooked my meals in a toaster oven and on a single-burner electric hot plate. And I was happy. I loved the crumbling bricks, I loved the olfactory weight of a century of different factory smells, and I loved my huge window that faced south, letting in pale light in the winter and blistering, full-throated sunlight in the summer.

There were approximately one million square feet of space in the factory complex—it was so huge, I had no idea how many other people lived there—and although I took up only one hundred of those square feet myself, I had access to the whole place. I would ride my friend Jamie's motorcycle up and down the empty factory floors, sometimes playing "motorcycle bowling": setting up bottles at one end of a factory floor and trying to knock them down with the motorcycle's wheels. When I was bored, I would go exploring: I'd find old propane canisters, barrels of industrial chemicals, giant rusty wrenches, spools of steel cable, and the occasional dead pigeon.

When friends and family visited me, they were dismayed. My five-year-old cousin Ben, visiting me with my aunt Anne, stood in the doorway to my small space and announced, "This is terrible." I smelled like a homeless person—because although I had a quasi-residence, I was functionally homeless. I didn't have running water or a bathroom or heat, but I had free electricity, which is the one utility I needed to make music.

When I needed to pee, I would use an empty water bottle. With no bathroom, I was bathing only once a week—if I visited my mom's house, or my girlfriend's dorm, I could use the shower there. I usually stank, but I'd stopped offending myself. I loved everything about my life in the abandoned factory.

Well, not everything. I didn't love that I'd been working on music for years and was still in a small city forty miles away from New York. I didn't love that no record label had expressed any interest in my electronic music, or that I had never actually played it for anyone except my girlfriend. But aside from my longing to live and make music in lower Manhattan, the abandoned factory was perfect.

Most days I would wake up in my loft bed around noon, make oatmeal on my hot plate, read the Bible, and work on music. When I wanted a break I would ride my skateboard up and down the long, empty hallways of the factory or walk to the local Dominican bodega, where I could buy oats and raisins.

Today, however, I was headed to New York City, my dirty mecca. There were a few ways to get to New York. Sometimes I would ride my old moped to Darien, where my mom lived, and borrow her aging Chevy Chevette. I would drive into the city, following the route that I learned from my grandfather when I was eight years old: he taught me how to get into the city without paying tolls, though it meant driving through the most crime- and drug-ridden parts of New York.

Sometimes I could find someone who was already driving into the city and get a ride with them. But usually I took Metro-North, a commuter train that connected New York to its suburbs. I spent my childhood fleeing Connecticut for Manhattan via Metro-North. My punk-rock friends and I would all put on our best punk-rock T-shirts and go into the city, hoping that real punk rockers would notice us and approve of our Black Flag and Bad Brains shirts. Heading into Grand Central Terminal in the morning, we'd sit next to sleepy white businessmen; coming home at night we'd sit next to the same white businessmen, who were now drunk and exhausted.

If the police were around when I left the factory I would climb out via one of the huge glass-and-steel windows to avoid the scrutiny of the cops. Today there was only a truck rumbling down the road, so I left by the back door, stepping outside and clenching my body against the cold. It wasn't a dry cold, but a wet cold that made my socks heavy and stabbed my bones. It had snowed three days earlier, covering the ground with a pristine and angelic blanket—quickly ruined by freezing rain. I walked under the gray sky, across the pitted and broken tarmac of the parking lot, picking my way through a maze of puddles. When I got to the chain-link fence, I let myself out through a hole in the corner and headed for the Stamford train station.

Walking to the train station I passed some storefront churches with hand-painted signs, a grocery store with bulletproof Plexiglas and a special on Schlitz malt liquor, the Cavalier Pool Hall, and some shuttered and abandoned buildings. Within a few minutes my hands and feet were already cold. The scattering of locals on the street looked homeless or scared, and they were nonplussed by the badly dressed white kid walking through their neighborhood.

The next train to Grand Central didn't leave for half an hour, so I stopped at the pool hall to play a game by myself. The room was dark, with a few dim lights over the five pool tables. Even low-wattage lighting couldn't conceal that the felt on the tables was scarred and burned from decades of cigarettes and spilled drinks. Aside from me there was one other person playing a midday game of pool, and the guy in the back who rented you your cue and rack of balls for $1.50. I often stopped by the pool hall on my way to the train station, even though I was a mediocre pool player. I consoled myself with the knowledge that if I were any good at pool I'd run the table quickly and not be able to play as long. As with so many things, there was utility in avoiding excellence.

The pool hall was always filled with cigarette smoke. That wasn't surprising—I worked in bars where everyone smoked and went to restaurants where everyone smoked. Even though I was a nonsmoker, and there were only two other human beings inside the pool hall, it seemed normal for the room to be filled with smoke. I never spoke with the other pool players, or the guy handing out cues and racks. I hoped that someday, they would say "How are ya?" or even give me a subtle nod, but they just tolerated me. Apart from me, the only white people around here were suburban kids buying crack and heroin. The irony was that even though I was sober, I was seen as part of the problem: another drug-addicted white kid ruining the neighborhood. Eventually the locals realized that I lived there, and while that didn't get me any friendly nods, at least it stopped the hostile stares.

I finished my game, hoping that if either of the other guys in the pool hall looked at me, they would think that I was a better player than I actually was. On the rare occasions when I sunk a tricky or satisfyingly loud shot, I would glance up to see if anyone had noticed; they never did. As a scrawny white kid I was an anomaly, but not so interesting that I actually warranted much of anybody's attention.

I shrugged on my thrift-shop winter coat, which now smelled like cigarette smoke and wet sheep, and trudged the last few hundred yards to the train station. I passed one of the storefront churches; they were having a service inside. I could hear tambourines, an electric organ, and a choir singing. Sometimes on Sundays, when the churches were in full swing, I would stop in and sit in the back. Or when the weather was nice, and all the churches had their doors open, I would walk down the street and it would sound like a beautiful Tower of Babel, with all of the churches filling the street with perfect competing versions of the gospel. Puerto Rican churches were next to Abyssinian churches, right along-side evangelical and Pentecostal congregations, and whatever other brand of church could justify renting a storefront and buying some plastic folding chairs. If I stood listening in the doorway too long I made the congregation uncomfortable, so I usually stood just to the side of the doorway, listening to the Casio organs and raised voices.

When I got on the train I immediately headed for the bathroom; in high school, I had learned that you could avoid paying the $5 fare if you hid there. I was heading to New York City to drop off a DJ mix cassette at a brand-new nightclub. I'd heard about it from my girlfriend Janet; we'd been dating for a few months. Janet had grown up riding horses in Greenwich, Connecticut, but now lived in the Columbia dorms—she was a sophomore at the university—and had an internship at *Interview* magazine. She looked like Katharine Hepburn circa *The Philadelphia Story*, but her heroes were the writers at *Paper* and the *Village Voice*, and she was obsessed with nightclubs and galleries.

A writer at *Interview* had told Janet that a new nightclub called Mars was hiring and that if I hurried down I could drop off a mix tape. So in the torn pocket of my wet jacket I had a sixty-minute cassette of my best DJ mixes: hip-hop on one side, house music on the other. I had worked on this tape for days, mixing grooves on my four-track cassette recorder and then overdubbing them with a cappella tracks from obscure hip-hop and disco twelve-inch records. I wanted to look less homeless than I usually did, so under my secondhand jacket I was wearing my coolest nightclub outfit: black turtleneck, black jeans, black dress shoes, all from Goodwill and the Salvation Army.

I sat in the bathroom of the Metro-North train for forty-five minutes, inhaling the smell of pee and disinfectant and studying the artwork my friend Jamie had drawn on the cover of my tape. Was it cool enough? Was it cool at all? Jamie had designed a logo for me, all elaborate graffiti swoops and jagged edges. He was an aspiring graffiti artist but he was also a white kid from Norwalk, Connecticut, who studied accounting at UConn. Would anyone else know that? Maybe the logo was cool. I had no idea.

I had started sending similar mix tapes to a radio promoter in California. I'd seen an ad in a DJ magazine: "Wanted: your mix tapes for NATIONAL radio syndication." I'd called the number listed and spoken to a surly man in Oakland, with the sound of a crying baby in the background. He told me that he could get my mixes played on the radio, so I'd been sending him thirty-minute hip-hop mixes. I hadn't received any money for the mixes, nor did he ever tell me if my mixes were being played, but I kept sending the mixes in the hope that someone, somewhere, was listening.

The train pulled into Grand Central; I got out of the bathroom and rushed past the commuters, through the vast space of the station, and into the subway system. Fifteen minutes later, after jumping two subway turnstiles, I was running down Fourteenth Street along the bloody sidewalks of the Meatpacking District. I made it to Mars, breathless with hope and excitement. Mars was a nightclub in an abandoned warehouse, huge and dirty and hulking. A club impresario named Rudolf had rented it with the intention of turning it into the biggest and best nightclub on the planet. Its façade looked out over the West Side Highway, some sex and bondage clubs, and the slate-gray Hudson River. There were no restaurants or bars in the Meatpacking District, but there was a line in front of the club, hundreds of cool New Yorkers hoping to get a job. I stood in line in my black nightclub clothes, hoping that the other people wouldn't notice that I was, in fact, a small and badly dressed white kid who lived in an abandoned factory in Connecticut.

After an hour of waiting I got to the front of the line. In the foyer of the nightclub there were three people sitting behind a big folding table, handing out paperwork. One of them asked, "What application do you want? Busboy, bartender, security?"

"Um, do you have DJ applications?" I asked.

There was a pause, and then they all laughed. "No, we don't have DJ applications," a disconcertingly calm woman behind the table told me. She was a beautiful African-American woman, wearing a long black coat over a weathered New York Dolls T-shirt. "Yuki's already hired the DJs," she explained.

"Oh. Well, can I just leave this tape?" I asked. "It's house music on one side and hip-hop on the other. Maybe you could give it to the person who hires the DJs?"

She looked at me with pity, but she accepted the tape. Then she directed her attention to the person in line behind me. I stood there, frozen. "Okay, thanks," I said, to no response. "Okay, bye."

I hurried out and walked to the corner to use the pay phone so I could call Janet. It was broken. I walked to the next pay phone, a block away; it was broken too. It was drizzling, I was cold, the sky was low and dark, and I had just humiliated myself in front of a cool and beautiful woman at what was going to be the best nightclub on the planet. I'd had the temerity to dream that I could be a DJ at Mars. I was a fool. And now I was standing with my feet in a slurry of rain and animal blood, staring at a broken pay phone.

I had a few dollars, so I walked to the health food store on Thirteenth Street and Eighth Avenue. When I had left the factory and rushed into the city I had been full of hope that I would finally be a New York City DJ. And now I was walking through the rain, hunched forward against the cold wind, to buy groceries from hippies. I purchased my soy milk and sprouted bread, jumped the turnstile on the F train, noted that F seemed like an appropriate grade for this trip to NYC, transferred to the Grand Central shuttle at Forty-Second Street, and splurged on a ticket back to Stamford so that I wouldn't have to sit in the bathroom. On the train I ate my bread and drank my soy milk, sometimes looking through the scratched windows at the South Bronx, sometimes reading a copy of *New York Rocker* that someone had left on a seat.

The bands in *New York Rocker* had record deals and played shows. They did interviews. They released records. People took their pictures. People listened to their music. It was everything I dreamed about. I wanted to play music for actual audiences. I wanted to DJ in dark, crowded rooms in New York City. But, in fact, I was a borderline-homeless twenty-three-year-old electronic musician whose only paying work was DJing Mondays at a tiny bar in Port Chester, New York, and every Saturday night at an all-ages club in a church in Greenwich.

When I got off the train in Stamford the rain had picked up, so I rushed back to the factory. I walked down a long hallway to my tiny studio and called Janet. It still amazed me that I had a phone. When I first moved into the factory I had called the phone company to see if I could get a phone. The very next day they sent someone, and five minutes after he arrived, I had a working phone. He didn't ask me if I was living in the factory illegally; he just laid down some wire and installed a phone jack. As he left I almost asked him what his name was so I could name my firstborn child after him.

"How was it?" Janet asked excitedly. "Did they hire you?"

"Well, there were a lot of people in line looking for work, but I left a tape with one of the women in charge," I told her.

"Great! How are you feeling?"

"I feel good," I lied.

We chatted for a few minutes, made plans to go to church together on Sunday, and hung up.

I'd done everything I could to get hired at Mars. I'd rushed to New York City in the rain. I'd left behind a tape decorated with an accounting student's idea of cool graffiti. Now it was in God's hands. Well, not the tape. I assumed the tape was in the garbage, or in someone's answering machine. But the situation was in God's hands. So I did what I always did: I turned on my studio and worked on music. I made quiet ambient house music until midnight, then I took off my headphones and turned off my equipment. I made some oatmeal and read a battered *Star Trek* paperback while listening to a Debussy cassette.

Sitting by the window, with the rain beating against my enormous factory windows and the space heaters on full blast, I was happy. I was unwashed and smelly, I lived in an abandoned factory in a crack neighborhood, and it had been an intensely disappointing day, but I was calm and happy. At four a.m., I went to sleep in my tiny loft bed, listening to the rain.

In the morning the rain had stopped, but it was still cold and overcast. I made more oatmeal on my hot plate and then went into my food stash for a few almonds and an orange. Almonds and oranges were luxuries, but the day before had been rough, and I wanted a treat. I was almost out of water, so after breakfast, I walked down the street to the bodega to buy two large plastic bottles of water. Walking back to the factory I noticed the huge mounds of dirt in the empty parking lot: once the beginnings of a construction project, they were now just big mud piles.

When I got back to my studio I saw that I had a message on my answering machine. I hit "play," the cassette rewound, and I heard the best message anyone had ever heard in the history of phone messages: "Hi, this is Yuki Watanabe calling from nightclub Mars. I'm calling for DJ Moby. I listened to your tape. Call me to see about DJing Mars."

I froze in place. I played the tape again. And then again.

Someone named Yuki with a thick Japanese accent had listened to my mix tape, and this same person was interested in having me DJ at Mars. I listened to the message once again to make sure it was real. And then again. And for good measure, again.

I picked up the phone, terrified. I had to call this Yuki and somehow convince him to give me a DJ job at Mars. Please. That was all I could say, to him or to God. Please.

I held the phone in my sweaty hand. I dialed the number.

"Hello, this is Yuki Watanabe," a rumbling voice said slowly.

"Hi, this is DJ Moby," I said, talking too quickly, "you called me about DJing at Mars?"

"Yes, I listen your tape. It's very interesting. Can you DJ Friday night?"

"Yes. Yes, I can DJ Friday night."

"Okay, you play in the basement. Ten p.m. to four a.m. It pays one hundred dollars."

"Thank you! I'll see you then."

"Okay, DJ Moby."

I hung up and thought about Walker Percy. There's a scene in his novel *The Moviegoer* when the protagonist is in a museum after an accident. He has a moment of clarity, and suddenly he sees tiny dust motes floating in the sunlight. My own life had just changed, on a larger scale than I could imagine, and I could see dust motes floating in the winter light that streamed through my oversized windows.

I sat on my carpet, still clutching the phone, my neurons firing like the whirling atoms in a PBS science video. Had this really happened? Was I hallucinating? Were ancient factory fumes corrupting my brain? I listened to the answering machine message again: it was real. I had just been hired to DJ in the basement at the coolest club on the planet.

The world around me evaporated. I no longer saw the abandoned factory, or the phone, or the sky framed by my window. In my mind's eye I saw the basement at Mars. I imagined a room, painted black, with low ceilings and a perfect sound system. A dark space filled with demonically cool people: I would stand at the elevated DJ booth, playing hip-hop and house music.

I called Janet. She was out, but her answering machine picked up. "Janet, you'll never believe what just happened," I blurted out. "Yuki from Mars called. I'm going to be DJing at Mars on Friday night. I can't believe it, I can't believe it. Call me! I can't believe it." I hung up.

I needed to thank God, so I got on my knees on my stolen carpet. "Thank you, God," I whispered. "Thank you. That's all, thank you."

2

VEGAN COOKIES

S omeone shot Jamie?" I asked. I was standing in front of the abandoned factory in Stamford on a sunny Friday afternoon, talking to one of the other squatters.

"No, he got stabbed," the squatter, Pedro, told me. "Someone heard screaming last night and then saw these two guys running down the hall. They looked in Jamie's room—he was lying on the floor in a pool of blood."

Pedro was a photographer and a graffiti artist. His graffiti tags were all over the factory complex: in the elevators, on the Dumpsters, on every inch of the loading dock. He always wore an old brown leather motorcycle jacket, and he'd been living at the factory for ten years.

"You're kidding," I said. "I saw him yesterday. Look, his motorcycle's still there."

Pedro eyed Jamie's Triumph, sitting between two Dumpsters. "Do you think someone will take it?" he asked.

"I'm surprised it's still there," I said.

"Am I stealing it if he's dead?"

There was a long pause as we both stared at it. Finally, I said, "I think it's kind of a gray area."

One of the advantages of living in the factory was that nobody paid attention to what we, as squatters, did. In addition to making electronic music and DJing I was playing drums in a punk-rock band called the Pork Guys and banging on metal cans in an industrial band called Shopwell—when we needed to rehearse, we took our equipment to some empty part of the factory and made as much noise as we wanted. Nobody complained. It was an abandoned factory in a crack neighborhood. As long as we weren't killing people, we were left alone.

But last month somebody had killed a homeless guy in the parking lot, and now Jamie had been stabbed to death. The other squatters and I weren't afraid that we'd be hurt; we were afraid that the police would figure out what was going on and that we'd be evicted. People dying in the abandoned factory wasn't good for our anonymity. "If you leave, where do you think you'll go?" I asked Pedro.

"I don't know," he said. "Maybe Brooklyn? Or the Lower East Side? I have some friends in a squat on Avenue C. But there are rats."

Most squatters lived in abandoned apartment buildings—and because abandoned apartment buildings had previously been lived in by people, they were usually filled with rats and roaches. The beauty of living in an abandoned factory, apart from one million square feet of unused industrial space, was that there were no rats or roaches.

"And you?" Pedro asked. "Where would you go?"

"I can't move home," I said. "So I'd probably move to New York somehow."

"Can you afford it? Or would you squat?"

"If I DJ more, I could probably pay a hundred fifty dollars a month for rent."

"That's a lot," he said.

"I know, but I need to be in New York."

"Word. Okay, see you later," Pedro said. "Don't get stabbed."

"Poor Jamie," I said, giving his Triumph one last look, as if I could say good-bye to Jamie through his motorcycle.

I had to be in Greenwich at four p.m. for Bible study, and after that I was going to the Episcopal church where I DJed on Saturday nights, to hold a microphone for my friend Chris while he shot his student film. If

I rode my moped I could get to Greenwich in about thirty minutes. I put on my helmet and headed west, past the pool hall, the storefront churches, and the drug dealers. I drove up to Route 1, passing the old Anthrax Club, where I'd seen Circle Jerks and Agnostic Front and countless other hardcore bands in the early eighties. I then headed west, passing the Villa Bar, where I used to get drunk when I was sixteen.

One time in high school I'd blacked out in the toilets at the Villa. A couple of off-duty cops had peeled me off the bathroom floor, thrown water in my face, and dumped me on the sidewalk. I emerged from my blackout with my friend Kitty shouting my name.

"What?" I said, opening my eyes and drunkenly looking around.

"I thought you were dying, you fuckhead!" she yelled at me.

I considered this. "I want a drink," I told her.

"You can't go back in. The cops will beat the shit out of you."

"But I love cops. Can we go to Port Chester and drink?"

Port Chester was in New York, and the bars there stayed open until four a.m. We got in Kitty's car and drove to Port Chester, where they served me more liquor. Then I threw up again and blacked out. When I woke up at dawn I was draped over a lounge chair by Kitty's parents' pool in New Canaan: sixteen, hungover, and proud.

Heading west out of Stamford on my moped I entered one of the wealthiest town in the United States: Greenwich, Connecticut. The check-cashing stores and housing projects in Stamford turned into leafy garden supply centers and mansions hiding behind giant pruned hedges. I arrived at the house where we were having Bible study and parked my moped—a twelve-year-old green Peugeot—between a Porsche Carrera and a Mercedes station wagon. After I took off my helmet I rubbed my head to get the dried foam rubber out of my hair. I'd bought the helmet at the Darien Salvation Army: it had been new in 1975, it didn't fit, and every time I wore it, I ended up with foam-rubber dandruff.

We were having Bible study at Catherine's house. Catherine was a shy, sweet junior at Greenwich High School who rode horses and listened to the Cure. Her family had moved to the States from Belgium a few years earlier; her father's finance company had rented them an eight-bedroom mansion with a swimming pool, a tennis court, and a horse paddock, on six acres in back-country Greenwich. Today I was going to be teaching Bible study in the basement.

For Bible study I wanted to talk about the Sermon on the Plain in Luke. It was almost like Jesus's greatest hits: "love your enemies," "judge not lest you be judged," but also "woe to you who are rich" and "woe to you who are well-fed now."

See, I was Christian, but I was also a dick. I was poor, I lived in an abandoned factory, I spent $10 a week on food. So when I read "Blessed are you who are poor, for yours is the kingdom of God. Blessed are you who hunger now, for you will be satisfied," I felt smug and justified and favored in the eyes of God.

Normally I felt like a subpar Christian, and I worked under the assumption that God was perpetually disappointed in me. I didn't do enough ministering to the homeless. I still wanted a career as a musician. I still had lustful thoughts. But when it came to poverty, I felt like I'd nailed it. I'd never met anyone as poor as I was now. Even the poor people I'd grown up around had indoor plumbing and walls made of stronger materials than salvaged plywood.

So I was smugly going into million-dollar houses in Greenwich to judge the children of the rich and make them feel bad about being born into wealth. I wasn't concerned for their spiritual health. I didn't want to lovingly guide them into seeing the error of their ways. I just wanted to make them feel bad for having money. I also wanted them to applaud the legitimacy of my teachings, since I had spent hours in my tiny room at the abandoned factory, memorizing Bible passages and figuring out new and interesting ways to use Christianity to make people feel bad about themselves.

I was also an expert at using Christianity to beat the shit out of myself. Three weeks ago I'd decided that my Christianity was inadequate: I felt like a fraud, for I was a Christian but I had a home. Admittedly, my home was a tiny space in an abandoned factory, but it was still home. I had read the teachings of Christ and understood from them that I was supposed to be homeless. Christ wanted me to get rid of my possessions and go out and wander the earth, ministering to people. I felt called. One day I decided to take my faith out of the realm of the cloistered and academic and walk into the world with nothing except for the clothes on my back and my Bible.

I picked up my Bible, left the room, and closed the front door. I held the key up to the lock, and then I stared at the key. I thought, *If I put the key in the lock and turn it, I leave and I don't come back. I commit to a life of wandering and doing my best to help anyone who needs it: the poor, the hungry, the bereft. I leave and I turn my back on home, career, ambition, everything.*

The key hovered an inch from my lock. In my mind I could hear the key sliding into the lock and turning. I imagined walking down the hallway, leaving the factory by the back door, going to the pay phone on the corner, and calling my mom. I'd say, "Mom, I need a favor. I'm leaving to wander and minister. Will you sell my stuff and give whatever money you make to the poor?"

But I couldn't do it. I stood at the door, key still outside the lock, and I prayed, "God, if this is your will, then please give me the strength to do it." It felt like such a clear calling, but minutes passed and I was still standing at my door. I couldn't give up the familiar, no matter how humble, for the unknown. I had no guidelines or personal precedent for becoming a mendicant. I put the key back in my pocket, walked back into my room, and sat in the fiberglass school chair that Paul and I had fished out of a Dumpster.

I prayed again. "God, I'm sorry. I can't do it. I can't leave everything and go minister. I'm sorry, God." I felt like a fraud. I knew my calling—to leave, to have no possessions, to minister—and I couldn't do it. But I still wanted to judge the rich and their soft children.

———

Catherine's little sister let me in, and I walked down the stairs to the basement of the mansion. There was a red-felt pool table at the bottom of the stairs, and some comfortable couches and chairs arranged in a circle. Seven of the eight Bible-study regulars were there, clean and smiling. They all lived with their parents, sleeping in the same quiet bedrooms they'd known since childhood. The boys wore button-down Brooks Brothers shirts; the girls wore Calvin Klein jeans and Fair Isle sweaters. We sat and one of the girls prayed, "God, thank you for bringing us here and thank you for giving us this place to meet and study. Please guide Moby as he brings us your teaching. Amen."

"Amen," we all echoed.

"Okay, let's open our Bibles to Luke 6:12," I said. "Tory, do you want to start reading?"

We went around the room, each of us reading a few lines, ending at Luke 7. And I was ready. I still had the smell of the factory in my unwashed clothes. There were specks of foam rubber in my hair from my ancient moped helmet. I was ready to bring the righteous judgment of God down on these soft suburban Christians. I went to bed listening to gunshots; they, I imagined, went to bed to the sound of snoring golden retrievers. Hadn't we just read "woe to you who are rich"? I felt justified, holy vengeance building up inside me.

Then I looked at a table where Catherine's mom had put out cookies and lemonade for us. Catherine saw my glance. "Oh, do you want a cookie?" she asked. "My mom went to the health-food store and got vegan cookies for you."

"Thanks," I said, and paused, the wind of judgment leaving my sails. Had I done anything selfless today? Had I gone out of my way to be kind to anyone today? Had I fed anyone today?

No. Here I was, the firebrand Christian, the self-styled voice of a judgmental God, staring at my failings in the form of a plate of vegan cookies. Catherine's mom had gone to some strange health-food store to get weird vegan cookies for a friend of her daughter whom she'd never even met. And I was the good Christian?

The thought came to me, from Hosea, "I desire mercy and not sacrifice." So I put my anger aside, and instead of judging these kind Christians around me I talked about my experience three weeks earlier, how I'd felt called to leave everything so I could minister to the poor, and how I felt that I'd disappointed God and asked for his forgiveness. Then I talked about how we could find the divine in the big gestures—grand statements and renunciations—but there was a quiet divinity in small things, like buying weird vegan cookies for a stranger. Or letting people into your house and serving them food. In that moment, those small gestures seemed more important to me, and more divine.

"So thank you all for being here for me," I finished. "And, Catherine, please thank your mom for the vegan cookies."

I left out the fact that the cookies were dry and terrible.

After Bible study, we all went to Greenwich's Christ Church to help the Episcopal minister's son, Chris, shoot scenes for his student film. Chris attended NYU, where his adviser was Martin Scorsese.

"Will Martin Scorsese be at the church?" I'd asked Chris.

"Probably," Chris had said, doing his Tom Sawyer best to get us all to work for free.

I pulled up to Christ Church at dusk and parked my moped under a spreading elm, next to the eighteenth-century cemetery. Chris was standing with a cluster of actors and extras, next to the portico that covered the entrance to one of the old stone chapels, explaining to all the volunteers what we'd be doing. As I was a musician, I'd been drafted to hold the microphone.

"Chris, who's that over there?" I asked, pointing to a long-haired guy walking in circles on the lush lawn and talking to himself. He was wearing a dark winter coat and gesturing with his hands, as if he were emphatically making a point to a ghost.

"Oh, that's Viggo Mortensen. He's goes to school with me, and he's the lead in the film," Chris told me.

"Why is he walking in circles? Does he have mad cow disease?"

"Ha, no, he's just intense," Chris said. "When he's getting ready to shoot, that's what he does."

We went up the ancient wooden stairs in the chapel and spent the next five hours filming Viggo on the roof. He and the lead actress kept going over the same scenes, with Chris pushing them to do minor variations on their lines. The night got later, the wind picked up, and it got cold.

"I thought movies were glamorous," one of the tired and shivering high school students on the roof said to me.

I was holding the microphone on a long, telescoping pole. One of Chris's film student friends asked me, "Do you work full-time as a boom operator?"

"What's a boom operator?" I replied.

"Ha, I guess not," he said, and walked away.

At one a.m., after we'd shot the same scenes a few dozen times, Chris announced, "Okay, everyone, that's a wrap." We all applauded for ourselves—something I'd never done before.

I walked over to Viggo, who hadn't spoken to anyone all night.

"Good job, Viggo," I said, holding out my hand.

He took my hand, looked intensely into my eyes, and asked, "Was it?"

3

NIGHT MOVES

You can't be a DJ in New York and live in Stamford," Damian had said to me, correctly.

"But I can't afford to live in Manhattan," I complained.

"Well, move to New York and get more DJ jobs," he told me.

He was right. I was scared, and poor, but he was right. So he and I were clearing out my tiny space at the abandoned factory. Leaving behind my plywood walls and my scavenged door, I packed everything I owned into my mom's car and moved to New York City with Damian, his girlfriend Alyssa, and our DJ friend Roberto.

I'd met Damian two years before at the all-ages club in Greenwich where I was DJing. He was a tall, blond aspiring artist. He smoked expensive British cigarettes and always wore black new-wave clothes. Every new-wave girl in Connecticut was in love with him. He couldn't afford art school, so he spent his time in different art museums, figuring out how people had painted in the eighteenth century. His girlfriend Alyssa was a tall, mantis-thin Asian model who had just graduated from Columbia. Our friend Roberto was a hip-hop DJ whose parents were modern-art dealers. Roberto dated beautiful women, DJed at downtown hip-hop clubs, and vacationed in the south of France in his family's villa.

A few weeks ago Alyssa had been looking at apartments in *Village*

Voice ads. She found a duplex on the corner of Fourteenth Street and Third Avenue, with three bedrooms and a big living room, for $1,200 a month. Lower Manhattan was filled with cheap apartments because lower Manhattan was filthy and dangerous, and most people didn't want to live there.

Damian and Alyssa were dysfunctionally dating, so they claimed the largest bedroom, in the basement. Their bedroom got no light and smelled like cheap building materials and mildew. Because it was perpetually dark, or maybe because they hated each other and were depressed, Alyssa and Damian both routinely slept until three or four in the afternoon. Roberto had the most money, being a working DJ and having villa- and gallery-owning parents, so he took the large bedroom in the back of the apartment that actually got thirty minutes of sunlight during the afternoon.

I was the poorest, so I took the smallest bedroom—but it was still bigger than my one-hundred-square-foot cube at the abandoned factory. The floors in my new bedroom were painted gray, my walls were faded green, and I had two grimy windows overlooking the garbage-filled shaftway between our building and the one next to ours. My boxes of books (*Star Trek*, Arthur C. Clarke, Kierkegaard) were on the floor, and my records (Joy Division, Derrick May, Public Enemy) were piled in one corner. I removed the closet doors and installed my small MIDI studio in the closet. I couldn't afford a bed frame, so my thin twin mattress sat on the floor. The apartment smelled like garbage, it got no light, and it was next door to a drug den and a Mexican restaurant specializing in deep-fried *cuchifritos*, but for me it was paradise.

New York City had long been the dark city on the hill for me, shadowy and ominous and perfect. I had been born on 148th Street in Harlem in 1965, and spent years in Connecticut dreaming of returning to New York, like a homing pigeon longing for the degenerate island of its birth. Gang violence and AIDS and drug overdoses weren't just tabloid headlines for us—we all knew people who had died way too young in New York City. Nevertheless, Damian and I and our roommates were in the filthy epicenter of the most remarkable city on the planet.

My share of the rent was $285, which was a huge stretch for me, since I'd previously been paying $50 a month to the security guards at the abandoned factory. But I was making almost $800 a month, as I was DJing at Mars and saying yes to any work that was offered to me.

The week before moving to the city I had borrowed my mom's car to drive across the Tappan Zee Bridge to Nyack, New York, where I DJed a wedding. The bride and groom were getting married without the blessing of their families, so they had rented the basement in the Nyack community hall and paid for it themselves. The basement was cold and damp and the twenty guests sat shivering on plastic folding chairs. The couple couldn't afford to rent turntables, so I played music on two cassette decks they'd borrowed from their friends, even playing "Wedding March" on a cassingle as the bride walked down the aisle between the folding chairs. They paid me $70, and I felt guilty taking so much money. But one of my goals in New York City was to avoid becoming a homeless prostitute, and to that end I needed to do anything that I could to make money, even DJing weddings with cassettes and taking money from impoverished newlyweds.

A month after my roommates and I moved in we decided to have a party. I played new-wave and house music records and cassettes in the corner of the living room, people danced, and everyone except me got drunk.

I had stopped drinking two years before, in 1987. I had my first drink when I was ten years old, on the last day of 1975. My friend Arthur's family lived in Darien on an estate by Long Island Sound, and his mom had invited me to their New Year's Eve party. At some point during the night Arthur's drunk mom had handed me a glass of champagne. I'd then gone to their huge marble-clad kitchen and stolen two more glasses of champagne from under the noses of the two European au pairs they had working for them. After I drank three glasses of champagne all my anxieties had melted away and for the first time in my life I'd felt genuinely happy. When I made it upstairs to Arthur's room after midnight Arthur was already asleep on the lower bunk of his bunk beds. I drunkenly climbed to my top bunk and lay down under a *Battlestar Galactica* blanket. "I always want to feel this good," I announced to the room. Arthur didn't say anything; he was sleeping.

In junior high school and high school I went to parties and drank anything I could get my hands on. I stole wine and beer from my mom and her boyfriends. I stole vodka and rum from the liquor cabinets of my friends' parents. And to top it off, when I was twelve my friend Jim and I would drink wine coolers and take the antipsychotic pills prescribed for his institutionalized brother.

"I'm an alcohol enthusiast," I'd tell my friends—sometimes at the very moment when I was hurling garbage cans at parked cars, drunkenly weeping, or throwing up on a sidewalk. I drunkenly crashed a few cars and lost my virginity in a blackout when I was sixteen.

I would also get drunk and go to straight-edge shows. Straight edge was a movement that had been started by the DC hardcore band Minor Threat. Most straight-edge kids wore big Xs on the backs of their hands and didn't drink, smoke, or take drugs. I loved the music, and I loved feeling like I was part of a secret society, but as a teenager, I had no interest in the actual philosophy.

When I was seventeen I went to see Minor Threat at Great Gildersleeves, a rock club in lower Manhattan one block away from CBGB. I drew the requisite X on the back of my hand, and on the way to the venue got drunk on rum with my friend Bill. In a blackout state after the show I introduced myself to Ian MacKaye, lead singer of Minor Threat, as he was loading equipment into the band's van.

"Mr. MacKaye," I said drunkenly, "I just wanted to say that I'm straight-edge too, and I love your band."

He shook my hand and said a wary thanks.

In 1983 I went to college and kept drinking, routinely waking up on the floor of my dorm room in a puddle of my own vomit. I also began having debilitating panic attacks. They were so bad I couldn't leave my dorm room or make it to class, so I dropped out and moved home. My friends from high school were at Ivy League schools sitting under hundred-year-old oak trees and discussing Kant and Foucault, and a year after graduating high school I was a nineteen-year-old college drop-out sleeping on his mother's secondhand couch.

Even though I was nineteen, and under the legal drinking age, I got a job DJing at a suburban bar called the Beat. At other bars being blind drunk at work might have been frowned upon, but at the Beat my bosses seemed to turn a blind eye to me drinking as often and as much as I could. I would drink a pint glass of vodka, throw up alcohol and stomach bile in the men's room, and then get a beer and head to the DJ booth to get back to work.

I was young, so the hangovers had been brief and almost charming— they made me feel a kinship with Dylan Thomas and Charles Bukow-ski. But consequences started to pile up from drinking and in 1986, at the age of twenty-one, I accepted that I might be an alcoholic, or at least a problem drinker.

In 1987 I became a vegan, started teaching Bible study, and decided that crashing cars and waking up covered in vomit wasn't in keeping with my values. My father had died of alcoholism. My friend Paul's mom had died of alcoholism. Most of the violence I had seen had been fueled by drinking. So I sat on the couch at my mom's house in 1987 and called up Paul, who had always been straight-edge. I told him, "I think I'm done. I don't think I'm going to drink anymore." I hadn't had a drink since, and our shared sobriety, and mutual love of *Star Trek* and David Lynch, had become the foundation of my friendship with Paul.

At two a.m. the housewarming party in our new apartment started winding down, so I turned on the lights and ended the night with a cassette of "Night Moves" by Bob Seger. My drunk friends sang along, finished their beers, and headed home. I went to bed and set my alarm for seven a.m. so I could wake up and collect all the empty cans and bottles before anyone threw them away.

After I slept for a few hours I woke up at dawn and filled three gar-bage bags with bottles and cans and lugged them down Fourteenth

Street to the Food Emporium. Even early in the morning there were a dozen homeless people standing in line outside the supermarket, all waiting to use the recycling machines. It was a cold March morning; I was wearing a Vietnam-era army jacket, thrift-shop jeans, old work boots, and a black knit cap pulled over my head.

It was starting to drizzle, my plastic garbage bags smelled like beer, and the people walking in and out of the Food Emporium were giving me and the homeless people in line pitying looks. When it was my turn I patiently inserted my bottles and cans into the recycling machines; each time I was rewarded with a loud crunch and five cents that clattered into the metal tray. After a few minutes my bags were empty and my pockets were full of nickels. I had made five dollars in loose change and I felt rich. All I'd done was wake up early and collect garbage that would have been thrown away. I'd put the garbage into a machine, and the machine had given me money. I felt like an alchemist, but instead of turning lead into gold, I'd turned beer bottles into nickels.

It was nine a.m. and I was newly rich with nickels, so I headed for Prana Health Foods on First Avenue. Prana was the only health food store in my new neighborhood, and it hadn't changed since 1970. It smelled like oats and brewer's yeast and stale spinach, and everyone who worked there was surly and thin and looked like a refugee from a Grateful Dead show parking lot. They even had the requisite hippie cat sleeping on the bulk sesame seed bin. I splurged on my favorite luxury indulgence: vanilla soy milk, which was $1.49 per carton. While the cranky hippie behind the counter watched, I counted out $4.90 in nickels and bought three containers of vanilla soy milk and an organic orange. Now I was an alchemist twice over: I'd turned beer cans and bottles into soy milk and an orange.

I walked up First Avenue and got home just as my roommates were waking up. Roberto was staggering around the kitchen in his Calvin Klein underpants and Adidas sandals, hungover. "You cleaned up?" he asked, confused.

"I took all the bottles and cans to the recycling place at Food Emporium," I said proudly.

"Ha, you're like a homeless dude!" he said.

I wanted to brag that I now had three cartons of soy milk and an orange, but his family owned a villa in Provence, so I didn't think he'd be impressed.

"Yo, what was that wack rock track you played at the end of the party?" he asked.

"'Night Moves' by Bob Seger?" I asked.

"That shit is wack."

I wanted to defend Bob Seger but said nothing—I just put away my groceries. Roberto had grown up in New York and he understood cool things in a way that I never would. We were both DJs, but he loved obscure jazz and Cozy Burger and I loved Bob Seger and soy milk.

"Yo, can I have some of your orange?" Roberto asked.

My orange. It had cost forty cents, or eight cans.

"Okay," I said. "It's organic."

"As opposed to synthetic?"

I peeled the orange and we sat down on our stained futon to play Mario Bros. on the Nintendo.

"Are you DJing at Mars tonight?" he asked.

"Yeah, in the basement. Klark Kent's on the main floor and Red Alert's on the second floor."

"Oh, word. Can you put me on the list?"

"Sure, you plus two?"

"Yeah, thanks," he said.

We sat on the futon, eating my organic orange and watching Mario leap around on giant mushrooms. I looked at the gray tenement wall across the shaftway from our apartment and smiled. For the first time since 1967 I was a New Yorker.

4

HANDS IN THE AIR

Janet and I were kneeling on the floor of her Columbia dorm room, praying. We had just finished having sex. I was twenty-four, she was twenty, and we were dating, but we were trying to be good Christians and not indulge our lust. "God, we're sorry that we have sinned. Please forgive us and please help us to do your will," we prayed in unison. "Through Jesus's name, amen."

Janet had decorated her Columbia dorm room with a U2 *War* poster and an André Kertész picture of a Parisian street scene. The room was tiny and had only a small single bed, which we would share—or, if I was feeling monastic or claustrophobic, I'd sleep on the floor. Last night we'd been in bed and had started kissing, but had managed to stop ourselves before we had sex. I'd gotten out of bed and lay down on the floor, reaching up to hold hands with Janet in her bed.

"I'm glad we didn't have sex, Moby," she said quietly in the dark.

"Me too, Janet. Good night."

Then this morning I'd gotten into bed with her after I woke up. We ended up transgressing and having sex. After our postcoital prayer for forgiveness, we lay on her bed spooning. "Do you think we can be celibate?" I asked, my face buried in her hair.

"I hope so, Mobe," she said. "I really want to do the right thing."

Janet wasn't allowed to have boys in her room—we were violating not only God's law but Columbia's dorm regulations—so after I got dressed, I snuck out her dorm room window and headed for the subway. Her dorm room was protected by Columbia University security guards, but it was still on 120th Street, so once I left her building I was back in Harlem, the land of my birth. The homeless lined the sidewalks, layered in dirty winter clothes and surrounded by old garbage bags filled with everything they owned.

I jumped the turnstile at the 125th Street subway stop and walked past the emaciated crack addicts propped up against the wall: nearly dead men and women, thin as knitting needles, nodding out and selling anything they could get their hands on. For sale on the subway platform I saw a used cigarette lighter, a five-year-old copy of *People* magazine, a Pat Benatar cassette, a single shoe.

I fished copies of the *New York Post* and the *Daily News* out of the garbage while I waited for the subway and read a MURDER CITY headline. Apparently the murder rate in 1989 was the highest in the city's history. The *Post* featured an article about teenagers running through Times Square and stabbing tourists with infected syringes. It all seemed normal: the emaciated crack addicts, the daily murders, the vicious, feral teenagers. New York had never been clean or safe, but in 1989 it was dirtier and more dangerous than it had been even two years earlier.

And it was my home. And I'd never been happier.

The train approached the station, announcing itself with a subtle change in air pressure. Then I could smell it: a distinctive combination of disinfectant, old concrete dust, rat poison, and dirty air. Soon I could see the small white light of the train in the distance, quickly getting bigger. Suddenly the station was filled with rushing noise and screeching brakes. I stepped back from the oncoming train—almost every week, I'd read about someone being pushed in front of a subway. As I retreated I tried to imagine if you died instantly when you were pushed in front of a train, or if you were trapped under the wheels, suffering while the rats stared at your death throes, trying to figure out if they were bold enough to get close and take a bite.

The train doors opened and I stepped inside. The car was old and covered with graffiti, both painted on the walls and scratched into the windows. There were a few passengers on the fiberglass seats, but at eleven a.m. on a cold Tuesday morning it wasn't crowded. I got a few stares from the people who had gotten on further uptown: Dominicans and Haitians and Jamaicans in huge down jackets, looking furtively at me. They probably assumed I was a drug addict; why else would a skinny white boy with long, stringy hair be getting on the 1/9 train at 125th Street? Nobody stared too long—that could get you killed. People got killed for their sneakers or their headphones, so no one on a subway in 1989 stared at anything or anyone for more than a cautious second.

The train headed south, its metal wheels loudly scraping against the tracks every time we pulled into a station. I always stood when I rode the subway, holding on to a strap or a rail, my eyes darting back and forth to make sure I was safe. There were no police on subways, and kids routinely walked through the cars stabbing people and stealing their watches and wallets and chains and sneakers. So I always stood, checking the doors, not making eye contact, remaining anonymous and unstabbed.

I wanted to go to Vinylmania, so I got off at Houston Street and walked east. The snow was melting on the sidewalks, and the taxicabs were speeding through dirty black puddles, splashing anyone standing on a corner.

The inside of Vinylmania looked like every other DJ record store in New York: everything was painted black, the walls were covered with metal racks holding all the new hip-hop and house records, and the floor was lined with long wooden record bins holding twelve-inch singles. At the back were the store DJs, with their turntables and huge disco speakers all shoved into a space the size of a small suburban garage. DJ record stores were never quiet. Sometimes there'd be one employee playing new hip-hop records at a deafening volume while five feet away another employee was playing new dancehall records at a deafening volume and ten feet away yet another employee was playing new house records at a deafening volume.

The best, or possibly worst, time to go to any DJ record store in New York City was on Friday afternoon. That was when the stores got most of their new records and when every DJ in the tristate area went vinyl shopping in Manhattan. On Fridays I'd walk into Vinylmania or Dance Trax or Disc-O-Rama and find a hundred other DJs crowded around the store DJ, who was loudly playing the new records. If a record was good everybody would know within the first thirty seconds. You could feel the collective shudder of longing and excitement as all the DJs in the store leaned into the new music. Then all the DJs would throw their hands in the air, scrambling to get a copy of the new record that would make the people on their dance floor scream.

I was at a disadvantage, being white and little; the majority of other DJs were Latino or African-American, and tall. I'd stand at the back of the store and hope that the man playing the new records would see my little white hand and maybe deign to sell me a copy of Raze's "Break 4 Love" or Precious's "Definition of a Track."

Sometimes on Fridays, Red Alert or Frankie Knuckles or Junior Vasquez or one of the other New York DJ legends would be buying records. The legend would be granted a spot right next to the DJ booth. The store's DJ would play a new record, look cautiously at the legend, and if the legend gave even the subtlest of nods, everyone in the store would clamor to get the vinyl that he had just blessed.

I had mastered the art of listening to three or four incredibly loud records at the same time, checking out the record bins while I figured out what my weekly investment was going to be. Buying twelve-inch vinyl was expensive. I was making $800 a month and spending about $350 of that on food and rent. That left $450 for records, studio equipment, and socks. A new domestic twelve-inch was $5.99 and a new import twelve-inch was $9.99. All I had to do was buy ten records, and in five minutes I had spent more on music than I would on food in an entire month. In buying records, I had to be selective and strategic. I wasn't just listening to the music and deciding if I liked it, I was also figuring out how the music might sound at Mars and whether it would help me keep my job.

At eleven thirty on a Tuesday morning at Vinylmania there were only a few other DJs there, poring over the selection in the bins. I was checking out the bin for the DJ International label when I heard the hip-hop DJ playing a new record. All of the rappers had started making house tracks—that way they could get played in hip-hop clubs as well as house clubs. This new crossover genre even had a name: predictably, it was hip-house. The Jungle Brothers had a huge hit with "I'll House You" and even Big Daddy Kane had deigned to make a hip-house track.

I listened to the new track. Some hip-house records were clichéd and obvious, but this one was subtle and understated—oddly, it was built around a sample of Latino bells. I walked over to the booth and got the DJ's attention.

"Hey, what's this?" I yelled.

He looked at me for a moment, then said, "Doug Lazy."

"Can I get a copy?"

He said nothing but handed me a twelve-inch wrapped in plastic. I held it up, reading the text on the label: Doug Lazy, "Let It Roll."

"When did this come out?" I asked.

"Today."

"Thanks!" I said, too white and enthusiastic. I bought a couple of other twelve-inches on the Strictly Rhythm and DJ International labels, but my instincts told me that "Let It Roll" was the one that was going to be huge.

After paying for my vinyl I walked down Carmine Street to Sixth Avenue. The park at Bleecker and Carmine was filled with dirty snow and crack addicts. Someone had taken the slats off a park bench and was burning them in a barrel. I kept walking.

I was excited by my new vinyl, so I stopped at Vesuvio to buy a celebratory cup of coffee and small loaf of bread. Vesuvio was a tiny bakery that had been in SoHo since the nineteenth century. For as long as I'd been going there the same old Italian man had always been behind the counter in a white apron, smiling and dusted in flour. "You want a whole wheat?" he asked me happily.

"Small, please. And a black coffee."

He smiled wider, wrapped my loaf in a thin piece of paper, and poured me a coffee. "Two dollars," he said.

"Here you go," I said, handing him three dollars and feeling like a Rockefeller, "keep the change."

"Thank you, gentleman!" he said, putting the money in the noisy metal cash register.

I sat at one of the two small tables at the front, eating my bread and drinking my coffee. SoHo was quiet—most of the art galleries weren't open yet—so I looked at my records in the sun reflected from the windows of the gallery across the street.

I was a sober Christian who worked in drug-fueled nightclubs. I was living in a filthy city that was being torn apart by drugs, AIDS, and gang violence. And I was sitting in quiet SoHo in reflected sunlight, drinking coffee at an ancient bakery while the man behind the counter smiled at me. I was so happy and so lucky. I had a perfect new record to play. I had a perfect little loaf of bread to eat. And I lived in a perfect city.

5

GARBAGE-FILLED SHAFTWAY

The Friday-night crowd streamed in as soon as Mars opened its doors at ten p.m. I started DJing on the first floor when the doors opened—but the evening got interesting around midnight, when some of the vogueing houses from uptown took over.

Vogueing was in the middle of a bizarre mainstream push, from Madonna's single "Vogue," but it had started years ago. The voguers were gay men, black and Latino, who would march proudly up and down the dance floor, turning it into their own ad hoc fashion runway. Vogueing wasn't really a dance, but rather a beautiful approximation of an idealized fashion show. Describing the phenomenon to a friend who drummed in a speed-metal band, I told him that the vogueing houses weren't actual buildings.

"It's more like 'house of Chanel' or 'house of Dior,'" I said. "They're inspired by French fashion houses."

"So they make clothes?" he asked.

"Um, no," I said, and I tried to explain again.

Just after midnight on a Friday I was playing house records for the beautiful vogueing queens when my friend Manuel ran into the DJ booth. Manuel was a busboy by night and a drag queen by other nights. At Mars he wore black pants and a black T-shirt and carried plastic trays filled with empty beer bottles and soggy cigarette butts. On his nights off, however, he became Carla, a delicate Latina drag queen with a long cigarette holder and dark eyes rimmed with kohl.

Last month I'd gone to a drag-queen club near Times Square to see Carla perform. She'd stood on the small stage and done an elegant and languorous rendition of "Bali Hai." After the show I said, "That was great! You're so beautiful!" Carla had batted her eyes, kissed me on the cheek, and walked away in a trail of perfume.

Now, as Manuel the busboy, he was in my DJ booth yelling, "Yo, Moby! You got Willie Ninja on your floor!"

Willie Ninja was his god. Or goddess. Willie Ninja ran one of the most famous vogueing houses in New York, and to have him and his house vogueing while I was DJing felt like a formal benediction. Mars was a demographically and musically complicated place: last night, when I had been DJing on the second floor, Kool Keith and the Ultramagnetic MCs had taken the mic and drunkenly and flawlessly freestyled over hip-hop tracks. Tonight Willie Ninja and his house were strutting down the middle of the dance floor to house tracks, their heads held high and their cheekbones like switchblades.

While they vogued I played "Love Is the Message" by MFSB. The crowd cheered and Willie Ninja beamed at me from across the room. I was straight, but he was so beautiful and his smile was so wide, at that moment I would have married that man. The night went on, the dance floor stayed packed, and at four a.m., I ended my set with "Set It Off" by Strafe. In front of me was a happy, sweaty sea of people: black, Latino, white, Asian, straight, gay. The song ended, the work lights came on, and everyone stumbled out of Mars and into the bewildering city.

When I got home around five a.m. I read some Arthur C. Clarke, curled up in my tiny bed, and tried to sleep—and then someone in the building opposite ours, a drug den, started screaming from the third floor.

"Fuck you!" he yelled, his voice slurred. "Fuck you, I'm gonna do it!"

I shut my window to keep out the sound of his yelling, which also had the advantage of reducing the stink of the garbage outside. The shaftway between our building and the drug den next door was about four feet wide and filled with garbage at least a yard high: rotting boxes, food scraps, aluminum cans, a mannequin, a suitcase. I asked my land-lord why he couldn't clean it up and he said that the shaftway technically belonged to the building next door—and since it was a drug den, the shaftway never got cleaned. And because it never got cleaned, everybody in our building and the drug den kept throwing trash out their window and filling up the shaftway, higher and higher.

"Fuck you, I'm gonna do it," the person next door kept yelling, over and over.

"Shut up!" someone in our building yelled.

Another sleepy voice echoed, "Shut the fuck up!"

"Fuck you, fuck you, I'm gonna do it!" the man shouted, for about the two hundredth time. And then he did it.

I heard a woman scream as the yelling man fell three stories down the shaftway. As he fell he had time to make a strange grunting sound— and then he landed with a sickening crunch. I jumped out of bed and opened my window. Two feet away, lying faceup in the pile of garbage, was a bloody, moaning man.

A woman was screaming, "Anton! Anton!" from one of the drug den's windows.

"Are you okay?" I asked Anton. He moaned, his bloody lips moving but not making words.

"Hold on, I'm calling 911." When I got through I told the operator, speaking quickly and very loudly, that a man had jumped out of a building and landed in the shaftway next to my apartment.

I could hear the operator smoking a cigarette and exhaling. "What's the address?" she asked, bored. I gave her my address and told her I'd be there to let the emergency workers in.

The woman next door was still yelling, "Anton! Anton!"

I stuck my head out the window and yelled back, "He's alive! The EMTs are on their way!"

Someone else in my building replied, "Shut up!"

And another person bellowed, "I'm trying to sleep! Shut the fuck up!"

"A guy is dying here!" I told them.

One of the voices responded, "Shut the fuck up!" The quality of mercy is especially strained when people are trying to sleep, even if a human being is dying in the garbage a few feet away from them.

"Anton," I asked, "can you hear me? Are you okay?" He just moaned. "The ambulance is coming," I said. "Hold on."

He moaned again. He was damp, from blood or perspiration or drizzling rain. Or all three. He looked like he was sweating oil.

After a few minutes our apartment's buzzer sounded. "EMTs!" a voice shouted through the static-heavy intercom. I let them in and three of them came down the hallway, carrying an aluminum gurney. I took them downstairs, opened the black steel emergency door, and let them into the shaftway. As I went back inside they were nimbly walking across the garbage with their gurney.

When I got back to my bedroom I looked through the window: they were checking Anton's vitals and shining a penlight into his unfocused eyes. I leaned out the window and asked, "Is he going to be okay?"

One of the EMTs laughed. "Yeah, the fucking garbage saved his life."

"What do you mean?"

"If the shaftway was clean, he would have landed on concrete. He'd be dead."

They strapped Anton onto the gurney and wheeled him into the waiting ambulance outside. And all was quiet. Nobody was screaming. I looked up the shaftway between the buildings and could see the faint gray of dawn.

6

GOAT-SKIN BUCKET

Working at Mars twice a week meant that I was meeting lots of random people, some of whom extended random offers for me to DJ at random places. Last week I had spun records in the basement of a restaurant called Cave Canem while a few drunk women danced naked in a filthy Jacuzzi. The week before that I had DJed a senior prom at an African-American vocational high school in Mamaroneck, New York. And tonight, a crisp Wednesday evening in November, I was scheduled to DJ twice in one night. The first event was a Balearic party at a Ukrainian cultural center; when I accepted the gig, I had no idea what "Balearic" meant. The second event was a sex party at a Chelsea loft.

The gig at the Ukrainian cultural center was within walking distance of my apartment. But I was bringing three crates of records, and vinyl is heavy. A few years before I had devised a good system for moving records: I stacked the cases on my skateboard and pushed everything down the street, slowly and carefully. A few months ago, late on a rainy night, I had been pushing my vinyl skateboard tower on the sidewalk outside of Mars. The cases toppled, I twisted my ankle trying to hold them up, and hundreds of records spilled into the mud and blood of the Meatpacking District. As the sun came up I spent twenty minutes hobbling around in the rain on my twisted ankle, trying to pick up twelve-inches from the wet bloody slurry of Thirteenth Street. Since then, I'd been a lot more careful about how I pushed the vinyl-laden skateboard around.

An added benefit to my system was that I had a skateboard for the anxious hours before people showed up where I was working. Usually I'd arrive at the nightclub or bar at nine p.m., set up my records, make sure everything was working, and wait. Sometimes I'd sit on a bar stool and read a science-fiction book. And sometimes I'd skateboard around the empty dance floor. This entertained both me and the busboys—especially, as often happened, when I fell off my skateboard and went sprawling on the dance floor.

I left my apartment with my unstable tower of vinyl and headed east on Fourteenth Street. It was a perfect New York autumn evening, the sort of night where people held hands and fell in love while walking in the park and stepping over homeless people. I pushed my skateboard under the leafless trees, past the wig store and the community bank, then past the Lebanese deli and the abandoned theater, and turned right on Second Avenue. A breeze kicked up, pushing the fallen leaves and garbage into an East Village pas de deux.

The venue, called the Sly Fox, was part of the Ukrainian National Home. As I opened the front door of the Sly Fox I heard the sound that all DJs fear: loud dance music in an empty room. I pushed my vinyl inside and saw that the first DJ was onstage, playing an Inner City record to an audience of five people: his girlfriend, one of his girlfriend's friends, the promoter, the promoter's business partner, and a sullen bartender.

The promoter was a Goa hippie who might have originally been Turkish or French or Swiss but whose nationality now was principally East Village. He had long bleached dreadlocks and hung out at Mars on Friday nights. One night he'd come up to me while I was DJing, thrown his arms in the air, and shouted, "Moby! We're going to bring love and ecstasy to New York!"

"Okay," I'd said, smiling nervously.

He'd rented the Sly Fox space and promoted the night as New York's first Balearic rave. (I'd since learned that "Balearic" referred to the Mediterranean islands that included Ibiza, the Spanish center of rave culture.) The problem was that Balearic music often was soft and driven by acoustic guitars and gentle keyboards, neither of which made sense in dystopian New York City in 1989. New Yorkers were more inclined toward the dirty sounds of hip-hop, dancehall, and lo-fi house music.

Now the promoter, high on mushrooms, was sitting on the stage at the Sly Fox and playing a piece of ethnic percussion that looked like a bucket covered by old goat skin. As he flailed away on his goat-skin bucket his eyes were closed—either in a state of rapture or as an ostrich-like effort to avoid the fact that his venue was empty and his Balearic rave night was a failure.

It broke my heart: he was sweet and well intentioned, and I had really wanted him to be right. I'd wanted to walk into the Sly Fox to find hundreds of sweaty ravers from the UK and Australia dancing to house music, waving glow sticks, and hugging everyone in sight. I'd read about raves, I'd heard about glow sticks being used outside of science class and traffic accidents, and I thought this was my chance to experience an actual rave just a few blocks from my apartment. And maybe rave culture would feel like home.

I knew that as a DJ in New York I was an outsider: a white twenty-four-year-old playing hip-hop and house music in black, Latino, and gay clubs. For the most part I had lost interest in white music, and I loved being in a world that wasn't my own. Some nights I'd visit the clubs when I wasn't working: I'd stand in the corner, loving that I was a minority of one, the only straight white person there, feeling grateful for how far away I was from suburban Connecticut. A few years earlier I'd read the Rimbaud quote "I is another" and taped it to my small bedroom mirror. I loved these worlds full of gay and black and Latino people, and I'd made casual friends there, but I always knew that I was another.

Maybe in this rave scene I'd heard about I'd feel less like an alien.

While the promoter pounded on his drum, his business partner came over and said, "Hey, Moby. I'm sure it'll get busier later." But I didn't have a later—I was on in fifteen minutes. Maybe the "later" would happen while I was DJing: suddenly the room would fill with beautiful sun-kissed people from Goa (I had no idea where Goa was— was it a Balearic island?) who were there for the ecstatic love vibes. Hope springs eternal, especially when you're a DJ getting ready to play records to an empty room.

The Sly Fox had been built by Ukrainian immigrants in the nineteenth century. For over a hundred years they'd used this room for weddings and union organizing. The wooden floors were worn down, smoothed by the thousands of Ukrainians who had come through to get married and start unions and dance in circles and congratulate themselves on living in this hard city of occasional hope and plenty. The Sly Fox was a room that was used to being filled with people, but I was pretty sure that in a few minutes the current DJ and his girlfriend would be leaving, which would bring its population to exactly four.

The DJ was playing his last song, so I did the polite DJ thing and stood behind him with my headphones while he nodded self-importantly and looked at the equipment. With a minute to go, he turned to me, unplugged his headphones, shook my hand, said, "Nice to meet you— good luck," and stepped away from the turntables.

I plugged in my headphones; grabbed my first record, "Bang Bang You're Mine" by Bang the Party; cued up the disc; and mixed out of the house track he'd been playing. I took the needle off his record and, completing our minuet, delicately handed it to him. As expected, he took his records and scurried away with his girlfriend, probably hoping that the night's failure wasn't contagious.

There were now four people in the room: the drug-crazed dreadlocked promoter, his stoic and hopeful business partner, the morose bartender, and me. I was scheduled to play for one long and painful hour.

And then during my second record, four happy dreadlocked white and black people came in, running up to the promoter and hugging him. A few minutes later, some more people came in. And then some more. Within twenty minutes, there were thirty people in the Sly Fox, some standing in the corners, but most of them dancing to house music. The promoter was still playing his unidentified percussion instrument, but now he had his eyes open and was running around the dance floor, his dirty blond dreadlocks whipping around his head.

By eleven thirty p.m. there were fifty people in the Sly Fox. Not really a respectable disco quorum, as the venue could hold four hundred people, but enough of a crowd to keep us all from staring hopelessly into the dance-music void. Plus, people were dancing. When people are dancing all seems right in the world to a DJ. I was playing the house records that had been released in the last year and become huge hits in the underground dance world: "Break 4 Love" by Raze. "A Day in the Life" by Black Riot. "It's Just A!!!" by House Without a Home II. "Follow Me" by Aly Us. These were remarkable, euphoric singles, all released on independent labels, sold only at independent record stores, and made by oddballs like me in small studios with drum machines, synths, and samplers. Outside of New York City, these records wallowed in obscurity, but here they were huge, newly iconic hits.

And they were organic: not produced by big producers working for multinational corporations, but made by the same people going out to the nightclubs. The record stores were owned by the people who made and played the records. The clothes were made by friends of the people making records. The drugs were sold by roommates of the people making clothes and records. Every night people were dying on the streets and New York City was literally setting itself on fire: landlords had learned that it was cheaper to burn down empty tenements than to pay taxes on them. And somehow the collective response of anyone in their twenties living south of Fourteenth Street was to ignore the despair and the fear and to go dancing until five a.m.

The end of my hour at the Sly Fox approached, so I played my favorite record that week: "Git on Up," the Fast Eddie remix, on DJ International. The fifty people in the Sly Fox were happily dancing, the promoter was spinning around with his goat-skin bucket, and before my record finished I stepped back and yielded my place to the next DJ, who was doing the polite DJ thing and standing behind me with his headphones in his hand.

I packed up my records, shook hands with a few people, and went to find the promoter's friend so I could get paid. "Good job," he told me, "but you can see we didn't do too well tonight."

I stood there, holding on to my skateboard vinyl tower.

"So here's twenty dollars," he said, handing me a crumpled bill. "We'll do another party and next time we'll be able to pay you more."

"Okay, thanks," I said, shaking his hand and taking the $20.

We had never discussed how much I'd be paid but $20 wasn't an insignificant amount of money. It was two taxi rides across town with record crates in the trunk. It was dinner for two at Angelica Kitchen. It was a week's worth of groceries. I wasn't insulted to be paid $20. I was living in New York City, making music, and being invited by Goa hippies to play in empty rooms.

My next stop was Chelsea. The week before I had been DJing at Mars when an older African-American man named Maurice asked me if I'd be interested in DJing a monthly swingers' party that he threw. I said yes, as I was interested in DJing anywhere. If a sanitation worker from Queens came to me and asked if I'd be interested in DJing in his living room for him and his grandmother, I probably would have said, "Yes, but only if you don't pay me."

I wanted to DJ at the biggest clubs on the best nights. I wanted to be a celebrated DJ and musician. But I was also indiscriminate when it came to the work I would actually accept. I didn't professionally say no to anything until 2002. My fear was that if I said no, the universe would send me back to Connecticut to spend the rest of my life emptying garbage cans at Arby's. Also I didn't know what a swingers' party was. Did it involve actual sex? Was it young and sybaritic? Was it old and sad? I hailed a taxi outside the Sly Fox. The cabbie popped the trunk and I stashed my two record crates and my skateboard. I sat on the stiff, cracked vinyl backseat and said, "Nineteenth Street and Tenth Avenue, please."

In New York cabs, there was always a little Plexiglas display where the cabbie's taxi license was displayed. I had an ongoing challenge with my friends to see who could find the best cabbie name. The week before a friend had ridden in the cab of Saddam al-Hussein. And my first week in New York City, I had a cabbie named Muhammad Ali. But tonight I hit the jackpot: the ne plus ultra of taxi-driver names. My cabbie was Fuk Man.

Fuk Man drove me across town. Chelsea in 1989 was empty, the long, desolate blocks stretching west to the Hudson River. For the most part there were no bars, no nightclubs, just shuttered loft buildings and warehouses. Nobody lived this far west, and the only people on the streets were the occasional transsexual hooker or homeless person, doing their best not to be seen.

I found the loft building where the swingers' party was happening, buzzed the intercom, and said what I'd been told to say, the password: "I'm here for a touch of class." The door buzzed open and I pushed my skateboard into the elevator. It was old and clunky, exhausted after decades of hauling garment workers and garments up and down. The doors closed, and I slowly ascended.

I got out on the eighth floor; down the hallway lined by dark office doors I could hear the soft thump of a kick drum. I knocked twice on the appropriate door. A Latino man, huge and bald, opened the door an inch and demanded, "What's the password?"

"A touch of class," I said again, feeling absurd and dirty at the same time.

"Okay, come in."

I walked into a four-thousand-square-foot loft. There was a dance floor at one end, abutted by some couches. There was a bar by the windows, mattresses scattered on the floor past the bar, and a Jacuzzi in the far corner. The DJ was playing an old disco single while a few chubby swingers dressed in bondage gear danced under some spinning red police lights and a lone Radio Shack strobe light.

Maurice, the promoter, came over to me. "Moby! Thanks for coming! Let me introduce you to Jacques, the DJ." We walked over to the DJ booth, where the current DJ ignored us. Then, after he had badly mixed two records together, he looked slowly up at us.

"Jacques, this is Moby. He'll be DJing with you tonight."

"Mmm-hmm," Jacques said, unimpressed.

"Moby plays at Mars," Maurice said.

"Mmm-hmm."

Maurice asked if I wanted a drink.

"Just water, thanks," I said, and he left us.

Jacques played another record and then said, "You can play at two. We'll see how it goes."

"Okay, great." He returned to ignoring me and then badly mixed a Peech Boys record into "Heartbeat" by Seduction. I put my records in the corner. Maurice came back and handed me a water.

"Jacques has been my DJ for years," he said. "He's great!"

"Okay," I said.

"Well, have fun. Thanks for coming." He walked off. I stood next to the DJ booth, ostensibly paying attention to Jacques's terrible mixing, trying to figure out whether I was allowed to look at the swingers in the loft. Finally I worked up my courage and went to find the bathroom. I assumed there were codes of behavior at sex parties, but I had no idea what any of them were. Could I look? What should I say if someone tried to have sex with me? Was I allowed to be straight? Was I going to be chopped into pieces and left in a Dumpster? These all seemed like legitimate questions and concerns.

I walked to the bathroom, surreptitiously watching the half-dozen swingers moving lazily on the dance floor. On the couches some African-American and Latino couples were languidly making out, with their hands between each other's legs. The couches were old and black, and probably caked with bodily fluids. Four people stood at the bar, drinking brown liquor and sparkling wine, with the Empire State Building framed priapically in the windows behind them.

Beyond the bar were the mattresses: a shadowy area, lit with only a few strands of Christmas lights dangling from the ceiling. The first mattress was occupied by a Latino woman going down on an African-American man while he stared blankly at the ceiling. On the second mattress a dominatrix was whipping the ass of a blindfolded pudgy white guy, while a group of people watched her. She was saying, "Pig. Fucking pig." On the third mattress a very skinny Latino woman was having sex with a large Latino man while a skinny white guy stood next to them, masturbating. They all looked bored.

There was a fourth mattress, and a fifth mattress, and a sixth mattress, all filled with people having listless sex. I had never seen public sex before. I had rarely even seen private sex. For most of my life when I had sex I had been ashamed and convinced that I was both doing it wrong and making God angry. The sex going on in front of me didn't seem deviant. There was no enthusiasm, no passion. The people having sex seemed lifeless, and the people watching them seemed lifeless too. The loft was full of scented candles and incense sticks; if you closed your eyes, you'd think you were in a discount candle shop. I had expected a sex club to be threatening and degenerate and challenging. This felt more like a randy group of Department of Motor Vehicles employees on their lunch break.

I walked into the bathroom, freaked out both by having seen people having sex and by how boring it all was. There was a woman standing in front of the sink, and she was the most beautiful naked woman I had ever seen: Nordic with short blond hair and a long, perfect body. She was cleaning herself off with an old pink towel and a bar of Ivory soap. I was smitten. She turned and looked at me, gave me a dismissive glance, and went back to cleaning off whatever had been left on her by the people on the mattresses.

I went into the toilet stall, wondering if any diseases would leap off the seat and energetically burrow into my urethra. I assumed the Nordic goddess had rejected me. Or was that part of sex-club protocol? For her to reject all comers and then wait to see who had the conquering temerity to pursue her? Would I? No. I had neither conquering nor temerity in me.

When I came out of the stall, she was gone. I made my way back to the DJ booth, where Jacques was pissed off. "Where were you?" he demanded. "You're on now. I'm leaving." He was playing "French Kiss" by Lil Louis, and I could see that I had about fifteen seconds left before it ended. I mumbled an apology, not saying that I had never seen people having sex in public before and that I had seen my semen-covered Nordic Dulcinea in the bathroom and that I felt that I'd never find true happiness because she had dismissed me. Instead I grabbed "Break 4 Love" and somehow seamlessly mixed it into the last four seconds of "French Kiss."

"Huh," Jacques said, and then he left.

I played my house and hip-hop and dancehall hits. When I played "Kiss" by Prince I actually got more than ten people dancing, which felt like success. It was hard to compete with the mattresses and the Jacuzzi.

Around four a.m. there were only a dozen people left in the loft; Maurice came over and told me I could play my last record. I put on "Sign 'O' the Times" by Prince and went for one last walk around the loft. On one of the mattresses my Nordic goddess was having a ménage a trois with two overweight guys who looked like they worked in a deli when they weren't befouling the love of my life. Her eyes were closed. They all looked bored. My soul died a little bit.

I had visions of being her Holden Caulfield, saving her from whatever demons compelled her to be at the "Touch of Class" sex party in a dirty loft late on a Wednesday night. I wanted us to eat breakfast together in our clean and sunny apartment, her reading Beckett and eating toast and gazing at me with love. But the reality was that we'd never spoken, she was underneath a sweaty stranger, and my Prince record was about to end.

Maurice came over, said, "Great job, thanks so much," and handed me $50. My $20 from earlier would cover my taxi fare, so this $50 would be my profit for the night. I almost asked Maurice about the Nordic goddess, but then I figured that the people here didn't want to be known. I picked up my records and pushed my skateboard down the hall to the elevator.

I looked over my shoulder at the "Touch of Class" door, hoping that it would burst open and that the Nordic goddess would chase me down the hall, tearfully saying, "I knew in my heart that you were my love. I don't know what I'm doing with my life—will you help me?" But it stayed closed. I rode the elevator down to the street.

As I left the building, I heard a garbage truck rattling in the distance, reminding me that everyone I knew was asleep.

7

TIC-TAC-TOE WITH A CHICKEN

B y the autumn our apartment had turned into a hostel. Damian's girlfriend Alyssa had moved out, soon replaced by his new girl-friend Christine, a nineteen-year-old Korean woman studying economics at NYU. Christine lived in the lightless basement with Da-mian for a month, then she moved out, too. After Christine moved out, Damian's friend Andy showed up with a couple of boxes and moved in.

Roberto moved out in October, and my friend Lee took his room. Lee was a nerdy Christian, but unlike me, he drank and didn't feel guilty about having sex with his girlfriend. We had met at the all-ages Christian club in Connecticut where I used to DJ, and with his thick glasses and love of *Star Trek* he had fit right in with our other awkward Christian friends.

Every night in the apartment there was somebody on the thin black futon in the living room. A friend of mine, a friend of Lee's, or a friend of Damian's, sleeping on the futon, playing Mario Bros., listening to Jane's Addiction, or having sex. After a while Lee and I put locks on our doors, since there were always total strangers staying in our apartment. Also, we didn't fully trust Damian's new roommate Andy.

Andy grew up in New Jersey and had been kicked out of high school a few years ago. Now he was living in the city, doing odd jobs, thinking about going to art school, and hanging out with crack dealers. He had curly red hair and bathed as little as possible. One afternoon Lee and I were sitting in the living room playing Nintendo when Andy appeared at the top of the basement stairs. He stood there in his underwear, not saying anything, just looking around and scratching himself.

"Um. Hey, Andy," Lee said.

"Hey."

"What's going on?" I asked.

He paused. "I just realized I'd been in the basement for forty-eight hours. I thought I should go out." He stood there, blinking, looked around some more, and then wordlessly headed down the black metal stairs, back to the basement.

"Lee," I whispered as I put down the video game controller, "Andy's getting weird."

Lee didn't say anything—he just started a new game of Super Mario Bros. We played a lot of Super Mario Bros. because it was the only game we had for the Nintendo (which we sometimes called the "No-friend-o"). A month ago I'd come home and found Paul and Damian and Lee, all sitting on the couch, watching Super Mario Bros. on TV. Lee had gotten to a new level and videotaped it, and then everyone watched it like a movie. We sometimes talked about buying a new game, but cartridges cost $15, and none of us had an extra $15 to spend. So we sat on the futon, playing Super Mario Bros. over and over again in our penury.

A week after Andy emerged from the basement, Paul (who now went to school at SUNY Purchase) was visiting the city and staying with me and Lee. Once again we were all on the futon playing Super Mario Bros. Paul stood abruptly, turned off the Nintendo, and said, "We need to have a dance party." He walked over to the stereo and put in a Jane's Addiction cassette. The sound of barking dogs filled the room as "Been Caught Stealing" started to play.

We had a rule: if somebody said, "It's time for a dance party," you had to dance. No exceptions. We jumped up and down in the living room to the music and heard Andy yelling from the basement. We couldn't understand what he was saying, but we stomped some more, because stomping on the floor while crazy Andy yelled seemed funny.

Then we heard Andy running up the metal stairs. "Shut up! Shut the fuck up!" Andy screamed when he got to the top. Paul turned off the stereo.

"I fucking hate this place!" Andy yelled. "I fucking hate this! Shut up! Just shut the fuck up! Fuck you! Fuck you!" He turned and ran back down into the basement.

The living room was very quiet. We all looked at each other, stunned.

"Your roommate doesn't seem very happy," Paul said.

"Or sane," Lee said.

"Should we keep dancing?" I asked. "Put on Black Flag?"

Paul laughed. "No," he said. "Let's go to Benny's and get burritos."

We tiptoed out of the apartment. "Bye, Andy," Lee whispered as we walked down the hall.

"I'm sorry you're insane," Paul whispered.

I started laughing. "Please don't stab us, crazy person."

After getting $4 vegan burritos at Benny's we walked to our favorite arcade in Chinatown to play tic-tac-toe with a chicken. I was a vegan and an animal rights advocate, but I couldn't resist playing tic-tac-toe with the chicken in her "Chicken Wins!" Plexiglas box. The arcade was in the bowels of Chinatown, and I assumed that a chicken playing tic-tac-toe was probably happier and better looked after than the chickens plucked and hung up in the windows of the restaurants on Pell Street. Over the years my friends and I had played countless games of tic-tac-toe with the chicken, and for some reason the chicken always won.

After losing to the chicken a few times we walked back up Mott Street and Fourth Avenue, getting home around eleven. Damian was in the kitchen, smoking cigarettes and looking concerned.

"You guys, Andy's really upset. What happened?" he asked.

"Andy freaked out," Lee said.

"Just give him some space," Damian said, putting out his cigarette in the sink.

"Is he going to stab us in our sleep?" I asked.

We heard a voice coming up from the basement: Andy in a singsong voice, saying, "I can *heeeear you.*"

"I'm going back to SUNY," Paul said, heading for the door.

"Coward," Lee called out. The door shut behind Paul and the apartment felt very quiet.

"What should we do?" I asked Lee.

"Nintendo?" he replied, predictably. So we turned on the TV and the Nintendo and quietly played some Super Mario Bros. I walked over to the basement stairs.

"Damian? Andy?" I called down politely. "You guys want to play Nintendo?" I could hear the Cocteau Twins playing on Damian's stereo. "Damian?" I called down again.

He came to the bottom of the staircase, smoking a cigarette. "No thanks," he said, and returned to his basement room. I played another game of Super Mario Bros. with Lee, then headed to my room, locked the door, and worked on quiet ambient music until two a.m.

In the morning I walked out to the living room. Andy was sitting on the futon and Damian was standing at the door to the kitchen. Next to Andy were two cans of gasoline. He was staring at the floor. "Get Lee," he said in a low voice.

I knocked on Lee's door. He unlocked it, still in his underwear, half-asleep. "What is it?" he said blearily, then saw the cans of gasoline. He walked into the living room and crossed his arms, suddenly awake. "Andy, what's going on?" he demanded.

Andy kept staring at the floor. Damian lit a cigarette. "Should you be smoking, Damian?" I asked, indicating the gasoline. He ignored me.

"I went out last night to get gasoline," Andy said. "I was going to burn you guys to death in your sleep." I looked at Lee; he looked at me. Both of us said silent prayers to the god of locked doors. "But I got back here and your doors were locked, so I sat down on the futon and fell asleep."

Lee and I looked at each other, not sure what to do or say in the presence of a potentially murderous psychopath. Damian broke the silence. "Andy and I have talked. He's not happy here. We're going to move out."

"Okay, when?" I asked.

"We're going to look at apartments today. So as soon as we find something."

"Andy, I'm sorry if we upset you yesterday," Lee said.

"Yeah, Andy, I'm sorry," I said.

"Too late for that," he muttered, not looking up.

"Andy," Damian said quietly, "let's go look for apartments, okay?"

Andy sat, clearly tempted by the cans of gasoline. Then he stood up and looked at Lee and me. "You should have burned to death," he said, and walked down the hallway. Damian followed him.

"Fuck!" I said after they left the apartment.

"What a fucking psycho!" Lee said.

"Do you think he can hear us?" I asked quietly.

"What a fucking psycho," Lee whispered. "What should we do with the gasoline?"

"I don't know—put it on the street?" That was our answer for everything. If you needed to get rid of a terrible book, or if you had an old pair of shoes, or a Bic pen with an eighth of an inch of ink left, you could leave it on Fourteenth Street and within five minutes someone would have taken it, hoping to sell it for crack. Fourteenth Street was like a dirty river, carrying away anything left on or near it. We picked up the gas cans and carried them to the street, putting them on the sidewalk by the L train stop.

It was a beautiful day: high white clouds against a pale blue sky. A good day not to be burned to death. "Do you think he would have done it?" I asked.

"I don't know," Lee said. "Probably?" We walked west down Fourteenth street. "How do we get new roommates?" Lee asked.

"I'll make an ad. 'Roommates wanted. Three-bedroom duplex overlooking a garbage-filled shaftway, no murderous psychopaths need apply.'"

8

L TRAIN CONDUCTOR

Michael Alig was the king of New York nightlife and the liege lord of the club kids. He'd created a world in lower Manhattan that was shiny and degenerate—years before he killed and dismembered his drug dealer and ended up in prison. Michael's club nights at the Limelight involved glamorous teenage trannies, drug-addled old queens, pee-drinking contests, people dressed as giant chickens, buckets of drugs, passed-out celebrities on filthy couches, random bathroom sex, and any forms of transgressive behavior that he and his club kids could borrow, invent, or appropriate.

There were riots in the East Village, people were dying everywhere of AIDS and crack and gang violence—and in the middle of this ruined city was Michael, a debased wunderkind who looked like a cherub from Indiana.

I started DJing sporadically at Limelight in 1990, and Michael and I became quasi-friends. "Quasi" because I worked for him, and also because I was a straight, sober Christian, while he was gay, drug addled, and as far as I could tell, in league with a consortium of at least a few devils. We had a strange and friendly rapport, and the Limelight was our shared world.

The Limelight was a nineteenth-century church that had been re-purposed in the early eighties as a cavernous A-list nightclub. By the end of the eighties it had lost its glamour and was generally seen as a sad place, turning a profit by hosting retro club nights for tourists. Then Michael Alig showed up at the Limelight in 1989 and reimagined it as a home for club kids, ravers, and goths. Club kids were generally urban and gay, ravers were generally suburban and straight, and goths lived in basements and spiderwebs. The ravers and club kids shared a love for techno and ecstasy, while the goths loved electronic music and old churches. So the Limelight became home for all three tribes.

At one of Michael's parties in 1990 I was hanging out in a back room surrounded by twenty-year-old club kids and ravers on ecstasy and ketamine. The club kids were wearing tight disco clothes and a thick veneer of glitter. The ravers were dressed in giant pants and oversized T-shirts with mutated corporate logos. The goths stood in the corners, drinking vodka and clad in black. I was in front of a Plexiglas booth, gazing up at the most beautiful woman I'd ever seen. She was a go-go dancer with long blond hair and an angelic, unblemished face. I was transfixed by the vision of her dancing to a Deee-Lite song under warm orange lights when Michael walked up to me.

"She's gorgeous, right?" he said as he sipped his cocktail.

"She's amazing," I agreed. "I've never seen anyone so beautiful."

"I think she might have a crush on you."

"What? Really?" I stammered as the go-go dancer smiled sweetly at me.

"Yes. Plus she has the most amazing penis I've ever sucked," he said, and walked away. The dancer blew me a kiss.

Later that night I watched the beautiful dancer pee into a glass on the club's main stage and convince a very high stockbroker to drink his/her pee while the audience and Clara the Carefree Chicken applauded. The stockbroker smiled in the disco lights, his teeth wet and shining from tranny pee, and then he and the go-go dancer started making out while DJ Keoki played a Lords of Acid track.

veryone in Michael Alig's world in 1990 was young and happy, and the constant degeneracy seemed almost sweet and benign. They were all doing obscene amounts of drugs and having sex with strangers, but they still seemed innocent. Michael had somehow created a consequence-free island of misfit toys, populated by fresh-faced NYU and FIT students covered in glitter and filled with MDMA. Being sober and Christian meant that I was excluded from most of the degeneracy, but I was still accepted as a fellow misfit toy.

Once a month or so Michael would organize an outlaw party: he and his business partner Steve Lewis would find an unused public space, rent a big sound system, and invite a thousand of their closest friends to get high somewhere that wasn't a nightclub. They had hosted outlaw parties under bridges and in shopping malls, but in early 1990 they decided to host one on a subway train. The instructions they gave were simple: meet at the L train at nine p.m. on Wednesday night. Bring drugs and music.

This was perfect for me and Lee, because the Third Avenue L stop was fifteen feet from our front door on Fourteenth Street. We left our apartment at 8:50, descended into the subway station, and jumped the turnstile. Then we waited on the platform with a few hundred club kids and ravers. A little after nine p.m. the L train limped into the station. We could see that the cars were already filled with hundreds of manic club kids and ravers, playing techno on giant boom boxes. When the doors opened we squeezed in. People were blowing whistles, banging on seats, and hanging upside down from the bars on the ceiling. The train wasn't moving, and every few minutes the conductor would get on the intercom and say, "The train is stopped in the station. All passengers depart here." The club kids and ravers ignored him, turned up their music, and kept dancing on the seats. Eventually the conductor closed the doors and got the train moving, with the dancers falling on top of each other when the train rounded the corner going into Union Square.

When the train reached Union Square the last terrified civilians got off the train and hundreds more club kids and ravers piled on. As the train left the station some of the ecstasy-fueled passengers decided that they needed to be naked on a subway train, so they took off their clothes and started dancing naked and jumping up and down on the seats. It was beautiful bedlam. Thirty different house and techno tracks coming from thirty different boom boxes. Naked ravers giving lap dances to Clara the Carefree Chicken. People doing lines of coke and ketamine off of fiberglass subway seats.

"This is amazing!" Lee yelled over a few different deafening techno tracks.

The train started moving again and a few of the club kids on our train started chanting, "New York! New York!" Lee and I and everyone else in the train car joined in, a hundred fifty club kids and ravers and giant chickens all stomping their feet and chanting, "New York! New York!" over the cacophony of competing techno and house tracks.

I was standing on an orange fiberglass subway seat, yelling, "New York! New York!" along with my fellow lunatics, when a club kid covered in silver body paint grabbed my hips and bit my penis through my pants.

"Aah! What, why did you do that?" I yelled over the din.

He smiled at me. "I don't know! I had to!"

The train pulled abruptly into the Sixth Avenue station. We poured out the doors and up the stairs into the night.

9

ORANGE SODIUM LIGHT

One Friday night I was DJing on the main floor at Mars when a white guy with thick glasses came into the DJ booth. After I cued up a Jungle Brothers track he handed me a business card and said, "I'm Jared Hoffman and I'm starting a record label. I was wondering if you ever produced your own music."

I'd spent my entire adult life, and most of my adolescent life, making music and trying to get a record contract. For the past five years I'd spent my free time either working on music or going around New York City with a bag full of demo tapes. I'd do my rounds, dutifully dropping off cassettes of my original music at Wild Pitch and Strictly Rhythm and Big Beat and Warlock and Profile and every other independent dance label in New York. No one had ever responded. But now there was a record-label president in my DJ booth.

"Yes!" I yelled over the music. "I was a musician before I was a DJ."

Later that week I met Jared at his apartment on Fourteenth Street. His building had a doorman, which impressed me; I had never set foot in an apartment building with a doorman. We sat in Jared's living room, which had views of downtown New York and the World Trade Center. He gave me a glass of water and I played him some of my music. He listened earnestly, tapping his fingers on the arms of his black leather couch. "This is good, Moby," he said after I played him a techno song I was working on called "Rock the House."

The next day he called me and told me that he wanted to sign me to an artist deal with his new label. Just as I'd never imagined that I would actually DJ in New York, I'd never actually imagined that anyone would offer to sign me to their record label.

There were a few caveats. For starters, his label lacked an office, a staff, money, any other artists, or even a name. "But we're thinking about calling it Instinct," he told me. "My business partner Dave even drew up a logo." He gave me a contract and I signed it the next day. I would have signed a napkin or an old Post-it note so long as it had the words "recording contract" written at the top. Upon signing I was given exactly $0, but I had a record contract, so I was ecstatic. They had never made records, and, apart from two punk-rock singles I'd released in high school, I'd never made records, so we were in the same boat.

Jared suggested that I move my studio into his living room so that we could get down to the actual work of finishing some of my songs and releasing them.

One week after signing with Instinct I was talking with Jared and he casually said, "We should go out to Newark to see Tony Humphries DJ at Zanzibar."

In 1990 every club I knew of—Limelight, the Tunnel, Mars, the Building, Nell's, the Palladium, Shelter, the Pyramid, Red Zone, and Sound Factory—was in Manhattan below Fiftieth Street. The exception was Zanzibar, in Newark, New Jersey. And the only DJ I knew of who didn't live in New York was Tony Humphries, who DJed at Zanzibar and lived in Newark.

Frankie Knuckles had invented house music, lived on the Lower East Side, and was deified. Junior Vasquez owned the floor at Sound Factory, where he played twelve-hour sets, and was a revered legend living in Chelsea. Danny Tenaglia was in the house-music pantheon: he too played long, remarkable sets and lived downtown. Larry Levan was a dance music god and he'd just started a residency at Choice in the East Village. Dave Morales was seen as the biggest of the New York house-music DJs: he owned the floor at Red Zone, and in an unconventional move, he lived in midtown.

But Tony Humphries existed in a strange, mythical realm of his own. His sets were long and legendary, his remixes were flawless, and he lived in the unknown recesses of Newark, New Jersey. Just on the other side of the Hudson River, Newark was a ravaged war zone that made New York City look like a bucolic suburb. The buildings in Manhattan might have been on fire, but the basic infrastructure of New York City worked, if barely.

Newark, on the other hand, was a failed state. Stories abounded of people calling 911 in Newark and the police never showing up, of Newark firemen drinking beer and laughing while buildings burned, and of emergency rooms where patients were raped by orderlies. Newark had the reputation of being the worst, nastiest city on the Eastern Seaboard. And that was where Tony Humphries lived and DJed.

When Jared suggested that we go to Newark to hear Tony Humphries, I was full of questions: *Do you actually know Tony Humphries? Does Zanzibar exist, or is it a mythical land, like the house-music version of Brigadoon? Will we die?* But I didn't want to be a neurotic killjoy. Instead, I just asked, "How do we get there?"

"Oh, I'll borrow my mom's car," Jared said. "She keeps it in a garage uptown."

On Friday at ten p.m. I walked over to Jared's apartment. Joining us for our pilgrimage to Zanzibar was his friend Romy, a gorgeous Arab Latina from Queens with short dark hair and perfect black eyes. Romy's entire world consisted of house music and nightclubs. She was friends with Larry Levan, she routinely hung out with Junior Vasquez in the DJ booth at Sound Factory, and, Jared told me, she actually knew Tony Humphries. Romy went out five nights a week, took a lot of ecstasy, drank a lot of water, danced until six a.m., and had never had a real job.

I was wearing my utilitarian nightclub outfit: black jeans, a black

T-shirt, and sneakers. Jared was dressed equally generically. Romy, though, looked amazing. Her hair was slicked back and she was wearing a thin white T-shirt, tight (but not too tight) jeans, and a pair of Adidas of the kind sold only to Japanese tourists and the stratospherically cool. I wanted to have a crush on Romy, but she seemed too unattainable. I thought that possibly she might be asexual or gay. Or she was straight but had no interest in dating nervous white musicians who could barely afford soy milk. Either way, there was no romantic tension between us—just unrequited worship on my part.

Romy and Jared sat in the front of his mom's big Oldsmobile as we drove up Tenth Avenue and talked about DJs they liked and records they adored and people they'd dated. I sat in the back, looking out the car window. We drove through Chelsea, passing tall, empty buildings and shuttered warehouses until we got to the Lincoln Tunnel. Flanking the entrance to the tunnel was a small army of defeated hookers. They were all skinny and unwashed, their gray skin sucking in the orange sodium light. And yet they were sexy.

I felt terrible admitting this to myself. They were all damaged and barely alive, deserving of my Christian sympathy and not my un-Christian lust. But the fact that they stood there, brazenly offering sex, was sexy. In my world, sex was concealed until it was had—awkwardly and on cheap futons or in suburban bedrooms. And here in front of me were hookers, letting the world know that sex was available, easily. I wanted to be a good Christian in a loving relationship, not someone who deep down was turned on by emaciated prostitutes hanging out at the entrance to the Lincoln Tunnel, hustling for enough money to score some crack.

We drove through the tunnel and emerged from the bright orange tunnel lights into the darkness of New Jersey. I knew New Jersey because every summer growing up I'd visited my grandmother at her retirement home in suburban Westfield. But this New Jersey was unknown to me: it was a land of empty gas stations and abandoned buildings and barren parking lots. It was where people went to give up, buy drugs, open a pawnshop, or die behind a Dumpster.

Somehow Jared knew how to get to Newark, which amazed me since every road looked like it went in an infinite loop or ended in a marsh full of bodies. We got off the freeway in Newark and rolled slowly down the unlit streets. Most of the stoplights didn't work, which was okay since there were no other cars on the roads. Clearly the apocalypse had chosen New Jersey for its test run.

We passed a few late-night delis, their fluorescent lights pale and blue behind thick bulletproof Plexiglas. By the time Jared found the Zanzibar parking lot Romy was almost bouncing with excitement. "I love Zanzibar, it's so great," she sang. I tried to think of something clever to say in return, but instead, I just sat in the backseat like a polite tourist, nodding and smiling.

Romy ran ahead of us to the entrance, hugging the doorman and saying, "Oh, Marcel, they're with me." Marcel looked at Jared and me like we were old socks, but he let us in. Romy disappeared into Zanzibar, hugging various friends. As Jared and I walked in it became obvious that we were the only white people in the building. A tall queen glared at me and said, "Oh, is it Ku Klux Klan night?"

I wanted to defend myself—*No! I love black music! I'm not a racist! I'm sorry I'm white!*—but I just walked down the hallway to the dance floor. I'd expected Zanzibar to be the Shangri-la of nightclubs, but on this Friday at eleven thirty p.m., it was just another club. A loud club, but still a club.

Jared and I headed for the bar, trying to be inconspicuous—but before we got there Romy grabbed Jared, said, "You have to see the DJ booth!" and ran away with him. I ordered a Coke and found a spot on the edge of the dance floor. From where I was standing I could dance a little bit and see the DJ booth. Romy was in there, talking with a DJ who clearly wasn't Tony Humphries. I'd heard of this phenomenon: superstar DJs had warm-up DJs who would play the first few and last few hours of the night. The superstar would show up at midnight or one a.m., when the crowd was ready for them. While Romy chatted, Jared stood behind her with his arms crossed, looking uncomfortable.

The music was generic house B-sides, nothing too exciting. The crowd danced languidly, pacing themselves, as everyone knew that they were here for a marathon. The legendary clubs like Sound Factory and Zanzibar and the Paradise Garage stayed open until eight or nine a.m., and DJs routinely played for ten or twelve hours at a stretch.

I started dancing by myself and felt something strange on my back. I reached my hand around, touching between my shoulder blades, and discovered that it was a gob of spit. I'd been spit on.

I was disgusted, but I wasn't offended. Fundamentally I felt that being white in a black environment was something to be ashamed of. Whenever I was allowed into hip-hop clubs or house clubs I felt grateful. I didn't want to go to straight white clubs where the people I grew up with drank Rolling Rocks and made cautious and ironic comments about *New Yorker* articles and Pavement records. I wanted to be on a dance floor, surrounded by black and Latino and gay people, getting lost in the euphoria that only seemed to happen there, when the perfect record came on and five hundred people cheered in a way that I'd never heard white people cheer. If the price of admission was being spit on or called a Klan member, then so be it. I had friends in New York who were dying of AIDS and being stabbed—I thought I could handle some spit and epithets delivered by glamorous queens.

Midnight came and went: no Tony Humphries. One a.m. rolled around: still no Tony Humphries, although I did get spit on again. At one thirty I felt everyone looking up at the DJ booth—and Tony Humphries was standing there, twice the size of the warm-up DJ. He looked down at the crowd like a benign dictator, made his way to the turntables, and started playing a tribal house twelve-inch, slowly mixing it in and out of the record the warm-up DJ had been playing. People streamed onto the dance floor, pointing at the DJ booth and yelling, "Tony!" He stood there, gently smiling at his turntables.

Then he segued into "New Beats the House" by Grey House, and the crowd went nuts. This was the genius of the best DJs: to take a simple, obvious record and make it sublime. They found the records that the rest of us ignored and made us realize that we were philistines. Tony mixed back and forth between two copies of "New Beats the House" for fifteen minutes, taking this repetitive electro-house track and turning it into an ecstatic celebration of life. The crowd was sweating and throbbing. The lights weren't amazing, the sound system was barely adequate, but at that moment, there was no better place on the planet than Zanzibar.

As Tony slowly mixed out of "New Beats the House" into an understated dub of "Just Want Another Chance" by Reese, Jared tapped me on the shoulder. "Isn't he amazing?" he asked.

"I'm so glad we came," I gushed. "I love it."

"Okay, should we get going?"

I was stunned. Tony Humphries was playing and I didn't want to leave, ever. "Leave?" I said, almost in a squeak.

"Yeah, I have to get up at nine to go upstate," Jared explained.

I looked around. "Where's Romy?"

"Oh, she's staying here. She'll get a ride back with someone at six or seven."

I wanted to stay and get a ride back at six or seven, ideally with Romy. I wanted to make out with her in the back of a car on the way to her loft in the West Village and wake up next to her in the afternoon, confident and less white. But instead I said, "Okay, let's go."

As Jared and I walked across the parking lot, I told him I'd been spit on a few times. "Ew, that's disgusting," he said. "Can you clean it off?"

"I don't think so—I don't have any tissues."

"Are you sure? I don't want to get spit on my mom's car."

I took off my spit-covered shirt, balled it up, and threw it into a Dumpster in a corner of the Zanzibar parking lot. We drove back to the city and Jared parked the car by his apartment. "Are you going to walk home like that? With no shirt?" he asked.

I shrugged. "I guess so."

He paused, maybe thinking about offering me one of his shirts, but he just said, "Okay, talk to you later."

I walked home. It was three a.m., I smelled like secondhand cigarette smoke, and I was shirtless. Lower Manhattan was full of drunks and partiers, but they all gave me a wide berth. In 1990 being shirtless in public in New York City was an announcement that you were a crack addict: they would sell their clothes, or anything, to buy more crack.

I quietly sang "New Beats the House" to myself as I walked, eager to get home so I could turn on my equipment and try to make a record that Tony Humphries could play for fifteen minutes at Zanzibar.

10

QUARTERS ON NEEDLES

By the summer of 1990 Mars had become a big hangout for rappers and drug dealers. The dealers would roll in, order bottles of champagne, and drunkenly throw crumpled $20 bills at the DJs to get them to play Audio Two's "Top Billin'" or Big Daddy Kane's "Raw." The dealers rolled in packs of ten or twenty, and they all carried guns, so these weren't really requests and I never considered refusing. When their favorite songs came on the drug dealers put aside their bravado—for a few minutes, they'd turn into happy kids, singing along to "Raw" or "Scenario."

Mars was also a hangout for gay black and Latino kids from the outer boroughs. They'd show up at ten thirty p.m., dressed in lightweight clothes, and dance until we closed at four or five a.m. They loved the melodic house tracks of the day: "A Promise," "The Poem," "Break 4 Love." When the dealers showed up and demanded hip-hop, the sweet outer-borough gay kids would look hurt and slightly defeated, but they understood. You didn't say no to crack dealers on the street and you didn't say no to crack dealers in a nightclub.

There were even a few songs that the crack dealers and the outer-borough gay kids agreed on: "I'll House You" by the Jungle Brothers, "Let It Roll" by Doug Lazy, and pretty much anything by De La

Soul. When the DJs played these songs there was relative dance-floor harmony.

One Friday at midnight I was on the second floor, spinning house records and hip-hop records, when suddenly I felt a frisson passing through the room. Terrance, the second-floor busboy, ran up to me, his eyes glowing, and shouted, "Yo, Moby, *Kane is here.*" I looked over at the bar: Big Daddy Kane was standing there, a glass of champagne in his hand, looking like a demigod. Kane and Rakim were the biggest stars in Manhattan; everyone played their records and revered them. Rakim might have been a slightly better rapper, but Kane was the reigning king.

In the previous few months I'd had visits in the DJ booth from the guys in 3rd Bass, De La Soul, and the Ultramagnetic MCs. They'd get drunk and get on the microphone as I played instrumental B-sides and they freestyled over them. I wanted to get Kane to rap over one of my tracks—I held up the microphone and tried to catch his eye. He just leaned against the bar with his fade and his linen suit, looking like a hip-hop Frank Sinatra, but cooler.

After thirty minutes Kane left, passing Joe and Darryl from Run-DMC as they walked in. I couldn't believe my eyes. Here we were, mere mortals, witnessing three of the mightiest rappers in New York shaking hands and nodding in the doorway. Run-DMC were the biggest hip-hop stars on the planet, but by 1990 they weren't nearly as esteemed among New Yorkers as Kane or Rakim or De La Soul. A few months earlier, though, they had put out a B-side called "Pause," and it was restoring some of the credibility they'd lost due to commercial success. Klark Kent played it, Duke of Denmark played it, Red Alert played it—the song was beloved and sanctioned.

Darryl marched over to the DJ booth and said, "Yo, boy, give me the mic!" I promptly obeyed. I had sampled the loop from "The 900 Number" on my sampler, so I played that and he started freestyling. Most MCs said the same things when they were freestyling—standard shtick, heavy on the "Oh shit!" and "Throw your hands in the air!"—

but Darryl was unique. He had grown up freestyling, and his skills were flawless. I segued into a loop of "Funky Drummer," and he lost himself in the flow, getting better and better. The crowd was yelling, the crack dealers were dancing and waving champagne bottles in the air—even the sweet gay kids from Queens were smiling and excited. Then I played the instrumental of "Pause" and the crowd exploded—this was his hit. Darryl was sweating and he had a manic gleam in his eye while he rhymed. He was doing his parts from the record; the crowd was screaming and dancing; I was dancing myself; and then I bumped the turntable.

The record skipped. Not a gentle "oops" hiccup of a skip, but the sort of skip that involved the needle bouncing loudly across the vinyl and ending up in the dead empty zone at the end of the record.

I had killed Christmas. I had stopped joy dead in its tracks. The crowd booed and Darryl looked at me with dismay and derision. He said, "What the fuck was that?" threw down the mic, and stalked away. The crowd kept booing. I tried to come back by playing "I'll House You," but in a room of five hundred people nobody wanted to dance. The drug dealers were loudly jeering: "Stupid white boy! Fucked up DMC!"

I stood before the crowd, wide eyed and ashamed, and felt my soul disappear through the top of my hairy scalp. Could I hide? Anywhere? The busboy came over, patted my back, and said, "Bro, you fucked up."

I knew. I had fucked up. My life was over. I would get fired, move back to Stamford, and hope that I could return to my old room in the abandoned factory. Or maybe I could put my twin mattress in my mom's basement and sleep there. At least I had options.

I kept DJing, without enthusiasm, and eventually the night ended. I packed up my records and my sampler and trudged upstairs to the office to get paid. Yuki had a voracious and legendary temper. He screamed at everyone, even people who didn't work for him. I had once watched him scream at a potential employee for what seemed like five straight minutes. The poor guy stood there, head bowed, while Yuki yelled at on him. And he was just applying for a job.

Yuki was sitting in the office with some friends. He saw me and said, "I heard you had a fuckup with DMC?"

"Yes," I said sheepishly. "I skipped 'Pause' while he was rhyming." I braced myself.

Yuki smiled and said, "Ha, maybe DMC was drunk! Maybe it was him!" The tension disappeared. I had caught Yuki on a good night: it seemed to me he was the right combination of drunk and high. Whatever the case, he had not fired me, stabbed me, or even yelled at me. He paid me and I went home.

After I unloaded my records and equipment into my bedroom I found Lee and some of his friends sitting on the futon, smoking pot and listening to a Klark Kent mix tape. I told them what had happened and they were stunned.

"Really?"

"Are you fucking kidding?"

Then one of Lee's friends asked, "Did you tape quarters to your needles?"

"Quarters?" I asked.

"Yeah, all the hip-hop DJs tape quarters to their needles. It makes them heavy so they never skip. You can use nickels too, but I like quarters."

So that was the trick. Tape quarters to your needles and your records won't skip. I vowed, like Scarlett O'Hara if she had been a stringy-haired DJ instead of an antebellum grande dame, that I would never skip a record again.

It was five thirty a.m. I'd humiliated myself in front of five hundred people and one of the biggest hip-hop stars in the world, but I still had my job and I'd learned something: tape quarters to my needles. It was time for bed so that this miserable night could come to an end, but first I needed to use the bathroom. I went down the hall to the bathroom, sat on the toilet, and picked up the toilet paper roll.

A huge cockroach fell out of the toilet paper tube and grabbed on to my penis.

"Aaaaah!" I screamed as I started swatting at the cockroach that was stubbornly clinging to my penis. Finally, I knocked it into the toilet and immediately flushed it. My harm-no-animals philosophy fell by the wayside: all I wanted to do was send this giant mutant cockroach very far away from my home and my penis.

I went to bed, still hyperventilating from my genital brush with the giant cockroach. I tried to calm myself down by imagining my obituary in the *New York Times*:

Local disc jockey Moby, best known for skipping a record while the most legendary MC on the planet was freestyling, died last week. He was crushed by the weight of his own terror and humiliation after a cockroach grabbed on to his penis. He is survived by his mother, his cat Tucker, and a few friends with whom he was known to play Super Mario Bros.

11

BLOODY SKATEBOARD WHEELS

The phone rang. It was Yuki, so I was immediately terrified.

"Oh, uh, Moby, can you play rare groove?" he asked.

"Of course, I love rare groove," I said, having no idea what "rare groove" actually was.

"Okay, you play on roof tonight. Bring rare groove records!"

"Great, thanks!"

I hung up the phone and panicked. What was "rare groove"? Did I have any rare groove records?

I called Damian. "I'm DJing on the roof at Mars tonight and I'm playing rare groove. Do you know what rare groove is?" I asked him.

"Is it a band?"

"Okay, you don't know either. I'll talk to you later."

I could call Roberto. He'd know what rare groove was, but would he tell me? If I showed up at Mars and played the wrong records I would get fired, and he could go to Mars and try to get my job. But I had to ask somebody. He picked up on the second ring.

"Roberto, do you know what rare groove is?" I asked.

"Hold on," he said. I could hear him yelling to someone in the background, and then he came back on the line. "We think it's James Brown and seventies funk," he said, "but we're not sure. Why?"

"Oh, I'm DJing on the roof at Mars and Yuki wants me to play rare groove," I said.

"Well, good luck. Let me know if you get fired."

We hung up. Maybe somebody at Vinylmania would know, and it was possible they would even tell me. (I worked under the assumption that the people who worked at Vinylmania wouldn't talk to me, largely because when I went to Vinylmania no one ever talked to me.) I walked over to Carmine Street. It was a slow afternoon and the DJ at the back of the store didn't look too busy.

"Hi, excuse me," I said politely to the DJ, "do you know what rare groove is?"

He just stared at me. "What?"

"Rare groove. It's a genre—do you know what it is?"

"Of course I do," he said, weary in the face of my ignorance. He walked out from behind the turntables and escorted me to the far back of the store. "Here," he said, pointing to the funk and soul section.

"Oh, so rare groove is funk and soul?" I asked.

"Basically," he said, and walked away.

I already had a bunch of James Brown records and a bunch of old northern soul records. Would I need more? I was getting paid $100 tonight, so I could afford to buy $100 of rare groove records. I flipped through the records: the Isley Brothers, the Meters, Funkadelic. I had all these records. Was I already an accidental rare groove DJ? I bought a few obscure funk compilations and headed home, almost confident that I'd play the right music and keep my job.

At three a.m. I was on the roof of Mars playing a Lyn Collins record. It was a warm and windy night; I'd taped quarters to the tops of my tone arms to keep them from blowing across the surface of the records. Flea and Anthony from the Red Hot Chili Peppers came over and stood in front of me, drunk and staring at the record I was playing.

"This is cool," Flea said. "What is it?"

"Lyn Collins," I said authoritatively. "It's rare groove."

"What's rare groove?" he asked, slurring and swaying a bit as Anthony was pulled away by a beautiful woman with bleached hair.

"Um, funk and soul," I said. "I think."

"Cool. Oh, I'm Flea." He stuck out his hand and I shook it.

"Hi, I'm Moby." He nodded his head and walked away. The Lyn Collins record ended and I played "Cissy Strut" by the Meters. The people on the roof cheered and Flea and Anthony started dancing drunkenly with their dates. Yuki came onto the roof, saw people dancing, and smiled at me. Once again, it looked like I wasn't going to be fired.

I checked my watch. In four hours I had to be on my way to Martha's Vineyard: I was driving with my on-again/off-again girlfriend Janet and some of her friends to a retreat organized by the Fellowship of Christians in Universities and Schools. I'd be sleeping in bunks with the other Christian men, while Janet would be in the women's bunks on the other side of the retreat center. Everyone at the Christian retreat had to have a service position, so I'd already signed up to be a dishwasher.

But at this moment I was playing rare groove on the roof of Mars. Flea came over again. "Awesome record, dude!" he yelled, and shook my hand again. I figured I'd go a bit obvious, so I played "Thank You (Falettinme Be Mice Elf Again)" by Sly and the Family Stone. Russell Simmons from Def Jam stumbled over, leaning on a drunken Asian model in high heels. He looked at me, looked at the record, looked at me, nodded, and stumbled away. Russell had signed and produced Run-DMC and LL Cool J. He was a legend, and he'd nodded at me for playing a Sly Stone record. Yuki was smiling, Russell Simmons was nodding, Flea and Anthony were dancing, and a warm late-night breeze was blowing from across the Hudson River.

Mars had to stop serving liquor at four a.m. but the music sometimes went on for an additional hour; there were never any complaints about noise, because nobody lived in or near the Meatpacking District. The police stayed away from the area around Mars unless somebody got stabbed or shot. Around four thirty a.m., as the sun was coming up, I played my last record, the Isley Brothers' "For the Love of You." There were twenty or thirty drunks left on the roof; a few of them ended their night by slow-dancing to the Isleys. I packed up my records and headed downstairs to get paid.

With $100 in my pocket I headed home, pushing my records on my skateboard. If I could do that for the nine blocks to our apartment on Fourteenth and Third I could save $10 in taxi fare. The sun was swelling over the horizon, casting long strands of orange light down Fourteenth Street. The meat packers were already busy, unloading sides of beef and dead lamb carcasses as I pushed my skateboard past them. I said a little prayer in my head for all the dead animals. *I'm sorry*, I thought, watching a meat packer head into a refrigerated warehouse, a dead pig slung over his shoulder. *I'm sorry.*

My skateboard slid through a puddle of blood. How could I be witnessing this horror—all of these dead animal bodies being thrown around—while the morning sun was on my face and when I'd just had a perfect night playing records on the roof of Mars? As I pushed my skateboard through another puddle of offal I silently vowed, *Trying to end animal suffering will be my life's work, no matter what.*

Eventually I got home, put my records away, and lay down for fifty minutes. The alarm went off at seven a.m.; I staggered out of bed, made a peanut butter and jelly sandwich, grabbed my backpack, and headed to Grand Central Terminal. I got off the train in Greenwich and saw Janet waiting by the red BMW her dad had bought her for her eighteenth birthday.

"Hi, Mr. DJ," she said as I walked off the train platform. "I didn't think you'd actually make it."

"I'm so tired," was all I could say. I got in her car and looked behind me: three strawberry-blond seventeen-year-old Christian girls were sitting shoulder to shoulder in the backseat and smiling at me. They were wearing khaki shorts, Esprit shoes, and soft pastel T-shirts. "Hi, I'm Moby," I said. "I hope it's not rude, but I might try to sleep on the ride."

They smiled politely and one responded, "Can we pray before we leave?" We bowed our heads as she said, "God, thank you for this time together, and thank you for this opportunity to get to know you better. Please look after us on this adventure. Through your son's name, amen."

Five hours later, we were all on the ferry from Woods Hole to Martha's Vineyard. The three Christian girls were sitting in a circle, praying with their eyes closed. The sun made their strawberry-blond hair glow, and the sky was endless blue, dotted with bone-white clouds. As the ferry pulled into the slip, Janet asked, "How are you doing, Mobes?"

"I'm okay," I said, my eyes red and burning. "Very tired." I'd napped briefly on I-95, but I'd had about seventy-five total minutes of sleep in the past thirty-six hours.

We all gathered outside the ferry dock in Vineyard Haven. Standing by some passenger vans was one of the leaders of our Christian youth group, but not the one I expected. The guy I expected was short, dark-haired, and average but thought of himself as an erstwhile Ralph Lauren model. He had almost lost his job the year before when it was discovered that he had been sleeping with a few of the Christian girls whose spiritual development had been entrusted to him. But after a tearful mea culpa he'd been allowed to keep his job and his house. I was relieved that this devout lothario wasn't going to be on Martha's Vineyard at the retreat.

We got into vans and drove down winding, shaded roads, past beautiful nineteenth-century Martha's Vineyard houses. As we passed a cobblestone path I realized that only twelve hours earlier I had been playing records for Russell Simmons and pushing my skateboard through puddles of blood. I looked at the young suburban Christians in the van: eight people, all kind and clean and well fed. Specifically, well fed on the animals I'd seen bouncing on the backs of the meat packers. I wanted to rail against the cloistered New England spirituality that dealt with abstract questions of faith when the world around us was full of horror and suffering. I wanted to scream inside the van, "You're all frauds! Your faith is like sending an L.L.Bean sweater to a concentration camp!" Instead I gazed at the mansions and the tall stone gates as we bounced along a sun-dappled vineyard road. I heard the van hit something small and the driver shout, "Crap!"

"What happened?" I asked.

"We hit a squirrel," he said.

"No!" all of the young Christians in the van cried. They were filled with grief for the little squirrel we'd just killed. I sat in the backseat, silent and judgmental, thinking, *You eat a few hundred dead animals every year, but a single squirrel being killed by our rental van makes you upset?*

Janet looked at me, concerned. "Everything okay, Mobes?" she asked.

"I just don't like us very much," I said.

"Us?"

"Us, the people in this van, our species," I said.

Laura, a curly-haired friend of Janet's from Greenwich, turned around and said, "But God loved us so much he sent us His only son."

Janet shook her head, as if to say, "Don't." I agreed with her. I didn't want to argue with a bubbly nineteen-year-old whose worldview had been formed by restricted country clubs and gated private schools. It wasn't my place to judge—it really wasn't. But I wanted to judge. I wanted to stop the van and scream, "What is wrong with us? Everything we touch suffers and dies. We are a scourge on this planet, and if God loves us, then God is delusional."

But I stared at the floor of the van, not screaming, not judging. At least not out loud. Eventually we pulled up to the retreat center. It was a wooden lodge from the 1920s: it looked like the bucolic set for a movie where all the teenagers end up dismembered. "When does the ax murderer come out of the woods?" I asked Janet.

"Ssshh, we're here on a retreat," she whispered.

I found the men's dormitory and threw my backpack down on an empty mattress in a metal-framed bunk bed. I wanted to lie down and sleep for a day or two, but we had a welcome meeting in the common room. I found it: a large wood-paneled room filled with one hundred young, white Christians. A clean Christian man who was demonstrating his youth and relatability by wearing an R.E.M. T-shirt greeted us.

Everyone quieted down and he said benign, unimpeachably friendly sentences about the retreat being a time for renewal and faith and community. He smiled and the young Christians smiled back.

The setting sun came through the windows, landing on the old stone fireplace like burnished gold. But in my mind's eye I kept seeing the blood on the wheels of my skateboard as I wheeled it through the Meatpacking District. Nothing had changed, and nothing would unless I did something. I raised my hand. Janet looked at me, alarmed, and shook her head.

The nice Christian man in the R.E.M. shirt smiled at me. "You'd like to say something?"

"Hi, I'm Moby." I took a breath. "I don't want to cause offense, but what are we doing here? This place is beautiful and everyone here is very nice—I can see that. But the world is out there, and it's full of unspeakable suffering. I think our faith calls us to go out and make the world better. I'm hoping we can all keep that in mind while we're here."

I could here a few people muttering, "Who is he?"

"Thanks for that," the man at the front said diplomatically. "This weekend will be about dialogue and sharing. So after dinner we'll meet back here for stories and games."

As the crowd dispersed, Laura made a beeline for me. "Can't you just relax, Moby?" she demanded.

"Laura," I said, "twelve hours ago I was walking through pools of blood in the Meatpacking District while men carried the carcasses of dead lambs and pigs into warehouses. So no, I can't just relax."

She turned away and stormed off.

"Everyone here is trying to do their best," Janet said gently. "Okay?"

"You're right," I said. "Okay." I took her hand and we walked into the dining hall. There was a blackboard by the entrance with the menu:

Beef stew or fried chicken
French fries
Green salad
Jell-O

I read the blackboard and felt my brain snap. I wanted to find some Semtex or C-4 and blow this whole meat–and–Jell-O–fueled suburban Christian retreat back to God. But I said quietly, "Janet, I need to leave and go for a walk."

I went outside, feeling like my brain was going to melt through my ears and eyes. How could I maintain sanity in a world that was indifferent to blood on the sidewalks? How could I be a Christian when Christians were shoveling beef stew and fried chicken down their little pink throats? I walked further away from the retreat center, heading into the darkening woods. Eventually I couldn't hear the sounds of people anymore, only birds and the breeze going through the pine trees.

I sat down on an old, fallen tree. A squirrel was standing on the other end, eating something and looking at me. "I'm sorry," I told the squirrel; it ran away. I wasn't sure whether it accepted my apology.

I looked around. The last light was touching the tops of the trees. "God," I said out loud, "what am I supposed to do?"

I listened, but all I could hear was the sound of the woods: the quiet hum made by wind and squirrels and a million bugs. And I thought, *I need to do what I can.* Everything here in the woods had its place and it did what it was supposed to do.

I didn't need to firebomb labs where they tested on animals. I didn't need to push vivisectionists and slaughterhouse owners and meat-filled Christians off cliffs. The world was full of pain, much of it avoidable. Death was inevitable, but suffering wasn't.

I prayed, "God, help me to do what you would have me do. Your will be done." In the dim light I made my way back to the retreat center. If I was going to be a lifelong animal-rights activist, I realized, I needed to be smart and strategic. All I wanted to do was yell at people and tell them they were wrong. But yelling made people hear less.

I walked back into the dining hall, and Laura came up to me. "I'm sorry I got upset with you, Moby," she said.

"I'm sorry too, Laura," I told her.

"Look!" she said, pointing to her plate of salad, french fries, and Jell-O, "I'm eating vegetarian!"

I didn't have the heart to tell her that Jell-O was made from the connective tissues and ligaments and hooves of cows, so I said, "That's great, Laura!"

An hour later, I was wearing an apron and washing dishes in the camp kitchen. I was sponging off plates covered in beef and chicken grease, shoveling bones and congealed fat into overflowing garbage bags. "This is my work and it's disgusting," I said to myself as I took off my blue dishwashing gloves so that I could tie a black plastic bag full of chicken bones and greasy paper plates. *I want this work to be easy*, I thought as I carried a greasy garbage bag to the Dumpster behind the kitchen, *but it isn't*.

12

WET SOCKS ON THE RADIATOR

The homeless were everywhere in New York City, and Jesus had been pretty clear in saying that Christians were supposed to look after the homeless: "What you do for the least of these, you do for me." So every day I'd leave my apartment with a bag of quarters, ready to hand them out to anyone who might ask me for money. I was DJing regularly and making around $8,000 a year, so I figured I could afford fifty cents or a dollar for every homeless person who asked.

Some of the homeless were mentally ill, walking down the street and cursing the air: "Fuck you get the fuck out shut up I said shut up fuck fuck fuck shut up." The mentally ill homeless rarely spoke to anyone except their personal demons. They were volatile and terrifying. Sometimes if you helped them you could catch a glimpse of who they were behind their illness. But then their face would become a rictus of pain and they'd start yelling, "Don't approach me, Satan! Get thee behind me! Motherfucker fuck!" I'd back away, hands raised in the universal gesture of "I mean you no harm, crazy person, please don't stab me." Plus, as a Christian, it was disconcerting to be called Satan.

The homeless drunks were the friendliest. Sometimes they'd say, "Can you help me out with some money? I need something to eat." You could tell it was a lie, because if you offered them food instead of money, they'd get offended: "Yo, just give me some money." Sometimes they'd try honesty as a tactic: "I could lie to you, my man, but I just need money to buy some beer."

The crack addicts were the hardest to face: They had lost their lives and their souls and were like staggering corpses. They were emaciated and ruined, with dead stares and open sores on their feet. They'd be on the subway platforms trying to sell anything they could scavenge. But I wanted to do God's will, and the Bible told me to give to everyone. I wasn't God, I wasn't omniscient, and it had been made clear that it wasn't my place to judge. It was just my place to have spare change in my pocket for anyone who asked.

Janet and I had been talking about trying to be better Christians and do more for the homeless. On a rainy Sunday night we decided we would meet at my apartment to make sandwiches and then hand them out to the homeless in my neighborhood.

"I just don't feel right giving them money," Janet said. "I don't know what they'll spend it on." We were in the apartment that Lee and I had just moved into, listening to a Nick Drake cassette and making peanut butter and jelly sandwiches. Our plan was to put the sandwiches in lunch bags along with some vegan cookies and to give them to any homeless person we saw.

Usually the homeless hated vegan food. I'd be walking down the street with leftovers from Angelica Kitchen, New York's oldest and most iconic vegan restaurant, and I'd see a homeless man by Cooper Union at Saint Mark's Place. "Spare some change?" he'd ask.

"I have some food," I'd say. "Do you want that?"

"Fuck that, I don't eat that shit," he'd say. "You got a dollar so I can go to Popeyes?"

Once a man by the 6 stop at Lafayette and Astor Place took my vegan food, but he looked heartbroken when he peered in the bag. "Aw man, I thought you'd have some goat," he said. "Goat's vegetarian."

I wanted to tell him "Well, no, technically goat's not vegetarian," but I just said, "God bless," and walked down Lafayette, leaving him forlorn with my adzuki bean and brown rice leftovers.

Peanut butter and jelly sandwiches and cookies seemed neutral: vegan without being blatantly vegan. Maybe, if we were lucky, nobody would throw our food on the ground and tell us to fuck off. Janet had brought over a J.Crew shopping bag; we filled it with sandwiches and cookies and headed out.

At eight p.m. on a late autumn Sunday it was cold. Not sharp Canadian cold, but a heavy wet cold that made my face hurt. We turned right on Mott and then left on Bleecker. There were always homeless people on Bleecker, but for some reason, tonight there were none. It was drizzling, and the J.Crew bag was getting wet. Our faces were numb and our feet were soggy, but we kept wandering around lower Manhattan, looking for homeless people to feed.

"It's like *Watchmen*," I said.

"What's that?" Janet asked.

"It's a comic," I said. "The homeless all disappear. Or maybe it's like *Soylent Green*? That would be ironic, if we were trying to feed the homeless and they were being turned into food."

"That's gross, Mo."

We walked west on Fourteenth Street and I thought of the Television song "Venus," where Tom Verlaine sings, "Broadway looks so medieval": tonight all of New York looked medieval. There was a cold mist over everything, making all of the lights look like halos and turning all the buildings into dark castles. "Where are all the homeless?" I asked as we walked down University Place.

"Maybe Washington Square Park?" Janet suggested.

"I'm not sure it's safe for us there."

"Well, we can look."

Washington Square Park was dripping with menace. We could see a few people in the park, but they were drug dealers, not the homeless. Dealers probably wouldn't be too keen on twenty-four-year-old white kids from Connecticut giving them PB & J sandwiches in paper lunch bags. Especially since most of the drug dealers were making more money than most twenty-four-year-old white kids from Connecticut. We walked east and sat down on a wet stone bench by the tall NYU buildings at Mercer. We still had all our sandwiches, and now the cold was leaching into us from the stone seat.

Janet and I had been dating on and off for two years. We'd met a few years ago at a Bible study group in Connecticut, and we'd been trying to be good Christians who dated. Our rapport was friendly but not passionate. We never ran down the street screaming, "I'm in love!" We never pined for each other. We had a calm, mainly celibate relationship. And somewhere I knew that twenty-four-year-olds weren't supposed to have calm, celibate relationships. Twenty-four-year-olds were supposed to have grand passions and sex ten times a day. We were twenty-four-year-olds having sex once a month and asking God for forgiveness afterward.

Sitting on the cold wet bench I admitted to myself something that I had been trying to avoid thinking about: I had to end our relationship. I paused, hoping that maybe God would miraculously intervene and end the world so I wouldn't need to have a breakup conversation, but no such luck. I broke the unhappy silence: "Janet, I need to say something."

"Oh," she said, her voice quivering. "What?"

"I really hate to say it, but this isn't working."

"Feeding the homeless?"

"That's not working, too. But no, our relationship. I don't think it's working."

"What do you mean?" Janet said, turning to me and starting to cry.

I paused. Janet was so kind, and she loved me, but I wanted to be alone. "I think I want to break up," I told her.

She stared at the ground, her shoulders rounded under her red, wet coat.

"I'm sorry," I said.

She just sat on the bench, crying quietly. I looked around. New York was empty. The freezing mist had become a steady, cold rain. My hat was wet and my gloves were soaked. "I'm sorry," I said again, "But I think this is what I want."

"You *think*?" she said with venom. "You tell me you want to break up because you *think* that's what you want?"

I swallowed. "No. I know that's what I want."

She started crying loudly, still staring at the ground.

"Shit," I said. "Shit."

She stopped crying and looked at me with some inner reserve of steel. "Well, you know what you want," she said, "so we should go." She stood up, brushing the cold rain off her jacket. "You want to break up, we're broken up," she said flatly.

I picked up the wet bag of sandwiches and cookies. "Should I walk you to the train?" I asked.

"Yes, Moby, you should walk me to the fucking train," she said.

We walked east, not saying anything. There were still no homeless anywhere. The bag of sandwiches and cookies was wet and heavy. "Do you want these?" I asked.

"No," she said, taking the bag from me. "Fuck this," she said, and threw it in an overflowing garbage can outside of a McDonald's.

I stared at her, offended. "I could have still fed someone with those," I said.

"There's nobody here to feed, Moby," she said. "And everything's wet."

We stood at the entrance to the N train on the corner of Broadway and St. Mark's Place. The rain was getting even heavier. "Do you think it'll snow?" I asked hopefully.

Janet just glared at me, exasperated. "Well?" she said.

"I don't know what to do, Janet," I said.

"We've broken up, Moby. You don't have to do anything." She turned and walked down the subway stairs, her wet red jacket glistening in the harsh white fluorescent lights.

I was free. Sad, wet, and free. I didn't know how to date, and I didn't know anyone who would want to date me, but I was free.

I turned and walked down the street, listening to the sound of wet taxi tires on Broadway. My face was freezing from the cold rain, and my hat smelled like a wet dog. I had done it: I had broken up with Janet. But why did it have to hurt? Why was being alone better than being with someone who loved me?

I walked south, passing the shuttered lightbulb stores and the sneaker stores. On the corner of Broadway and Bleecker, there was a homeless man standing in the rain, smoking a cigarette. "Help me out? Spare some change?" he asked.

"Here you go," I told him, and I handed him all of the quarters I'd brought with us.

"Hey, thanks, man!" he said.

"God bless," I told him.

"I'm going to buy some KFC, thanks!" he said, and hurried off through the rain.

I walked past the entrance to the 6 train at Lafayette and Bleecker. The lights above the entrance were broken and it looked like a tired steel mouth. I turned right on Mott Street and arrived home. Before putting my key in the lock, I checked left and right: you always needed to look both ways, because while you were unlocking your door, people could rush out of the shadows, push you into your building, and rob you or stab you. But it was ten p.m. on a wet Sunday night; no one was around.

The aged Chinese couple in the apartment next to mine were cooking something that smelled like dog food mixed with aluminum foil. And I could hear their muted voices through the door: they were arguing. Should they have broken up fifty years earlier so they wouldn't find themselves at age seventy, arguing in a tiny apartment?

The steam heat was rattling the radiators in my apartment. I put my hat, gloves, and jacket on the radiator in the living room, and soon the apartment smelled like a bunch of wet dogs. I was single. Shouldn't that involve sex and love and bad dates and holding hands on trips to Coney Island? For me I expected that being single would involve not talking to girls and going to sleep alone after reading a few pages of *Dune*.

I thought of Janet changing trains in Times Square. I thought of her crying on the way up to Harlem. The thought of her crying on the train under the blinking fluorescent lights made me unspeakably sad. I sat on the futon and took off my socks: they were wet and had to go on the radiator too. I was awful. I had hurt someone who didn't deserve to be hurt. I wanted my next relationship to last forever. It would be a relationship of small hurts, maybe even big hurts, but not these final hurts that ended with me alone in my apartment with wet socks on the radiator while my ex cried her way up to 125th Street on the 9 train.

13

SMEARED BLACK MAGIC MARKER

The Palladium was the biggest club in New York City. Red Zone had better music; the Tunnel had better architecture; Mars was cooler and stranger; Nell's was more glamorous. But the Palladium was the ne plus ultra mothership of nightclubs in New York. It was the largest. It had the loudest sound system. It had the biggest stage. And it was the most intimidating.

On weekend nights the sidewalk on Fourteenth Street in front of the Palladium would be filled with club kids, college kids, aspiring ravers, and bridge-and-tunnel kids, all in their best Manhattan nightclub clothes and trying their hardest to get past the velvet rope and get in. Disaffected club kids called it the "Get-laid-ium," because it was a hotbed of cheap and meaningless sex. In the autumn of 1990, however, nothing was a hotbed of sex for me, either cheap and meaningless or valuable and meaningful.

I'd lived in the Palladium's shadow, almost literally, as it was a few hundred yards from my first apartment on Fourteenth Street. Every day I'd walked past its front doors and wondered, *Will I ever play there? Will I ever DJ there? Will I be allowed in the next time I stand in line?*

I had started going to the Palladium when I was in high school and it was still a theater. Through the mid-eighties the Palladium had been a great place to see punk-rock and new-wave shows, one of New York's run-down but still grand theaters. My punk-rock high school friends and I had a Palladium routine: Get on the Metro-North train in Darien and try to hide in the bathroom to avoid paying the fare. If the bathroom was occupied, or too disgusting, we would use the money we'd made from cutting lawns to buy a $4.25 train ticket into Manhattan.

Once in Grand Central we'd quietly congratulate ourselves on being allowed into New York City; breathing the very air of Manhattan seemed almost overly aspirational for teenage punk rockers from Connecticut. We carried the taint of suburban frustration and loneliness; by all rights, we should have been stopped at the border of Manhattan and sent back to Connecticut with our new-wave tails between our Wrangler-jeans-clad legs.

We spent hours wandering around Grand Central, getting lost at the ends of platforms and exploring the levels below the station that weren't supposed to be open to the public. Walking through the hidden lower levels, we'd hope to find communities of the troglodyte zombies from *The Omega Man*—but the only life we'd ever encounter were rats or an occasional homeless person trying not to be seen.

Jim was the bass player in our high school punk band, the Vatican Commandos, and our leader. He wore a leather jacket and a spiked leather belt, and he knew how the New York subways worked. We'd follow him to the cool parts of downtown: he'd lead us on the 6 train from Grand Central to Canal Street, where we would go to Canal Jeans. We never had enough money to buy anything, but we loved to look at the punk-rock T-shirts and the beautiful employees with purple Mohawks. We'd stand around, arguing about our favorite bands and T-shirts, and wonder if someday we could borrow enough money from our moms to buy a Crass or Agnostic Front shirt.

Then we'd go uptown to Union Square Park. Our parents had all given us the same instructions when we went into the city: "Be back on the last train, and stay away from the parks." So we'd walk around the edges of Union Square Park, which was full of junkies and leafless trees. Then we'd go to the nearby Nathan's to get hot dogs and Cokes. We'd sit at the stained Formica tables and stare at the junkies and punk rockers and cops and transvestites. After a few hours of nursing our Cokes in paper cups, we'd walk the fifty feet from Nathan's to the Palladium. A bored Palladium employee would tear our ticket and we would run as fast as we could to get to the front of the stage.

It didn't matter who we were seeing, whether it was the Boomtown Rats or Simple Minds or OMD or the Clash—we loved them all unconditionally. These were real musicians on a real stage. They'd made records and they came from a different country. After standing for five hours at the front of the stage and dancing to punk-rock and new-wave bands we'd take the 6 train back to Grand Central Terminal. At midnight, Grand Central was an empty cavern, populated only by the homeless, a few drug dealers, and some drunk businessmen stumbling onto the last trains to Larchmont, Brewster, and Darien.

We'd get on the local Metro-North train, it would start moving, and our friend Chip would throw up. Every time. During shows at the Palladium we'd all drink Cokes, and water from the drinking fountain in the men's room, but Chip would go to the bar, buy beer, and get drunk. Leaving New York always involved the sound of Chip's partially digested hot dogs and beer splattering on the floor of the train beneath his feat. He'd throw up and the rest of us would move a few seats away and pretend we didn't know him.

When the train got to Noroton Heights I'd get off and run all the way home. My ears would be ringing, and I'd be queasy from hot dogs and Coke, but I'd be glowing from seeing punk-rock bands and a day spent in the most perfect city on the planet.

Now it was 1990 and Union Square Park was being cleaned up; the dead trees had been carted away and the struggling trees were being cared for. The junkies had relocated to Tompkins Square Park and East River Park. And the Palladium had been turned from a theater into the biggest nightclub in the world.

I was sitting on the filthy futon in our living room and eating breakfast when the phone rang.

"Hello," a British woman said, "I'm looking for Moby."

"This is Moby."

"Oh, hi, this is Olivia from the Palladium. I got your number from Jared Hoffman."

"Hi, how are you?" I said professionally.

"Okay, good. I wanted to see if you'd be interested in opening up for Snap!. They're playing their first US show here."

My brain needed to have a quick conversation with itself. Opening up for Snap!? They had released "The Power" a few months ago and it had gone to number one around the world, making them one of the biggest dance acts on the planet. My first solo twelve-inch hadn't yet been released and I'd played exactly one solo show, for an audience of fifteen people.

Keeping those thoughts to myself, I said, "Oh, playing live or DJing?"

"It would be a live gig. Jared says you have a great live show."

Jared said that?

"Sounds good," I said calmly.

Olivia gave me the details for the show. After we hung up I calmly walked to the kitchen with my cereal bowl and put it in the sink. I stood by the refrigerator, paralyzed: my brain was on fire.

I was going to be playing live at the Palladium.

For thousands of people.

After a few minutes I realized I needed to call everyone I knew: Damian, Janet, Paul, Jared, Dave, my mom. But I couldn't use our phone: Lee was on it, talking quietly to his mom about something important.

I grabbed a handful of quarters and ran outside to the pay phone by the 6 train. I called Damian; he wasn't there, so I left a message. I called Janet, even though we'd broken up, and left a message. Nobody seemed to be picking up the phone. My mom and Paul were both in Connecticut, which counted as a long-distance call, and I didn't have enough quarters for that. I decided that I'd go to the Instinct office (a.k.a. Jared's apartment) and call them from there.

I ran up Lafayette, and then Fourth Avenue, and soon I was standing in front of the Palladium. I looked up at the giant façade, the same one that had been there when I was in high school. In a few weeks I would be standing on the same stage that the Clash had stood on. I started running west across Fourteenth Street. I dodged some cars on Broadway and then crossed Fifth Avenue. My lungs were cold and raw, but I couldn't stop running, impelled by the mantra "I'm going to play at the Palladium!"

Jared's doorman let me in—I was a regular visitor—and I ran up the stairs. I opened the door at his apartment and yelled, "Hello!" but nobody was there. I was so manic, I felt like my cells were made of twitching glass. I went out to Jared's balcony, looking at lower Manhattan and the Twin Towers, and yelled, "Aaaaaarrrrrrghh!" It felt good. I did it again: "Aaaaaarrrrrrghh!"

Somebody below me opened a window and said sullenly, "Ah, shut up."

Of course. This was New York, my home.

For the next three weeks I worked on my twenty-five-minute live set, figuring out what songs I should play and how they should be arranged. I decided that to sound good I'd have to bring all my equipment and set up my studio onstage at the Palladium. I also practiced jumping up and down in front of a mirror and tried on different stage clothes.

Two weeks before the show huge yellow posters went up everywhere. They were very simple: in big letters, FIRST U.S. PERFORMANCE— SNAP! And in little type at the bottom, PLUS: MOBY. Every day I would pass the giant yellow posters on the street and marvel at them. That was my name, on a concert poster in New York City.

And then it was the day of the show. Damian met me at Jared's and helped me carry my equipment down to the street. We put it all in the back of a cab and drove the five blocks to the Palladium. We carried everything onto the stage and I stood there, looking out at the empty nightclub. From the stage the Palladium looked huge and still. It held three thousand people, but right now, there were just two janitors mopping the floor and one busboy working behind a distant bar.

I set up a folding table, found an outlet for my power, and rebuilt my studio on the stage. I hooked up the MIDI cables from my sequencer to my drum machines, my sampler, and my keyboards. I plugged in the audio cables that connected my sixteen-channel mixer with the keyboards, Oberheim sound module, sampler, and drum machine. I connected my Alesis QuadraVerb multieffects unit to the mixer. And then I turned everything on. The longest part of this process was loading the samples into the sampler. I had a slow Yamaha sampler, and for it to work I had to load four floppy disks. Each disk was about three inches square and took a minute or two to load; I stood onstage, feeding them into the sampler one by one. After five minutes, everything was ready. I put on my headphones, pressed "play" on the Alesis, and miraculously, everything worked.

I adjusted the levels on the mixer and went to find the soundman. Olivia had told me that his name was Johnny and that he showed up at four p.m. I found him in the DJ booth, which had four turntables—I'd never seen four turntables in the same place before. The booth was suspended thirty feet over the dance floor and its walls were lined with brand-new equipment. It was a sacred space.

"Hi, are you Johnny?" I asked.

He turned to look at me, all long hair and tattoos. "Yeah, can I help you?"

"I'm Moby, and I'm opening up for Snap! tonight."

"Okay, what setup do you have?" he asked mechanically. "Reel-to-reel? A DAT?"

"No, I brought my whole studio. It's set up onstage."

That got his attention—he started laughing. "Are you kidding me? Your whole studio?"

As we walked down to the stage, I said, "I think everything's ready to go. I just need two XLR cables and a microphone. Do you have a microphone?"

He laughed. "Yeah, I think we have a microphone." Onstage, he surveyed my equipment with a smile. "You have one of those Oberheim 1000s? Those are great. How about the Roland 106? Is it like the Prophet?"

We talked about gear while he located the XLR cables and microphone. I plugged the cables into my mixer. "Okay, let me go to the booth and turn you on," he said. I stood on the stage, trying to breathe in every molecule of oxygen in the room. I had assumed that the soundman would be bored or hostile, certainly not a friendly man who loved analog synths.

Johnny interrupted my reverie with a shout from the DJ booth: "Okay, turn it on!"

I hit "play." Johnny brought up the volume. And brought it up some more. And then some more.

The Palladium's sound system was legendary. There was no louder club sound system in New York City, or the world. And now the entire empty venue was shaking with my music. I was too stunned to smile. Johnny turned down the volume and shouted, "Sounds great!"

I hit "stop," and the music ended, reverberating in the huge room.

Johnny walked back to the stage. "How was that?"

"That sounded amazing! I've never heard my music in a big place!"

"Cool. Snap! are just using a tape and two microphones, so you can keep your equipment set up 'til showtime."

"Will it be safe here?"

He laughed again. "I'll make sure no one steals it."

"Hey Moby!" I heard someone yelling from just in front of the stage.

My boss from Mars, Yuki, was standing at the front of the stage with a friend. I walked down, confused as to why Yuki was at the empty Palladium in the middle of the afternoon.

"Hi Moby, I was here for a meeting and I heard you sound check," he said, shaking my hand and smiling. He gestured to the diminutive man standing next to him, and said, "Oh, Moby, meet Miles Davis."

I looked at Miles Davis, standing a few feet away from me in the middle of the afternoon at the empty Palladium for my sound check.

He was smaller than I'd imagined, and was wearing a dark brown silk suit that looked like it cost more money than I had made in the previous ten years. He stood very still and looked almost predatory.

"Hi Miles, Mr. Davis," I said, extending my hand.

Miles Davis looked at me, barely nodded his head, and kept his hands at his side.

"Okay, Moby, good show tonight!" Yuki said, turning and walking away with Miles Davis.

I walked back up on the stage and watched Yuki and Miles Davis leave through one of the Palladium's side exits.

"What was Yuki doing here?" Damian asked.

"I have no idea," I said, haltingly, "but he was with Miles Davis."

After I thanked him, Damian and I walked out the back door, letting the bored security guard know we'd be back later. We went east, heading for Angelica Kitchen, trying to figure out why Miles Davis had been at my sound check.

We ate dinner and headed back to my apartment on Mott Street. I had decided to wear black jeans onstage, and no shirt. For some reason going shirtless in front of three thousand people for my first show seemed like a good idea. I took a Magic Marker and awkwardly tried to draw a cross on my chest. Damian got exasperated and said, "Here, let me do it."

When he finished, I looked at myself in the bathroom mirror. My long hair was slicked back, I was wearing my best black jeans, and I had a big black cross on my chest. And my pupils were dilated with sober fear.

We headed for the door. "Don't you want to wear a jacket?" Damian asked. "It's cold outside."

"No, I don't want to smudge the cross," I said. "Let's go."

At the Palladium the security guard remembered us and grudgingly opened the door. Johnny spotted me. "Your dressing room is downstairs," he said. "I'll show you where." He led us to the basement.

I had been in a dressing room only once before. In 1985, I had gone to see Sonic Youth at CBGB with my girlfriend Margaret. We had drunkenly snuck into their dressing room and stolen some of their beer. We'd talked about having sex on the disgusting CB's dressing room couch, but before we could take our clothes off Sonic Youth's tour manager had come in and yelled at us and thrown us out.

This dressing room—my dressing room!—was a small yellow cube in the basement with a mirror and an old black leather couch.

"You're on at ten," Johnny told me. "Break a leg!"

Damian and I sat on the leather couch. I got up to look at myself in the mirror. I sat down again.

There was a knock on the door. It was Olivia—she was in her thirties and dressed all in black. "Hi, Moby," she said in her clipped British accent. "I have some bad news. Snap! missed their flight, so they're not playing tonight."

"Uh, what?"

"Snap! won't be here, so you're the only one performing."

I blinked. "So what does that mean?"

"You're the only performer tonight," she said patiently, as if addressing a simpleton.

"Won't people want their money back?"

"No, they just want a good night out. We've got some DJs tonight too. Now you'll be going on at eleven. Good luck!"

After she left, Damian and I looked at each other. "You're headlining the Palladium!" he said.

"No one knows who I am!" I yelled. "It's going to be a disaster!"

"Calm down," he said. "Your set is great. People will love it." I started pacing in the room. Then I switched to pacing in the hallway. Then I decided I needed to talk to my new analog-synth friend, Johnny. I walked upstairs to the DJ booth. The crowd was coming in and Mark Kamins, a legend who'd discovered Madonna, was DJing.

Johnny saw me. "Hey, I heard Snap! canceled. Do you know Mark?"

Mark Kamins turned around. "You're Moby, you DJ at Mars. Nice to meet you."

"Nice to meet you too," I said, baffled that he knew who I was.

"Do you want a drink or some weed?" Mark asked.

"No thanks, I don't drink."

He looked at me like I was an alien lizard and got back to DJing.

"Johnny," I asked, "should I cancel, too?"

He stifled a laugh. "No, Moby," he said kindly. "This crowd just wants to party. Trust me, you'll be fine."

I went back to the dressing room and started running in place, doing jumping jacks, anything that would pass the time and keep the panic at bay. At last, it was 10:55. Olivia came to get me: "Okay, you're on." I walked to the side of the stage and looked out at the crowd. The Palladium was packed, the walls were glowing with strobes and colored lights, and Mark Kamins was playing "Vibrations" by Supernova. And I was about to die.

The music stopped and the crowd cheered. An MC walked onstage and took the microphone. "Ladies and gentlemen," he said, "some bad news. Snap! missed their flight and won't be here tonight." He took a breath, and the crowd started booing. "But now, from right here in New York City, Moby!"

I hurried across the stage to my equipment. The crowd was booing loudly and yelling "Snap! Snap! Snap!" Some people threw plastic cups and slices of limes at me. I looked at the three thousand people booing at me, picked up the microphone, and said, "I'm Moby." Then I hit "start" on my sequencer.

Nothing happened. The audience kept booing. I hit "start" again. Nothing.

There's a word missing from the English language. Maybe it exists in other languages. It describes the unspeakable, incomprehensible panic that comes from standing onstage to play your second-ever solo show in front of thousands of hostile fans who've just found out the headliner canceled and then hitting "start" on your sequencer with absolutely no result.

I looked to see what was wrong. Was everything plugged in? Yes. Was everything on? Oh no. The sampler had been turned off. I turned

it on and began the laborious five-minute process of reloading its samples. I fed floppy disks into it with my left hand while I played drums
on my keyboard with my right hand.

After a couple of minutes the audience stopped booing. They just
stood there, trying to figure out why this shirtless guy didn't seem interested in doing anything but playing drums on a keyboard. I loaded the
third disk, and then the fourth disk. After five eternal minutes, the
sampler's tiny green LCD screen said "READY."

I hit play once again, and this time there was music. My set stared
with "Electricity," a hip-hop techno song. All of my anxiety and terror
suddenly left me. I grabbed the microphone and ran to the front of the
stage and screamed into it as loud as I could. *You can hate me*, I thought,
*but right now I don't care. The headliner canceled. My equipment failed.
I've been consumed by panic and fear. But right now I'm here and I'm
going to scream at the top of my lungs.*

I got through "Electricity" and the crowd actually applauded. Then
I played "Besame," banging on the keyboard and yelling, and they
started dancing. I was covered in sweat—the black cross on my chest
was smeared, making it look like a bad prison tattoo. Next was a new
song, "UHF," and it worked, the crowd dancing and even some cheering at the end. Then for the finale I played "Rock the House," and I
could feel the crowd turn. They were with me. I was pacing around the
stage, screaming, "Rock the house," along with the sample—they
shouted it out too. The song ended and the crowd cheered.

The MC came onstage and put his arm around my sweaty naked
shoulder. "Give it up for Moby from New York City!" And they cheered
again.

I walked offstage, depleted and catatonic, and returned to my yellow
dressing room. My new friend Johnny came in. "Dude! That was great!"

"Really?"

"Really! Everyone was dancing!"

When he left I walked into the bathroom. It was a relic from the beginning of the twentieth century, with black-painted stalls and chipped
black and white tiles. I leaned my head against a metal stall, not sure

whether I was going to cry or throw up, feeling the beads of sweat work their way down my forehead.

After a couple of minutes I went back upstairs to the stage and disassembled my equipment. Mark Kamins was DJing and the club was throbbing, the legendary Palladium sound system sounding like a thousand Valkyries flying into war. When I finished packing up Olivia came up to me and handed me two hundred dollars, the first money I'd ever been paid to play live.

"That was really great, Moby!" she said, giving me a hug and a kiss on the cheek. "Well done!" she said. "Let's do it again sometime!"

I needed to get my equipment back to Jared's apartment, but I wanted to be virtuous and save the $10 it would cost to take a taxi. "Olivia, do you have a cart or something I could borrow?"

"Sure, no problem." She got the security guard to find a plastic laundry cart with four wheels. Damian and I loaded my equipment and pushed it down the street to Jared's apartment. After we got my equipment into Jared's living room Damian got very serious and shook my hand.

"You were really good, Moby," he said earnestly, "I'm proud of you."

"Thanks, Damian."

"You do know you're going to be huge?" he asked.

"No," I said.

"It's all going to get weird," he said. "You'll see."

MOBY GO!, 1990–1992

14

YAMS

When I became a vegan in 1987, in one fell swoop I extended my life expectancy and annoyed most of the people in my life—my mom most of all. For most of my childhood my mom and I had lived on food stamps and welfare, but she had done her best to get me to eat healthfully. One night in 1980 she'd even had the temerity to make brown rice with tofu and vegetables for dinner. I was appalled.

Growing up in Connecticut I ate like a suburban American teenager, largely because I was a suburban American teenager. I lived on meatloaf, pizza, ice cream, salami sandwiches, steak sandwiches, ground beef tacos, more ice cream, more pizza. When I could afford them I loved the local Burger King and McDonald's and Wendy's and Chi-Chi's. I loved french fries dipped in milkshakes. I loved hamburgers dripping grease onto plastic fast-food trays. How dare my mother try to feed health food to her only son? It was like child abuse.

"Just try it," she pleaded.

"No," I said, looking at the tofu and broccoli in the pan. "It's disgusting."

"It's good for you," she said, a rubber spatula in one hand and a cigarette in the other.

"I don't care."

She glared at me, served herself a plate of rice and tofu and vegetables, and sat in front of the TV, watching *The Muppet Show*. After a minute, I went into the kitchen and made a Stouffer's French-bread pepperoni pizza in the toaster oven. Then I made a big glass of chocolate milk and joined her in the TV room. We ate in sullen silence while the Muppets and Carol Burnett sang together.

Now, on Thanksgiving 1990, I was at my grandmother's house in Connecticut. My grandmother had sold her big antique-filled house in Darien and moved to a smaller antique-filled house in nearby Norwalk. My family was sitting around the table in her wood-paneled dining room. There was a nineteenth-century sideboard against the wall, covered with Wedgwood serving plates of ham and turkey and gravy and mashed potatoes and stuffing. My aunts and uncles and cousins were eating happily and talking between bites.

For this Thanksgiving, my three-year vegan anniversary, I had decided to fast. It was a strange experiment, to fast on the one day when most Americans ate to the point of exploding, but it seemed like a good way to step back from the gluttony, since there wasn't much for me to eat on Thanksgiving anyway. I wasn't fasting as a criticism of my family, but my mom was livid.

"Just eat something!" she said. "I'll go make you a sandwich, just eat something!"

She was wearing a brown and orange homemade sweater and a pair of burgundy corduroys. Her blond hair fell in curls on either side of her face.

"No, I'm okay," I said. "I like fasting and watching you guys eat."

"It's not right!" she said.

"I'm okay," I told her. "I'm just not eating."

She stormed out of the dining room, her new husband, Richard, following to placate her. My family looked at me.

"What? What did I do?" I asked.

My aunt Jane put down her fork. "Just go talk to her," she said.

I sighed and stood up. My mom was in the living room with Richard, smoking a cigarette. She and Richard had met at the hospital where they both worked. After dating for two years they'd gotten married in 1988. Richard was a Republican and a meat eater, but he was kind and he made her happy, and I loved him for that. Richard was in a blue button-down shirt and a pair of Levi's, holding my mom's hand on my grandmother's couch, which was covered with a green and yellow floral pattern.

"Are you okay?" I asked my mom.

She exhaled smoke. "Why can't you just eat something? It's Thanksgiving!"

"Why is it so important to you?"

"I'm your mother!"

"But I'm not doing anything! I'm just fasting."

"It's Thanksgiving! It's not normal!" she yelled.

"I don't know why that's so important to you," I said, confused.

We sat on the couch underneath a Currier and Ives print of foxhounds. Richard stared at the floor. There was a long silence.

"If I have a sandwich and some cranberry sauce, will that make you feel better?" I asked.

"Yes!" she said.

"Is cranberry sauce vegan?"

"Of course it is," she said, putting out her cigarette in a crystal ashtray.

We returned to the dining room and sat down. I sat next to my uncle Dave—bearded, seven feet tall, wearing suspenders—as he put a buttered roll in his mouth. "Everything okay?" he asked.

"Yup," I said. "I'm going to have a peanut butter sandwich and some sweet potatoes and cranberry sauce."

"Why are you a vegan anyway?" my eight-year-old cousin Benjamin asked.

"Well, I like animals and I don't want to hurt them."

"I like animals too," my five-year-old cousin Noah said.

"But you also like turkey," my aunt Anne, his mother, quickly said.

Noah stared at his plate and looked confused. "I do," he said.

"I just don't understand why you have to be so militant," my mom said. "It's Thanksgiving. Can't you get off your high horse and eat turkey with your family one day out of the year?"

"Honestly, my veganism is too important to me," I said. "What if I just sit in the corner and eat a yam?" I grabbed one from a serving bowl and relocated to a corner of the dining room, where I started gnawing on my yam.

"Can I eat in the corner?" my six-year-old cousin David asked.

"It's only for vegans," I told him, hunched over my food.

"How's your yam?" my aunt Jane asked, unfazed. She looked like Joan Baez and was wearing an L.L.Bean sweatshirt.

"Don't talk to me," I told her. "I'm eating my yam."

"Sorry, I didn't know vegans were so sensitive," she said.

My cousins were laughing. "A yam is kind of like a vegan rat," I told them.

"Moby's eating a rat!" Noah yelled.

"What if you accidentally ate some turkey?" Benjamin asked.

"I'd throw up everywhere," I said from the corner, my yam almost finished.

"Oh, stop it," my grandmother said. "Moby, come back and sit down at the table." My grandmother was the benign matriarch at the head of the table. Even though it was Thanksgiving she was wearing a red-and-green Christmas sweater. She'd grown up in Scotland and India, and although she was getting smaller with age, we all unquestioningly did what she asked.

"But, Grandma, I'm in my vegan corner of shame," I said.

"There's no vegan corner of shame," she declared. "Now come sit down and no more fighting, you two," she ordered, pointing at me and my mother.

I sat at the table, mock-chastened. "How's your turkey?" I asked Jane. "Does it taste like suffering?"

"Mmm, suffering," she said, and took a big bite of turkey.

"Stop it," my grandmother said, pretending to be stern.

When she looked away, Jane made a face at me. Then my cousin

David started giggling. Noah and Ben started laughing too, soon joined by the whole family.

"Excuse me, Grandma," I said. "Can I go back in the corner and eat my yam rat?"

"No," she said. "Just sit there and be normal."

"Ha, he can't be normal," Jane said.

"*You* can't be normal," I retorted.

"Can so."

"Cannot."

I turned to Richard. "Did you know this is what you'd be getting when you married my mom?"

He put down his fork and sighed. "I had no idea."

We all started laughing again.

When we finished eating Richard and my mom gave me a ride to the train station. I sat in the backseat while Richard drove and my mom smoked a cigarette. All the stores in Darien were closed. The streetlights were draped with Christmas lights that glowed in the rain.

"Mom, I'm sorry if I made you upset," I said from the backseat.

"I'm sorry too," she said, exhaling. "But I'm your mom. I worry about you."

"Thanks. But I'm okay," I said. "Do you remember when you'd try to feed me health food when I was growing up?"

"You hated it and accused me of child abuse," she said, laughing.

"And now all I eat is brown rice and tofu and vegetables," I said.

"Ah, irony. Just eat enough protein and I won't worry."

"Okay. And thanks for worrying, Mom."

"My pleasure," she said with a smile.

"Do you want to stay over?" Richard asked. "The bed in your old room is made."

"Thanks, Richard, but I'm going to head back to the city and work on music."

"Okay, but any time you want to stay, you can," he said. "It's still your house." He pulled up to the Darien train station and I got out.

"Bye, Mom," I said through her open window. "I'm sorry I argued with you."

"Bye, Mobes. I'm sorry I argued with you too. I love you."

"I love you too. See you guys later."

I walked to the platform. There were a few other people standing there, running back to the city after their own suburban Thanksgivings. A gust of wind hit my back as the train pulled in, pushing me onto the train and back home.

15

CROSSED ARMS

a Palace de Beaute?" I asked, not sure I had heard right. I was in my friend Gigi's apartment. He was a tall French DJ who'd moved into a huge loft on Broadway and Bleecker with his wife, Maripol.

"Maripol's friends with the owner—we can do a party there next Tuesday," Gigi said. He was smoking a cigarette and drinking an espresso, and was gently backlit by the late-afternoon sunlight coming through his west-facing windows.

"Is that enough time to promote?" I asked.

Maripol walked into the room, her stiletto heels clicking on the floor. She was also French, but much more intimidating than Gigi. She declared, "It's enough time."

Lighting a Gitane, she said, "You get your list and Gigi and I have our list. I'll get Madonna to come and it'll be full."

"You played at Palladium for three thousand people," Gigi said. "This club only holds five hundred."

"You played at Palladium for three thousand people?" Maripol asked.

"Well, yeah," I said cautiously, "but I was opening up for Snap!."

"But they never showed up," Gigi said, "and Moby was the head-liner."

Maripol looked at me, wary. She was a sophisticated European with jet-black hair who was friends with Madonna and had been friends with Andy Warhol. I was a twenty-five-year-old kid from Connecticut who lived in a cheap apartment that smelled like deep-fried cats.

"Also, Moby's new record just came out," Gigi said.

"You have a new record?" she asked.

"Yeah, my first single," I said.

"What label?" she asked skeptically.

"Instinct Records," I said. "They're on Fourteenth Street."

"I never heard of them," she said, and walked out of the room, trailed by French perfume and French cigarette smoke. Gigi and I looked at each other.

"So . . . next Tuesday?" I asked.

"Yeah!" he said. "It'll be great! I'll make flyers and you can give them out at Mars."

The next day I went to Gigi and Maripol's loft to pick up a stack of flyers. "Maripol Presents: DJ Gigi and Moby at La Palace de Beaute," they read.

On Thursday and Friday night I walked up and down the stairs at Mars, going into different rooms and handing flyers to everyone. "Gigi is DJing and I'm playing live!" I yelled over and over. "And Madonna will be there!" At the end of the night I stood outside Mars in the rain until five a.m. and thrust the flyers on people as they left the club. Most of the flyers ended up in the street or on the sidewalk, but a few people actually put them in their pockets.

Saturday I was DJing at Mars, so I gave a stack to Paul and Damian, who also walked from the basement to the roof and then back down again, handing out flyers all night. Normally handing out flyers for a rival club inside Mars would get you tossed out on the street, but Mars was closed on Tuesdays, so Yuki said it was okay. Also, he seemed to think it was cute, his little DJ Moby making a twelve-inch single and being a club promoter.

A few days passed and all too soon it was Tuesday. I'd handed out around two thousand flyers, and I assumed Gigi and Maripol had distributed a couple of thousand more. Maripol knew everyone, and Gigi was a cool and glamorous French DJ, so I assumed it would be an amazing night. I had a dreamy vision of arriving at La Palace de Beaute around ten p.m., walking past the long, snaking line of people waiting to get in, and hearing people say, "Oh, that's Moby. He's playing tonight and he's the promoter." I'd get to the front of the line and the beautiful doorwoman would say, "Moby, come in, everyone's here!" I'd play my show and Madonna would be watching from the side of the stage. When I was done, she'd hug me and say, "You're amazing! Let me help you! I believe in you!"

At four p.m. I arrived at La Palace, on Broadway and Nineteenth, with all my equipment stowed in the trunk of a taxi. I asked the cab driver to wait, ran to the entrance of the club, and banged on the door. Nothing. I banged some more. Still nothing.

"Yo, you gotta get your stuff outta the trunk," the taxi driver yelled.

"Okay, can you give me a hand?"

"Can't leave the cab," he said, staring straight ahead through his filthy windshield.

I unloaded everything, leaning my equipment against the front of the club, and paid the taxi. I sat with my equipment, waiting. After half an hour I experimentally banged on the door again: once more, nothing.

A homeless guy walked by and stopped when he saw me sitting on the sidewalk, surrounded by all my equipment. "Yo, play me a song!" he said.

"I can't. No power."

"Okay, I'll play you a song!" He started dancing and singing his version of "White Wedding." While people hurried past, he punched the air and sneered like Billy Idol: "It's a white wedding for you and me, can't you see, bay-bee, bay-bee, you and me!" Tired office workers ignored him as they walked by.

Gigi walked up in the middle of the song, nodding his head. "Hey, Moby," he said.

"Weren't you supposed to meet me at four?" I asked.

"Oh, what time is it?"

I looked at my watch. "It's five. I've been sitting here for an hour."

"Oh, sorry. Let's go in."

I gave the singer a dollar and Gigi unlocked the front door. "What's your name?" the homeless singer asked as he put the dollar in his pocket.

"Moby," I said.

He thought about it for a moment. "That's kind of fresh," he decided. "Moby." Then he yelled, "Yo, everybody! This is Moby! Moby!" The commuters walked by him, heading home, staring at the sidewalk. "Yo, Moby!" he shouted. "Give me another dollar and I'll shut up!"

I laughed. "Here you go—what's your name?"

"I'm Sancho Panza!" he said, accepting the dollar. "I'm a hero!" I shook his hand and he walked across Nineteenth Street, yelling, "I'm Sancho Panza! Sancho Bonanza!"

Gigi and I walked inside. "Do you think anyone will come tonight?" I asked.

"It'll be great. You gave out flyers at Mars?"

"Yeah, Thursday, Friday, Saturday. Where'd you promote?"

"Oh, I left some flyers at Tower Records and Dance Trax."

I paused. "And where else?"

"Oh, that's it. But Maripol called some people, so it should be great."

I'd spent three nights running up and down the stairs at Mars and begging people to even look at the flyers, and Gigi had just dropped off some flyers at two record stores. But Maripol knew Madonna, even if it felt like we were starring in an update of *Waiting for Godot*, with Madonna as Godot and Gigi and I as Vladimir and Estragon.

Down two flights of stairs, in a warren of dark rooms, there was a small stage and a DJ booth. "Is Madonna coming?" I asked, channeling Samuel Beckett.

"Oh, I don't know," he said. "Maripol left a message with her assistant."

I found a folding table in a utility closet and set up my equipment on the small stage. I didn't know when the soundman would show up, so I did sound check in my headphones. It sounded fine. Maybe I'd do the show in my headphones and no one would listen. Maybe I'd go home.

Gigi walked over and eyeballed my equipment. "Whoa, cool," he said. "Can you show me how it works?"

"Okay," I said. "The sequencer controls the synths and the samplers. The keyboards make MIDI and audio. The audio from the synths and samplers runs through the mixer, and the QuadraVerb gives reverb and delay."

"Cool," he said, suddenly bored. "Well, I'm going home to get my records. See you later."

"Sure, I'll just hang out until the soundman gets here." Gigi walked up the metal stairs and shut the door. I put my headphones back on and ran through the songs I was going to play. After thirty minutes I heard someone yelling, so I took the headphones off.

"Who the hell are you?" a man was screaming from the back of the club. "You can't be in here!"

"Oh, I'm Moby. I'm promoting tonight with Gigi and Maripol?"

"So what the fuck are you doing here now?"

"Setting up my equipment, waiting for the soundman."

"So you're a band?"

"No, I make electronic music. Do you know when the soundman shows up?"

"Yeah," he said, calming down. "Around nine."

"Can I wait here?"

"I guess so."

I went back to working on my show. Apart from the angry manager, the club was empty. I felt protected underneath the city. I knew that above us people were walking and eating and fighting and crying and hurrying home in the cold. But here in the basement it was quiet, like a dark womb that smelled like spilled drinks.

The soundman showed up at eight; we ran audio cables from my mixer into the sound system. At nine thirty, Gigi returned with his records. "Ready?" he asked.

"Yup. I just hope people show up."

"Oh, it'll be great!"

I left to get dinner, lingering over a vegan burrito on Twenty-Second Street. When I walked back to the club, there was no line. Broadway was cold and empty, and the woman working the door at the nightclub was clearly bored.

"Hi, I'm Moby," I said. "I'm one of the promoters tonight."

She said nothing—just opened the door and let me in. I walked downstairs to an almost-empty room. A few people were bravely trying to dance. I walked up to Gigi, playing records in the DJ booth. "How's it going?" I asked.

"Still early!" he said. "Don't worry!" And he played another house record.

At eleven fifteen, Maripol showed up, looking Gallic and terrifying in a black vinyl dress. She headed straight for Gigi and started yelling at him, her hands flying in the air. He stared at the record he was playing, saying nothing back.

She stormed over to me. "This is fucked up! No one's here!" she yelled over the music.

"I know," I said. I was going to tell her about the two thousand flyers I handed out, but before I could, she left in a cloud of fury.

I returned to the DJ booth. "What time should I go on?" I asked Gigi.

"How about now?" He stopped his record cold and walked away.

I ran to my equipment, picked up the microphone, said, "I'm Moby," to the empty dance floor, and hit "play" on the sequencer. "Electricity" filled the almost-empty club. Twenty people came out of the shadows and wandered onto the dance floor that held two hundred fifty. I jumped around and yelled; I banged on my keyboard and my Octapad (a drum pad that could trigger eight different sounds, depending on where you hit it). After each song, I got a gentle rain of polite applause.

When I got to the last song, "Rock the House," Gigi started scratching records over the track. When I looked over, he had a big smile and he gave me two thumbs up, so I smiled back and yelled into the microphone some more. When the song ended, I got one final round of tepid applause.

I walked to the side of the stage. I had taken off my shirt and my hair was drenched with sweat. Maripol was standing on the side of the stage; next to her was Madonna. "Moby, Madonna," Maripol said. "Madonna, Moby."

I reached forward to shake Madonna's hand, but she stood back with her arms crossed. "Hi," I said, sweaty and awkward. "Thank you for coming."

This was Madonna, legend of legends, the biggest star on the planet. She was wearing black clothes; her hair was bleached and pulled back from her face. She was smaller than I'd imagined, and she didn't look very happy. She gazed at me for a second, the way a doctor inspects a potentially infected toe. "You're very talented," she said curtly, and then she walked away, Maripol following one step behind.

I saw Damian at the bar, flirting with the bored Asian bartender. I ran over to him. "I just met Madonna," I gushed. "She said I was very talented!"

"Cool," he said. "I just spotted O. J. Simpson on the dance floor."

"O. J. the Hertz rental-car football player?" I asked. "Here?"

"Yeah, he was dancing during your show."

"O. J. Simpson? Are you sure?"

We walked over to the dance floor, and sure enough, there was O. J. Simpson in a beige suit, dancing badly to house music with a white woman. "O. J. Simpson dances like a black comedian imitating white people," I yelled over the music to Damian.

"Just like us," Damian said.

I walked over to the DJ booth. Gigi looked depressed. "You want to DJ?" he asked.

"Sure. Can I use your records?"

"Okay. I want to get drunk. Maripol's really mad at us."

She's mad at us? I thought. *I went out Thursday and Friday and Saturday and gave out two thousand flyers and she's mad at us?* But I just went through Gigi's records and found the Mayday mix of "Good Life." It was an obvious choice but a crowd-pleaser, and I loved it. I segued into it. The backward drum edits and sampled synth stabs filled the empty club. O. J. and his date walked off the dance floor and headed for the exits.

16

SILVER RADIO

Janet had left a message on my answering machine: "Mo, this might seem weird, but the guy I'm dating is playing at Sin-é tonight. It's folk music, but he's really good. If you're free, you should come by."

Janet and I had broken up a few months ago, and now she had a new boyfriend who was a musician. Should I be jealous? I poked around inside my brain and endocrine system, looking for jealousy. I couldn't find it. I was painfully single, but I wasn't bothered by Janet's having a boyfriend.

Sin-é was an Irish café on St. Mark's Place owned by one of Janet's friends. After we broke up, Janet had moved away from my world of hip-hop and house music—and the furthest away she could get from club kids taking drugs with rappers was a tiny café for folk musicians where they served cappuccinos and closed at eleven p.m.

It was a cold Tuesday night and the streets were quiet and black with rain. I left my apartment and walked up Second Avenue as the cold wind pushed and pulled at my hair and clothes. I loved nights like this. The rain had driven people inside, and Second Avenue was still, aside from some lonely taxis. Another gust of cold wind hit my face and tried to push me backward.

I reached the block between Seventh and Eighth Streets, a criminal bazaar. This block was where the addicts and dealers sold crack, mescaline, stolen bicycles, and more benignly, weed. Because it was cold and wet, most of the criminals and addicts were somewhere else. But there were still a few emaciated junkies and crack addicts sitting on the sidewalk, trying to sell lone shoes and water-damaged eight-track tapes. I looked down and saw that next to a stained pink bathrobe one addict was selling an old bass machine, a Roland TB-303. I already had one, but I figured it wouldn't hurt to have a spare.

"How much for the TB-303?"

The crack addict looked up and stared at me blankly.

I tried again: "How much for the drum machine?"

He looked around, confused. "The drum?" he asked haltingly. "I don't got a drum."

"No, the drum machine," I said, pointing at the TB-303.

"Oh, the radio?"

I paused. "Yeah, that radio."

"It's a silver radio," he said. "It's ten dollars."

Since I already had one, I bargained. "I'll give you five," I said.

He looked around at the rest of his waterlogged junk. Then he looked up at me, pleading in his eyes. "You can't do ten?" he asked meekly.

"Okay," I said. "I can do ten." I handed him a ten-dollar bill.

His eyes lit up. "Okay, man, here's your radio!"

"Thanks, man," I said, taking my TB-303 and walking away. After a few yards, I turned around. He was already scurrying down Second Avenue, heading for a tenement on Seventh Street where he could buy and smoke crack. I'd just enabled him to buy drugs. But, I reasoned with myself, he had free will and it wasn't my place to make decisions for other people. However, I continued Socratically, he didn't have true free will, because he was an addict. I realized that part of the reason I felt guilty was that I had bought a superfluous bass machine while walking to see a folk musician.

I got to the corner of Second Avenue and Saint Mark's Place. "Yo, you wanna buy a bike?" some guy asked me. I looked over: he was wheeling an old rusty bike with peeling paint and no gearshift. Eh, what the hell.

"Five dollars?" I asked.

He nodded. "Five dollars." I took a five-dollar bill out of my wallet and handed it to him. He said nothing. As soon as I was holding the handlebars, he walked away down Second Avenue. I was down $15 but I had a rusty bike and a wet Roland bass machine.

The bike was heavy and it seemed to be held together by rust, but the tires were inflated and it felt reasonably sturdy. I got on and rode down St. Mark's, with my $10 bass machine in my jacket pocket, feeling liberated on my new bike. When I got to Sin-é I leaned my bike against the window. I didn't have a lock. Maybe someone inside had some string or a rope?

I walked in. Janet was in the corner, helping her new boyfriend set up his equipment. "Oh, hi, Mo," she said. "This is Jeff."

"Hi, Jeff," I said, shaking his hand. "Nice to meet you. Janet, do you think they have any rope here? I just bought a bike and I want to tie it to the gate out front."

"You bought a bike? Is it nice?"

"Not really. It only has one gear and it's kind of falling apart."

She went behind the tiny bar and asked her friend Karl if he had some rope. "I need it to tie up my bike," I explained.

Karl laughed. "You really think the crackheads will be slowed down by some rope?"

I laughed with him. "Well, if they steal it, I'm out five dollars."

He looked in a drawer. "Nope, sorry, no rope."

I looked around for anything I could use to secure my bike. Next to the door was a coatrack, and on top of the coatrack were some wire hangers. I took two of them and twisted them into two makeshift bike locks. At the very least they would slow someone down just enough that I could walk outside and politely ask them not to resteal my stolen bike. I attached the bike to the front of Sin-é and went inside to sit down with Janet.

The café wasn't crowded—there were maybe fifteen people there—

but the room was filled with cigarette smoke. "I hope your boyfriend's good," I told Janet. "The air in here is disgusting."

"Well, I'd rather breathe secondhand smoke and be with my friends than breathe clean air at home by myself," she said with a small smile.

"Really? Clean air at home by myself sounds pretty good."

Karl turned off the stereo behind the bar and we all stopped talking. Jeff tapped the microphone a couple of times. "Hi, everyone," he said, looking uncomfortable. "My name's Jeff Buckley. Thanks for coming out tonight."

He started playing. Janet sat, rapt and transfixed. I noticed that Jeff had all the women in the room rapt and transfixed. His voice had a high and beautiful quality to it, but he was anxious and his performance was awkward and rushed. When he finished his first song, all fifteen of us clapped. He played a second song; we clapped politely again.

For his third song, he started playing "Hallelujah." I turned to Janet and whispered, "Did he write this? I know this song." She shushed me. While playing "Hallelujah," Jeff finally calmed down. His guitar playing smoothed out and his voice opened up and filled the room. In the far background we could hear the sounds of the city: rain on the sidewalk, distant car horns. But the fifteen of us were in a little smoky cave with this awkward boy and his beautiful bell-tone voice. His eyes were closed as he sat on his café chair, singing to us and the ceiling and his hidden angels. When he finished, we cheered and whistled.

"'Hallelujah' is a Leonard Cohen song," Janet said. "It's a cover."

"Wow. It's great."

As he started singing his next song, I asked, "How long have you been dating?" She shushed me again. I looked out the window. An addict was circling my bike, trying to figure out if he could steal it. I got up and went outside in the middle of Jeff's song.

"Hey, man, that's my bike," I said.

"All right," he said. "I'm just looking at it. Kind of a piece-of-shit bike."

I laughed.

He peered through the small, steamy window. "What's this place?" he asked.

"It's an Irish café."

"They got beer in there?"

"No, no beer."

"That's fucked up," he said, and walked away. I watched him go, protecting my $5 bike.

I walked back inside as Jeff started a fifth song. "I just stopped some guy from stealing my bike," I told Janet.

"Sshh!"

"Plus I bought a bass machine."

She stared daggers at me. "Shut up, Moby."

Jeff was playing one of his own songs with his eyes closed. His guitar playing was choppy and strange, but his voice was beautiful and his strangeness was compelling. When he finished and everyone was applauding, I said to Janet, "He looks like the guy from *90210*."

She said nothing, ignoring me to get me to stop talking.

"Or James Dean," I added.

When Jeff finished his set we all applauded. A few people went up to congratulate him while he gathered up his equipment. He smiled hugely at everyone, saying, "Hey, thanks! Thanks for coming!" I walked over.

"That was really great," I said. "Your singing is beautiful."

"Thanks, Moby!" he said loudly. "Janet played me some of your records—they're cool!"

"Oh, thanks," I said, searching for something to say. "Oh, on my way over, I bought this bass machine." I held out the TB-303.

"Whoa," he said. "That is *so cool.*"

"It doesn't have MIDI, but it was ten dollars, so how could I say no?" Jeff laughed, a bit too loud.

"Janet, thanks for inviting me," I said. "I'll talk to you tomorrow. And it was nice to meet you, Jeff."

"Nice to meet you too, Moby!" he said, pumping my hand.

I untied the wire hangers from my bike. The wind had picked up and it was raining harder. I rode across St. Mark's and down Avenue A, dodging puddles and singing "Hallelujah" to myself. I was reflecting on how beautiful Jeff's voice was when a cab pulled in front of me on Houston. I hit my brake, but it was wet, and I slammed into the side of the cab.

There was a loud boom as I hit the cab door with my bike, and then I fell backward onto the street, my bike on top of me. As I stood up the cab driver slammed his door and ran around his cab. How considerate; he was coming to see if I was okay.

"What the fuck!" he yelled. "You fucking hit my cab, you asshole!"

Oh, he wasn't coming to see if I was okay. "You almost killed me!" I yelled.

"Fuck you!" he responded, getting in my face and pushing me backward. "You fucking asshole! You hit my cab!"

I wanted to push back, but I was supposed to be a pacifist. Plus, I didn't actually know how to fight. "Look," I said, "your cab's okay."

He looked at his door, which was unscratched and undamaged. Reluctantly, he headed back around his taxi to the driver's side. "I should kick your ass, motherfucker!" he shouted as he walked away.

A taxi behind us honked a couple of times, trying to motivate him to move. He spun around like a crazy rooster. "Fuck you, motherfucker!" he shouted at the other cab. He gave me a parting "Motherfucking fuck you," got into his cab, and sped away, tires squealing.

I pulled my bike onto the sidewalk. The bike seemed to be okay—I supposed it was indestructible. I pulled myself onto the sidewalk. I was not indestructible, but I thought I was unhurt. I pulled up my pants— my legs were scraped and bleeding. With the adrenaline rush, I hadn't noticed.

I checked the bass machine in my pocket—it was fine. I got back on the bike and rode home, staying on the sidewalk. My heart was racing, and part of me wanted to find the cab driver and beat him senseless with a crowbar. But I was a Christian, and Christians weren't supposed to beat people to death with crowbars.

I got back to Mott Street and tried to figure out where to put my $5 bike. It was too heavy to lug up and down four flights of stairs. And the insane superintendent would kill me if I tried to leave it in the area under the stairs. I parked it in the entryway and ran upstairs to see if Lee had a bike lock.

"How was it?" Lee asked from the futon, where he was talking on the phone with his girlfriend in London. "Did you meet Janet's new boyfriend?" Lee had met a woman at Max Fish, a new bar on Ludlow Street, and had fallen drunkenly in love. She had just moved to the UK and he was talking to her for an hour every night, spending all his money on long-distance calls.

"It was good, he seems nice, I bought a bike, I got hit by a cab, do you have a lock?" I replied.

"What?"

"Do you have a bike lock?" I asked again.

"I think so, hold on." Lee finished his phone call, went into his room, and emerged with an old bike lock and chain. He started to ask, "You got hit by a cab?" but I ran downstairs before he could finish.

There was an old dead tree in front of our building, so I locked my bike to it. It was as safe as a bike could be in New York City in 1991. I went back upstairs.

"You got hit by a cab?" Lee asked again as I walked in the door.

"Well, technically I hit him, but it was his fault. He cut me off. I want to find him and hit him with a crowbar."

"Ha," he said. "Wait, what's the story with Janet's boyfriend?"

"His name is Jeff Buckley and he's a folksinger. He's really nice but kind of awkward."

"Any relation to Tim Buckley?"

"I doubt it," I said, "but that would be cool."

"Didn't Tim Buckley write 'Song to the Siren' on the This Mortal Coil album?" Lee asked.

"I think so," I said. I walked into my room and looked out the window to check on my bike. It was gone. I started laughing and then ran back down to the street, Lee right behind me. In the five minutes we'd been talking someone had ripped the dead tree out of the ground and stolen my bike—and Lee's bike lock, which was probably worth more than the bike. The dead tree was lying on the sidewalk.

"I thought crack addicts were weak," I said.

"Do you want to go back to Second and Seventh and buy it back?"

"No, it wasn't meant to be," I said. "The crack gods have taken my bike."

I went back inside and left a message on Janet's answering machine: "Thanks for inviting me to Sin-é. Your boyfriend seems nice and I really like his voice. I got hit by a cab on my way home, but don't worry, I'm not dead. Thanks again."

17

BLACK LACQUER

Over the summer of 1990 I'd produced a slow R & B single
called "Time's Up" for a singer named Jimmy Mack. It sold
fewer than two hundred fifty copies. When I released my first
solo single, "Mobility," it had sold around fifteen hundred copies, which
felt like a huge success compared to "Time's Up."

The B-side of "Mobility" was a minimal techno track called "Go." It
was poorly mixed and no DJs were playing it. Even I wasn't playing it
when I DJed. It was too subdued and too poorly mixed to be played
alongside any other house or techno records.

Jared had been talking to Outer Rhythm, a label in the UK, and the
head of A & R for some reason liked "Go" and had expressed interest in
releasing it. Jared warned me, "They'll only release it if you make some
new mixes so it doesn't seem like an old record."

After signing with Instinct I had moved my studio into Jared's place.
He had a big one-bedroom apartment; we set up the Instinct Records
office and my studio in his living room. The walls of his apartment
were painted pink and covered with black-and-white pictures he'd taken
of Boston-based indie-rock bands in the early eighties.

Having my studio set up in his big living room made more sense
than trying to work in the closet of my tiny bedroom on Mott Street.

Jared worked full-time and made $80,000 a year doing data entry for Citibank. So from nine a.m. to six p.m. every weekday while he was at work I would go to his apartment, where I would make music, do office work, or clean the kitchen.

On a Monday morning I went to Jared's apartment and made myself oatmeal with raisins in his microwave. I sat at his black lacquered dining room table and thought about how to do a remix of "Go" for Outer Rhythm records. When I finished my oatmeal I put the bowl in the sink, walked past Jared's black leather sofa to my equipment, and loaded in the samples for "Go," still having no idea what to do.

First I tried an even more barebones version of the song, stripping down the already minimal elements and putting reverb on the bass line. It was interesting, but would anyone play it? Would Tony Humphries play it? I assumed not, so after a couple of hours of work, I scrapped it.

Then I tried to work up a tribal version, adding lots of bongos and congas and making it even more repetitive. I sat in Jared's black office chair in front of my equipment and added digital delay to the percussion. It almost sounded good, something that a DJ might consider playing. But it needed more. A breakbeat, maybe? I went to the turntables and started playing breakbeat compilation albums while listening to the tribal version of "Go." None of them worked—until one stood out.

It was too slow, but I sampled it and sped it up and somehow it fit. The kick drum to my new remix was just a traditional 4/4 pattern. The bass line had very little low end and sounded more like a percussive bass pattern played with an analog synth. This new breakbeat was driving the song. It wasn't finished, but I recorded it to a cassette to take it home and listen to it later with fresh ears.

After working on the remix it was time to do the office work. I ran envelopes through the preloaded postage meter. I stamped and addressed cardboard shipping boxes for promo vinyl. I sorted the faxes that had come in, arranging them in the wire "in" basket on Jared's desk. I checked the phone messages to see if there were any I should respond to. Then I cleaned my oatmeal bowl and put it in the drying rack. I was basically running the Instinct Records office five days a week and making the music for the label even though I hadn't been paid anything in the year since I signed my deal with them. But I was happy and living in New York and making over $8,000 a year DJing, so I couldn't really complain.

It was three p.m., and I wanted to get to UPS and FedEx and the post office before they closed. I loaded up two messenger bags with promotional vinyl, ready to be shipped to DJs and distributors and radio stations. I left the building and turned the corner by the L train stop on Fourteenth Street and Eighth Avenue. I looked up and a giant walked straight into me. He was about six foot eight and wearing dirty work clothes. There was a crash. I looked down: he'd dropped his forty-ounce bottle of Olde English malt liquor, and there was red fury in his eyes. He had a little Ratso Rizzo–esque friend who started laying into me: "Whoa, you fucked up, man! You broke his beer!"

I started apologizing. "I'm sorry, I'm sorry."

"What the fuck," the giant said in a deep voice. "You broke my bottle."

"I'm really sorry," I said. "It was an accident."

"Yo," his friend said, "you gotta get him a new bottle."

"Okay," I said. "Let me go into the deli and get you a bottle of Olde English."

"Fuck that," the giant rumbled. "Just give me five dollars."

"Okay." I took out my wallet and handed him five dollars. "Here you go."

He took the money and stormed off. His friend followed, saying, "Yo, watch where you're walking, dickface." With my heart racing I looked at the broken bottle on the sidewalk and realized the liquid didn't look like beer. There were no bubbles, no foam. It just looked like water. I'd been scammed.

I smiled. They'd bought a bottle of Olde English, drank it, filled it up with water, and bumped into an unthreatening guy walking down the street. Then they'd dropped the bottle, threatened me, and gotten me to give them five dollars—and, presumably, gone off to buy more Olde English. I almost wanted to chase them down and congratulate them on a well-executed con. Kudos to you, small-time grifters—for a second you had me believing that you were going to rip off my arms.

The owner of the deli stepped out his door and glared at me. "You gonna clean up that bottle?" he demanded. Oh, you're kidding.

"No, I didn't break it, they did," I said.

"I saw it! You broke it, clean up that glass!" he yelled.

"Nope, I have to go," I said, and walked across Eighth Avenue.

He started yelling at me, "Hey, fuck you! Clean up this bottle!" His voice faded as I walked away. "Fuck you, motherfucker! Fuck you!"

I was pretty sure that every person in New York City had Tourette's. I wanted to yell something equally Tourette's-y back at him, but I had records to ship and the post office was closing soon, and post offices always smelled good.

When I was seven years old I would hang out with my grandmother in her office at the Noroton Heights Presbyterian Church, where she volunteered and worked on the church's weekly news circular. I would sit in the closet with the office supplies and play with the pens and paper while she typed up the weekly church information and ran it off on the mimeograph. The soft cardboard and old stone smell of post offices was like Proust's madeleine for me, bringing me back to the office supply closet in my grandmother's office at her church. I walked into the post office on Fourteenth Street and Eighth Avenue and got in line. After twenty minutes I got to the front of the line and handed my packages to the woman behind the counter.

"You know, you don't have to stand in line to drop these off," she told me.

Did I know that? Or had I conveniently forgotten so I could stand in line and smell the post office?

"Okay, thanks!" I said.

When I was fifteen I wanted to work for a dry cleaner in Darien because I loved the way it smelled. One day I walked in and asked if they had any job openings. The old Italian-American man behind the counter was nonplussed. "You want a job? Here?"

"Yes, I've always wanted to work here," I told him sincerely (not adding "because it smells nice").

"Okay, come in Saturday."

I was so happy: I was going to work in my favorite-smelling place, the dry cleaners by the Noroton Heights train station. I came in Saturday ready for work, and he said, "Oh, how old are you?"

"Fifteen," I said.

He shook his head sadly. "You have to be sixteen to work. Come back when you're sixteen." I went back when I was sixteen, but he didn't have a job opening, so I got my first real job: washing dishes at a restaurant in a shopping mall. I was at the bottom of the restaurant totem pole. At the top was the African-American manager, then below him were the Caucasian waiters, and below them were the Latino busboys and cooks. At the bottom was me, the sixteen-year-old white kid who washed the dishes, got scalded by boiling rancid water for six hours at a stretch, and left smelling like a bag of rotten lobsters.

After leaving the post office, I dropped off some packages at FedEx and then went back to Jared's. As I walked into his apartment, the phone was ringing. I picked it up. "Instinct Records, can I help you?"

"Hi, Moby, it's Jared."

"Hi, Jared, how's it going?"

"Good. Any messages?"

"Guy from Outer Rhythm faxed, your mom called, someone from *Mixmag* called, Dave sent a fax, and a distributor from California faxed too."

"Cool, thanks. Oh, did you see *Twin Peaks* last night?"

"No, I was out and Lee and I don't have a VCR. I'm hoping Paul taped it and I can see it at his dorm."

"Oh. I taped it if you want to watch it."

"Really? Thanks! When are you coming home?"

"Probably around seven. Talk to you later." He hung up.

I ran to the television. *Twin Peaks* was my religion. Well, *Twin Peaks* and Christianity. But at present, *Twin Peaks* was winning. I loved God, but at the moment I was more obsessed with Bob and Dale Cooper and Audrey Horne. I rewound Jared's tape, sat on his black couch, and hit "play." Angelo Badalamenti's score filled the room and I was happy. For the next hour I could live inside David Lynch's head.

The bird was in the tree. The saw blades were being sharpened. The falls were cascading slowly past the Great Northern Hotel. The camera panned over the dark, still water. When they cut to Leland Palmer's house, "Laura Palmer's Theme" started playing—the best and darkest piece of music in the Twin Peaks score. I needed something to add to the remix of "Go" I was working on and wondered if I could sample "Laura Palmer's Theme" and use that.

When the episode was over I went to Jared's CD carousel and took out the *Twin Peaks* score. It was too slow and too long to be sampled, as my Akai S950 sampler had only about eight seconds of sampling time. But maybe I could play it myself? It was simple, only three notes of a modulating E-minor chord and a low E note on the piano.

I'd started studying music theory when I was ten years old and had continued until age fourteen, when I heard the Clash for the first time. After falling in love with punk rock I'd decided to forget Dorian and Mixolydian scales and instead learn how to play three-chord songs by the Damned and the Sex Pistols. Some of my formal musical education still sat in the back of my head, though, helping me to understand chord voicings and transposition.

I turned on my Yamaha SY22 keyboard and found a string sound I liked. I played the three notes in "Laura Palmer's Theme" and it almost sounded like Angelo Badalamenti's recording. I cued up the tribal remix of "Go" I'd been working on and played "Laura Palmer's Theme" on top of it. And it worked. The chords were long and languorous, but they worked with the skittish bass line and the looping drums.

It was missing something: Badalamenti's low, droning piano. I added the low piano part with my Oberheim piano module, and the remix suddenly came together. Now it needed arrangement. I'd start the remix with the Twin Peaks strings and piano. Then add a kick drum. Then bring in the percussion and drums. Then the strings went out and the weird digital synth swoop came in. And it was basically done.

Or did it need something else? In the late eighties there had been a brief period of Italian house records based on big, bouncy disco pianos. They'd been huge in the British rave scene, and almost all British rave tracks involved that piano sound. I went to the middle of the remix and muted the strings and improvised a bunch of percussive E-minor seventh piano chords.

The remix of "Go" didn't need much else. I dialed in some high end on the strings, some reverb on the vocal samples, some low end on the kick drum. With its long, slow strings, it was an odd remix, but I thought it worked. I hit "play" and recorded it to a DAT. I left the DAT on Jared's black lacquer table with a Post-it note: "a remix of 'go' i did today, what do you think?"

I looked at the clock. It was getting close to seven. Jared really didn't like my being in his apartment when he got home from work. I knew that musicians signed to record labels didn't usually work for free and clean the kitchen and go to the post office and send faxes, but I still wanted to respect his desire for me not to be around when he came home.

I was free labor, but I was also the only artist on Instinct. When I was going to FedEx and the post office to send out vinyl I was usually sending out my own records. Also I liked working. I'd been raised by my mom to do whatever work needed doing. When I sat on the futon and played too much Nintendo I ended up feeling like a greasy vegan slug. Work was fun and made me feel sharp and virtuous.

I turned off my studio equipment, put my oatmeal bowl back in the cupboard, turned off Jared's lights, and went home.

At eight p.m. my phone rang. "Moby? It's Jared." He paused. "This remix of 'Go' is really strong."

"Really? I just made it after watching *Twin Peaks*."

"Is it finished? Can I send it to Guy?"

"Well, if you think it sounds good, then sure. Do you think he'll like it?"

"We'll see. Oh, what should we call it?"

"How about 'The Woodtick Mix'?"

A moment of silence on Jared's end. "The Woodtick Mix?" he finally said.

"When Dale Cooper got shot his vest was riding up 'cause he was chasing a woodtick. So, 'The Woodtick Mix,'" I explained.

"Okay. Moby, again, this remix is really strong."

"Thanks, Jared. Oh, did you get the messages and the faxes?"

"Yeah, thanks. Are you coming in tomorrow?"

"Around ten a.m. Do you need me to go to the post office?"

"No, all the vinyl's been sent out. Probably not sending out more until Thursday or Friday."

"Okay, have a good night."

"You too. I'm going to listen again."

This was the first time Jared had sounded this excited and the first time he had called me to tell me that he liked something I'd done. I doubted that anyone would play this remix of "Go," but at least Jared liked it.

18

BABY FOOD

was standing in Jared's living room, holding a fax. It was from Outer Rhythm records in the UK and it read: "'Go' is huge! Love, Guy."

I read the first three words again: "'Go' is huge!"

The "Go" remix had come out a few months earlier, and it kept getting bigger and bigger. I knew something was happening when I went to Limelight to hear Derrick May DJ and he played the "Rainforest Mix" of "Go." Around that time, Guy from Outer Rhythm had sent a fax saying, "'Go' is big! You need to come to England!" So with Guy's help I booked my first UK tour: I was going to spend two months playing at clubs and raves. Real raves! I'd seen pictures of raves in magazines: ten thousand people on ecstasy in a field at dawn, dancing to 808 State and Adamski and Guru Josh and Orbital, everyone wearing smiley-face T-shirts and waving glow sticks and hugging each other. And, in theory, I was going to be onstage in front of them. In England. Where I'd never been, as I'd only left the country twice before: once to visit France in 1987 and once in 1989 to go to Canada to visit lakes.

I'd been packing for two weeks and my luggage contained:

Star Trek books
other science-fiction books

the red vinyl Bible I'd had since the sixth grade
DATs
vinyl
T-shirts
socks
jeans
sweater
keyboard
drum machine
Octapad
MIDI cables

And in my carry-on:

brand-new passport
an economy round-trip ticket on Air Pakistan
another *Star Trek* book
vegan cookies
sandwich
baby food

I'd been in a health-food store on Prince Street wondering what I could buy to eat on the plane. I was standing in front of a display of organic baby food, and I checked out Earth's Best Organic Oats and Bananas. The ingredients were oats, bananas, and water. I bought a jar, tried it at home, and it was delicious. I bought a few jars for the plane. It was organic and simple and portable, even if there was something odd about a twenty-five-year-old man eating baby food as he flew over the Atlantic Ocean en route to play at drug-fueled raves in London.

The next day I carried my keyboard case and suitcase and knapsack and record case and carry-on bag to the curb outside my apartment. I got a taxi and went up Lafayette and Park Avenue, getting off outside Grand Central Terminal to catch the airport bus. I stowed my luggage in the bus's undercarriage and sat down, almost bouncing in my seat with panic and excitement. We drove through the Midtown Tunnel and finally arrived at JFK.

I felt a bit inadequate when I got to the terminal, as I was alone and almost everyone else flying on Air Pakistan seemed to have brought their extended families. People were weeping and hugging each other, kids were running around, and a man was arguing with an airport employee about why he couldn't check a refrigerator as part of his luggage. I waited in a long, snaking line for an hour and finally reached the economy check-in desk. I checked all my luggage, got my boarding pass for a middle seat, and went to the gate. Eating my apple butter and banana sandwich while I waited, I spotted Laurie Anderson reading a magazine. It was an omen. She was the patron saint of weird New Yorkers, and if she was on my Air Pakistan flight to London, then my trip had to be blessed.

The flight was bumpy but uneventful; I landed in London exhausted and full of organic baby food. I'd tried to sleep on the plane, but I was too excited to close my eyes for more than a few minutes. I went through immigration, got a luggage cart, and wheeled my stack of luggage to the Heathrow tube station. I was staying at a house in Wood Green, which was a neighborhood in north London. When I booked my trip, Lee and Janet had decided to go to London as well. Lee was there to visit his girlfriend, and Janet was there to be a tourist; we were all staying in the same house. It was an old Victorian, and Sally, the publicist for Outer Rhythm, lived there with her dogs and kids and whichever of her friends were in town.

I piled my luggage and equipment onto the tube, changed trains a few times, and ended up sweaty and exhausted in Wood Green at two p.m. When I arrived at the house, Sally and Janet were standing at the front door. Sally was wearing a long batik skirt and holding a cup of herbal tea. Janet was wearing a Columbia University women's tennis jacket over a Police concert T-shirt.

"Welcome to London!" Sally said.

"Hi, Mo," Janet said.

Standing next to Janet, gazing up at me, was a curly blond four-year-old girl chewing on a sock and clutching a worn Paddington Bear. "And this is Cinnamon!" Sally said.

Cinnamon took my hand and showed me to my bedroom. There she helped me unpack my luggage and equipment. She then took my hand again and escorted me to the kitchen. The whole time she had a sock in her mouth and was humming wordlessly to herself.

Cinnamon pulled out my chair at the kitchen table and Sally handed me a glass of orange juice. "How are you feeling? Are you ready for your big tour?" she asked.

"I'm tired, but I can't believe I'm in London," I said. "Oh, where's Lee?"

"He's in the pub with his friend Adam," Janet said.

"The pub?" I asked. It seemed a bit early in the day for him.

"He's depressed, Mo. When he got here, his girlfriend broke up with him and told him she was sleeping with the guitar player in her band. He's been drunk ever since."

The phone rang: it was Guy calling for me. "Listen, I know you just arrived," he said, "but would you be up for DJing tonight?"

"Tonight? Okay, where?"

"A friend of mine from Kiss FM is having a party at a club in Soho and he really wants you to DJ," he said.

"How does he know who I am?" I asked.

Guy laughed. "Kiss FM is playing 'Go' ten times a day."

After I slept for a few hours Guy picked me up to drive me to his friend's party. I got into Guy's car with a shoulder bag full of house and techno twelve-inches. Guy was a dance-music fanatic who DJed at underground clubs and ran Outer Rhythm, one of the coolest dance labels in the world. He was my height, with short blond hair. He was wearing a black polo shirt, an Arsenal windbreaker, and a brand-new pair of Adidas.

We drove through London in his Renault, switching between Kiss FM and some of the other, pirate radio stations. London, and the rest of the UK, was full of unlicensed pirate radio stations. There were the official, licensed radio stations, which were generally quite conservative, playing Top 40 records and classical music. And scattered throughout the dial were the unlicensed pirate stations, operating out of abandoned offices and warehouses and playing cutting-edge dance music and reggae.

As Guy drove, and Kiss FM played on the car radio, I stared out the window, thinking, *I'm in London. I'm in London. I'm in London.* Growing up I'd been obsessed with everything and anything that came out of the UK: Joy Division, the Sex Pistols, Benny Hill, Monty Python, Peter Saville, Peter O'Toole, John Peel. And now I was here, making casual conversation with Guy while driving past British supermarkets and British bus stops. The sun had set in London two hours ago, and in New York, where I had been twenty-four hours ago, it was late afternoon. It all seemed like intercontinental magic.

Then "Go" came on the radio. "Ha, see!" Guy said, turning it up. We sped through London listening to "Go." We passed a century-old pub as the breakbeat I'd sampled kicked in. We passed a tube station as the disco pianos kicked in. The same disco pianos I recorded in Jared's apartment while my oatmeal bowl was drying. I was trying to be urbane and jaded, but I wanted to roll down the window and scream at the top of my lungs, "I'm in London and this is my song! On the radio! Not even on a cassette, but on the radio!"

"I told you," Guy said, "they're playing it ten times a day."

We pulled up to the club in Soho and parked in the alley at the back. The club was small and run-down and had the dank pheromone of every club I'd ever been in: cigarettes and spilled drinks, with a faint reek of urine and cleaning products from the toilets.

"On Saturday you're playing a proper rave," Guy said, "so consider this the warm-up."

"How many people will be at the rave?" I asked.

"I dunno," he said. "Five thousand? Ten thousand? It's a big one, near Bath. Make sure to play 'Go'! People will go mental."

I started playing records at his friend's party at midnight, and it was like any night DJing in New York, except that everyone in this British club was straight and white. At one a.m. I played "Go," and the two hundred people in the small club cheered.

Guy's friend from Kiss FM came over and drunkenly slapped my back. "Wicked tune, mate!" he shouted in my ear. The night ended around two a.m. and Guy drove me back to Wood Green.

"So what'd you think?" he asked.

"It was good, but weird to be DJing for straight white people," I said.

"Oh, none of my business," he said, "but are you gay?"

"No, I'm straight, but the dance scene in New York is mainly black and Latino and gay."

"I lived in New York, so I remember that. Not sure the punters here know," he said, pulling up to Sally's house. "See you tomorrow bright and early. You have interviews at Outer Rhythm at nine a.m."

"Which is four a.m. in New York," I said, exhausted.

Sally's house was dark, but Janet was awake, drinking tea and reading by a faint light at the red-painted kitchen table.

"Hi, Mo," she said. "How was—"

She was cut short by Lee, who stumbled through the kitchen door and fell on the floor. He was wearing a beer-stained Jesus and Mary Chain T-shirt and he hadn't shaved in a week. "She fucking hates me," he drunkenly moaned from the floor.

"Lee?" I asked. "Are you okay?"

He looked at me, his eyes unfocused. He pulled himself up from the floor and started punching himself in the face.

"She fucking hates me," he said over and over again, hitting himself each time.

"Oh shit," I said.

Janet ran over to him and he accidentally punched her in the face, sending her crashing into a kitchen chair.

I ran over and grabbed Lee's arms to stop him from hitting himself. He started slamming his head against the wall.

"Lee!" I said. "Lee! You're drunk, stop it!"

"Why does she hate me?" he said, and started crying. I let go of him and he lay down on the floor again, weeping and saying, "Why does she hate me?"

"Janet, are you okay?" I asked. She was sitting on the floor, holding the side of her face where Lee had unintentionally punched her.

"I've never been hit before," she said, stunned.

"Everything okay here?"

I looked up. Sally was in the kitchen doorway, in sweatpants and a Primal Scream T-shirt, half-asleep. Cinnamon was standing next to her, the sock in her mouth and Paddington Bear in her hand.

"Oh no, I'm sorry," I said. "Lee's drunk."

She looked at him crying on the floor and shook her head, regretting letting her house be used as a hostel for Americans. "Try to get him to bed," she said. "The kids have school in a few hours." She and Cinnamon headed back to sleep.

"Let's take him to his room," Janet said. We hoisted him up and walked him down the hall to his bedroom. We laid him on his side in his bed, so he wouldn't choke on his vomit if he threw up in his sleep. He passed out immediately.

"Can we pray, Mo?" Janet asked.

We kneeled on the floor by Lee's bed and asked God to look after Lee. While we were praying, Lee farted and started snoring.

"Our prayers are answered, he's alive," I said as Lee farted again.

"Welcome to London," Janet said.

19

GIANT LOOP OF KEYS

P lay it again."

I was sitting on our battered black futon and Lee was standing by the answering machine. He hit "rewind" and then "play." A manic, irate voice came out of the tiny speaker: "This is your landlord, you can't fucking change the locks! It's my apartment! I will fuck you up if you don't fucking change the locks back! You can't fucking do this!" Lee hit "stop" and looked at me.

"I think everyone in New York has Tourette's," I said.

Nine months earlier Lee and I had moved out of Fourteenth Street and into a two-bedroom apartment on Mott Street that cost $800 a month. It was on a quiet block and we each had a small but nice bedroom with south-facing windows looking out onto Mott Street. We'd signed a yearlong lease, but we both liked the apartment and had talked about staying longer.

Two weeks ago we'd heard about some burglaries in the building, so we'd had a locksmith come and put a new Medeco lock on our door. The locksmith said that this was the one lock burglars hadn't figured out a way to get past. Then yesterday Lee and I had come home to find that someone had used an iron pry bar to try to break into our apartment, hacking at the locks and trying to remove our steel door from its hinges. We assumed it was one of our friendly neighborhood crack addicts, but now it seemed as if it was our landlord.

"Let's look at the evidence," I said, trying to sound like a TV detective. "One: you saw our landlord on the street a few weeks ago and you said she'd lost a lot of weight. Two: someone got into the building and tried to break into our apartment yesterday. Three: our landlord called us for the first time in six months, knowing that we'd changed the lock."

"So you think our landlord tried to break into our apartment?" Lee asked.

"Technically, our crack-addict landlord tried to break into our apartment," I said.

"What should we do?"

"Move?"

"But I love this apartment. Where will we go?"

"I saw a sign down the street for lofts for rent," I said. "I might go ask there."

"Are we breaking up?"

"Sniff," I said. "Hold me."

"Fuck you, do you want to go to Benny's Burritos?"

After lunch I walked to the old building on Mott Street that was renting lofts. It was a nineteenth-century industrial building across the street from Old St. Patrick's Cathedral. I stepped into the building's loading dock and knocked on the office door in the back wall.

"Come in!"

I opened the door. A round sixty-year-old Italian-American man was sitting at a metal desk under bright lights reading the *Daily News* and eating Chinese food. He was wearing a light-gray short-sleeve button-down shirt with some ballpoint pens in the breast pocket.

"I'm interested in the sign out front about lofts for rent?" I said.

"Come on in." He stuck out his hand. "I'm Joe Chinnici. My son Russ and I own the building." We shook hands and I sat down at his desk. "So what are you looking for? Oh, and what's your name?" He closed the lid on his Styrofoam Chinese takeout container.

"I'm Moby and I'm a musician. I'm looking for a space for a small electronic-music studio," I said.

"Electronic music? What's that? Is it loud?"

"It's not that loud. I mainly work in headphones."

He nodded. "Okay, you want to see some spaces?" He gathered up his giant loop of keys and we walked out of the office. "You want to know about the building?" he asked.

"Sure."

"Well, it was built in 1840 and during the Civil War it was a prison and a hospital. Then it was a meat-processing plant for about seventy-five years, which is why the floors all slope, 'cause there were drains for the animal blood. Now it's mainly artists' studios, although a lot of bands play in the basement. Maybe you know some of them?"

"Huh, maybe. Which bands?"

"To be honest, I don't know," he said. "Okay, here's the first space, 201." He unlocked the door and I stepped inside. It was about six hundred square feet and it had four giant windows looking out into the cathedral churchyard. It was beautiful, with filtered light coming through the leaves of the huge elms across the street. Looking around, I could see it didn't have running water or a kitchen or a bathroom, but it was still perfect.

"Is there a bathroom nearby?" I asked.

"Down the hall. Everyone on this floor shares it."

"And what's the rent?"

"Well, it's six hundred square feet and it's got nice windows, so five hundred dollars a month?" he proposed.

I was paying $400 a month for the apartment up the street. Could I afford $500? And did I want to once again live in an old factory with no bathroom or running water?

"Or if you pay up front, maybe six months, we can give you a deal," he said.

"How much of a deal?"

"I don't know, maybe twenty-five hundred dollars for six months?" he asked, unsure of himself.

That was almost exactly what I was paying now, only I'd have a six-hundred-square-foot loft with huge beautiful windows looking out at giant trees and a nineteenth-century churchyard. I had made a few thousand dollars from touring over the summer, and I'd put it all in the bank. I could just about afford to give him $2,500 for six months' rent.

"Okay, great, I'll take it. Should we sign a lease?" I asked.

"No, we don't do leases here. It's not that kind of building."

We were in Little Italy and I was going to rent a loft from a round Italian-American man named Joe Chinnici. Maybe I shouldn't ask too many questions. But I had one more: "Can I put bars on the windows? I have a lot of expensive equipment."

"No, you don't need no bars on the windows," he said.

"What do you mean?" I asked.

He considered his words. "Well, you see, this block is safe. It's protected."

I looked confused.

"There are a lot of Italian grandparents on this block, and their sons and grandsons make sure nothing happens to them. This block is protected," he said.

Oh, I understood. It was a Mafia block, so even the crack addicts and drug dealers knew to stay away. "When can I move in?" I asked.

"I don't know, today? You seem like a nice guy—here's the key." He handed it to me. "Also, let me tell you more about the building," he said, warming to his role as landlord and ad hoc historian. "I told you it was a prison and a hospital during the Civil War. It's also got three sub-basements that we rent out to bands and people. Across the hall from you is a guy who sells truffles, and down the hall is some clothing company, 555 Soul. You'll see Joe around, the superintendent. He don't talk much, but he's okay." He shifted his weight uncomfortably. "Okay. So welcome to the building." We shook hands again.

I casually left the building and then ran up the block to my old apartment. "Lee!" I yelled as I came in the door. "I just rented a new loft!" He was on our filthy futon, eating the rest of his lunch.

"When?" he asked, his mouth full of burrito.

"Just now!" I yelled. "Want to come see?"

We walked down the block, crossed Houston, and came to my new home. We walked up one flight of stairs, and I opened the door to 201. "Whoa," he said, "you can see the churchyard. How much is it?"

"Well, I'm paying six months in advance, so it's around $400 a month. You want to ask if there's another one for rent?"

He looked around. "Where will you shower?" he asked.

"The gym, on Broadway."

"No running water? And you'll cook on a hot plate?"

"Yup, it'll be like Stamford again."

"I think I want an apartment with a shower and a real kitchen," he said.

"Pussy. Want to go down to the basement?" We walked downstairs. The ceilings of the first subbasement level were just six feet high and the walls were old, dark brick. We wandered down a long, low hallway lit with a few twenty-five-watt bulbs and came to another staircase heading down.

"This is creepy," Lee said. We walked down again and came to the second basement level, with slightly higher ceilings. We could hear a band playing behind a sheet-metal door. "There are bands here?" Lee asked. "Do you know who?"

I looked at the door: it was covered with Sonic Youth stickers. "Sonic Youth?" I guessed.

"Cool."

We walked down two more long brick hallways, looked at an old boiler room, and found another staircase heading down.

"Three basement levels?" he asked.

"That's what the landlord said."

We walked down as someone else was coming upstairs. Lee and I mumbled "hey" and the person walking past also mumbled "hey." When we got to the bottom of the stairs, we looked at each other.

"Was that Iggy Pop?" Lee whispered.

"I think so," I whispered back.

"What is this place?" he asked. "Are we in indie rock heaven?"

We walked down more narrow brick hallways and came to a different set of stairs heading up. We returned to the second basement level and explored another long hallway we hadn't seen the first time. There was almost more basement real estate under the building than in the building itself.

A very tall bearded guy was standing in a doorway, smoking a cigarette. "Hey," he said.

"Hi," I said. "Excuse me, do you rehearse here?"

"Yeah," he said, extending his hand and saying, almost formally, "Gibby Haynes. I'm in the Butthole Surfers."

I shook his hand. "Moby," I said. "I just moved in upstairs."

"Are you an artist?"

"No, a musician."

"Oh, cool. Welcome to the building."

"Do you know who else has spaces here?" I asked.

"Well, there's us and Iggy and Sonic Youth and Helmet and Sean Lennon and the Beastie Boys and some other people," he said as someone behind him started making a wall of feedback. He stubbed out his cigarette and headed back into his rehearsal space. "Okay, Moby, see you later," he said, and disappeared into a fog of noise.

Lee and I walked up another staircase to the first basement and then up one more to the ground floor. When we were finally standing on the sidewalk, he said, "I feel like I've been down there for a year."

"I know, it's like the catacombs. What else do you think is down there?"

"Nazi gold?"

Across the street from my new building some old Italian ladies were sitting on the street in lawn chairs, while potbellied men played dominoes at a folding table behind them. Some guy in a tight white T-shirt had set up a hibachi barbecue on the sidewalk and was cooking sausages.

"You live in *Goodfellas*," Lee said.

"With the Butthole Surfers," I said.

20

THIN GRAY CURTAINS

was flying to London for the third time in two months, to play a show for Kiss FM and to perform on *Top of the Pops* for the first time. "Go," this oddball song that I recorded in Jared's living room on a few hundred dollars' worth of equipment, was now a top-ten pop hit in the UK.

I was tucked into a tiny blue British Airways seat, reading an Arthur C. Clarke book and eating a peanut butter and jelly sandwich I had brought from home.

The person next to me was reading the entertainment section of a British newspaper. I looked over his shoulder while he read a profile of Bryan Adams. There were the top ten movies. The top ten books. The top ten albums. And on the list of top ten singles, there was "Go," in between Michael Jackson and Phil Collins.

We were somewhere over Nova Scotia; the lights were dimmed so people could sleep as they flew over the North Atlantic. I turned off my overhead light and closed my eyes, listening to the low roar of the airplane. I couldn't sleep. I felt like a monkey on crystal meth, my brain bouncing between blind excitement and blind panic. I was going to be on *Top of the Pops*, the biggest and most iconic music TV show in the history of big, iconic music TV shows.

Trying to sleep was pointless, so I turned on my overhead light. Maybe reading Arthur C. Clarke would calm me down. I'd be distracted by aliens, forgetting how in thirty-six hours I was going to be miming on camera by myself with a rental keyboard and a broken drum machine. I read Arthur C. Clarke as we flew past Iceland, over Ireland, and eventually landed at Heathrow.

I stood under the gritty lights in the immigration line, looking at all the exhausted travelers, and assumed that I'd be sent home. This was a new phobia for me: I'd been to Europe a few times now, and whenever I went through immigration I expected that I'd be kept out of whatever country I was trying to get into. But after ninety minutes I was waved through UK immigration and walked outside.

The record company had sent a car to pick me up. I sat in the back and watched London unfold before me: The British cars with their big yellow and white license plates. The run-down Tudor-inspired houses between the airport and outer London. The newsagents selling tabloids with lurid headlines: PRIME MINISTER RAPES THE POPE AT THE WHITE HOUSE! SHOCKER! MADONNA EATS HER GAY BABIES! HORROR!

After two hours in traffic we pulled up to the hotel. Except it wasn't a hotel. It was a sad gray house on a sad gray road in a defeated part of London. The sort of place where British directors made grim movies about working-class hopelessness: "Shut up, Violet, I can't get my job back, the mine's closed."

Eric, my new manager, met me outside the house. He and I had met in New York a year ago and I'd asked him to be my manager, even though he hadn't ever really managed anyone. He was tall, German, and seemed trustworthy. Plus I'd never met any actual full-time managers. "Welcome to sunny England!" he said in the drizzle.

"Is this the hotel?" I asked.

"It's a B & B; my office is nearby. It seemed like a good choice," he said.

"Okay," I said, staring at the front of the sad gray house. We walked in and I got my key from an old woman in the entranceway. She was wearing a worn beige dress and reading the *Daily Mirror*. "Here's your key," she croaked. "Your room's on the second floor and the bathroom's down the hall. Here's your towel." She handed me a towel that clearly had been used in World War II to mop up diseased blood from the basements of infirmaries.

"Okay, pop star," Eric said. "I'll pick you up at one to go to Kiss FM." That was in one hour.

"One?" I asked. "Can I sleep a bit more?"

"Didn't you sleep on the plane? We have a big interview at one thirty at Kiss."

I stood there, holding my scratchy towel. "Okay, I'll just take a shower," I said.

The woman in the beige housedress said, "Shower's fifty p for five minutes."

I was confused. The shower cost money? "Fifty p?" I asked.

"You put fifty p in the shower and you get five minutes of water," she said brusquely.

I walked upstairs. My room was cold and had one small window facing the wall of the house next door. I walked back down. "Um, how do I turn on the heat in my room?" I asked.

"Heat's not on yet. We don't turn on the heat 'til winter." She returned to her tabloid.

I almost said, "But it's November and it's cold," but I didn't want her to ridicule me for being a soft American.

I went back to my room. It had two single beds, separated by a cigarette-scarred bedside table. The only light came from a small light fixture on the ceiling and the dirty little window. *It's only two days*, I thought. I lay down on the small bed and fell asleep.

An hour later, Eric was banging on the door. "Moby, come on, we have to go!"

I woke up, disoriented. Where was I? Oh, London. "I'll be down in a minute," I yelled.

I got my toothbrush and walked to the shared bathroom. Someone had just been in there, and it smelled like cigarettes and diarrhea. I brushed my teeth quickly and walked downstairs.

"How's the hotel?" Eric asked.

"It's not a hotel, Eric. It's a sad Dickensian workhouse."

He laughed. "So the pop star is a prima donna now?"

Eric lived nearby in a nice home with his wife. He didn't have to pay fifty p for a five-minute shower, and he didn't have to brush his teeth while breathing a stranger's diarrhea fumes. "Let's go," I said.

At Kiss FM I sat in the radio booth in my jeans and hooded sweatshirt, blinking and trying to string sentences together. The DJ probably thought I was hungover and exhausted after a night of partying with groupies in the Four Seasons. I wanted to tell him, "I'm jet-lagged and staying in a charnel house that should have been leveled during World War II."

After the interview we went to Neal's Yard to get lunch. I ordered vegan pasties and vegan cookies and vegan couscous and vegan everything I could get my hands on. We sat outside in the cold and ate.

"You eat a lot for a little person," Eric said.

I laughed. "Maybe one day I'll be big and fat like you."

He laughed, too.

"What's the schedule?" I asked.

"Well, tonight we have dinner with the people from Outer Rhythm, then the Kiss show at eleven p.m. at the Astoria. Tomorrow we have to be at *Top of the Pops* at nine a.m. and it goes out live at eight p.m."

That didn't sound right. "We have to be at *Top of the Pops* for eleven hours?"

"That's the way they do it."

We finished our food and Eric dropped me back at the sad gray B & B. I decided to invest in a shower. There was a coin-operated electric water heater in a moldy vinyl shower stall. I put a fifty-p coin into the water heater and it started to rumble and hum. Eventually a lukewarm trickle came out. I took off my clothes and stepped into the shower stall, trying not to touch the walls, but only ended up damp and cold. I stepped out and tried to dry off, pushing the cold water around on my skin with my scratchy green towel.

Someone knocked on the door and growled, "Hurry up!"

"Just a minute," I said. I threw on my clothes. I was wearing what I thought was a cool rave T-shirt, jeans from Kmart, and a black sweatshirt. I opened the door: an old man with a giant head stood in the hallway scowling at me.

"Don't take so fucking long," he said, pushing past me into the bathroom.

I walked back to my room, lay down on the bed wearing all of my clothes, and slept like a dead person.

A few hours later, Eric was banging on my door again. "Come on, pop star! Time to go to dinner!"

"Just a second," I said. I put on my shoes and opened the door. Eric looked in at my room.

"Well, this is depressing," he said.

We went to a vegetarian restaurant called Manna in Primrose Hill. It was clean and warm and half the menu was vegan. "Can I stay here tonight?" I asked Eric.

"Don't be such a baby," he said.

After dinner we drove to the Astoria for the radio show. My dressing room was a small closet with a black plastic chair and two bare lightbulbs over a mirror. "It's just as depressing as your hotel," Eric the German comedian said. "You should feel right at home."

I looked at the running order. I was on for ten minutes, after Dream Frequency and before K-Klass. "I play for ten minutes?" I asked.

"Yeah," Eric said. "You play 'Go' and then maybe play 'Go' again."

"I'll play 'Go' and 'Rock the House,'" I said. "Does that seem like a good idea?"

"You're the pop star."

Eric and I walked up to the stage. The show was in an old, venerable theater but it felt like a rave. The air smelled like Vicks and the crowd was waving glow sticks and blowing air horns and whistles. Onstage, Dream Frequency were playing their hit "Feel So Real." It was a quintessential rave track, with bouncing pianos, wailing disco vocals, and synthesizers that sounded like buzz saws. The stage was full of singers, dancers, and keyboard players, and it was manic. The song sounded amazing and I was petrified.

"How do I go on after this?" I asked Eric.

He grinned. "You'll be fine."

Dream Frequency finished "Feel So Real," waved at the crowd, and walked off. The MC said, "Wicked! Top tunes from Dream Frequency!" While he was speaking, they were taking Dream Frequency's equipment offstage and replacing it with my one sad Yamaha SY22 rental keyboard. "Now from New York, Moby Go!" I had gotten used to being introduced as "Moby Go": because of the design of my single's sleeve many Britons thought that "Moby Go" was my name.

I ran onstage as "Go" started. The crowd roared, but I panicked because my keyboard wasn't plugged in and I didn't even have a microphone. The crowd didn't care: three thousand people were dancing and yelling "Go!" at the top of their lungs. I banged on my unplugged keyboard and yelled "Go!" even though I didn't have a microphone.

The song ended and the MC returned. "Wicked! Top tune from Moby Go! Next up are Manchester favorites K-Klass!" Some roadies ran onstage, grabbed my keyboard, and rushed it offstage. I stood there, confused. Wasn't I supposed to play a second song?

"Come on, mate, get off the fucking stage!" one of the roadies barked at me. I scurried off.

"That was great!" Eric said. "They loved it!"

"But my keyboard was unplugged and I didn't have a microphone and what about my second song?" I asked.

"Oh, they're running behind schedule so they're cutting people's second songs. They told me while you were on."

I considered that. "The song was okay?" I asked.

"It was amazing! Didn't you see the crowd?"

"But I wasn't really doing anything."

"It doesn't matter. They loved it."

I hung out and watched the rest of the show: Orbital, 808 State, the

Prodigy. It was like listening to my record collection. After the show Eric dropped me back at my alleged hotel. It was one a.m. and I had to be up at eight thirty for *Top of the Pops*. Sleeping would be wise, but even though I hadn't slept much in the last thirty-six hours I was now wide awake. I went for a walk.

I headed for what I thought would be a busy street, but all the shops were closed. A few cabs and buses rolled by, leaving the smell of diesel in the air. I walked for a mile or so before it started to rain. The only shops open were Pakistani groceries: little beacons of light on the wide empty streets. They sold milk, juice, vegetables, VHS tapes, magazines, and Pakistani pop music cassettes. I stopped in one, bought an orange juice, looked at a few foreign newspapers, and kept walking.

I came to an overpass and looked at the railway lines beneath me. London was spread out in front of me, sleeping. Why was this city so quiet? London was where music was born and then disseminated through-out the world. Growing up I'd imagined London to be like Times Square, with every inch a riot of noise and activity. I thought of a Clash lyric in "London's Burning," "I run through the empty stone because I'm all alone," and it made sense.

A night bus went by, the few people inside facing forward and lit by the cold, fluorescent light. My shoes were getting squishy from the rain. I walked for another hour and got back to my hovel. It was five a.m. and I had to wake up in three hours. There was a thin gray light coming through the thin gray curtains. I kept my clothes on, got under the one smallpox-ridden blanket, and willed myself to sleep.

"Pop star! It's your big day! Wake up!" It was Eric, yelling on the other side of the door. I was already dressed, so I put on my damp sneakers.

I'd grown up seeing two different Englands on TV. There was the bucolic England with witty university students floating on slow boats alongside waterborne flower petals on gentle rivers and sunny ponds. Then there was this England, the rainy, cold England that was the back-ground for every movie about defeated people waiting to die in public housing estates. This was the country that gave birth to Joy Division. If

Ian Curtis had been born in Palo Alto he'd probably be managing a chain of organic coffee shops and married to a yoga teacher.

I walked downstairs. Eric was waiting, looking big and cheerful. "Morning!" he said. "You ready to be a big star?"

"I want to go to sleep," I said.

"Oh, come on, it's *Top of the Pops*!"

We got in the car and I closed my eyes. Eric turned on Radio 1; they were playing "Go."

"See, it's a huge hit!" he said enthusiastically. I dozed in the car as we drove to the BBC studio, my head bouncing against the cold window. When we got there, Sally from the record company came to meet us. "Welcome to *Top of the Pops*!" she said. "First run-through is in two hours, then there's a second run-through at one p.m., then camera rehearsal at four, a final run-through at six, then the show at eight."

I asked, "Is that normal? To have so many run-throughs?"

"Well, no. But it's *Top of the Pops*."

She walked me upstairs to my dressing room and I almost started crying with joy. The dressing room was small, but it had a radiator and was warm. It had a bank of windows looking over the rainy studio roof, but most importantly, it had its own bathroom and its own shower.

"Can I stay here all day?" I asked.

She laughed. "It's all yours."

"I'm going to take a shower and sleep for a few minutes. Is that okay?"

"I'll just get you for the first run-through," she said, assenting.

I took off my stinky travel clothes and stepped into the shower for ten uninterrupted minutes. The water was hot, and for the first time in days, I was clean. I dried off and lay down on the couch. The rain was pattering against the old windows, the steam heat was clanking in the old radiator, and I felt at peace. I closed my eyes, and there was a knock on the door. "Moby? First run-through in five minutes!"

We walked to the studio via a warren of huge windowless hallways. "Who else is on the show?" I asked Sally.

"Bizarre Inc., Dream Frequency, New Order, U2, and Phil Collins," she said.

"U2? New Order? Really?"

"I think so. We'll find out in a minute."

We arrived at a giant door with a red light blinking above it. The security guard said, "Welcome to *Top of the Pops*," and swung it open for us. I'd never been in a TV studio before.

The studio was vast, with forty-foot-high ceilings and six different stages. There were cameras everywhere, and cameramen practicing their movements with giant black camera cranes. Eric joined us and handed Sally a sheet of paper. "This is the list," she told me. "Tonight you're on with New Order, Bizarre Inc., Dream Frequency, Slipmatt and Lime, Phil Collins, and U2 will be performing remote."

"So U2 aren't here?"

"No, they're in New York."

"Apart from Phil Collins, it's all dance music," I observed.

I ducked under a swooping camera crane and climbed onto the tiny stage where I'd be performing. There was my rental keyboard and my borrowed drum machine and Octapad. None of the gear was plugged in. "Do they plug in the equipment before the broadcast?" I asked.

"No," Eric said. "Some people sing live, but everyone mimes their equipment."

I looked across the room: New Order were rehearsing on their stage. I'd loved Joy Division obsessively and loved New Order just as obsessively. Now Bernard Sumner and Peter Hook and Stephen Morris were standing forty feet away from me. After New Order, Dream Frequency did their sound check, and then Bizarre Inc.

Then it was my turn: I stood behind my unplugged equipment and jumped around a bit and yelled "go" into the unplugged microphone. I didn't understand the need for a sound check if everyone was just miming to a track, but I'd never been on TV before and maybe there were variables I didn't know about.

When I was done I looked at Phil Collins; he was staring at me with annoyance and confusion. He'd been on *Top of the Pops* countless times, but always with bands with drums and guitars. Now he was surrounded by DJs and synthesizers and disco singers. A few months later he released "I Can't Dance" with Genesis—I like to think it was inspired by his time on *Top of the Pops* surrounded by me and my fellow electronic musicians.

When sound check ended, a voice boomed over the PA, "Okay, ladies and gents, next rehearsal is one p.m." I walked casually back to my dressing room, pretending that this was normal. New Order were walking next to me. I couldn't talk to them. I felt strange even looking at them. They were New Order. They had been Joy Division. I wasn't fit to clean gum from their old shoes. Had I tried to speak to them I would have blathered incoherently, possibly falling on the floor and writhing like a Baptist snake handler.

I went back to my little dressing room and fell asleep. Three naps and two rehearsals later Sally came to my dressing room with Guy, who had driven over after work. "Do you have your clothes ready?" she asked.

"Yup, just give me a minute," I said. I was going to wear a pair of yellow pants that I'd found at a Salvation Army and a green T-shirt covered in arrows. I thought it looked cool and futuristic, possibly like something Marinetti would've worn if he'd been a balding techno musician and not an aspiring fascist.

I stepped out of the dressing room and Eric guffawed. "That's what you're going to wear?" he asked.

"Yes," I said defensively. "It's okay?"

"Well, um," he said.

Sally looked concerned.

"Is this okay?" I asked her.

She said nothing.

Guy came to the rescue. "The guys from a club called Rush gave you a T-shirt if you want to wear it?"

I took off my futuristic arrows shirt and put on the proffered Rush T-shirt.

"Much better," Eric said. "You look almost modern."

We walked into the TV studio for the live broadcast and the energy was completely different from the rehearsals: the lights were flashing, all of the musicians were dressed up, and the studio was filled with audience members. At eight p.m., the lights dimmed and the hosts started the show. "This week, in at number thirty-seven, New Order with 'World in Motion'!" The audience crowded around the New Order stage, the song finished, the audience clapped, and the hosts moved on to the next stage, until finally, "In this week at number ten, from New York City, Moby Go!"

My song started. I jumped around, banged on my keyboard, yelled, "Go!" and whacked the Octapad. And in three minutes, before I even knew what was happening, it was done. I was hurried off my little stage by a *Top of the Pops* stagehand and walked down the hallway and back to my dressing room.

A moment later, Eric came in. "How was that?" I asked.

"It looked good, but maybe next time you want to dance a little less?"

"You think so? But what should I do?"

"I don't know, just play keyboards and hit the drum machine."

"Okay," I said, slightly chastened.

Guy and Sally came into my dressing room. "That was great!" Guy said.

"Well done, Moby!" Sally said, smiling.

After some more congratulations, Eric said, "We'll leave you alone so you can change." I took off my futuristic yellow pants and my Rush club shirt and stepped into the shower. The adrenaline left me and I deflated like a balloon at the end of a six-year-old's birthday party. None of this made sense to me. What was I doing here? Living in an abandoned factory in a crack neighborhood made sense to me. Playing punk-rock shows for ten people in a dingy bar made sense to me. Walking around New York dropping off cassettes at record labels made sense to me, even if I knew that they'd never be listened to. But flying to England and being on TV shows confused me to the core of my soul. *Top of the Pops* was New Order's world. It was Phil Collins's world. I loved it, maybe too much, but it wasn't my world.

Suddenly I felt lonely. I imagined what this day would have been like if I had a wife or a girlfriend, someone who would sit with me on my dressing room couch and stroke my head while I tried to sleep away the jet lag and anxiety.

I knelt down in the shower stall under the hot water and prayed. "God, I don't know what I'm doing. Please help me."

The Outer Rhythm people took us to dinner, and after dinner Eric drove me back to my Dickensian hovel. "You just played to half the population of England," he said, suddenly earnest. "Congratulations, Moby."

The next day I went to Heathrow to fly back to New York. I'd been on *Top of the Pops*, an idol-making institution. I walked into the terminal expecting a throng of people asking for my autograph, but no one noticed me. I went through security and walked to my gate; nobody threw themselves at my feet begging for a photograph or wanting to touch the hem of my Kmart jeans.

We boarded and I sat in an economy aisle seat, reading my Arthur C. Clarke book. About two hours into the flight the people around me were sleeping or watching the movie *Robin Hood: Prince of Thieves*. A flight attendant knelt down in the aisle next to me. "I don't want to cause a scene," she said sotto voce, "but you're Moby Go?"

I was startled. "Yes, that's me."

"I saw you on *Top of the Pops* last night. I'm a raver, your track is wicked." She touched my shoulder and walked away.

21

BROWN FLORAL BEDSPREAD

Suddenly I felt like a professional.

In six months I'd made six trips to the UK, playing live or DJing. I'd brought my keyboard and Octapad to California and played raves in LA and San Francisco. I'd been to Berlin and Paris and Amsterdam (twice). For my first show in Amsterdam the promoter had hung actual dead-goat heads over the dance floor, dripping blood on the crowd.

"They think it's fake goat heads," he had whispered in my ear before the show, "but they're real!" He had a giggling fit and then disappeared into a utility closet to do drugs with his dominatrix girlfriend.

Now I was going to play a club in Cleveland on a Sunday night.

"There's a rave scene in Cleveland?" I asked my booking agent. Apparently so.

I took my keyboard case to Grand Central and got the bus to LaGuardia Airport. LaGuardia was New York's smaller and dumpier airport, the runty little brother to JFK. With low ceilings and faded blue walls, LaGuardia felt more like a regional bus station than an international airport. In fact, it was an international airport only because it had forty-five-minute flights to Toronto. You'd never fly from

LaGuardia to Paris or Tokyo, but you'd for sure fly from LaGuardia to Cleveland.

I checked in my keyboard case, went through security, sat in a 1970s fiberglass airport chair by the gate, and read *Dune* while eating a tomato sandwich I'd made at home. I was happy: I had a sandwich, a science-fiction novel, and a brand-new $49 Nintendo Game Boy. I had splurged on it the day before, but I was saving it for the flight because I didn't know how long the batteries would last.

We taxied down the runway and took off into the sun. We banked left at Rikers Island, and then all of Manhattan was in front of me, surrounded by rivers. Far to the south I could see Zeckendorf Towers, the tallest things close to my apartment. We passed over the Upper West Side, flying over Columbia Presbyterian Women's Hospital in Harlem, where I was born in 1965.

In second grade I'd told some other kids that I'd been born in a women's hospital. They all laughed and told me that I was a girl: "They don't let boys into a women's hospital!" Their seven-year-old logic was hard to refute, so I fought back as best I knew how. "I'm not a girl!" I yelled, and went home to sulk and watch cartoons.

As we flew over New Jersey I turned on my Game Boy and started playing Tetris. I turned it off as we started descending, picked up my keyboard case at baggage claim, and walked out to find my ride.

Touring in 1991 was based on hope, goodwill, and faxes. Everything was communicated by fax: the hotel information, the name of the venue, the flight information. I felt especially professional, because I now had my own fax machine, full of new, curly fax paper. When I flew somewhere I would land in an airport, clutching a sheaf of faxes from the promoter. Usually a seventeen-year-old raver would meet me outside the airport, listening to techno cassettes in his mom's minivan as he drove me to my hotel.

When I walked out of baggage claim in Cleveland, a pretty woman in her twenties wearing a Lou Reed *Transformer* shirt waved at me and asked, "Are you Moby?" I conceded that I was.

"I'm Jenna—welcome to Cleveland."

I peppered Jenna with questions about Cleveland as we drove to the hotel: "Does the river still catch on fire?" "Has the river ever caught on fire?" "How could a river catch on fire?"

She laughed and explained that the Cuyahoga River had, in fact, caught on fire in the past—but that for the last thirty years, it had been fire-free. As we pulled up to the hotel, Jenna said, "There's a really great vegetarian restaurant near here, so I'll pick you up at seven and we'll get dinner and go to the venue?"

"That sounds amazing, thanks," I said.

I was staying in a generic businessman hotel. My room had a painting of ducks on a pond, a beige bedspread with a floral pattern, and new bars of Dial soap in the bathroom. I washed my hands with the new soap, sat in the office chair by the desk, and read *Dune*.

At seven the promoter and his girlfriend were with Jenna in the lobby to escort me to the local vegetarian restaurant. Until recently the promoter had been in the industrial scene, booking shows with Skinny Puppy and Front Line Assembly. Then a year ago he'd been in Los Angeles and had gone to a rave, and his world had changed. He still had an Einstürzende Neubauten tattoo on his arm, but he was a pure raver now, in big pants and a long-sleeved Fresh Jive T-shirt. His girlfriend was still more of an industrial goth, with an asymmetrical black haircut and a Bauhaus T-shirt. They were both vegetarians, so we ordered hummus and talked about the rave scene. I'd just met them, but they were so nice I decided they were my new best friends and that I loved Cleveland. Maybe I'd leave New York and move there and eat hummus with them every day.

We headed to the venue, a dance club below some huge iron bridges in the industrial area called the Flats. It was nine p.m. and I had a few hours before I went on, so I went for a walk along the river. Trucks drove by on the bridges overhead, and the solid brown river moved indifferently past me, saying resignedly, "I've had better days." I sat happily on a dock by the edge of the river, smelling the chemicals and the decay.

Back at the club there were a few hundred people inside, all dancing to T-99 and James Brown Is Dead and other Belgian rave records. There were some goths with asymmetrical haircuts in corners of the club. The goths didn't like the disco elements in rave music. And they certainly weren't wearing smiley rave shirts and waving glow sticks, but they had started to embrace new electronic music, even if it wasn't bleak enough for them.

The DJ played "Energy Flash" by Joey Beltram and I started dancing between some ravers, some goths, and a lone hippie with his eyes closed. The cool ravers had mastered dances that looked vaguely like they were measuring a fish or building a box with their empty hands. I just took up space on the dance floor, not measuring fish but dancing badly to the techno.

The promoter found me as I was dancing. "Hey!" he yelled. "It's eleven, do you want to go on now?"

"Sure!" I yelled back.

I walked onstage and eventually the DJ stopped playing. The promoter grabbed the microphone and boomed, "Cleveland! All the way from New York City, Moby!" I started my set with "Ah Ah," then the "Rainforest Mix" of "Go," "Electricity," "Voodoo Child," and "Next Is the E," ending with "Rock the House." I ran around the small stage, jumping on top of my keyboard, beating my Octapad half to death, and screaming at the top of my lungs. The audience were measuring fish and waving glow sticks. During and after each song they blew whistles and cheered. At the end of the set I walked offstage, soaked in sweat.

I was leaning against a wall backstage when a goth woman with dyed red hair walked up to me. "Hi, I'm Kim," she said.

"Hi, I'm Moby."

"I really liked your show."

"Oh, thanks," I said, feeling sweaty and self-conscious and gross.

"Can I get you a drink?"

"I don't drink, but I'll take a club soda."

As we walked to the bar, random ravers and goths stopped me to say that they liked my show. I was glowing. This had been my first US show not in New York or California, the ravers had cheered, and now I was being led to the bar by an attractive goth woman with pierced cheeks.

Jenna came over in her Lou Reed shirt and she was radiant, telling me how much she loved the show. Then she saw Kim and the light went out in her eyes. "Oh, hi, Kim," she said tersely.

"Hi, Jenna," Kim said, equally tersely.

There was an awkward pause. Trying to sound like a grown-up, I asked Jenna, "Do you want a drink?"

"No, I'm going to get back to work. Let me know if you need a ride."

"Oh, I'll give him a ride," Kim said territorially.

Jenna walked away. Kim pulled me close and asked, "Do you want an E?"

I wanted to say, "Oh, ha, I'm a naïve sober Christian who reads *Star Trek* books. I've never had ecstasy or a one-night stand on tour." But I just said, "No, I'm good, thanks."

Our drinks arrived; she swallowed her pill and washed it down with a white-wine spritzer, leaving dark red lipstick on her glass. Then she took my hand and said, "Let's go dance." We walked onto the dance floor, surrounded by ravers and goths who were now sweaty, drunk, and high. Some of them patted me on the back and shouted, "Great show!" Everyone was smiling and I felt like a puppy, basking in the attention of these happy Cleveland strangers.

The DJ played the "Woodtick Mix" of "Go" and the people on the dance floor cheered. Kim pressed in close to me. I could smell the white wine on her breath and feel her breasts pressed up against me. She said, "Let's go, okay?"

It took me a moment to figure out whether she was making some rudimentary wordplay on the song title or if she wanted to leave. "Go? To my hotel?" I asked. And she nodded.

Kim led me off the dance floor, holding my hand. She walked me past the bar, past the doormen, and into the parking lot. When the door to the club closed, it was suddenly very still and quiet.

"What's the name of this river?" I asked, making conversation and pointing to the dark river flowing by the parking lot.

"Oh, I don't know."

"Didn't a river catch on fire here?" I asked, not sure what people talked about before having one-night stands.

She didn't respond. We got into her blue Saturn and she put a Nine Inch Nails cassette into the stereo.

"Oh, you like industrial?" I asked. "I really like Nitzer Ebb and Test Dept."

"I love Trent," she said, starting her car and pulling out of the parking lot. As she drove, she sang along to "Sin," and she took my hand. Her hand was sweaty and she started gripping my hand like she was kneading bread dough.

We got to my hotel and I didn't know what to do. I was single and allowed to have one-night stands, even if I was unsure about the eternal theological ramifications of having sex with strangers in hotel rooms.

I worked up my courage and asked, "Do you want to come upstairs?" Six simple words, so hard to say.

"Okay," she said, turning off her Saturn and putting the keys in her black leather purse.

Up in my room, she asked, "Do you have anything to drink?"

"Um, there's a minibar." I opened the fridge. She inspected it, took out a tiny bottle of Jack Daniel's and a can of Coke, and made herself a drink, leaving the can and bottle on my bathroom counter, next to my Tom's of Maine toothbrush and dental floss.

Kim looked at me, her eyes a little unfocused from ecstasy, white wine, and Jack Daniel's. She smelled too much like generic perfume, but I wanted to kiss her. I didn't want to fall in love with her or buy a house with her or raise little vegans together. I just wanted to kiss her Coke-and-whiskey lips in my quiet hotel room. I was a Christian, but I wanted more nights like this, with drunk and high women leaving empty bottles of Jack Daniel's next to the little wrapped bars of Dial soap in the bathroom.

Kim sat on the brown floral bedspread with her drink and started talking. She told me about her job as a hairstylist. She told me about her ex-boyfriend whom she'd just broken up with, and how he was a DJ and an asshole. She told me about growing up in Ohio, and how she wanted to move to LA, but she didn't want to leave her friends in Cleveland. I sat on the bed and listened, wondering when I could kiss her.

She stopped talking, so I leaned forward and kissed her bright red lips. She didn't kiss back, so I stopped, confused.

"I have to tell you something," she said, finishing her drink. "When I was growing up, I was sexually abused by my stepfather."

"Oh my God," I said. "I'm so sorry."

She spent the next thirty minutes telling me about growing up in the suburbs outside of Cleveland and being abused by her stepfather. I sat next to her, mute. When she was done, she got up and made another Jack and Coke. She drank half of it, put it on the nightstand, and asked, "Will you lie down and hold me?"

"Of course." So we lay down like spoons on the brown floral bedspread. After a few minutes I realized she was crying, so I stroked her stiff red hair and held her. Eventually she stopped crying, and we lay there in the strange quiet of a hotel room at two a.m.

Kim got up, finished her drink, and adjusted her dress. "I have to go," she said. She looked down at me and said, "Good-bye, Moby. You're sweet."

She took her purse and left, quietly closing the door. She had left behind a glass printed with her dark lipstick, two empty bottles of Jack Daniel's, and a half-full can of Coke. I could smell her perfume on my shirt, mixed with the cigarette smoke and the rave fog from the club.

I went into the bathroom and emptied the half-full can of Coke into the toilet.

22

LIGHTS THROUGH THE TREES

My UK booking agent had decided it would be a good idea for me to play three shows in one night—as opposed to the traditional, bourgeois, and lazy one-show-in-one-night. His logic, I assumed, was: England is pretty small, the motorways are empty at three a.m., and three shows meant three fees.

This was long before the days of cell phones and Google Maps and computer navigation. It was the age of going around suburban roundabouts countless times, buying maps in petrol stations, and asking homeless junkies under bridges in Birmingham for directions.

I was staying in Maida Vale, in the guest bedroom of Mark Moore. He and S-Express had a number one dance hit, "Theme from S-Express," and he was the biggest pop star I'd ever met or had a real conversation with. Like everyone else in the dance scene he was young and had stumbled into his success. His one condition for my staying in his guest bedroom was that I cook for him.

My first night in Maida Vale I walked to the local grocer's and bought tofu, brown rice, ginger, broccoli, and sesame oil. I made him a stir-fry. He ate one-quarter of it, looked at me with baleful eyes, and said, "Okay, you can stay here, just please don't cook for me anymore."

Mark and I were sitting in his living room with his boyfriend and

Jeff Mills from Underground Resistance, talking about Berlin and new techno records. The doorbell rang and my driver came up the stairs. My booking agent had a few people on his payroll whose sole job was driving DJs and rave acts to clubs and raves around the UK. The only qualifications for the job were that you had to have a car and you had to be able to stay awake.

The driver came in, spotted Mark and his boyfriend holding hands on the couch, and curtly said, "I'll be in the car."

"Uh-oh, dear, your driver might be a homophobe," Mark said.

I put my equipment in the back of the car and sat up front with the driver. Neither of us mentioned the fact that he was probably a homophobe and that I was staying with a gay pop star and his boyfriend. The driver's only job was to get me to the gigs on time and to collect the money. His being a homophobe might have been loathsome, but it didn't make him unfit to drive me around England in the middle of the night.

We headed east out of London, got on the M25, and went to Mr. B's, the first club of the night, in Essex. Mr. B's was a legendary rave spot, as the Prodigy and every other Essex-based dance act had started out there, taken drugs there, or had sex in the Mr. B's parking lot. I was scheduled to go on at eleven p.m., which in raver terms was the beginning of the night, almost dusk.

Traffic was light, so we arrived in Essex at ten fifteen. We parked and I carried my keyboard case and Octapad into the club. I had expected Mr. B's to be an imposing rave warehouse on par with the Hacienda in Manchester. Instead, it was a bar/disco from 1975 with surly black-clad security workers and a very loud sound system. Like almost every other bar/disco in the UK, Mr. B's was painted black and had stained red carpeting most likely stolen from a brothel in Croatia.

I set up my gear onstage and waited in the closet that one of the security guards politely referred to as "backstage." There were two folding chairs, and a small fridge with a half-full jar of mayonnaise and some beer. It was cold; every backstage area in England was, without exception, cold. A venue might be hot and steamy and filled with sweaty ravers, but backstage in English venues would always feel like a filthy mortuary where you could see your breath.

I sat by myself for a while, and then at eleven p.m. got onstage and played my twenty-five-minute rave set. There were fifty people in Mr. B's. Some of them were carrying glow sticks and dressed in oversized long-sleeve raver T-shirts. Some were carefully groomed and dressed like office workers. The venue was 80 percent empty, but I jumped around, banged on my Octapad, yelled, "Go!" a whole bunch of times, broke a microphone, and ended the show standing on my keyboard. The fifty people clapped politely and waited for the DJ to resume playing techno hits.

After the show the promoter came backstage to introduce himself. He was a little bit older than me and wearing a tight black T-shirt. He was so high he was grinding his teeth and his eyes were like polliwogs, darting around the room. "Oh man, too bad there weren't more people," he said in a drug-fueled staccato. "You should come back at three a.m., that's when it's really fuckin' wicked!"

"Thanks, but we have to drive to Coventry and Birmingham."

"Tonight? Fuck me, mate, three shows in one night? What's that about?" His eyes swiveled from the fridge to the door to my face.

"Good question," I said.

He clapped me too hard on my shoulder. I packed up my equipment and put it back in the car.

We headed to show number two, which was at the Eclipse in Coventry. The UK is relatively small, but it feels unspeakably huge when you're driving for two hours with a laconic, homophobic driver and no radio.

"The radio doesn't work?" I asked.

"Someone stole the xmrsmmga," he said. I assumed he was using some technical car-radio term, but I couldn't figure out what it was.

"Stole the what?"

"The xmrsmmga," he said again.

"Okay," I said.

We arrived at the Eclipse at two a.m. My driver parked the car and leaned back in his seat to take a nap; I got my equipment and walked inside. The club was wall-to-wall people. The DJs were playing blindingly fast techno, the air was thick with smoke and Vicks VapoRub, and everyone and everything was covered in sweat. I wandered through the crowd, bumping into wide-eyed ravers on E. I found a security guard and as politely as I could while yelling asked if he knew where the promoter was. He pointed casually to a sweaty guy by the toilets with his hands down the pants of a chubby rave girl.

I walked over, cautiously interrupted them, and introduced myself.

"Oh wicked! Moby Go, nice!" the promoter said, his pupils as wide as manhole covers. "Just find Blackie, he'll sort you with sound. Do you need any Es or whizz or charlie?"

"No thanks," I yelled over a Grooverider track. "Where's Blackie?"

"Back by the DJ."

He went back to putting his hands down the pants of the chubby rave girl. I pushed my way through the crowd and found Blackie behind the DJ booth, asleep on a speaker box.

In New York, my nightclub friends and I sometimes played a game called What Drug Is He On?

If someone in a nightclub touches your face and tells you that you're beautiful, it's a safe bet they're on ecstasy.

If someone is dancing slowly and staring at the lights shining through their hands, they're probably on acid.

If someone is sitting on the floor staring at their shoes, they're likely on ketamine.

If a white person tells you how much they love Haile Selassie, they've almost certainly been smoking too much pot.

And if someone, in this case a soundman, is asleep on a thumping speaker box at two a.m., it's safe to conclude that they're a junkie.

I woke up Blackie and asked him, loudly, "Where do I set up for the show?" He just sat there, clearly wanting to go back to sleep.

I asked again. "I'm Moby. Where do I set up my keyboard?"

He sighed. Or I thought he did—you can't really hear a tired junkie's sigh in a club at two a.m. He got up and slowly walked me to the stage. I unpacked my keyboard, drum machine, Octapad, and DAT machine and set everything up on the top of metal stage cases.

The DJ was playing ultra-fast 180 BPM jungle, and my set was a 135 BPM techno set. I was afraid that even though I'd had a couple of Top 40 dance singles in the UK the transition to my slower tempo would make my live set feel like a sinking stone. I imagined the 1,500 E'd up ravers in front of me staring at me with a disdain so strong it would even pierce their MDMA love haze.

At two thirty a.m. the DJ stopped and an MC dressed like a homeless mime introduced me: "Eclipse! Coventry! All the way from New York! Moby Go!"

I played my twenty-five-minute rave set, shuffling the song order a bit, and it wasn't the sinking rave stone I'd feared. The pilled-up crowd danced like lunatics. The lights were chaotic and blinding. The sound was deafening. It was about 105 degrees onstage and on the dance floor, and everyone was sweating through every menthol-slathered pore. It was a big, Vicks-scented, anarchic, flawless, Dionysian mess.

Flying to the UK and eating bad food and trying to play three shows in one night suddenly seemed like the best thing I'd ever done. I finished the show shirtless and standing on my keyboard. The audience cheered and blew whistles as the homeless mime MC yelled, "Moby Go! NYC in the house!" I went to the parking lot and woke up the driver. He came in and collected the money while I put my sweat-and-rave-fog-covered equipment back in the car.

We drove silently to the third show of the night, outside Birmingham. This show promised to be the most exciting one, as it was an actual old-school rave in a field in the middle of nowhere. Playing in a big field miles away from everything was the best part of touring: driving down a country lane somewhere in the UK and hearing techno in the distance and seeing lights flashing through the trees was magical and primordial.

I was scheduled to go onstage at five a.m., but at four thirty a.m. we were lost somewhere outside of Birmingham. Being lost was a routine part of being on tour. But this wasn't a quotidian wrong turn—we were really lost. Our thirty-minute trip from Coventry to the outskirts of Birmingham had now taken ninety minutes. We'd seen the same roundabout ten times. The driver was looking at his map and cursing.

"Is there a hill somewhere nearby?" I asked. "If we get to a hill, maybe we can look at the horizon and try to find something that looks like a rave."

We drove around the roundabout for the eleventh time and found a hill next to an old village. At its summit I stood on top of the car and could see rave lights, hovering on the dark horizon, past trees and fields.

The driver sped down little country roads in the general direction of the lights we'd seen, until we started to hear techno in the distance. As we got closer, we could see the lights above the trees. And suddenly we were there, surrounded by ten thousand people in a field on a warm British night. There was the techno stage, where I'd be playing. Next to the techno stage was the house stage, next to that was the jungle stage, and on top of the slope of a gentle hill, there was a chill-out tent filled with people on ecstasy, touching each other's hands and looking lovingly in each other's eyes.

By five fifteen a.m. my equipment was set up and the DJ stopped playing. I looked out over the sea of thousands of ravers as the ragga MC introduced me: "Techno massive! From New York! Moby Go!" I played my twenty-five-minute techno set, starting with "Rock the House." Green lasers were skittering over ten thousand people and touching the tall trees at the edge of the field. The sun was coming up and the sky was slowly turning from gray to pink and light blue.

In front of me the crowd danced like ecstatic monkeys. They threw their hands in the air, and when my set was over and I was standing on top of my wet and damaged keyboard, they cheered like I'd always imagined an audience could cheer. It was the sort of sound you hear at a football game or a Bon Jovi concert. I walked offstage into gentle dawn light and a soft breeze blowing from the east.

In the car at six a.m., heading back to London, the driver's homophobia didn't seem as pernicious, and the lack of a radio didn't seem as stultifying. My ears rang with the sound of ten thousand ravers in a field at dawn, all yelling their joy and approval.

23

YELLOW HARD HAT

was standing on the side of the stage at a rave in midtown Manhattan, shirtless and covered in sweat. I'd just finished my set and was drinking a bottle of water when a woman walked up to me wearing a tiny halter top and oversized raver jeans. She stuck out her hand and said, "Hi! I'm Cara!"

She was tall and pretty and had bright white hair, so as I shook her hand I asked if she was a model.

She grinned and said, "No, but I'm a model citizen." And I was smitten.

Cara was a fashion designer who went to raves and clubs five nights a week. After a month of dating and going to raves and sleeping over at each other's apartments she took me to Louisville, Kentucky, where she'd grown up. I met her parents and her sister, and Cara and I slept in the bed she'd slept in when she was in junior high school. Her bedroom in Louisville was still festooned with her old 4-H ribbons, and the walls were still covered with her David Hasselhoff and New Kids on the Block posters. But her mom was trying to raise chinchillas for profit, so the room was also filled with chinchillas in cages.

"Is your mom going to kill the chinchillas?" I asked.

"No, she'll probably end up letting them live here as furry pets," Cara said.

So we had sex in her childhood bedroom and fell asleep surrounded by 4-H ribbons and mangy chinchillas.

At the end of our Louisville weekend we visited her grandparents' farm. Her tall, laconic grandfather showed me around his pasture as the sun was setting over his sorghum crop. We stopped to admire one of his cows and he asked me where I was from.

"I grew up in Connecticut, but I'm from New York," I said.

"The problem with New York is all the Jews," he said genially, while petting a goat.

At the airport I told Cara, "I like you but your family scares me."

The day after we returned to New York from the chinchillas and her anti-Semitic grandfather I went to Dance Trax on Third Street. Frankie Bones was there with a messenger bag full of flyers for one of his Brooklyn Storm Raves. The Storm Raves were legendary, and Frankie Bones was even more legendary. He had started as a hip-hop DJ in Queens in the eighties and had gradually become the most well-known techno DJ in New York City. He handed me a flyer for his Storm Rave.

"It'd be an honor to have you there," he said to me.

"Can I bring my new girlfriend and a friend?" I asked.

"Sure, I'll put you on the list plus two. See you Saturday," he said, and walked down Third Street with his bag full of flyers.

The Storm Rave was in a distant part of Brooklyn, further east than Williamsburg. It was 1992 and I didn't know anyone who had ever ventured that far east into Brooklyn. I knew only one person who lived in Williamsburg; he had moved there in 1991 because it was so cheap. He and his girlfriend rented a three-thousand-square-foot loft overlooking the East River for $750 a month. They loved the space, but they had to bring their food on the L train from Manhattan, since the neighborhood didn't have grocery stores or delis.

Williamsburg was as far east as I'd ever been, and for the Storm Rave we were supposed to be going much, much further east, to the part of Brooklyn where old-timey cartographers drew "Here there be dragons."

On Saturday night Cara and Paul and I got on the L train at First Avenue. In the station we looked up at the subway map.

"We go where?" Cara asked. I pointed to the end of the gray L train line on the map, a stop that I'd never heard of until that week.

"There," I said. I checked the map on the flyer. "And then we walk a few blocks."

"Where are you taking me?" Cara asked forlornly as the L train pulled into the station.

After twenty minutes heading east we were the only people left in our car on the L train, so Paul and I climbed onto the bars and hung upside down. "Get down, you're going to kill yourselves!" Cara said, laughing.

Paul and I started wrestling upside down, hanging like monkeys from the subway bars and singing the *Star Trek* fight music.

Paul yelled, "Khan!" We laughed and got down.

"Are we there yet?" Cara asked.

I looked at the subway map behind the scratched glass. "Only three more stops," I reported.

"Are we still in New York?" she asked.

"No, we're in Rhode Island now," I told her.

"I've never been to Rhode Island," she said. She then told us a story about a friend of hers who'd been attacked on the F train the week before. A few kids had jumped her friend, beaten and stabbed him, and left him bleeding on the platform. People just walked past him, and one woman spat on him and said, "Stupid white boy."

"But that was in Fort Greene," I pointed out. "Out here in east, east Brooklyn we'll probably just get mugged for our body parts."

The train came to the end of the line. We got off, walked down the crumbling platform, and walked upstairs to a desolate street. "It's eleven p.m. on a Saturday night," Cara said, surveying the street. "Did everybody die?"

Following the map even further east, we walked past empty warehouses and vacant lots. When we turned a corner past a shuttered factory we heard the *thump thump thump* of techno. "I guess that's the rave," Paul said.

Ten or twenty ravers in giant pants were outside a warehouse, smoking cigarettes. Adam, Frankie Bones's cousin, spotted us. "Hey, Moby!" he shouted. "You're here! Come in!" We walked into the warehouse and the air was thick with fog and techno.

"Adam, who's playing?" I yelled over the din.

"Lenny Dee!" he yelled back.

I could see turntables up on a platform in the corner of a huge room, with Lenny Dee playing super-fast techno to a thousand ravers. The Brooklyn and Queens ravers were shirtless, muscle-bound guys with hair gel and gold necklaces; the suburban ravers were skinny nerds wearing giant rave pants and smiley-face T-shirts.

"There's also a house room!" Adam yelled. "Down that hallway!"

"Thanks!" I said. "See you later!"

We left the main room and walked down a dark hallway and found a room with a hundred ravers dancing to house music.

"I like this!" Cara said, and started dancing. Paul and I started dancing too. The DJ played "Housewerk" by Airtight. Cara shouted, "Moby! I love this song!" and started dancing like an excited Muppet.

After dancing to a few more house records we decided to explore the factory complex. We walked down another long hallway, past a few ravers making out in the corners, and through a metal fire door. On the other side of the door was a parking lot full of trucks and bulldozers. "This is great!" Cara said, running across the lot toward the bulldozers.

"Why isn't anyone else out here?" Paul asked, looking around at the empty parking lot.

"Come on!" Cara yelled, climbing up on a backhoe. She found an old yellow hard hat and put it on top of her short, bleached hair. She was covered in glitter and wearing a small halter top made out of an American flag.

"You look like an alien construction worker!" I yelled.

"I do!" she agreed. "Oh, hey! They left the keys in it. Should I turn it on?"

"Um," Paul said.

"Yes!" I said.

She turned the key and the backhoe rumbled and came to life.

"Woohoo!" Cara yelled. "Let's go!"

Paul and I jumped up on the backhoe and looked at the levers and pedals.

"How do we make it go?" I asked.

"I drove a backhoe at my uncle's house," Paul said. "Let me try." Cara got off the old vinyl seat and Paul sat down. His hair was dyed blue and pink, and he was wearing a sarong and an old Sex Pistols shirt. "There are two brake pedals," he said, testing them with his feet, "and one gas pedal."

He pumped the gas, making the engine roar a bit more. "And these levers make it go." He pushed a lever and the front of the backhoe lurched forward.

"Yay!" Cara yelled.

"Can you steer?" I asked Paul as we slowly headed toward a chain-link fence.

"No!" he shouted.

We heard someone behind us, yelling and blowing a whistle.

"Is that a raver?" Cara asked.

An out-of-breath security guard ran up alongside us, furious. "What the fuck are you doing?" he shouted.

"Stealing a backhoe," Cara said.

"Get off that! Get down!" he yelled.

Paul turned off the backhoe and we climbed down.

"I should fucking arrest you!" the security guard yelled, spraying spittle in our faces.

Paul mumbled, "Arrest us? And put us in security-guard prison?" We left the guard to marinate in his fury and walked back to the rave.

"Let's go steal it again when he's not looking," Cara proposed.

"We could drive it back to New York," I suggested.

"Technically, we are in New York," Paul said as we went back through the metal fire door.

We danced for a while in the house room and then went back to the giant techno room, where Frankie Bones was DJing and playing very fast Belgian techno. I went over to say hello. "Hey, Frankie!" I yelled over the music.

"Moby! Hey!" he yelled, shaking my hand. Then he stopped the record and picked up his microphone. "Storm Rave, you out there?" he said on the mic.

One thousand Brooklyn and suburban ravers yelled back.

"I said are you in the house?" he bellowed.

One thousand Brooklyn and suburban ravers yelled again.

"We got Moby in the house!" And the ravers screamed as he dropped the needle on the "Rainforest Mix" of "Go."

Cara started dancing and Paul said, "Moby, this is insane." I just smiled. A few years earlier I'd been wandering around New York City in the rain, toting a soggy bag full of cassettes and trying to get a record contract or find work playing records at a bar or a nightclub. And now a thousand ravers were dancing to music I had made and yelling their love for me into the smoky air. I looked around the crumbling warehouse at my beautiful, smiling girlfriend and the happy throng of ravers, all dancing with their arms around each other. A huge smile started at my mouth and filled my entire body.

I wasn't just happy for me—I was happy for us. No big companies were doing this for us; we had created all of this—thousands of us, in different cities around the world. We had learned how to make electronic music and how to DJ and how to press vinyl and how to start record companies and how to start clothing companies. We were renting clubs and warehouses and putting on events for thousands of ecstatic, dancing people. We were starting magazines and radio stations and inventing new musical forms: joyful, futuristic music that was the soundtrack to this new world we'd created. I wasn't succeeding as a musician playing by rules that some old person had created decades ago: I was succeeding in a musical landscape that my peers had gleefully invented yesterday.

"Go" ended and Frankie Bones played an older record, T-99's "Anasthasia." The crowd yelled and I yelled with them.

We danced until three a.m. and then Paul asked, "When should we go back to the city?"

"Let's steal another bulldozer!" Cara said.

The music was getting faster. The ravers around us were bathed in sweat and their eyes were wide and unfocused. At some point during almost every night out a line got crossed where the drugs took over. People would start dancing more listlessly or collapsing in corners. The conversations would get slower and the music would get darker. And that was usually when I went home.

"Okay, it's probably time to go," I said.

Outside the warehouse there were about a hundred kids, smoking cigarettes and looking out of place in this empty urban no-man's-land. A few police cars were out front, but the policemen looked bored. I walked up to a policeman. "Do you know where to get a taxi around here?"

"Ha!" he said to his partner. "He wants a taxi."

"I think we had a taxi here in 1970," his partner said.

"So no taxis?" I said.

He relented. "You walk five blocks that way and you'll come to a deli. Around the back there's a Haitian minicab. It's not licensed, so wear your seat belts."

"Thanks, officer," I said.

"How's the party?" he asked.

"It's great," I said. "Really fun."

He chuckled. "You kids get home safe."

We walked five blocks down the desolate streets and found the deli, and then the minicab service, located in a tiny storefront. "How much to go to Manhattan?" I asked the Haitian man behind the bulletproof glass.

He put down his cigarette and stared at me. "You want to go to Manhattan? It's three thirty a.m. Manhattan?"

"Yes, please."

"Okay, twenty dollars?"

"Sounds good," I agreed.

"Hey, Jean, you want to take these nice white people back to Manhattan?" he asked a driver sitting on a chair, reading the *Daily News*.

Jean stood up. "Sure thing."

"What are you kids doing way out here in Brooklyn?" the dispatcher asked.

"Going to a rave!" Cara said.

"A rave?" he asked. "What's a rave?"

"It's a big drug party!" she said.

The dispatcher scowled. "Drugs be bad, ruin your life," he said. "You get back safe to Manhattan now."

24

TRILLIONS OF MILES

y flight from New York to Brussels landed at ten a.m. in a sea of fog. I went through immigration and was sitting on the curb outside the airport with my keyboard case, a small overnight bag, some soy milk, and a loaf of whole-wheat bread. A tall, slow-moving man in a long brown jacket came up to me. "Are you Moby?" he asked.

"Yes, are you my ride?"

He said nothing, just turned and walked toward his car. I followed him. We left the airport and drove with the windows down for ninety minutes, ending up in a small Belgian village surrounded by fields and cows. He dropped me off at a small hotel, said, "I'll be back at nine p.m.," and left.

The hotel was tiny, and my room was tinier. One twin bed, a wooden chair, a little window, and a bathroom. I put my keyboard case in the corner, lay down on the tiny bed, and fell asleep. At six p.m. I woke up, looked at the small Magritte print next to my bed, and reminded myself that I was in Belgium. I had a bowl of cereal and soy milk, and, as it was a beautiful summer evening, left the hotel to walk around the village.

Everything in the village was closed, so I headed back to the hotel and read one of Frank Herbert's later *Dune* books.

Nine p.m.: the sun went down, and the driver didn't show up.

Ten p.m.: I ate some bread and peanut butter I'd brought from New York, and the driver didn't show up.

Eleven p.m.: I fell asleep again, and the driver didn't show up.

Midnight: the driver showed up.

"Where were you?" I asked.

"Late," he said, lighting a cigarette and walking to his car. We drove in silence down empty lanes through the Belgian countryside and finally came to a parking lot by a river.

"Where's the rave?" I asked.

"The boat," he said.

"Which boat?"

"That one." He pointed to a long barge. I unpacked my keyboard case and walked with him through the parking lot to the long, dark barge.

"I've never played on a boat before," I told him.

He said nothing.

I walked over a metal gangplank, headed across the deck, and opened a door. The bowels of the boat emitted a deafening blast of techno. "Here, give me your keyboard," the driver said. He took it down a metal staircase, disappearing into artificial fog.

"It's Stygian!" I shouted at the bottom of the stairs, over the echoing techno. He looked at me and I realized that was a weird thing to say to a stranger in Belgium. "Stygian," I said awkwardly. "Like the river Styx."

"I know what 'Stygian' means," he said, and walked down a metal hallway.

I walked across a crowded low-ceilinged dance floor at the bottom of the boat and set up my keyboard on a makeshift stage. The promoter introduced himself, let me know I was going on at four a.m., and disappeared into the smoke. The sweaty dancing bodies were writhing, the sound was deafening, and I couldn't see more than five feet in front of me. There were hands and bodies and faces in the fog, but everything was obscured. I had a couple of hours until I went on, and I didn't want to breathe secondhand smoke in the bottom of a rusty barge, so I found

the exit and stepped outside. The inside of the boat was like a Hierony-
mus Bosch painting, whereas outside was a quiet, bucolic night.

I walked away from the boat, the sound of techno receding behind
me. After five minutes I couldn't hear anything: no car sounds, no
techno sounds, no city sounds, just a few bugs squeaking.

My wallet and passport were in the hotel; all I had in my pockets
were a hotel key, a pair of earplugs, and a DAT. I stood at the edge of the
river and wondered what would happen if I just stepped in and disappeared. I wasn't sad. I wasn't depressed. I didn't want to die. I just wanted
to fall in the river and let it push me out to sea. Being alive was nice, and
usually interesting. But something about giving up and sinking into the
dark river was seductive. Existentially all choices seemed arbitrary, and
who was I to claim an understanding of a fifteen-billion-year-old universe, so how was drowning better or worse than not drowning?

I stood at the edge of the water in a reverie for thirty minutes. It was
calming to stand in one place, feeling the air on my skin and not moving. In the distance, I saw a glow of lights; I assumed it was Brussels, but
I squinted and pretended it was New York. If I fell in the river, would
I open my eyes and magically be looking up at the FDR Drive?

No. I was hallucinating from jet lag. If I fell in the river I would just
be cold and wet. I turned around and went back to the boat. The music
was even louder, the air even thicker. The promoter found me on the
side of the ramshackle stage. "You ready to go on?" he asked, smoking a
joint.

I walked onstage and checked my keyboard. I tapped the
microphone—it was on. I looked at the crowd dancing in the fog and
imagined the boat filling with water and all of us peacefully drowning.
Not rushing for the exit, not clawing at each other to escape, but quietly
letting the dirty river water fill our lungs.

Paul had just made an experimental movie set on another planet. At
the end of his short movie the characters all happily drowned in their
spaceship. The drowning was supposed to represent grace. Thinking of
this made me want to play a different set tonight: a long, slow ambient

set. Not even music. Just long Tony Conrad–style tones, echoing in the underwater metal basement of this strange old barge. I would play my long slow tones, and we would all sink to the bottom of the river, our lungs full of dark water.

"From New York!" The promoter was suddenly onstage, yelling into the microphone. "Moby!" I snapped out of my reverie and started my show with "Ah Ah." The first synth stabs of the song were loud and menacing, and I started banging on my Octapad when the drums kicked in. I couldn't really see the audience, but through the fog I could see that people were dancing. "Ah Ah" ended and "Electricity" started. I yelled, and through the impenetrable fog, I heard the audience at the bottom of the barge yell back. "Go," "Next Is the E," "Rock the House," two other rave songs, and thirty minutes later the set was over, the audience clapping and the DJ playing "Evolution" by Speedy J.

I packed up my keyboard and Octapad, both covered with a miasma of fog and sweat, and found the driver. "Hotel?" he asked.

"Yes, thanks."

We left the Stygian barge and got to the small village hotel at five a.m.

"I'll be here at seven to take you to airport," he said.

"It's really important," I said. "I have a big show in Washington tomorrow night. I can't miss my flight."

"Okay," he said, and drove away.

I wasn't tired, the sun was starting to come up, and I had to leave in two hours. So rather than trying to sleep I walked out of town, strolling down a tree-lined lane. After ten minutes I came to a field of cows. "Hi, cows," I said, not sure how one was supposed to address cows. I whistled to see if they would come over. They just stood there, staring at me, chewing grass. So I stood there, too.

The ravers were still in the basement of the boat, staring at strobe lights. In Manhattan it was twelve thirty a.m. and millions of New Yorkers were getting drunk and dancing and having sex. And I was in a field in Belgium, standing in the soft dawn light and talking to cows. After a while, I checked my watch: it was six a.m.

"Bye, cows," I said. They stood there, blinking.

Back at the hotel I made some peanut butter sandwiches for the flight and carried my keyboard down to the entryway of the little hotel. The sixty-year-old woman who owned the hotel was sitting at a desk, drinking coffee. "Good morning, do you need a taxi?" she asked.

"No thank you, I have a ride coming." I went to the curb, sat on my keyboard case, and watched the grocery store across the street open for business. At seven fifteen I started to panic. The driver had been three hours late last night, and if he was even thirty minutes late this morning, I'd miss my flight.

I walked back inside and asked, "Can you call me a taxi to go to the airport?" She got on the phone and spoke Flemish to someone; ten minutes later, a yellow Mercedes taxi pulled up.

"You need to go the airport?" the elderly cigarette-smoking taxi driver asked me.

"Yes, please, in a hurry," I said.

We sped to the airport and I made it onto the plane with a few minutes to spare. Once I sat down I built a little nest against the window. I was like a rat, padding my bed with a pillow, two blankets, earplugs, and a sleeping mask. All I needed to complete my rodent nest was some torn-up newspaper and an exercise wheel. The travel gods had given me an empty seat to my right and a passed-out obese man in the aisle seat. Soon we would be over the Atlantic Ocean and I would be asleep. Every part of me ached from exhaustion. My hair hurt. My spleen hurt. I just wanted the gentle benediction of sleep.

I put on my sleeping mask as a voice came over the intercom and in English, said, "Ladies and gentlemen, just a few words about our flight. Your safety is our number one concern, so . . ." This would end soon enough and I could sleep, I told myself. Four minutes later, it concluded with, "Thank you for flying Sabena. Have a good flight." I closed my eyes, only to be jolted awake by a blast of German: "*Beste damen und herren* . . ." They then proceeded to give the preflight message in four additional languages, ending in Japanese.

After twenty minutes it seemed like the announcements were over, so I peeked out from under my eye mask. Would there be one more preflight announcement? Was there somebody from the Hindu Kush who needed instructions on how to fasten his seat belt translated into Urdu? I knew that God had smitten Babel just because He was annoyed by all the talking. I assume that before letting loose, He said, "Everyone shut up! Just please just shut up!"

The obese man on the aisle was snoring. Japanese tourists were reading books back to front. I leaned against the window. I was sitting up in a cheap, lumpy seat and I smelled like other people's European cigarettes, but I slept.

Six hours later we descended into DC with the requisite twenty minutes of multilingual "we are landing" messages. I was no longer annoyed by the polyglot soundtrack—I was just giddy that I would soon see my girlfriend and play euphoric songs at a rave in a field. I was an uptight WASP from Connecticut, but in the rave scene I had been reborn, unashamed and happy. Growing up I'd learned that there were culturally acceptable emotions, and joy wasn't one of them. Happiness in New England had been suspect unless football or alcohol or money was involved.

And now I was part of a scene that was about unapologetic joy. The song titles reflected this: "Everybody's Free," "Feel So Real," "Strings of Life." For a lot of ravers the joy was facilitated by drug use, but the underlying ethos was still celebratory and unashamed. After decades of hunching my shoulders and keeping my feelings under wraps, I could suddenly throw my hands in the air on a dance floor with a hundred or a thousand or ten thousand other people and be happy.

The car pulled up to the hotel in Georgetown, the sun shining through the giant windows in the atrium. I walked through the sliding doors, and there was Cara running across the lobby toward me. We hugged and took the elevator up to my room. I told her about flying to and from Belgium in the last twenty-four hours, and she told me about eating sandwiches on Amtrak on her trip down to Washington. In my room, she pulled the curtains open. In the near distance we could see the Washington Monument. "Oh jeez!" she said. "You can see forever!"

I grabbed her and threw her on the bed and started kissing her. She laughed. "Don't you want to jump in the shower?" she asked. "You're all covered in airplane!"

"Okay, I'll shower," I said. "But don't try to join me."

"I promise," she said earnestly. I took off my clothes and got in the shower. Five seconds later, I heard the bathroom door open.

"Hello?" I said. "If that's Cara, I told you, stay out of the shower."

"It's me, Cara," she said. "You sure I can't come in?"

"Those are the rules," I said.

"Are you sure?"

"Well, just this once," I said as she pulled back the shower curtain.

At nine p.m. we left the hotel and drove to the rave, an hour out of DC. We parked behind the stage and got out of the car as the DJ was playing "Everybody's Free" by Rozalla. It was a warm night, with a huge field of ravers blowing whistles and throwing their hands in the air. Cara and I walked onstage and gazed out at the field of ravers and neon glow sticks. "I want to go dance!" she said, pulling on my hand like a seven-year-old.

I laughed. "Okay, go dance, see you later!"

She ran off into the crowd. I walked to the hill behind the rave, sat down in the grass, and tried to spot Cara in a sea of ten thousand ecstatic ravers. I located her in the distance, dancing with some kids wearing backpacks. The DJ played a track I had never heard before, full of breakbeats and pianos. I lay back in the grass, closed my eyes, and felt the beautiful weight of the music and the heavy mid-Atlantic summer air pressing down on me.

I opened my eyes and stared into the sky. Through the light pollution I could see four or five stars. *All this emptiness between here and there*, I thought. *And here we are, skittering around in the grass like happy bugs.* The DJ played a Prodigy song, and the crowd cheered.

Ooof. I opened my eyes. Cara had jumped on top of me and was straddling me. "I found you!" she said. "Your manager said you're on in half an hour!"

We stood up. "Doesn't the air feel heavy?" I asked.

"No, it feels like air!" she said.

I looked at the strobe lights flickering on the stage. These tiny infernos, burning for a fraction of a second, filling the heavy air with more light. Goethe's last words were "More light." Maybe he was a prescient raver.

Cara and I stood on the side of the stage as Scott Henry finished his set. Tonight's rave was called Future, and the promoter, Michael, walked onstage and took the microphone. "Hello, Future!" he yelled, and the future yelled back. "Welcome to the summer of love!" The crowd went crazy, even blowing air horns. "He just got off a plane from Belgium! Here he is, from New York City, Moby!"

I ran onstage as "Ah Ah" started, grabbed the microphone from Michael, and yelled. I yelled at the top of my lungs, trying to contact both the ravers and the little points of light trillions of miles away in the sky. Sound didn't travel through space—but we could pretend that it did. Sound died without atmosphere. It ended in the void. So we filled the void with our lives. With wide Belgian rivers and piano anthems and joy and sex in hotel showers.

I felt the love of the audience washing over me. When I played "Next Is the E," ten thousand ravers exploded as one, bursting with joy.

"I feel it," I sang.

"I feel it," they sang.

We were pinned down by the weight of everything: history, heredity, God, air. So we sang and danced in fields and boats and basements. I looked over at Cara, on the side of the stage. She was dancing and smiling.

"I feel it," I yelled to the ten thousand ravers standing underneath the night sky.

"I feel it," they yelled back.

DISTORTION, 1992–1995

25

BEANBAG CHAIRS

Two years earlier there hadn't been a rave scene in the States. And now, seemingly overnight, the world had changed. Every decent-size city in North America now had DJ record stores and rave-clothing stores. Musicians were trading in their guitars for synths and making techno records that were becoming globe-spanning anthems. It was 1992 and the rave scene was blossoming like a shiny, DIY flower.

Almost everyone I knew was trying to be a promoter. So with my managers; my lighting designer, Scotto; and my friend DB I decided to try it myself, organizing a rave in Chelsea the day before Halloween. DB was a British DJ working and living in New York, and when I was first introduced to him in 1988 I thought he was the coolest person I'd ever met. He was tall, darkly handsome, flawlessly dressed, and somehow always had better records than I did.

First DB, Scotto, and I came up with a terrible Halloween-themed name: "Mask-a-Rave." Then we needed a venue. DB had some experience promoting raves, but my managers and I were clueless. "Let's find something small and start small," I suggested timidly, visions of the empty dance floors at Sly Fox and La Palace de Beaute running through my head.

"We could rent the Sound Factory," my manager Marci said.

"Marci, the Sound Factory holds three thousand people," I said.

"We'll start big! It'll be great!" she said. "Don't worry, Moby."

"I worry," I told her.

DB and my other US manager, Barry, both thought that renting the Sound Factory was a good idea, so we rented it for October 30. We got a friend of DB's to design the artwork and we made twenty-five thousand shiny and simple flyers: MASK-A-RAVE. OCTOBER 30, 1992. ALTERN8 & MOBY LIVE. DJS D.B., MR. KLEEN, KEVIN SAUNDERSON. CYBER-LIGHTS BY SCOTTO. DB and I picked up the flyers from the print shop and met at my managers' office with thirty baby-faced ravers who made extra money by handing out flyers at clubs and record stores.

"Do you think people will come?" I asked a green-haired eighteen-year-old raver named Mike.

"With this lineup? Yeah, it'll be great," Mike said, somewhat assuaging my fears.

Now it was the day before Halloween, the day of our rave, and I was nervous. Would our rave fail? Would I be jumping around onstage at midnight in front of twenty people and a janitor?

I was in my new loft at nine p.m. looking out the windows at Mott Street. At dusk the buildings across the street looked like sharp teeth against the new night sky. I could hear cars honking up the block, and beyond that the ineffable hum of a few million people on a Friday night in Manhattan, all out looking for love and chaos.

I walked out the front door of the building, saying hello to Joe, our homeless handyman. Joe had been a boxer in his youth and ended up homeless on the Lower East Side, sleeping on the sidewalk in front of this loft building. The Chinnicis took pity on him and gave him a job and a place to sleep in the basement, next to Sonic Youth's rehearsal space. Joe kept his eyes to the ground and shuffled around the building, mopping and cleaning and not talking.

"Hi, Joe," I said as I left the building.

"Hmm," he mumbled in return.

"Happy Halloween."

He shuffled away down Mott Street, saying nothing.

Traffic was backed up on Houston, cars futilely honking at each other while drivers punched their steering wheels. It was only nine p.m., but there was already a drunk girl dressed like Minnie Mouse throwing up on the corner of Mott and Houston. She leaned against a mailbox while she vomited on her red shoes. Her two friends were standing a safe distance away from her, wearing sexy Ninja Turtle outfits and laughing under an amber streetlight while their friend vomited mixed drinks onto the sidewalk.

I walked down Houston past Ballato and Milady's and the Knitting Factory, all of which were already spewing drunks onto the sidewalk. Somebody outside of Milady's was wearing a Bill Clinton mask—the election was five days away, so I took a moment to hope that after November 4 this saxophone-playing former hippie would be our new president.

I went up Lafayette and turned left on Fourth Street. There was Tower Records, the mother ship of all record stores. Even at nine p.m. on the night before Halloween it was crammed with people. But then, it was always crammed with people. Tower Records was an institution, the giant anchor of downtown at Fourth Street and Broadway. I bought my twelve-inch vinyl at Dance Trax and Disco Mania and Vinylmania, but I bought my CDs and cassettes at Tower Records.

Two weeks earlier I'd gone to Tower with Damian and we'd walked upstairs and down a long hallway to what everybody called "the dance ghetto." There, in the same rack as the David Morales remixes and the Ultra Naté singles, were two of my singles. It was like seeing my newborn in the delivery room of a legitimate hospital, except that this delivery room had Stone Temple Pilots playing on the stereo and my newborns had been birthed in a CD pressing plant in New Jersey and were swaddled in plastic.

I walked past Tower Records and NYU and came to Washington Square Park. It was full of drug dealers, all melodically repeating variations on the refrain "Weed, smoke, sense, Buddha," over and over again.

I walked past the fountain and toward the dark and stained Washington Square Arch. At one point, possibly in the nineteenth century, the arch had been white. Now George Washington's face was pitted and black with pollution.

At the base of the Washington Square Arch, under the grit and soot, was my favorite hidden part of New York, a tiny unmarked door. In 1917 Marcel Duchamp and some of his Cubist and Surrealist friends had broken the lock on this door, climbed to the top of the arch with a case of wine, and at dawn proclaimed lower Manhattan to be its own sovereign country. Whenever I saw this door I thought of Duchamp and his drunken friends dancing on top of the arch at dawn, in the newly christened country of Lower Manhattan.

I walked up Fifth Avenue, passing a few of the only nice buildings in lower Manhattan. A handful of rich people lived downtown, even though 99 percent of downtown was filled with crack addicts and burning buildings. Whenever my friends and I walked past these fancy buildings, we'd always wonder, "Why would any rich person want to live south of Fourteenth Street?"

I headed west on Fourteenth Street: past the abandoned storefronts, the discount electronics stores, the vast emporiums selling cheap handbags and bootleg Disney T-shirts. I reached Cara's apartment, stared up at her dark bedroom window, and kept walking. Cara and I had broken up two weeks before. I'd gone to her apartment and told her that I adored her but that I didn't feel enough of an emotional connection to keep dating her. She sat on her bed and cried; I held her underneath her framed Roxy Music concert poster. After a while she turned away from me and said, simply, "You should go."

I let myself out quietly and hadn't spoken to her since.

Now I passed the shuttered check-cashing store next to Cara's building and crossed Eighth Avenue, walking into the desolation of the Meatpacking District. A restaurant named Florent had just opened, but otherwise the neighborhood was a wasteland of blood-covered cobblestones, crack-addicted hookers, and Hasidic masochists. Counterintuitively, the very worst blocks were the safest, as apart from the occasional hooker with fifty cents in the bottom of her soggy shoe, there was no-body to rob.

I turned up Ninth Avenue, walking past abandoned buildings and housing projects. Some drunk girls in bright green wigs were standing outside an Irish bar. Their faces were flushed, they had pints of Guinness in their hands, and they were laughing too loud for this neighborhood. There was public housing nearby, which meant crack and predators. These girls in their neon-green wigs were oblivious, protected by a low fence and the warm glow of the Irish bar. But the predators were there, waiting just outside of the light.

I continued up Ninth Avenue; two kids in hoodies came around the corner at Eighteenth Street. "Crack?" they asked. "Crack?" I kept walking. "Fucking white boy," one said behind me.

I looked up ahead. There were two more kids in hoodies heading toward me, holding knives at their sides. I couldn't go back; I couldn't go forward. So I ran into the street. Traffic was light and I was lucky. I ran around taxis and buses, some honking, but the kids didn't follow. I had become too much trouble for them, so they let me run away.

On the west side of the street I kept running. More kids in hoodies made their sales pitches: "Yo, crack?" "Base?" "Crack?" I sprinted past Nineteenth Street and Twentieth Street, eventually getting to bright and wide Twenty-Third Street. I looked back. Nobody had followed me.

My heart was pounding. What if I'd been killed en route to a rave? I'd end up as a footnote, one more dead New Yorker, to be talked about by hungover hipsters at the dog park as they drank lattes. *Remember that guy Moby? What happened to him? Wasn't he a DJ?* I didn't want to die yet, and I especially didn't want to be stabbed by eighteen-year-old crack dealers to bleed out on a sidewalk.

I kept jogging uptown, reasoning that a weird guy in oversized rave pants jogging up Ninth Avenue was less attractive prey than a weird guy in oversized rave pants walking. As I got closer to Twenty-Eighth Street I suddenly remembered to be nervous about the rave. Would anybody show up?

I turned the corner, filled with fear and trepidation that our event was going to be a failure. And it was a Halloween miracle. A line of a few thousand ravers went down the block from the Sound Factory, around the corner, and down Tenth Avenue.

Marci was standing at the front door with DB. "Did you see the line?" she asked, as if I could have missed it. We all walked into the club with wide smiles.

I heard music even though the doors were just opening. "Who's playing now?" I asked.

"Jason Jinx," DB said. "He's a friend of On-E's—we thought he'd open the night."

The club we'd rented, the Sound Factory, was a hallowed space for dance music. This was where Junior Vazquez and Danny Tenaglia played their legendary ten-hour sets. I still didn't understand how we'd been able to rent the Sound Factory for our little rave. It was akin to renting St. Patrick's Cathedral for a swap meet.

The dance floor was empty, but we knew there was a line of three thousand ravers outside. Soon they'd all come inside, take ecstasy, and dance for seven or eight hours. At six a.m. they'd spill outside, chemicals rushing through their blood, and race to an after-hours party before the sun came up. At ten a.m. they'd go to breakfast and sit in the park for a while before stumbling to their dorm rooms, where they'd sleep until eight p.m.

Jason Jinx played Blame's "Music Takes You," and even in this empty space it sounded like a warm hug. The city was dying, but in here we were creating our own little Day-Glo, consequence-free world.

I walked back outside to look at our line. It felt like a beautiful living creature, our line of three thousand people in Fresh Jive T-shirts. By eleven p.m., the dance floor was filled and Kevin Saunderson was DJing. At midnight, Altern 8 came on. They stood behind their keyboards wearing anoraks and dust masks. They barely moved, but their songs were anthems and the crowd roared their love and approval at them. Everything was peaking. The music was loud and joyful. The walls were sweating, and when one of the guys in Altern 8 finally raised his fist in the air the crowd lost their minds.

DB went on after Altern 8, starting his set with "Music Takes You." Everyone yelled and blew their whistles under the green lasers. Import twelve-inches were $10, so it didn't make sense for DJs to buy too many records that nobody else was playing. You'd hear the same rave anthems played by different DJs a few times each night, and each time you heard them they sounded like a revelation.

I walked down the hall and into the jungle room. The music here was darker, the kids tougher. The DJ was playing a jungle twelve-inch with sub-bass that made my toes vibrate in my shoes. I went down a back hallway to the chill-out room. The DJ here was playing a Future Sound of London B-side. Seventy-five ravers were lying in beanbag chairs that I assumed Scotto had borrowed or stolen. The walls were lit pink and blue, making the beanbags and the ravers all look like jelly beans. There were beautiful short-haired raver girls in oversized raver pants, but they were all cuddling with beautiful short-haired raver boys in their oversized raver pants. It was almost androgynous, except that the girls were so beautiful in their baby-doll T-shirts that I wanted to become a polygamist and marry all of them.

It was almost time for me to go on. I walked onto the stage in the main room, checked my equipment, and waved across the dance floor at DB. He gave me a thumbs-up and stopped the record he was playing—a dead stop. Suddenly the dance floor was silent.

I started my set with "Ah Ah" and the ravers erupted, dancing and waving glow sticks. The lights and strobes were behind me, shining in the ravers' wide eyes, and all felt right with the world. I played "Rock the House," "Voodoo Child," "Go," and "Next Is the E." In the last few months "Next Is the E" had become a rave anthem for 1992. During the chorus, as the sampled female vocal sang "I feel it," I looked out at the audience. In the front row a beautiful girl with blond hair was dancing and crying. Her face flickered in the red and blue and green lights. She opened her eyes, looked at me, and yelled, "I love you."

I played two more songs and ended with a new song, "Thousand." The distorted 909 kick drum came in; the track got faster and faster, Scotto's strobes and Vari-Lites were pulsing, and the ravers just stood there, quivering. When the first breakdown came, they cheered and the joyful zeitgeist of the rave scene flooded over me. I locked eyes with the beautiful crying girl in the front row. The song got even faster and I climbed on top of my keyboard, shirtless and raising my hands over my head.

When the song ended, DB took the mic and yelled, "New York! Give it up for Moby!," the crowd gave a full-throated roar of love, and I walked offstage. I had broken two drumsticks banging on my Octapad. My keyboard was covered with footprints and was probably ruined. But I was numb with happiness. I stood on the side of the stage, sweaty and breathing hard, and the beautiful crying raver came over. I opened my arms, and she fell into them, weeping. I held her for a minute.

Finally, she gasped, "I just want you to know how much I love 'Next Is the E.' The chorus is so beautiful."

"What's your name?"

"Rachel." She was about five foot three and wearing giant raver pants and a small black T-shirt. "I just wanted to tell you how much I love your music, Moby," she said, looking me directly in the eyes, and walked away.

I packed up my battered keyboard and Octapad and hid them under the stage. Then I went looking for Rachel. As I walked through the room ravers stopped me and hugged me. But I couldn't find her. I looked everywhere—the jungle room, the chill-out room—but she had disappeared. I wanted to find Rachel and walk across the Manhattan Bridge at dawn with her while everyone else in the world was asleep. I wanted to see where she lived. I wanted to know what books she loved. I wanted to sit on the edge of her bed and look at her high school yearbook, discussing the Duran Duran pin she wore in her senior portrait. But it was four a.m. and Rachel was gone.

I carried my equipment outside and my friend Gabe helped me get my keyboard in the trunk of a cab. The party was a success, but I couldn't find Rachel, my little rave Dulcinea. "Gabe," I asked naively, "if you see a woman named Rachel, could you get her number for me?"

Gabe smiled sweetly. "Okay, Moby, I will."

I slid into the cab's backseat. "Where to?" the driver asked.

"Mott Street, between Houston and Prince," I said.

"Oh, Little Italy," he said. "You Mafia?"

I laughed. "No. I'm not even Italian."

He was playing music softly as we drove away from Sound Factory and the three thousand ravers.

"What's this music?" I asked.

"It's a cassette from my church in Haiti. You like it?"

"It's beautiful. Can you turn it up?"

He did. It sounded like baby angels.

26

PLYWOOD DANCE FLOOR

was drinking organic carrot juice, eating a bowl of oatmeal, and reading the *New Yorker*. Because of jet lag after my last trip to Europe I'd woken up at five a.m., put on some old sweat clothes, and gone to the gym. Now it was eight a.m. and I felt clean and civilized, eating breakfast at the yellow kitchen table I'd found a month ago in a Dumpster in front of my building. The dappled sun was coming through the giant trees at Old St. Patrick's Cathedral and filling my loft.

Outside, people were shouting; I thought I heard my name, so I went to the window. Twenty wide-eyed ravers were standing on the sidewalk, chanting, "Moby! Moby!" I opened the window, leaning on the old stone windowsill. Ani, a DJ whose name was a pun for taking ecstasy, yelled, "Moby! You're up!"

"I've been up since five," I said. "What are you doing?"

"We're going to an after-hours on Fourth Street! Come with us!"

I looked at my bowl of oatmeal and my glass of carrot juice. "Okay!" I shouted. "I'll be right down!"

"Where are you coming from?" I asked Ani a few minutes later as we walked up Mott Street.

"NASA, Shelter," he said, referring to a weekly club night that DB and Scotto had started recently. "At eight a.m. Soul Slinger's DJing an after-hours in a loft on Fourth Street."

We crossed Houston and got to Bleecker. It was a jewel box of an autumn morning: the sky was cloudless and the sun was warm. The other ravers shuffled alongside us, their pupils wide and their jaws clenching. They were all in their giant raver pants and Liquid Sky T-shirts. The raver pants kept getting bigger and bigger; most of the ravers now wore jeans that would have comfortably fit a three-hundred-pound man. Some of the ravers wore their jeans low, like hip-hop gangbangers, but most of them wore belts, making their billowing jeans look like cotillion dresses. None of the ravers were talking, just wandering next to each other like a laconic tribe on narcotics.

We walked up the Bowery, past CBGB. "Have you ever seen a show at CB's?" I asked Jason Jinx. He had grown up in the New Jersey suburbs and had been a hip-hop DJ before discovering the rave scene a few years earlier.

"I don't think so," he said. "Have you?"

"Hundreds," I said. "The best show I ever saw there was Bad Brains in 1982. HR, the lead singer, was doing backflips off the stage." Nineteen eighty-two was ten years ago, and ten years ago Jason had been nine years old. He looked at me suspiciously, doing math in his head and trying to figure out if I was old.

"Did you ever go to any of the hardcore matinees at CB's?" I asked Ani. He had grown up in the city; his parents were art dealers who lived in a five-bedroom apartment on the Upper West Side.

"No, my brother went," he said. "I was too young."

"Too young for a CB's matinee? Most of the kids there are fifteen."

"Yeah, my mom wouldn't let me go."

We walked up the Bowery, past the homeless shelters, the restaurant-supply stores, and the fenced-in lots covered in garbage. We stepped around a few homeless drunks passed out on the sidewalk. "Here's the White House," one of the ravers said, pointing to a homeless shelter on the west side of the street. "That's where I stayed when I first came here."

"You stayed in a homeless shelter?" I asked, curious.

"It's an SRO," he said, a little defensively. "SRO" stood for "single-room occupancy"; SROs were generally safer and cleaner than homeless shelters. "You live in that factory?" he asked.

"Yeah," I said.

"Do you have a bathroom?"

"No, I pee in the bathroom down the hall."

"Where do you shower?" he asked.

"I go to the gym."

"I don't know if I could live without a shower," he said.

"But you lived in a homeless shelter," I pointed out.

"An SRO. And it had a shower. Plus my apartment now has a real bathroom."

We got to the loft where the after-hours party was happening. "What is this place?" I asked.

"I don't know," Ani said, stepping down a few steps to a scratched, red metal door. "A theater? A studio?"

We walked through the scratched red door and down a long, dark hallway. We could hear the thump of house music coming through the old wooden floor. The hallway ended at an industrial green metal door. Jason opened it and the hallway was filled with loud electronic music. It was an experimental theater or art space, with a balcony open to a plywood dance floor below. A hundred ravers and club kids were wandering around under a few pulsing disco lights. Another twenty or thirty were passed out on cushions, and a few people were dancing on the plywood dance floor.

I walked to the DJ booth, where Carlos, known professionally as Soul Slinger, was playing a Brazilian techno record. He owned Liquid Sky, a store that was the epicenter of the New York rave scene. They sold import twelve-inches, drum machines, giant rave trousers, and lots of oversized Liquid Sky long-sleeve T-shirts. "Hey, Carlos!" I said.

He gazed at me, his eyes as wide as manhole covers. "Moby! What are you doing here?" Everybody knew that I was sober, and as a sober person I never went to after-hours parties.

"I was eating breakfast and Ani and Jason came by and brought me here!"

"Cool!" he said, and turned his attention to the record he was cueing up.

I walked across the dance floor and spotted Keoki in a corner, staring into space. "Hey, Keoki!" I yelled. It took him a minute, but eventually he followed my voice to me.

"Moby!" he yelled back. "Do you have any drugs?"

"No, I'm sober."

He looked at me quizzically. "Why are you here?"

He was hanging out with Michael Alig's club kids. Ravers and club kids liked the same music and the same narcotics, but over the last year they'd stopped socializing together. The rave scene was generally straight, and the club kids were generally gay. There wasn't any animosity between club kids and ravers, but they kept to their respective scenes. The only exception was the Limelight, where ravers, club kids, and goths all danced and took drugs together.

The club kids in the corner with Keoki looked strung out and terrifying. In 1989 these same club kids had been innocent fashion students in colorful clothes, looking like flowers and pixies. But just three years later they looked like scary monsters, with faces painted white, steel spikes piercing their cheeks, and fake blood smeared around their eyes. They used to take a hit or two of ecstasy when they went out, but now they were smoking crack and shooting heroin. They didn't really speak very much anymore; they just went out and stood there, expressionless and terrifying and tall in their seven-inch heels.

Carlos played "Plastic Dreams," and some of the club kids and ravers started dancing. I awkwardly danced with them. I danced about as well as O. J. Simpson, but it was nine a.m. and nobody was paying attention because they were all so high. I closed my eyes and danced for ten hypnotic minutes to "Plastic Dreams." Then Carlos played "Pancake," my favorite new twelve-inch.

I opened my eyes and saw Ani dancing with Chloë Sevigny. I'd known Chloë since she was thirteen; we'd both grown up in Darien.

When I started DJing at all-ages clubs in Connecticut I'd given rides to her and her brother, picking them up at their parents' house by the beach. Chloë had been shy and preppy, sitting quietly in the back-seat while my friends and I listened to Nitzer Ebb cassettes. Now she worked at Liquid Sky and hung out at NASA with her raver boyfriend, Harmony.

"Hi, Chloë," I yelled. "How's your brother?"

She stared at me with hooded eyes and answered slowly, "He's good."

I kept dancing on the plywood dance floor, surrounded by ravers and passed-out drug casualties. After half an hour the music got even darker. The bass lines had more echo and the vocals sounded like they were coming from the bottom of a deep well. Half the crowd had passed out, and those who were upright were moving very slowly. It was ten a.m.; I decided it was time to leave.

"How late does this go?" I asked Jason on my way out.

"I don't know," he said. "Noon? One?"

I loved the same music and shopped at the same record stores as these people, but I was always home in bed by three a.m., which was the beginning of the night for most ravers. The only thing that changed in a nightclub after three a.m. was that the music got darker and more and more kids passed out in corners.

I walked up from the basement, opened the red door, and stepped back outside into the morning light. It was still the same flawless autumn day. I looked up and saw a remote blue sky, staring back at me like a sea of glass. I wanted to go home and turn on my 909 and my 303 and write something sinewy and dark and laden with reverb for a DJ to play for a basement full of drug-damaged ravers. But when I got back to my apartment my glass of carrot juice was waiting for me, glowing in the sun.

I sat at my yellow Formica table and finished my carrot juice, reading the *New Yorker* in the dappled light.

27

SUNBURN

The drunk businessman sitting across the aisle from me was pretending to be indignant. "An entrée?" he asked the stewardess. "An entrée should be first!"

"Yes, it's your entrée, sir," she said. "The beef."

"I'm not trying to give you a hard time," he said, leaning into the airplane's aisle and patting her arm. "I studied French at the lycée. 'Entrée' means 'first.' We say 'entrée' when we should say 'main course.'"

"Well, do you want your main course, sir?" she asked.

"When you say it like that, of course I do," he said loudly, his smile broad and wet.

"And would you like another Dewar's and soda with your main course, sir?"

He thought overly long. "No, I'll have a glass of red. What reds do you have?"

"We have a cabernet and a pinot noir."

"I'll have the cabernet, and thank you, beautiful lady!"

I'd been upgraded to business class, and it was wasted on me. I wasn't eating the beef or chicken; I wasn't drinking the wine; I wasn't even using the complimentary headphones to watch a Nicolas Cage movie playing on the tiny screen by the bathroom. I was even too small to fill out the expansive seat. These business-class seats were designed for obese businessmen, not skinny vegan ravers.

"Are you sure I can't get you anything?" the stewardess leaned over and asked me.

"Orange juice?"

"Sure. What's that you're eating?"

"Oh, vegan ravioli." Before leaving my loft I'd made vegan ravioli on my hot plate and put it in a tomato-sauce jar. I was eating it with a plastic fork I'd taken from a restaurant near the departure gate. I was flying to San Francisco to play a rave with Young American Primitive, Mark Farina, and Doc Martin.

"Miss!" the drunk businessman yelled to the flight attendant. "This cabernet isn't so great. Can I get the pinot?"

"Of course, sir," she said, taking his glass.

He looked over at me. "No point drinking bad wine!" he said, boozy and convivial.

I smiled, unsure how to respond. Before I got sober I hadn't known the difference between cabernet and pinot noir. Pre-sobriety I drank beer and vodka. I didn't care what the beer or vodka tasted like; I just loved them for the fact that they made me drunk. Wine always tasted like syrup to me, unnecessarily thick, the slow lane on the road to getting drunk.

I smiled a meek vegan smile at the businessman, hoping he'd stop talking to me.

Yesterday I'd been in upstate Connecticut, on a lake with Paul, Lee, and our friend Tarquin, the hockey-fanatic son of Latvian immigrants. Lee had never water-skied, so we taught him. "How do you all know how to water-ski?" he asked on the boat. "You're all losers."

We threw him overboard with some water skis and told him he couldn't get back on the boat until he learned how to water-ski. He kept falling down, surprising us with his utter inability to get up on skis. "Good try!" we yelled as he fell on his face again. "You almost got up!"

Eventually he stayed upright, briefly, and we decided to let him back on the boat.

One of the benefits of growing up in Darien was that my friends all had rich parents, and rich parents tended to have nice boats. I'd grown up watching my mom borrow money so that we could eat, but then riding my bike to Long Island Sound and spending a lot of time on my friends' parents' boats. I was the only poor person most of my friends had ever met, and inviting me to their houses and onto their boats served as a form of easy charity for them.

Paul had grown up poor, too, but his uncle had a house on a lake in Newtown, Connecticut, and we had been coming up here to go water-skiing since high school. The day was winding down, so Paul went skiing, then Tarquin, and as the sun set, I jumped over the edge of the boat for one last ride. "Throw me the boogie board!" I yelled to Tarquin.

He hurled it over my head. "Swim, monkey!" he yelled. I swam to the board, holding the ski line in my left hand. Once I had it the boat slowly pulled away from me, tightening the line. Once it became taut I gave the "okay" hand sign and expected the boat to lurch forward, pulling me up and out of the water. But Paul sped up only a little, dragging me through the water. I was laughing and getting lake water in my mouth.

"Go faster!" I yelled. He sped up another mile per hour, pulling me through the water like a worm on a hook. Eventually, he punched it. The boat leaped forward and I was skimming over the water, going twenty miles an hour, the glassy water an inch below me. I reached down and touched the water; my fingers were like little blades, cutting the surface.

I gave Paul the thumbs-up signal, which meant "Go faster." He sped up to twenty-five miles an hour. I gave him the signal again. Thirty miles an hour was dangerously fast for a boogie board. I was singing Bad Brains' "Pay to Cum" at the top of my lungs as I flew over the water. This was pure, simple joy, a rave on a lake. I gave Paul the thumbs-up again.

At thirty-five miles an hour my arms were being pulled out of my shoulder sockets and I was bouncing behind the boat. The happiness coursed through me—I wanted more. I raised my hand and made a fist, which meant "Go as fast as you can go." Paul sped up a little. I pumped my fist, and he brought the boat up to its top speed of forty-five miles an hour. I was screaming. The happiness was exploding through me like God and disco. I raised my hand and made the circle motion that meant "Go around so I can jump the wake." Paul started to turn, but the boogie board caught the edge of a wave. I was thrown off the board, bouncing across the lake at forty-five miles a hour like a skipping stone in a bathing suit. I rolled across the surface of the water, laughing uncontrollably, and finally I sank.

I raised my hand above the waterline and made the "okay" hand signal. When you fell you had to let the boat driver know you were okay. People broke ribs and limbs and necks water-skiing. Water was ostensibly soft, but it sent countless suburban kids to the emergency room.

The boat pulled up to me. "That was amazing!" I yelled. "Let's do it again!"

"It's getting dark. We should head in," Paul said.

"No!" I yelled, and swam for the towline.

"Get in the boat, boatmate!" Paul yelled, which made me laugh even harder. I swam to the boat and sat on the ledge at the back. I wrapped myself in a towel; my limbs were shaking. As Paul headed back for the dock, I threw off my towel and jumped off the boat again. He turned the boat around.

"Do you want to swim back?" Paul asked, stern.

"No, sir," I said, climbing back onto the boat. The sun was balanced on the horizon, but the air was still warm. I was sunburned, I smelled like algae, and I had a belly full of dirty lake water. "That was the happiest I've ever been," I said.

Do you want a hot fudge sundae?" the stewardess asked the drunk businessman.

He thought deeply. "Yes, with chocolate and strawberry sauce," he decided. "Oh, and a Dewar's and soda."

"Any defibrillator paddles?" I wanted to ask. "Some interferon for your metastasizing tumors, sir?" I sat smugly, thinking of him succumbing to obesity, diabetes, cancer, and heart disease, possibly simultaneously. "Why, God?" he would cry on his deathbed. "It's so unfair!"

Five scotch-and-sodas, two glasses of wine, airplane beef and greasy egg noodles, and a pile of ice cream with chocolate and strawberry sauce. How dare the fates punish you after leading such a virtuous life? I knew I was being a judgmental dick, so I looked out the window, away from the businessman with the ice cream dripping down his chin.

We were flying over the Rocky Mountains. The valleys had disappeared into darkness, but the setting sun was touching the peaks, some of which were still covered in snow. I took out my CD player, my headphones, and my wallet of CDs. I flipped through the discs—what should I listen to? Nick Drake? Kraftwerk? U2? Debussy? The Clash? Mission of Burma? Dvořák? The Gun Club? Brian Eno and David Byrne? Roxy Music? Gershwin?

Okay. Gershwin. "Rhapsody in Blue." I settled the disc on the little spindle of the CD player and hit "play." The music started, reserved and familiar. I'd heard "Rhapsody in Blue" a thousand times and it always amazed me. It was so humble and then so bombastic. It was beautiful, bright, and terrifying: old and new, European and American. At times it sounded like Debussy, at times it sounded like Stravinsky, and at times it sounded like the Lower East Side in 1910.

"Rhapsody in Blue" was a quintessentially New York work of art, but it was also about moving from east to west, from the old world to the new. I was flying over mountains at six hundred miles an hour, the west far beneath my feet. The world didn't even notice me, or any of us. We measured the earth and tore at it. We built edifices and brought water to barren plains, but the Earth barely noticed that we'd been here. We measured our time in decades. The Earth measured its time in millions of years. We were a blip. I was a blip.

Somehow this wasn't fodder for existential despair. My insignificance felt like weightlessness. Eventually my cells and molecules were going to succumb to entropy and fly apart. They'd be free to turn into an ether that had no relation to anything I'd ever been. At some point I'd die and drift back into the crucible that had formed me.

My skin was still burned from my day at the lake. But the land beneath me had been baking in the sun for hundreds of millions of years. I stared at the dark mountains, my forehead leaning against the cold plastic window. "Rhapsody in Blue" ended.

I hit "play" again, trying to hang on to transcendence. The day before I had been skimming over a lake like a bullet, and now I was skimming over mountains in a metal tube. If I thought too hard about "Rhapsody in Blue," I'd conclude that I could never write anything even approaching its beauty and majesty. But I could sit here, full of vegan ravioli, listening to the most perfect music ever written as I stared at the West through a tiny window.

Later I would eat vegan food with friends in San Francisco and DJ at an amazing rave and marvel at the thousands of people packed together and hurling their hands into the lights and lasers. But nothing would touch the beauty of "Rhapsody in Blue" at dusk above dark, towering mountains.

28

MONOCHROMATIC STROBES

As I walked down Hudson Street with my record bag slung over my shoulder, on my way to DJ at NASA, my sixth sense for nightclubs was tingling with some small, banal dread.

The night before I'd finished DJing in Berlin at five a.m., gone to my hotel to shower off the patina of cigarette smoke and rave fog, and rushed to the airport for a nine a.m. flight. I'd slept for fifteen minutes in the Berlin airport, then I'd sat in my economy seat for the two-hour flight to London, my head bouncing around with hypnagogic exhaustion. I'd stumbled through Heathrow and made my flight to New York, sleeping sporadically like a junkie at an NA meeting.

Both the rave scene and my trips to Europe were changing. Two years ago everything had been new and celebratory. I had been making happy techno records for audiences on ecstasy, and even when the travel was crushing and I was debilitated by illness and exhaustion, I was still happy to be part of a scene that was built on a foundation of joy. Now, by 1993, the music was getting darker and the drugs were getting heavier. Audiences were dancing less and passing out in corners more.

Last night at Tresor I'd felt like I was in a subterranean bunker full of medicated zombies. The music was cool and adventurous but also menacing and otherworldly. The shiny, idealistic days had seemingly drawn to a close. Acen's "Trip II the Moon" and Underworld's "Rez" were the big records, and I loved them, but they were the soundtrack to this encroaching darkness. The drugs fueled the music and the music fueled the drugs, pushing each other further down the dark rabbit hole.

Flying home, I'd been thinking about NASA. Whenever I played there the ravers gave me hugs and candy bracelets; the year before they had all signed a giant birthday card for me and adorned it with pastel hearts and blue unicorns and spaceships. Even as I traveled around the world, NASA had been my refuge in New York. I hadn't played there for a few months, and tonight would be a homecoming: I was booked for one a.m., between DB and Soul Slinger. My plan was to play joyful records, to remind people that music could be celebratory, not just ominous. Between my fleeting naps on the flight I made a list of the records I'd play. The obvious hands-in-the-air anthems were off-limits: no Rozalla's "Everybody's Free" or "Don't Go Lose It Baby" or Altern 8. They were great records, but they were too dated. I could play Blame's "Music Takes You." I might be able to play Bizarre Inc.'s "Playing with Knives." It was only two and a half years old, but it felt like an artifact from a distant, idyllic past.

After my flight landed I went home, had dinner, watched a *Simpsons* episode on my VCR, and gathered up my records. Walking through Tribeca, I turned the corner onto Hubert Street. Outside NASA there were ravers lined up to get in, ravers skateboarding, ravers already passed out on the sidewalk. I stepped over an unconscious raver leaning against a mailbox and walked to the front of the club. Gabe was working the door; he had worked at Limelight for years, but a few months ago he had moved over to NASA. He had short blond dreadlocks and was dwarfed by the two hulking security guards flanking him.

"How is it inside?" I asked him.

He shrugged. "A lot of people," he said, "but they're all sitting on the dance floor. I fucking hate ketamine."

"Well, I'm going to play some rave records. Maybe they'll wake up."

He looked at me skeptically. "Good luck," he said.

As I walked down the black hallway the kick drum got louder and the fog got thicker. I was used to walking into NASA and seeing people in smiley shirts dancing and hugging each other, but this looked like a refugee camp. The lights were strobing through the clouds of fog and smoke, and when they flashed, I could catch glimpses of ravers sitting on the dance floor hugging their knees, or lying on their sides. I made my way through the ketamine-disabled crowd and went to the DJ booth. DB was there, playing some very dark progressive house, the perfect soundtrack for comatose ravers. We nodded at each other. I walked over to the lighting booth and said hi to Scotto. He had been my lighting designer for two years, and had toured with me in the States and Europe. He had long brown hair and always wore huge, striped raver pants.

"Are the lights different tonight?" I asked Scotto.

"We wanted to make things darker," he said. "More strobes and less color."

"Okay," I said, surveying the nightclub. The music sounded sepulchral and the dance floor looked like a primordial soup. The darkness was palpable. "I'm going to play rave records," I told him.

"Okay," Scotto said, his attention on his lighting board.

Gathering my records earlier in my apartment, I'd felt like a zealous rave evangelist. I'd go back to NASA and single-handedly usher in a new era of joyful techno. Now, standing in the DJ booth and looking at the ravers in their K-holes, I felt like a deluded idiot. And I was so tired. It was twelve thirty a.m. in New York, or six thirty a.m. in Germany. In the last thirty-six hours, I'd had about two hours of airplane-damaged sleep. I had brought only happy records, but the cool DJs now played as dark as possible: dark jungle, dark house, dark breakbeats.

I walked to the turntables, where DB was finishing up. He gave me the "You ready?" head gesture. I gave him the "Okay, I guess so" shrug. I didn't want to be there. I wanted to go back to the celebratory NASA of a year earlier, where I'd been loved and relevant. Or I wanted to go home and go to sleep. I flipped through my records to find something to start my set with: something that wasn't too dark, a track that would let me segue into the happy records I wanted to play. I took Gypsy's

"Skinny Bumblebee" out of its sleeve. It was enough of a rave record to make me happy but progressive enough that the crowd wouldn't pelt me with garbage.

I played "Skinny Bumblebee" and the audience was unmoved. I played some newer progressive house records, trying to push the mood toward joyful techno, but with each selection I could feel the ravers' antipathy washing over me like cold fog. What could I do? Stare at the happy record I was playing and pretend I wasn't losing an already lost crowd? I was so tired. The jet lag was like a bird of prey sitting on my shoulder and snapping at my face.

I snuck in one of my records, "Go." I got a ripple of acknowledgment but nothing more. I'd lost the crowd to Special K and dark lights and a sea of impenetrable fog. I wanted to play one purely joyful record to see if I could pierce their class-A carapace. I mixed from "Go" into Bizarre Inc.'s "Playing with Knives," and it fell flat. No euphoria, no exuberance—not even recognition. Just narcotic apathy for yesterday's DJ playing yesterday's rave record.

Carlos, a.k.a. Soul Slinger, came over to the booth. "Hey, you want to finish early?" he asked. I'd been playing for thirty-five minutes; I was supposed to play for an hour. I couldn't tell if he was being rude or kind. He could have been telling me that I was failing in front of eight hundred kids on drugs, which I knew, or giving me an easy way to end what was clearly a DJ disaster. Or maybe Carlos was letting me know that he and NASA had moved on.

The darkness here hadn't just randomly happened; it had been created and cultivated. While I mourned the end of hands-in-the-air celebratory techno, everyone else seemed thrilled that the era of happy anthems had come to an end. The rave anthems of a year ago were an embarrassment to the other NASA DJs, who were now dark and sophisticated. "Did we ever hug each other and throw our hands in the air?" they seemed to ask. "Clearly not. Or if we had youthful indiscretions, we've clearly grown up and left naïveté and joy behind." I felt like the rave equivalent of Comrade Trotsky, a blotted-out figure from an era that had now officially never happened.

I stood back from the turntables and let Carlos cue up his record. Normally when you're DJing you let the last DJ's record play for a while, and then you gradually mix from his last record into your first. It's a way of maintaining cohesion and keeping people dancing, but it's also a sign of respect. Fifteen seconds after I stepped back from the turntables, Soul Slinger hit stop on the Technics 1200, bringing the exuberance of "Playing with Knives" to an abrupt and awkward end.

Two seconds of dead air followed, and then he started his first record, a dark and dubby jungle twelve-inch. People woke up. Some of the reclining ravers stood up and started dancing. Some people even cheered.

DB came over and clapped me on the shoulder. "Rough set, Mo," he said. I nodded, sad and jet-lagged.

I stood behind Carlos as he played a few more jungle records, the crowd getting more animated with each selection. Suddenly it all made sense: the monochromatic strobes, the dark and angular music, the drugs. This was their world now. I was politely tolerated, but it was 1993, and I was a sober relic from 1992. Or maybe 1991.

Heading for the exit, I stopped in the lighting booth to say good-bye to Scotto. He was dancing as he manipulated the lights and strobes. I tapped him on the shoulder—he turned around, saw me, and turned back to his lights. I stood there, looking around to see if everyone else knew how irrelevant I was. But nobody was paying attention to me or my exhausted shame. I walked out of the back of the club, onto Laight Street.

The door closed behind me and suddenly the world was quiet. Tribeca was a no-man's-land, especially after midnight on a Friday. I wanted to say good-bye to Gabe—he had seemed sad too. I walked around the block to the front of the club. The ravers had stopped skateboarding; now they were just sitting or sleeping on the sidewalk. One rave couple was leaning against an abandoned car, making out. The boy had his hand up the girl's shirt, but neither of them were moving or excited.

Gabe was standing by himself at the entrance. "You're done?" he asked, confused. "I thought you finished at two."

"Yeah, Carlos took over." I looked at the passed-out ravers. "I guess it's not really my scene anymore," I said.

He could see that I was defeated. "I'm not sure it's my scene anymore either," he confided.

I needed that moment of solidarity. DB and Scotto and Soul Slinger and the ketamine-blasted ravers had moved on, and if I thought about it, I couldn't begrudge them. The dance scene had always been about the new, and I was no longer new. But NASA had felt like my soul's home. I'd imagined playing happy rave anthems for happy ravers at NASA for years and years. Eventually we'd get older and welcome the new millennium together, forever throwing our hands in the air to blissful techno songs punctuated with wailing female vocals.

"Well, good night, Gabe," I said. "You're a good guy. Thanks."

"You're a good guy too, Moby," he said, and shook my hand.

I walked away, looking for a cab. By the time I got to Hudson Street I couldn't hear the echoing drums anymore.

29

JUNIPER BUSH

The last time I'd visited East Hampton on Long Island, with Janet in 1988, the thing that had impressed me the most had been the doughnut robot. It made doughnuts in the window of the doughnut shop while kids and an aspiring techno musician stood outside and watched. It looked more like a small factory assembly line than C-3PO, but I was fascinated by it because they called it a robot. It spit lumps of dough onto a conveyer belt, pushed them into frying oil, dried them under red lamps, and delivered them into a little cart.

Now, five years later, I was returning to East Hampton to escape my crumbling life. My situation with Instinct Records was falling apart, so I was distracting myself by wondering if the doughnut robot was still at work in East Hampton. I was a vegan and couldn't eat the doughnuts, but what better way was there to spend a beautiful summer day than watching a giant robot make doughnuts?

Paul and his friend James were on the train to East Hampton with me. Paul had shaved the front half of his hair and dyed the back half pink; James was six foot five and had a yellow Mohawk.

After four years on Instinct Records I'd decided it was time to leave. My dream label, Mute records in the UK, the home of Nick Cave and Depeche Mode and Boyd Rice and Nitzer Ebb, wanted to sign me.

That was perfect, except for one small problem. Instinct wouldn't let me go.

Discussing record contracts is, by definition, dull. Even record-company bosses and music-business lawyers and people who write books about record contracts would agree. So suffice it to say that my contract with Instinct was vague, unfair, and crummy, but legally binding.

I asked Instinct politely, "Can I leave?" and they said, slightly less politely, "No." Then I asked again, via my lawyer, "Can I please leave?" and Instinct said, "Okay, but you need to pay us a lot of money."

This confused me, because Instinct had never paid me a lot of money—which meant I didn't have a lot of money. I asked them for clarification: "I have no money but you want me to pay you a lot of money?" They replied, "Get your new label to give you a lot of money. Then you can give it to us."

At this point months started passing and the lawyers started racking up hundreds of billable hours and Mute began to lose interest in me. I wanted to leave Instinct, I had a golden door open, and through it I could see Nick Cave and Depeche Mode saying, "Come join us! Make records for the best label in the world!" And I was standing on the other side of the threshold, with downcast eyes, saying, "I can't, I'm stuck in legal purgatory."

So in an advanced state of panic I decided to go to East Hampton for the weekend with James and Paul. James's sister was going to meet us at the train station and take us to their parents' house.

"Tell me more about your sister," I said.

"She goes to Cornell, she's premed, and she won't date you," James said.

"But is she single?" Paul and I asked in unison.

"Yes, but she would never date either one of you."

"Why?" Paul asked.

"Because she's smart and pretty," James said.

"Okay," I conceded. "Fair enough." Then I wondered, "How do you have a house in East Hampton?"

"My parents bought it in the sixties for fifteen thousand dollars. It's not much, but we went there every summer when I was growing up."

"Where will Paul and I sleep?" I asked.

"You guys will be in sleeping bags on the floor of my bedroom," he said.

"That sounds fancy," I said.

"What about your sister's room?" Paul asked. "I could always stay there."

"And I would kill you in your sleep," James told him.

James's sister, Mandy, was waiting at the train station in khaki shorts and a polo shirt. She had long blond hair and a gentle Ivy League glow. She looked like every girl I'd loved from afar in junior high school and high school.

"James!" she yelled, and ran up and hugged him. He introduced us and we walked off the platform to Mandy's Volvo. James and Mandy led the way, talking about well-adjusted things like school and parents and holidays. Paul and I hung back like trolls, saying sotto voce, "I love her," "She's mine," "No, fuck you, she's mine," "I love her," "No, I love her."

We got in Mandy's Volvo, she put on a 10,000 Maniacs cassette, and she drove us to their house.

James, this sleeping bag smells like a dead Cub Scout," I observed as we carried old sleeping bags up from the basement.

"Did you steal these from a homeless shelter?" Paul asked.

"Fuck both of you," James said.

"I can just stay in Mandy's room," I volunteered.

"I bet her sheets smell like clean strawberries," Paul said.

"Or you sleep in the basement with the rats," James said.

After midnight, we made spaghetti and an iceberg lettuce salad; sat in the TV room, carpeted with brown shag; and watched a rerun of *Late Night with David Letterman*. Then we played Ping-Pong in the basement, inventing a game where three people run around the table hitting random balls, yelling at each other and laughing like happy idiots. We went to bed—technically, Paul and I went to sleeping bag—and woke up seven hours later to steady rain.

"What should we do?" I asked.

"What's Mandy doing?" Paul asked. James ignored him.

"What about croquet in the rain?" I said. We went in the backyard and put croquet hoops everywhere: behind sheds, around corners, under bushes. Normal croquet was dull, but we called this "Rainy East Hampton guerrilla croquet."

"So what's going on with your record label?" James asked as he sent my ball past the driveway and behind a juniper bush. I explained how I wanted to leave Instinct and sign with Mute—and Elektra in the United States—but how for the last nine months Instinct had been holding me hostage and how I was going to spend the rest of my life in record-label purgatory.

"Can you do anything in the meantime?" James asked.

"I can do remixes for other people and I can tour, but I can't release any new music."

"That sucks."

"You're right."

"Tell James about the compilation record," Paul said.

"Well, last year Instinct put out *The Best of Instinct Records*. The thing is that I'm their only artist, so the album was just music by me under five different names."

Paul said, "Also, Moby used to clean the Instinct office and take all the packages to UPS. He was like their musician intern slave."

"Well, it was good for a while," I said.

We played more croquet in the rain while I fought off panic attacks over the notion of never being able to release new music again. Then we walked into town, talking about girls and record contracts and the merits of the *Star Trek* movies. In town we bought coffee and watched the doughnut robot for a while.

It gave me a sense of peace knowing that it was still there, tirelessly making doughnuts for the preppy tourists. The last time I'd been here, in 1988, I'd been living in the abandoned factory in Stamford and trying to get anyone to listen to my demo cassettes. Now I lived in New York and had expensive lawyers who were fighting with a record label who desperately wanted to keep me. In 1988 I'd been DJing to around forty or fifty people a night and making $5,000 a year. Now I was playing at raves for thousands of people a night and making close to $100,000 a year. These changes in my life could've comforted me, but my panic remained ensconced at the base of my brain stem.

We reluctantly left the doughnut robot and sat on a wet park bench with our coffee, Paul with his pink hair and his Siouxsie and the Banshees shirt, James with his Doc Martens and his yellow Mohawk. The perfectly clothed and moneyed preppy people vacationing in East Hampton gave us a wide berth, possibly assuming that being interesting was contagious. We sat silently for a while, drinking our coffee and pretending that we were extras on *Twin Peaks*.

"If it keeps raining, I might head back to the city," I said, suddenly wanting to jump up and flee. My friends were great, but the panic was chewing on my brain like an angry squirrel. "Do you think I'll ever be able to make records again?" I blurted out.

"Of course," Paul said. "Sure."

"Sure" meant a lot.

We had a friend in Connecticut who was habitually vague. Rather than say "yes," he would always say "sure." So a few years earlier, we had decided that "sure" meant "100 percent emphatically *yes*." Paul had just said "sure," which meant that he was confident and omniscient and that I would make records again someday. My brain was not yet released from the viselike panic, but I accepted that it would be, hopefully soon. I finished my coffee and stood up.

"Should we go play croquet again?" I asked.

"Sure," Paul said emphatically.

"Sure," James said equally emphatically, and we walked away from East Hampton in the summer rain.

30

BIOLOGY TEXTBOOK

I n high school my biggest dream had been to fall in love with the perfect punk-rock girl. After I did my homework I would drive my moped around Darien late at night, listening to Joy Division or X, dreaming of my imaginary punk-rock girlfriend. She would be kind and have pink or green or blue hair. She would love Joy Division and sometimes jump in the pit at hardcore matinees. And she would love me and have sex with me in her parents' living room while they were upstairs sleeping.

As I cruised past the Noroton Heights train station on my moped, John Doe would sing in my headphones: "I'll replace your drunk old man / Sit in the parking lot and hold your hand." In high school that was all I wanted—a kind and smart pink-haired punk-rock girlfriend with gentle hands.

In the late eighties my friend Jamie started dating a punk-rock girl named Sarah. She was pretty, wore vegan Doc Martens, had short hair dyed pink, and loved Minor Threat. She even jumped in the pit during hardcore matinees. I had spoken to her only once or twice, but I decided that she was perfect. She was my friend's girlfriend, so I kept my longing to myself, loving her pink fuzzy Easter-egg head from afar.

Then, in June 1993, Jamie broke up with Sarah. Two months later Sarah called me to say that she was going to be in New York. We went out to dinner at Angelica Kitchen—I worked up my courage and told her that I'd always had a crush on her. She blushed, looked down at her plate of soba noodles, and said, "I have a crush on you, too."

After dinner we walked around New York in the August heat, holding hands and eating vegan ice cream. She stayed over at my apartment and in the morning took the train back to Connecticut.

"I'm leaving for Hawaii in two days to teach," she told me.

"How long are you going?"

"Six months."

"I'll write every day," I promised.

"That seems a bit much."

"Okay, every week."

We kissed in Grand Central Terminal and I watched her walk down the platform.

Sarah went to Hawaii; I went on tour and we wrote to each other every week. We didn't actually know each other very well, as we'd spent only one night together, but I convinced myself that she was the perfect punk-rock vegan woman I'd always longed for. Her letters were brief to the point of being terse—but to me the brevity seemed confident and profound. She was in Hawaii, teaching environmental education to junior high school kids, learning to surf, and going on nature hikes every weekend. She sent me pictures with her letters, radiant pictures where she was tan and freckled, smiling on the beach in Kauai. And I swooned.

I sent her pictures with my letters: me onstage in the UK jumping off my keyboard or lost in a German airport. I wrote that I missed her and described how hard it was to be a straight-edge vegan on tour. And she swooned.

My letters got longer and longer—even though I barely knew her I felt like I'd finally found my soul mate.

In November I was going on tour with Aphex Twin and Orbital. At the end of the tour I was scheduled to play a show in Japan before heading back to New York. Before the tour started I called Sarah from a hotel room in Köln, Germany, at six a.m. She picked up the phone in Hawaii, where it was six p.m.

"So I have an idea," I said. "What if I came to Hawaii after the tour ends?"

"That would be great," she said.

"Then I have a show in Japan—we could go together?"

"Okay."

"The tour ends in November, so I'll come around November twentieth?"

"Great," she said. "And I wanted to let you know: I'm moving back to the East Coast in December."

"Really?" And then I said without thinking: "Should we move in together?"

"We'll have a vegan apartment in New York?"

"Of course. Bye, Sarah!"

"Bye, Moby."

I hung up and started to panic. What had I done? I didn't really know Sarah, since we'd spent only one night together. I remembered that she was a vegan and a punk rocker and an environmental-education teacher, and I calmed down a bit: this was the right decision. I was an adult and I'd never actually lived with a girlfriend, but living with girlfriends was what adults did. And I had decided that she and I were soul mates even if we'd spent less than fifteen hours together.

I lay down on the twin bed in my German hotel room and tried to sleep, but I was too afraid and excited, so I just watched the wan morning light coming through the curtains.

I flew back to the States for the tour with Aphex Twin and Orbital, and from the first day it was disappointing. I wanted to like Aphex Twin, because I loved his records. But he rarely spoke to anyone, and when he gave interviews he criticized me for playing guitar onstage and accused me of not being a true electronic musician. At the start of the tour we were all traveling together on the tour bus, but I couldn't sleep well so I started flying from show to show. He called me elitist in the press, when actually I just had crippling tour-bus-inspired insomnia. After an awkward and unhappy month the tour ended and I flew to Hawaii to meet Sarah.

When I got off the plane in Kauai Sarah ran up to me and embraced me, her skin smelling like salt and coconuts. We got into her car and drove down dark, winding Hawaiian roads.

"Everything smells like flowers," I said.

"It's mainly jasmine," she said.

"I can't believe I'm here."

She smiled.

"Have you seen any sharks?" I asked, looking at the moon over the ocean.

"Not yet," she said.

"And how's school?"

"Good," she said. We drove by a run-down hamburger stand and I waited for her to elaborate.

"Good?" I finally asked.

"Yeah, it's good."

We got to her rented house and I carried my luggage inside. "I rented us an apartment on Tenth Street," I told her. "It's really cute. It has a loft bed and a living room and a little room you could use as an office. And it faces south."

"Okay," she said.

"Also, it's right around the corner from two health-food stores and two blocks away from Angelica Kitchen."

Sarah said nothing.

"Is everything okay?" I asked. "You seem quiet tonight."

"No, I'm happy to see you," she said.

"Me too," I said, panicking.

The next day, we hiked to the Napali coast, found an empty beach, and swam naked in the surf. Afterward, we were lying in the sun, the sound of the waves like kettle drums at our feet. "You sure you want to leave all this?" I said.

"Yup," she said.

"I mean, this seems like the most beautiful place in the world," I said.

She said nothing.

"The surf sounds like explosions," I said.

She said nothing.

"What's your favorite place here?" I asked.

"The beach near the school."

"Oh, why's that?"

"I don't know," she said. "I just like it."

We hiked back to her car and drove to her house, listening to a techno compilation in her cassette deck—and not talking. "Do you like dance music?" I asked.

"Yeah," she said.

"A lot of my old punk-rock friends hate it," I said.

She said nothing.

"I kind of see dance music as being like punk rock, though," I pontificated. "I mean, it doesn't sound like punk rock, but the spirit's the same."

She said nothing, so we sat and listened to the cassette as we drove past waterfalls and palm trees.

The next day we woke up, had a quiet breakfast outside, and headed to the Lihue airport. "The world's quickest Hawaii vacation—forty-eight hours," I said. When she didn't reply, I changed the subject. "Are you sure you're all set to leave?"

"I packed up my books and clothes and sent them to Connecticut before you got here," she said.

"I can't believe we're moving in together," I said. I looked out of her kitchen window, where the palm trees were swaying gently in the wind.

"Me too," she said.

We flew from Kauai to Honolulu and transferred to our nine-hour flight to Tokyo. Three hours after we took off everyone on the plane was asleep. I was reading a book of Flannery O'Connor stories, and Sarah was reading a biology textbook.

"Sarah," I whispered.

"Yes, Mobe?"

"Have you ever had sex on a plane?"

"No."

"Me neither," I said. "We should."

She smiled. "Okay."

"You go to the bathroom. I'll come in a few minutes and knock twice."

"Really?"

"We'll join the mile-high club."

She got up and went to the bathroom. After two minutes I walked to the bathroom and knocked twice, quietly. She opened the door and I squeezed into the bathroom with her.

"How should we do this?" she asked.

"I could sit on the toilet," I suggested.

"Eww, it's gross."

"Standing?"

We pulled down our pants and had perfunctory sex standing up in the tiny airplane bathroom. After a few minutes we finished and leaned against the wall, breathless and sweaty. "Now we're mile-high club members," I said.

Sarah pulled up her pants and said nothing.

"Was that weird?" I asked.

"No," she said, opening the door and walking back to her seat. I left a minute later and sat down next to her.

"Good night, Mo," she said, closing her eyes.

"Good night," I said, taking her hand.

She pulled it away. "I can't hold hands and fall asleep," she said.

"Okay," I said. I tried to read my book, but I was freaking out. I was moving into an apartment with a woman who didn't talk and didn't like to hold hands. Talking was how I connected with people—it was like dancing for people who didn't know how to dance.

Maybe over time Sarah would get more comfortable and open up and start talking. Or maybe I could learn to be in a relationship without conversation. Or maybe I was making a huge mistake. I closed my eyes and panicked as we hurtled toward Tokyo, flying over the dark Pacific.

We landed at Narita; the local promoter was waiting for us after customs. He was an Australian club promoter who had moved to Japan to teach English as a second language three years ago but had started promoting raves instead. As we got in the taxi, he said, "Tonight's show is sponsored by NKTV, a big Japanese TV company."

"Wait," I said. "Tonight's show?"

"Sure," he said. "That's why you're here."

"I thought the show was tomorrow."

"No, today, November twenty-third."

"But today's the twenty-second."

"Mate, you flew over the dateline. It's the twenty-third."

I blinked. "When am I on?"

"Three hours," he said, and grinned.

After ninety minutes in the cab we walked into a disco full of Japanese club kids waving multicolored fans. "Why are they waving fans?" I shouted over the techno.

"Oh, it started a few months ago. They all do it now," the promoter said. He showed us to the small red dressing room behind the stage.

After he left, I told Sarah, "I can't believe I'm playing tonight."

She said nothing.

"So, I forgot to ask you, are you okay playing keyboards?"

"What?"

"To get your plane ticket, I had to say that you were in my band."

"You want me to play keyboards? Onstage? I don't know how to play keyboards."

"No, you just have to pretend. All the keyboard parts are on tape."

"I guess so," she said.

"Thanks. It was the only way I could get the promoter to pay for your ticket. It should be fun. You can jump around and play fake keyboards."

"I'm not going to jump around," she said.

The promoter escorted us to the side of the stage. Onstage were three new Roland synths, a brand-new Roland Octapad, and two brand-new microphones. "Do I get to keep the equipment?" I asked him.

"Ha, nice one, mate," he said. "Nope, all loaners from Roland."

"It's nicer than the equipment I have at home."

"It's Japan, mate. You ready?"

I nodded. He walked onstage and announced, "From New York City, Moby!"

I ran onstage, while Sarah walked to her designated keyboard at the back of the stage. "Ah Ah" started with a roar of synths. I banged on the brand-new Octapad and ran around the stage, screaming into the microphone. One thousand Japanese ravers were dancing and waving multicolored fans like a school of rainbow fish. I looked at Sarah; she was staring at her keyboard, pretending to play. I ran over and smiled at her. She looked up at me and then looked down at her keyboard again.

"Go" started. I was about to yell "Go!" for the first time when I was tackled from behind. I fell face-first on the stage and squirmed around so I could see who was on top of me: it was a huge person dressed in a nine-foot-tall tree costume. Most of his body was covered by the costume, but through the branches, I could see his sweaty Caucasian face. I tried to get up, but he grabbed me and wrestled me back to the stage.

I looked over at the side of the stage: the promoter was smiling and dancing. He gave me both thumbs up. "I need to play!" I yelled at the guy in the tree costume. He smiled and pulled me back down. While I wrestled with the tree, I tried to get Sarah's attention. She was looking at me and the tree, bewildered. "Help!" I yelled. She kept pretending to play the keyboards.

The audience was waving their red and yellow and orange fans, assuming that my wrestling a tree was part of the show. Finally I broke free from the tree and ran to the promoter. "Get him off me!" I yelled as the tree person followed me across the stage to wrestle me again.

"That's Chaz, mate!" the promoter yelled. "He does this to everyone!"

"Get him to stop!"

The promoter looked hurt and disappointed. "Chaz!" he yelled.

"Cut it out!" Chaz the tree person ran over to me and gave me a big hug. Then he jumped into the audience, dancing with the Japanese ravers waving fans.

After the show Sarah and I were recovering backstage when the promoter came in, looking a little sheepish.

"What was that?" I asked.

"The tree guy?"

"Yeah."

"Oh, he started doing that and the audience loves it," he said.

"And why you didn't tell me before?"

"I didn't tell you?"

Sarah and I went to our hotel and tried and failed to have sex in a tiny Japanese bathtub. The next day we flew thirteen hours to JFK.

On the flight Sarah read biology textbooks and I read science fiction. At one point I looked over at her: the sun was coming through the window, kissing her book and her hair. She looked so earnest and pretty as she turned the pages of her textbook.

On the good side, I thought, *she's a vegan and an environmentalist and sober and a punk rocker.*

On the bad side, I thought, *she doesn't like to talk.*

But maybe it would change. We would live together in our sunny apartment on Tenth Street and go to vegan restaurants and adopt a dog. She would open up and talk to me for hours about biology and environmentalism and old punk-rock records and we would fall in love and enjoy life together.

"I'm happy, Sarah," I said, taking her hand in the sunlight.

"I'm reading something important," she said, taking her hand back and turning away from me.

31

DENTAL FLOSS

Sarah and I had been living together in a drug-infested area of Tenth Street for four months. Our communication had been stilted at the beginning, and after we moved in together it had deteriorated even further. She was comfortable not talking. And I was not. I loved to talk. Talking was how I connected with my friends and my family. Without talking I felt lost and unseen.

Maybe Sarah was enlightened and didn't need to fill empty spaces with chattering conversation. Or maybe she was just very quiet. We'd sit across from each other at our black, wooden breakfast table and I'd ask her questions that started with the word "so."

"So," I'd say, putting apple butter on a piece of toast, "you're working today?"

"Yes."

I'd slowly refill our cups with green tea.

"So how is work going?"

"Fine."

I'd study the toast and think of other questions I could ask that started with the word "so."

So do you think the International Monetary Fund should operate with more transparency?

So are you more of a fan of Wittgenstein's Tractatus *or his Blue and Brown Books?*

So do you know this lack of communication is killing me?

I'd keep studying the toast, or look out the window, and eventually our quiet breakfast would end. We'd say good-bye and I'd head to my studio, where I'd sit in my broken studio chair and panic and try to write music.

What was I doing? I'd hoped that over time Sarah would open up and talk more, but now she was talking even less. I wanted our relationship to work. I wanted to be a grown-up who lived with his loving, kind, beautiful vegan punk-rock girlfriend. I couldn't admit defeat and accept that I was miserable and our relationship was dying a slow death. I spent long hours in the studio and did everything I could to avoid going home. The less time Sarah and I spent talking, the more time I had to work on music or to walk Walnut, the dog we had adopted from an animal shelter uptown.

Walnut was the world's sweetest little pit bull. She was a lot smaller than most pit bulls, and she had delicate almond-shaped eyes that always seemed innocent and kind. She was white and brown, and unfailingly happy. Tenth Street between First and Second Avenues, where we lived, was a notorious drug block, the sidewalks lined with crack and heroin dealers in giant black down jackets. Every day when I took Walnut to the dog park in Tompkins Square she and I would walk past the menacing drug dealers. They would spend the day looking as tough as possible, intimidating everyone who walked by. When I walked past them alone I would get the barest of nods from them—but when I walked by with Walnut they turned into happy little boys.

"Hey, it's Walnut! Hi, Walnut!" And Walnut would get excited, run over to them, and give them little dog kisses. The super-tough drug dealers would laugh and pet her and ask the same questions every time: "Is she a pit?" "She's pretty small for a pit, right?" "Is she a pit puppy?" "What's she crossed with—beagle?" And then we'd walk away and the dealers would say, "See you later, Walnut!" The dog run we went to in Tompkins Square Park was an egalitarian field of dirt in the middle of the park. The junkies would bring their dogs, the queens would bring their dogs, the stockbrokers would bring their dogs, the old ladies would bring their dogs, the homeless punk rockers would bring their dogs. The dogs would run around like speedy rubber balls, sniffing butts and digging holes and chasing each other in circles. The humans generally kept to themselves, their heads buried in newspapers, sometimes having shy dog-centric conversations with each other.

On a rainy day in March the dog park was mostly empty: just me and Walnut and a Latino gangbanger and his damp pit bull. I sat on a cold bench and Walnut sat next to me. "Come on, Walnut," I said. "Run around, go poop." But Walnut just wanted to sit next to me and stare at the empty, muddy dog park. "Don't you want to go play with the pit bull?" I asked.

Walnut stared up at me, as if to say, "Really? Do I want to play with the giant psychopathic pit bull that eats glass for breakfast? Best-case scenario, I get cold and muddy and the pit bull ignores me. Worst-case scenario, I get slowly eaten by that monster. So no, Moby, I don't want to go play in the cold mud with the pit bull."

I gave up and reattached Walnut's leash. We walked back along East Ninth Street. When we reached First Avenue, Walnut finally decided that she wanted to poop. In the 1970s New York City had passed "curb your dog" laws, compelling people to pick up and dispose of their dogs' poop. And somehow these laws had worked. Most dog owners were prepared and responsible, bringing plastic poop bags with them whenever they went walking with their dogs. I preferred to trust fate, assuming that the universe would provide an old plastic bag or napkins from a nearby garbage can with which I could pick up Walnut's poop.

Walnut did her "walk around in a circle to find the perfect spot on the sidewalk on which to poop" dance. I watched, mildly annoyed, as it was early March, cold, and drizzling, and I was being slowly killed in a soul-destroying relationship. "Come on, Walnut," I said, "poop."

Walnut started pooping. Then she stopped, looking startled. And then she started to run in circles, confused and scared. I looked and saw the problem: somehow she had eaten dental floss, and her poop was dangling from her butt, attached by a long piece of floss. She kept trying to get away from her poop, but the floss held firm.

I laughed, assuming the poop would soon fall out and we could continue our walk back to our home and my joyless relationship. Then I realized the poop wasn't going anywhere: it was stuck. Poor Walnut was terrified and didn't understand why she was being attacked by her poop.

Shit, I thought, without intending any wordplay. I needed to help Walnut, but I didn't really want to reach behind her and grab a handful of poop and dental floss. I needed a tool of some kind. In the nearest garbage can, I found a greasy plastic fork in a Styrofoam box from a local fried-chicken restaurant. "Hold on," I told Walnut, and used the fork to try to pry the poop out of her butt. And she bit me.

"What?" I said, more offended than hurt. Walnut looked chastened and scared. So I calmed her down, went to work with the fork, and eventually managed to dislodge the poop and floss. When the job was done I sat next to her on the curb and took stock of the situation. I had chicken grease and dog poop on my hand. I was cold. I was wet. I was in a loveless relationship. And my sweet beautiful dog had just bitten me.

"Is this my life?" I asked Walnut. She looked at me, confused, but mostly grateful that the poop was no longer attacking her butt. I found a dirty napkin; threw away the poop, floss, and fork; and walked home with little Walnut in the rain.

32

LEMON ZINGER

B ut it's only a three-second sample," I said.

"I know," Barry said, "but that's what they want."

I had written a rave anthem that sounded like a hundred buildings falling down and being built at the same time. It sounded like a herd of ecstatic elephants. It was huge and joyful and full of longing. I had visions of this song shaking the ravers out of their ketamine-induced stupors and reminding them that techno could be joyful. That dance music could be explosive and beautiful, not just background music for teenagers in giant pants passed out on dance floors.

This new song I'd written was based on a perfect vocal sample from an obscure disco song from the late seventies. I loved the way the vocal sample sounded, so I decided to do the right thing and get permission to use it.

After months of legal rancor, I had finally left Instinct and signed with Mute and Elektra, and now I was making my first real album. Musicians who had real record deals had to do the right thing and get permission to use samples. Which I supported in theory, but in this case, the people who owned the recording from which I'd taken the sample had absurd ideas about what their sample was worth.

"Let me try to understand," I said to Barry, who, along with his partner Marci, was managing my career in the United States. "The sample is three seconds long, but they want fifty percent of the recording, seventy-five percent of the publishing, and an advance of fifty thousand dollars?"

"Yes. They originally wanted one hundred percent of the publishing and an advance of seventy-five thousand dollars, but we talked them down," he said.

I couldn't believe it. I had my huge beautiful rave anthem, and it was being taken away from me. Ironically, it was being taken away from me by the people who'd made the sample that I was trying to take. I appreciated the irony, but I was still panicking. "I can't afford to pay that," I said. "And I can't give up seventy-five percent of the publishing. That's nuts."

"Can you find a different sample?" Barry asked.

I hated to admit it, but I probably could. But this vocal sample was so beautiful and it worked so perfectly. It took my big beautiful anthem and it made it bigger. And more beautiful. "I can try," I said, resigned and sad at being unable to successfully use someone else's sample.

I spent the rest of the day going through my record collection, trying to find better samples. Hour after hour I listened to my old disco and funk and R & B records, trying to find the vocal sample that would replace the current sample. Nothing worked. A few things weren't terrible, but almost everything just sounded arbitrary and flat. By the end of the day I was despondent. I sat in my broken studio chair in front of my studio computer.

I'd found my studio chair in the garbage in front of my studio building. Every week I'd wander around the neighborhood, looking for interesting things that people had thrown away. In the last few years I'd found an old wooden ladder, three Japanese shoji screens, a table that might have been designed by Ray and Charles Eames, a ceramic bulldog statue with only one ear, a collection of Philip K. Dick books, and this broken, squeaky office chair. The seat was busted and it squeaked when it rolled, but it had been free and was almost comfortable.

I stared at the fax machine. Maybe a magic fax would appear: "Good news! They've decided they love the song and they'll let you use the sample for free!" But it stayed stubbornly quiet. I looked at the giant pile of vinyl stacked next to my turntable. All of those records, all of those amazing singers and writers, and I couldn't find a single thing to steal.

The phone rang. "Any luck?" It was Barry.

"No luck," I said. "Maybe it could be an instrumental?"

"I met with an Israeli singer," he told me. "She'd like to come by and try to sing on the song. Would tomorrow be okay?"

"Sure. What's her name?"

"Myim Rose. She's sung on a bunch of house records for Strictly Rhythm, I think."

"Okay, noon here tomorrow?"

"Sounds good. I'll call her now."

Maybe this Israeli singer would save my song. I listened to it again without the sample to see what was left. It had the lunatic and propulsive breakbeats and the giant strings and the huge sawtooth synth parts. It had the Juno-106 sub-bass. It had the insistent 4/4 Roland TR-909 kick. With the vocal sample it had been an A or an A+, but without the vocal sample it was, charitably, a B.

I turned off my equipment and stood in my little studio. It was eight p.m. on a beautiful summer night, and the orange light of the setting sun was slanting through my window. I locked the door and headed home to Walnut and Sarah on Tenth Street, filled with dread at the thought of another quiet, awkward night with Sarah. But underlying that was anticipation at the prospect of seeing Walnut. I'd get home and Sarah would be reading on the futon. She'd say, "Hi, Mobe," and get back to her book. Walnut, on the other hand, would be tearing around the kitchen in tiny circles, a little bundle of constant pit bull joy.

When Myim arrived at my studio the next day she clasped both my hands and beamed, and instantly made me feel less anxious about my terrible relationship and my problematic disco sample. Myim was short and blond and radiated kindness.

"So you've done some records with Strictly Rhythm?" I asked as she walked in.

"Well, no," she said. "But I'd like to."

"And you're Israeli?"

She laughed. "No, I was born in Washington Heights."

Apparently Barry had been confused. But Myim was here and we were both enthusiastic. I was ready to record her vocals and take my beloved-but-unusable disco sample behind the woodshed and put it out of its misery. "Can I get you some tea or some water?" I asked.

"Sure, I'd love some tea and some water," she said with a smile.

"Both? Or tea with water?"

She laughed merrily. "Both would be good, thanks." I turned on my hot plate and poured water into the little saucepan I kept in my studio for making tea and oatmeal.

"Did Barry play you the song?" I asked.

"Yeah. I really like it."

"Well, I need to replace the vocal sample. Do you want to give it a try?"

"Can you play it again?"

I hit "play" on my Alesis sequencer. The song started with break-beats and Koji Banton's raga samples. Then the keyboards came in, sounding emptier now that they weren't supporting any vocals.

"Oh, the water's boiling," she said.

I turned down the volume on the mixer. "Do you want green tea or herbal?" I asked.

"What herbal tea do you have?" she asked.

"Let me see," I said. "I have Lemon Zinger and Red Zinger and kava and valerian and hibiscus and peppermint." She settled on hibiscus; I let the teabag steep in a *Star Trek* mug that Paul had given me for Christmas last year. Myim sat on a milk crate while I sat in the broken studio chair. I started the track again at the beginning. "I've got the microphone set up," I said. "Do you want to try some ideas?"

"Do you have headphones?"

"Only one pair. You can wear them and I'll just keep the speakers really quiet so I can hear a little bit."

She stood in front of my SM57 microphone and ad-libbed some vocals so I could get a level. "I'm not very good at recording vocals," I said sheepishly.

"Don't worry, it sounds fine," she said kindly.

"Maybe for the first pass you could just sing the sample that we're replacing," I said.

She sang the sample, but it just wasn't the same. She had a good voice, but she wasn't a black disco diva from 1979.

"That sounds good," I said, "but let's try some new ideas." For the next twenty minutes we tried new vocal ideas. Some almost worked, most didn't.

"Do you think one of those will work?" she asked. She was visibly tired, and I could hear her voice was starting to break.

I thought about it. "Possibly," I said. "But I have one last idea. I keep thinking of a really simple disco vocal, just three notes." I sang it for her. "Do you think you could try that?"

"It's high, but I can try." And she sang the short, simple melody. There was something to it. It was at the top of her range, and she was straining, but somehow it worked. "Do you have any ideas for lyrics?" she asked.

"How about something really disco, like 'I'm, feeling so real'?"

"Okay, let me try." And at the top of her range, she sang, "I'm, feeling so real."

"That sounds good. Does it feel okay?"

"My voice is about to break, but I think I can do it a few times," she said. I hit "record" on the sampler and she belted it out a few times. The first couple of times her voice cracked on "real," which was just outside of her range.

"It sounds good," I told her. "But let's do it again, and this time close your eyes. Imagine you're in a field somewhere. It's dawn, the sun is coming up, and you're singing to fifty thousand ravers."

She smiled. "Okay, let's try it." The keyboards kicked in, she sang, "I'm feeling so real," and it was perfect. Then she sang it again, and it was even more perfect. Then a third time, and it was still perfect.

"How was that?" she asked.

"It was great!" I said, beaming. "I think I got it. Now I just have to see how it works."

She sat down on the milk crates and drank some hibiscus tea while I edited her vocals. "It's so funny," she said. "I ended up in Barry's office yesterday somehow, and he asked me if I could sing disco samples. I said yes, and here I am, singing disco samples."

"Well," I said, "inventing disco samples."

She finished her tea. "I have to get uptown for a meeting," she said. "Are you sure you got it? I could do it again."

"No, it's great," I told her. She hugged me and walked down the stairs. I went back to working on Myim's "feeling so real" vocals. All the takes were good, but the third one was the most emotional. Her voice was on the edge of breaking when she hit the highest note. It sounded vulnerable and celebratory, and the slight distortion from the microphone sounded great. I edited the front and the back of the sample and triggered it with my keyboard.

I laid Myim's vocal over the keyboards, and it worked. I added the drums and the sub-bass and the strings, and it worked even more. I looped the whole chorus, jumped up, and started dancing around my studio while the track played. I was pretty sure the people walking by on Mott Street could hear me singing along badly with my own track; I didn't care. I'd lost my original sample and found something better. Actually, I hadn't just found something better—I'd written something better.

I picked up the cheap phone attached to my fax machine and called Barry to play him the track. "Barry, listen!" I said, and held the phone up to the speaker.

"It sounds great!" he said. "So Myim worked out?"

"Yes, she was great!"

"Okay, go finish it. I'll talk to you tomorrow."

I jumped around my studio and listened to the whole track from start to finish, reliving the magic moment when Myim had been both in my tiny studio with the hot plate in the corner and with her eyes closed at a rave in front of fifty thousand people at dawn.

33

CRACKS BETWEEN THE FLOORBOARDS

S arah and I had nothing to talk about in New York, so we went upstate for the day. It quickly became obvious we had just as little to talk about there.

We found a lake near Bedford, New York, and went hiking. The sun was shining and Walnut was happy, running around and sniffing everything. Sarah and I talked about Walnut and the heat. After five minutes we had exhausted our topics of conversation, so we walked under the trees in silence, Walnut happily running around our legs.

At some point as we walked around the lake a deer tick found its way onto my skin and bit me. I felt nothing, since the tick was the size of a stunted poppy seed. But when it bit me it passed spirochetes from its filthy deer-tick mouth to my blood. And the enthusiastic spirochetes spread through my body. A week later I had Lyme disease and a 104-degree fever.

It was August in New York City, which meant it was 95 degrees outside. Sarah and I were deep environmentalists who didn't believe in air-conditioning, so it was 100 degrees in our apartment. I'd wake up in the morning, deliriously recognize that I still had a fever, stagger to the old futon in the living room, and lie there, sick and sweating. Walnut would hop up on the futon next to me, look at me with pity, and fall asleep as fire engines drove screaming in the heat past our window.

After five days of fever I decided to go the doctor. I was a left-wing vegan raver punk rocker, so rather than go to a Western doctor I decided to go to a traditional Chinese medicine practitioner. I got dressed and managed to get out of our building. Yesterday had been hot; today was hotter. The sky was the sickly color of spoiled milk and the air felt like the inside of a vinyl glove.

I took a taxi to Chinatown and walked up the three flights to Dr. Lee's office. The receptionist was an elderly Chinese woman sitting under a lithograph of Chinese mountains. There was a good-luck ceramic cat on the desk next to her typewriter, and framed calligraphy on the walls of the waiting room. Next to my seat was a small statue of a Chinese peasant standing by a broken waterwheel and a pine shrub. After five minutes she escorted me into a tiny room with a small metal bed, where I sat and waited some more. Ten minutes later a young Asian man in running shorts, sneakers, and a sweaty polo shirt came in.

"Mr. Hall?" he said with a preppy Massachusetts accent. "I'm Dr. Lee."

I'd expected a sixty-five-year-old man in a white coat. This guy was younger than me and smelled like runner's sweat and cheap cologne.

"So what's the problem?" he asked, wiping his brow with his shirt.

"I have a fever that won't go away. But it's August, so how can I be sick?"

He chuckled. "You have summer flu. Happens all the time." He felt the glands in my throat, peered in my mouth, and checked my pulse. "Okay, I'll give you some pills. You'll be fine soon."

"Oh, I'm a vegan. Do the pills have animal products in them?"

He considered this. "Well, they have deer antler in them. Is that vegan?"

"No, I can't take pills with deer antler in them."

He nodded. "Okay, I'll give you other pills. No deer antler." He went to a cabinet and opened a big container, shaking out a bunch of gray pills into a bag. "Here. Take these three times a day, Mr. Hall, you'll be fine."

Four days later my fever was still at 104. I was lying immobile on the futon with Walnut curled up next to me. "Shit, I'm really sick, Walnut," I said.

Walnut just looked at me, as if to say, "I know. I'm sorry. What can I do?"

"You're doing enough, Walnut. Thanks." I fell asleep on the futon, the fan blowing hot air on my skin. I was woken by the phone ringing.

"Hello?" I croaked.

"Hi, Moby, it's Barry. How are you feeling?"

"I'm really sick."

"I'm so sorry. I don't want to bother you, but I'm calling because the head mastering engineer at Western-Young can master your record tomorrow. He had a cancellation and can fit you in."

The chief mastering engineer at Western-Young was one of the most successful mastering engineers in New York, and I'd been told he didn't have an opening for months. "Okay, great, I'll be there," I said. I hung up and passed out on the futon.

Again I was woken up by the phone ringing. "Hi, Mobe." It was Sarah. "I'm going out to dinner after work—can you walk Walnut?"

"Sarah, I'm really sick," I said.

She exhaled, annoyed. "All you have to do is walk her."

"Okay," I said, my eyelids burning with fever. "Good-bye."

She hung up without saying good-bye. Sarah didn't like sick people. When we first started dating I'd gotten the flu and she'd acted like Leni Riefenstahl, cold and clinical and disappointed in my exhibition of human frailty.

There were no more phone calls, so I slept through the day. At dusk I walked Walnut for five minutes—and then collapsed back onto the futon.

The next day I woke up in the heat and Sarah had already left for work. I didn't even remember her coming in the night before; I had been passed out from whatever illness was killing me.

"Hi, Walnut," I said as I walked into the kitchen. Walnut was lying on the kitchen floor. "Walnut, are you okay?" She looked up at me and wagged her tail but stayed on the floor. I brought Walnut her favorite toy, a green stuffed squid. She ignored it and closed her eyes. "Okay, Walnut, I need to get dressed and go out. I'll be back."

I stood in the shower. The hot water was too hot on my fevered skin, and the cold water burned. I leaned against the shower wall and closed my eyes. But there was a ray of hopeful light: I was going to master my album with the chief engineer at Western-Young. He would take my poorly mixed record and make it amazing. I was sure of it. He was going to save my record and save me. Maybe he'd even give me the courage to end my loveless relationship.

I toweled off, got dressed, and sat on the futon, trying to gather my strength. "Walnut, are you okay?" I called. She walked slowly to the futon and looked up at me. I lifted her up onto the futon, and she closed her eyes. "I'll be back in a few hours, Walnut," I told her.

I got in a taxi, looked out the window as it headed uptown, and almost threw up. The world was moving too fast; it was too hot; I was too sick. August is the cruelest month in New York, mouth-breathing on you with its heavy, fetid air.

When I got to the mastering studio in midtown the receptionist told me, "Go on in, your engineer will be here soon." I sat in the back of the mastering studio on a big black leather couch, looking at the platinum records on the walls.

"Hey! Hi! You Moby?"

I opened my eyes. A short, skinny wild-eyed man with long stringy hair was standing in front of me, smiling manically.

"Hi, are you the engineer?" I asked.

"I am! Hey, you want coffee? Tea? Beer? You want anything? I can get you anything you want, Moby! You have the tapes for me? I'm going to nail this! It's going to pump!"

I wondered why he was talking so much and so loud and so fast. "Maybe some water?" I said.

He jumped up and ran out of the room. "I'll get you some water!"

Five minutes passed before he returned. "Here's your water!" he said, wiping his nose.

Oh. Now I understood: he was on coke. I was sober and naïve, but I knew that when someone talked a mile a minute, disappeared for five minutes, and came back wiping his nose, he was on coke.

He sat down in front of his equipment and spun around on his chair. "Okay, let's do this! I'm going to make this pump!"

"Well, some of the tracks are dance tracks," I said meekly from the black leather couch. "But there are a lot of quiet songs, too."

He wasn't listening to me—he was setting up his equipment and humming to himself.

"Moby, you like to party?" he asked.

"No thanks, I'm sober."

He ignored me and went back to his equipment.

"Where should we start? Let's do this! I'm pumped, Moby, are you pumped?" he yelled.

I felt like I was sinking further and further into the couch. "I'm excited," I said weakly. "Thank you for taking the time to master my record."

"Ha!" he said. "Do you want another water? I'm going to go get a water!" He bolted out of the room. I closed my eyes. They were getting hotter. I thought of Walnut passed out on my old futon, just like me, wanting to pass out on this crappy black leather couch. Poor Walnut. Poor me.

Five minutes passed, and the engineer returned. "Here's your water!" he yelled, handing me a bottle of Poland Spring that I put next to the other full bottle of Poland Spring.

"First track! 'Feeling So Real'! I like that! Good name!" He hit "play," and I'd never heard music so loud. He added low end and he added high end. Then he added more high end. He stopped it, rewound it, and played it again, somehow making it even louder. He added more low end and more high end.

Then he shouted, "We got it! It's pumping! Right? You like it?" He spun around in his chair, staring at me with his wild eyes.

"Sounds good," I said cautiously, not sure if it sounded good or bad or better or worse. I just knew it was loud.

"Okay! Let's print it!"

I drank my water and blinked my hot eyelids, watching the room swim in front of me.

This went on for every track on the record. He would listen at ear-splitting levels, add low end, add high end, run out of the room to do more coke, come back, add low end, add high end, and yell at me about the music "pumping!" even for the quiet songs without drums, like "When It's Cold I'd Like To Die." Three hours later the record was mastered.

"We're done! Moby, we're done!" he yelled, jumping out of his chair. "Great working with you, Moby! Great day! This shit is pumping!" he said, grabbing my hand and shaking it vigorously.

"Thanks again," I said. "I'm looking forward to hearing it at home."

"We'll send a CD today! Let me know what you think! I think it's pumping! Totally pumping!"

"Okay, talk to you soon," I said, stumbling through the door and back to the lobby. I was confused. I'd never mastered an album before—was this how it happened? Had the mastering engineer worked his magic? Or did it just sound like loud music as mastered by a crazy person on coke?

When I stepped outside the heat hit me like a giant fist. I wanted to lie down on the sidewalk and die. But Walnut was at home and I needed to take care of her. I took a cab to my apartment, stepped inside the lobby, and was hit by a smell that was a cross between a sewer and a bucket of rotten seafood. I walked upstairs, and the smell got stronger.

Oh no.

I made it to our apartment door: the stench was coming from inside.

Oh no no, really oh no. I opened the door and gagged.

Walnut had thrown up and had diarrhea. Everywhere. The floors were covered with yellow vomit and diarrhea, all cooking in the hundred-degree heat.

"Walnut? Walnut?" I asked. I walked in, unavoidably stepping in the ubiquitous vomit and diarrhea.

I found Walnut in the bathroom, lying on the tiles, trying to get cool. She looked past me, her eyes unfocused.

I had two options. Option number one was to leave, lock the door, and never come back. Leave my terrible relationship and this unair-conditioned apartment filled with dog vomit and diarrhea. It was tempting, but Walnut was here and I loved her and she was sick.

So option number two: take care of Walnut. I picked her up and carried her down to the street, where I flagged a cab. "Can I bring my dog in the cab?" I asked.

"No dogs in cab," the driver said.

"I'll give you fifty dollars," I said.

He weighed the offer. "Okay. But no mess!"

We drove up First Avenue to the animal hospital on Ninetieth Street, and I rushed Walnut into the emergency room.

"My dog is passed out and she threw up and had diarrhea every-where," I said to the receptionist behind the Plexiglas window.

"Have a seat," she said.

I sat on a brown vinyl couch with Walnut on my lap, saying com-forting things to her, and me, like "It'll be okay," over and over again.

A female African-American vet came out, looked at Walnut, and said, "Who's this?"

"Walnut," I said.

"Did she get her parvo vaccination?" she asked.

"What's that?"

She shook her head. "Okay, so she has parvo. Just to let you know, sir, she might die."

"What's parvo?"

"It's a virus that dogs get from other dogs. It has a fifty percent mor-tality rate. Here, let me take her." She picked up Walnut and carried her through metal swinging doors, leaving me with a clipboard and a bunch of forms.

I left Walnut in the hospital's care and took a taxi home. The smell had gotten worse. I got sponges from under the sink and spent two hours mopping up vomit and diarrhea. It was under the fridge and on the futon. It was even in the cracks between the floorboards.

While I was rinsing out a diarrhea-soaked sponge in the bathroom sink the phone rang and the answering machine picked up: "Hey, Mobe, it's Sarah. I'm headed out after work. Can you walk Walnut again?"

I wanted to pick up the phone and say, calmly, "I can't walk Walnut because she's dying uptown. There's vomit and diarrhea everywhere. I have a one-hundred-four-degree fever and I just spent the day with a coke addict who probably ruined my album."

But I stood at the sink with the sponge in my hand and listened to Sarah's voice until a fire truck went by, the sound of the siren filling the apartment. Sometimes when fire trucks went by Walnut would howl along with the sirens. Sometimes she'd try to chase the emergency lights as they bounced on the walls and ceiling of the apartment.

I sat on the corner of the futon where Walnut hadn't thrown up. My body was burning hot from fever and the air was hot and smelled like dog vomit. I thought of Walnut, sick and alone and terrified. Nothing was working. Everything was wrong.

34

DUST MOTES

Sarah and I had broken up and gotten back together and broken up and gotten back together. And then broken up. And then, for good measure, gotten back together.

We'd experimented with dating other people, which only led to jealousy and despair, mainly for me. In theory, the thought of her being with other people had seemed fine. We ate in multiple restaurants and watched multiple TV shows, so why not date multiple people? But the first night she spent at another man's apartment made me want to rip my face off. I sat alone all night in our apartment and the jealousy sat with me, a leering old demon with waxy yellow skin.

At midnight I realized that Sarah wasn't coming home. I tried to sleep or write or watch TV, but the jealousy kept whispering to me: "Do you think they're having sex now? Or maybe they're finished and his semen is drying on her breasts? I'm sure she's laughing with him about how good it is to finally have sex with a real man." I tried to wave the jealousy away, and it smiled, its pale skin stretched around its long teeth. "You want me to leave? Ha, you invited me here, you idiot."

So jealousy and I sat, wide awake, until seven a.m., when Sarah came home smelling like sex and someone else's sheets. I cried and we yelled and decided to date exclusively one more time and see if we could somehow make things work. She promised to communicate more and I promised to be more relaxed. Which for both of us was akin to Aesop's scorpion promising not to be a scorpion.

Things hadn't gotten better between us, so I was spending as much time as I could in my studio. It felt small and safe and calm, whereas home felt like a claustrophobic and horrifying Skinner box.

I was starting all our conversations with the word "so" again: "So . . . how was work?" "So . . . do you want to have spaghetti tonight?" "So . . . would you do me a favor and kill me in my sleep so I can be spared the pain of waking up in this terrible relationship?"

After listening to the masters that had been done for my album I realized that, as much as I wanted it to be, my album wasn't finished. Some of the songs needed more work, and I needed to record some new songs. This was going to be my first real album, and I wanted it to be a lifeboat for everything that I'd always wanted to put on an album. I wanted it to be a joyful rave that was also a night in a punk-rock club that ended with delicacy and beauty, leaving you crying under a sky full of stars.

So day after day and night after night I went to work in my tiny studio on Mott Street, avoiding Sarah and trying to finish an album that I might love. I spent a lot of time in my studio sitting at the window, looking out at the empty lot across the street. This lot had been vacant for years, and it was an accidental piece of land art, something that Michael Heizer or Robert Smithson might have made. Isolated by a chain-link fence, the undisturbed lot was filled with native trees and weeds and rats and garbage. Because it was neglected it was one of the only spots in lower Manhattan that was entropic and seasonal. In the summer it was an explosion of locust trees and weeds. By December the trees had stoically dropped their leaves and the brick tenement walls on either side of the lot were dark and brown from months of rain.

The sun was setting through the winter clouds, the last rays of sideways light casting long shadows and turning my studio into a Lower East Side Stonehenge. I was working on a piece of quiet classical music, not knowing if it would find its way onto the album. Perched carefully on my studio chair—it now squeaked like a bag of scared mice if I moved around too much—I was working on a cheap Yamaha keyboard set up on a plywood table next to a computer monitor.

I played a simple piano arpeggio in A minor, recorded it, and looped it. Then I listened to its three simple notes, over and over, wondering what I could or should add to it.

I overlaid a second piano part in C major, adding a hopeful counterpoint to the plaintive A-minor arpeggio. Now I had two delicate piano loops bouncing around with each other. I wondered: *Should this become a dance track? Should I add a kick drum, a bass line, and high hats, and make it something a DJ could play at three a.m.?* But the way the sadness of the A-minor arpeggio pulled against the optimism of the C-major arpeggio made me want to keep it simple. Adding drums felt almost heretical.

I turned on an old string synthesizer and played a long, slow cello part under the arpeggio. Then I added some sevenths and thirds to the cello part. My brain started tingling, telling me, *This is good, keep going, Moby.* I wanted to add some high string parts, almost filigreed, so I turned on another string synthesizer, took the C-major arpeggio, and played it with high violins, creating something delicate but insistent. I didn't want to anthropomorphize the parts I'd written, but it felt like I had two piano parts that were like two excited people: the polyphonous cello parts that were like slow-moving earth or water, and the filigreed violins that were naïve angels watching over everything. The light slanting through my window seemed palpably slower than it had thirty minutes earlier. I could see the dust motes floating in the fading sunlight and each dust mote seemed like its own quiet world.

I added some long orchestral chords, loosely following the cello parts. Then I added some more orchestral chords, filling out the areas that felt empty. It still needed drums—but not dance drums. I was sure now that I didn't want this to be a club track. I wanted it to be orchestral. I took a bass drum, a low tom, and two crash cymbals, and played them as an orchestral accent at the beginning of each measure. It was bombastic and harsh, so I added reverb to soften the drums and make them quieter.

Then I arranged the track. I let the whole piece start delicate and empty, with just the piano arpeggio. I added the orchestral elements, slowly letting the track build. In the middle I removed those elements one by one until there was just a delicate arpeggio and a plaintive, austere viola part. Then everything came back in.

While I listened to this arrangement I thought about God moving over the face of the waters, when the Earth was new, before there was land and before anything was alive. The spirit of God, full of prescience and omniscience, seeing the emptiness and expanse of the new world, aware of all that's there and all that's going to follow. The life that will come, and the death that will end each life. The trillions of creatures who will come out of this ocean, all wanting to live as long and as well as possible, resisting death until the end. All the life and death and longing and heartbreak and hope.

I listened to the music, put my head on the plywood table, and cried. Then I lay down on the floor and curled up underneath the table, listening to the sound of God moving over the empty oceans, following a sun that never stops rising and setting. I couldn't think of anything I could do to make the track better, so I decided to record it as it was. I didn't want to ruin it by overcomplicating it. I got up, found a tape, wrote "god moving over the face of the waters" on the label, put it in the tape recorder, and pressed "record," listening and crying with my head on the plywood.

35

SNAKES IN CAGES

Some of my raver friends from New York had moved to San Francisco, discovered alcohol, and become drunks. On New Year's Eve I'd DJed a rave in Los Angeles; now it was the first day of 1995, and I'd flown up to San Francisco to visit them.

My friends were all chewed up from New Year's Eve, so they'd gone to a bar to drink away their hangovers. Even though I had been sober for eight years I was happy to sit in a dirty vinyl booth in a dive bar, listening to Iggy Pop on the jukebox and watching my friends drinking cheap beer and whiskey.

My friend Joey was the ringleader. In 1993 he and his boyfriend had moved to San Francisco from New York to start a clothing company, and a bunch of their raver friends had followed them. In New York they had been happy ravers; in San Francisco they were happy drinkers.

I judged my friends. I claimed that I wasn't judgmental when it came to drinking and drugs, but I was. I felt evolved and sober. I sat in bars and laughed with my friends, but I was secretly self-satisfied, judging my friends for being sloppy drunks. I selectively forgot the few thousand times pre-sobriety when I'd been the sad drunk in the corner of a bar, listening to Hank Williams and blinking tears into my beer.

Before I'd gotten sober I'd loved dive bars. I'd loved the way they smelled, the ex-cons and ex-cops who hung out in them, the tautological and pointless bar stool conversations, and most of all, the cheap liquor served quietly and without judgment. I loved sitting down on a bar stool, happy and defeated, and handing my brain and body and soul over to a disinterested bartender and the warm gods of liquor.

Tonight we were in a windowless dive bar in the Mission, with thick cigarette smoke in the air and an alphabet of hepatitis in the toilets. The walls of the bar, dotted with old neon beer signs, might have been brown at some point, but now they were black. At nine p.m. my friends were on their third drink, talking about what they'd done on New Year's Eve. How many hits of ecstasy they'd taken, who they ended up going home with, who threw up on whom, what DJs they heard, what time they did or didn't go to sleep. I stood up to use the bathroom and find a pay phone. It was a new year, so I decided to call Sarah.

We were finally, officially broken up—she was living in a new apartment—but I wanted to be a good ex-boyfriend and wish her a happy New Year. I peeled myself off the sticky vinyl seat and found the pay phone on a wall by the toilets. I punched in my phone-card info and called Sarah's new apartment. It was midnight in New York, but I knew she'd be up. After three rings a man picked up the phone and said, "Hello?"

That was all I needed to hear. His "Hello?" told me that he and Sarah had been repeatedly having sex in the last twenty-four hours, that she was naked in bed at that moment, that they had been ridiculing me and my receding hairline, and that this new guy had made her realize that I was the worst sex partner she'd ever had. Whether or not any of that was true, I was acutely aware that I was alone and she was not.

I said nothing and hung up the phone. Then I walked over to the bar and calmly said, "A pint of Anchor Steam, please."

I took my pint of beer back to the booth, where my friends were talking loudly. I sat quietly, holding the glass and looking at the beige foam on top of the brown beer. The glass was cold and wet; it fit in my hand like an old, comfortable bowling pin.

I lifted the glass to my mouth, smelling the beer just an inch away from my nose, and I drank. My first drink after eight years of judgmental sobriety.

My friends stopped talking and looked at me. There was a moment of stunned silence, and then they started shouting at me: "What are you doing?" "You're sober!" "No, Moby!" "You don't drink!" I held up my hand to stop them, lifted the glass to my mouth again, and finished my pint. I put the glass firmly back on the table, exhaled loudly, and said, "Delicious!" They laughed and applauded.

Joey's boyfriend said, "Moby's drinking!"—awestruck, as if he had just witnessed a small malignant miracle.

My friend Mary asked me, "Why are you drinking?"

"I called Sarah," I said. "Some guy she's fucking picked up the phone. So now I'm drinking. Plus I love beer."

She smiled. "Good reason. Or, reasons."

Joey went to the bar and got me another beer. In an instant everything had changed. The music sounded better and the filthy bar had become the most interesting place on earth. After only one drink my constant awkwardness abated and I felt like my true self. Sobriety was complicated and difficult and sad. Drinking offered salvation and safety. When I drank, the world felt welcoming and simple, and I was happy.

I ordered a third Anchor Steam, and then a fourth. The beer was beautiful coming out of the tap, elegant like polished wood in the pint glass, laden with promise when I carried it back to the table, and sublime as it filled my stomach and wound its way through my body, healing my wounded synapses.

By midnight I'd had seven beers. I was slurring my words and flirting with a tattoo-covered dominatrix who was sitting next to me in the booth. She was morose because the guy she was dating had bailed on their New Year's Eve plans and hadn't called her in the last forty-eight hours. She had left him a message earlier that she was in this bar with her friends, and that he should come meet her, but it was getting late and he hadn't shown up.

While Mazzy Star played on the jukebox I said, with drunken sympathy and self-interest, "Okay, he's a dick. If he doesn't show up, let's go home together. I just called my ex-girlfriend and the guy she's sleeping with picked up the phone. You and I are alone and our exes are having sex with other people. We need each other."

She smiled and kissed me. I walked to the bar and bought us more drinks. As I was standing at the bar, watching the bartender carefully fill our pint glasses, I looked up and imagined the ceiling parting and a sky full of smiling Celtic angels welcoming me back into the fold of drunkenness. "You're probably an alcoholic," I imagined these hereditary angels saying, "and this is going to end badly for you at some point, but for now just be drunk and happy."

I carried our beers back to the booth and "Oh! Sweet Nuthin'" came on the jukebox. I looked at my drunk dominatrix and my drunk raver friends, all happily singing along to the Velvet Underground. I smiled a wide smile and sang along.

At three a.m. the music stopped and the harsh overhead bar lights came on. The night was over; we were being weaned from the beer taps and expelled onto the street. I got in a cab with Joey, his boyfriend, and the dominatrix, and we went back to Joey's house. Joey and his boyfriend lived in a small house near the Mission, and they collected snakes: big, little, benign, venomous. They had a greasy kitchen that was filled with snakes, a living room filled with snakes, a bedroom filled with snakes. Snakes in glass cages everywhere.

"When did you start collecting snakes?" I asked Joey, sitting down on their green thrift-shop sofa. He answered, but I was too drunk to pay attention.

We put on a Suicide CD, and then Joey and his boyfriend took a bottle of wine and disappeared into their bedroom. The dominatrix and I got two Miller Lites from the fridge and sat on the floor as Alan Vega sang "Cheree."

"I'm sorry your boyfriend didn't show up," I said, taking her hand. "But I'm glad you're here with me."

"You're sweet," she said. "I'm sorry your girlfriend had a guy in her apartment."

I put down my beer and started kissing her. We lay down on the thin carpet and slowly, drunkenly, took off our clothes. I pushed aside Joey's Pier 1 coffee table and had my first fumbling, drunken one-night stand in eight years. After sex we passed out on the floor but woke up around six a.m. because the heat was off and the apartment was freezing. I found a thin blanket on the sofa and we wrapped ourselves in it.

"It's still cold," she said, her breath smelling like cigarettes and beer.

"Hold on," I said. I took all the cushions off the sofa and piled them on top of us. "Is that better?" I asked.

"I think so," she said, and fell back asleep. I lay next to her, cold and drunk. The dawn light leaked through the curtains, and I heard a lonely ambulance siren somewhere far away. On the wall, in between some of the snake cages, there was an old framed absinthe advertisement. There was a green devil fairy in the ad, staring at me with a faded green smile. I looked at the snakes in their cages and the dominatrix snoring next to me. I smiled at the green absinthe devil fairy and whispered to her, "I'm back."

ALCOHOL ENTHUSIAST, 1995–1997

36

THOUSANDS OF LEATHER JACKETS

came home drunk at four a.m. on a Saturday night. To remind myself that Sarah and I were 100 percent broken up I put on Black Flag's *Damaged* and took a black Magic Marker and started writing "DO NOT CALL HER" on the inside of my apartment door. The first few "DO NOT CALL HER"s were written in big block letters in the middle of the door, but by the thirtieth "DO NOT CALL HER," the text got smaller. I ended up lying on the floor, writing at the base of the door to make sure it was covered.

When I was done I stood up and looked at my work. I had black ink all over my fingers and a door covered top to bottom with over a hundred "DO NOT CALL HER" inscriptions. Now that Sarah and I were broken up she was sleeping with Matt, a cool and handsome twenty-one-year-old who worked at the health-food store where she and I had bought our lentils. And I was jealous.

Matt was everything I wasn't. He was tall, young, had beautiful blond surfer hair, and even looked sexy in a green "Commodities Natural Market" apron. I'd see him when I was buying soy milk at the health-food store, and my stomach would implode. I didn't want to date Sarah, but I didn't want her to date anyone else. Or at the very least, I didn't want to know about her dating anyone else, especially if that someone else was tall and had healthy hair.

I could have done the rational thing and shopped at the competing health-food store three blocks away. I also could have reminded myself that I was the one who had broken up with Sarah, and that I was a twenty-nine-year-old musician signed to a major label while Matt was a twenty-one-year-old slacker working in a health-food store. But instead I convinced myself that Sarah had rejected me and that I was a worthless failure.

Since we'd broken up there were no more painfully awkward breakfasts at my mom's old black sewing table. Wasn't it better that my debilitating panic attacks had been replaced by debilitating spasms of jealousy?

So I was going out, trawling bars in the East Village and flirting with tourists. On the rare occasions when I got someone to overlook my tawdry desperation and come home with me, she'd spot my lunatic "DO NOT CALL HER" door and promptly leave. So at the end of each night out I would drunkenly crawl alone into the loft bed that Sarah and I had shared. She was across town having sex with her young, blond Adonis and I was in bed with an old quilt that my mom had sewed in the 1970s.

But I wasn't powerless. I decided that I could compete with Matt the blond god. My hair was receding, but I could dye what was left of it blond. I could get rid of my Wrangler jeans from Kmart and get the big raver pants and shirts that Matt and his cool friends wore. I called my friend Jenna and asked her to help me become Matt.

"You want to bleach your hair and buy trendy rave clothes and you want my help?" she asked. "Do I get lunch?"

Jenna lived on the Lower East Side and worked as a receptionist at *Rolling Stone*. She was pretty, with shoulder-length blond hair and floral tattoos circling her wrists. She came to my apartment and escorted me to her friend's hair salon. It was cold and raining as we walked down Ninth Street, and all the snow was hunkered down in gray and brown piles on the sidewalk.

I hadn't accepted that I was losing my hair. I'd decided that I had a high forehead, which for some reason was getting higher. At some point it would stop. It had to. Other people, as a form of karmic punishment, lost their hair. I was a good, albeit confused, person. Therefore I wouldn't lose my hair. Or so I'd decided.

Jenna's friend was named Abi, and his salon was tiny, with walls painted gold and black, and four chairs in front of four sinks. There was house music on the stereo and a bored woman sitting in the corner, smoking a cigarette and reading a European fashion magazine. Abi was lithe, Persian, and gay. His fingers smelled like tobacco. I sat down in his chair and he put the bib around my neck. "You want to bleach your hair?" he asked, running his fingers through my thinning hair. "Are you sure? Your hair is very, um, small."

"Yes, let's bleach my hair," I declared.

He leaned me back into the sink and spent the next hour bleaching and washing my thin and rapidly disappearing hair.

One time in high school I'd tried to dye my hair, giving myself unfortunate orange leopard spots and scalp lesions that lasted for a week. Which was why I was going to a professional this time: I didn't want a scalp covered in orange leopard spots and lesions.

After the bleaching, the washing, and the neck shaving, Abi spun me around in the chair and I looked at myself. I was a blond and pale stranger. "What do you think?" Abi asked.

"I have blond hair," I replied.

"Do you like it?"

"Yes, I can't believe I have blond hair."

Abi pushed my newly blond hair around and made me feel like I was cared for. I knew he had helped me to be more attractive and lovable.

"How much do I owe you?" I asked.

"Oh, nothing, honey, just keep making your records," he said magnanimously. (Not surprisingly, his salon went out of business six months later.)

I handed him $40 as a tip and Jenna and I stepped back outside into the cold rain. We walked down Second Avenue to St. Mark's Place, and then downstairs to Trash and Vaudeville.

In high school St. Mark's Place had been my aspirational paradise.

On this one shitty and filthy block were record stores, clothing stores, bookstores, homeless punk rockers, actual members of new-wave and punk-rock bands, drug dealers, cheap food, and beautiful new-wave girls. St. Mark's was where the Velvet Underground came to fame, via Andy Warhol's parties on the north side of the street. It was smelly and chaotic and threatening, and it was the center of New York City for me and my friends from 1980 to 1988.

After that, we moved on, realizing that maybe St. Mark's Place was not the epicenter of new wave and punk rock we'd imagined it to be, and that in fact it mainly existed to sell ironic T-shirts and hash pipes to tourists.

Trash and Vaudeville was where suburban punk rockers since the seventies had bought their leather spiked belts, New York Dolls and Misfits T-shirts, bondage trousers, and super-skinny black jeans. Everyone in Trash and Vaudeville looked like a junkie in training, but Jenna told me that, surprisingly, they also had raver clothes. No matter the year, my age, or my status, walking into Trash and Vaudeville made me feel like an uncool high school student. The twenty-three-year-old woman behind the counter with jet-black hair and a Bauhaus T-shirt probably lived with her aunt in Queens, but I still wanted her approval. I wanted to walk up to her and say, "I might not look cool, but I grew up playing in punk-rock bands and I own every Bauhaus record, so please will you think I'm cool? I could really use your validation."

The store looked the same as it had in 1981: low-ceilinged rooms overstuffed with rack after rack of bondage trousers, tight black jeans, punk-rock T-shirts, old rockabilly suits, and thousands of leather jackets. Trash and Vaudeville's smell was like Proust's madeleine for me: the aroma of leather jackets, hair spray, and basement asbestos sent me directly to 1981, when I had $5 and a Metro-North train ticket in my pocket, and a secondhand Public Image album in a brown record bag from the record store next door.

But now it was 1995, and I was here to buy cool raver clothes. As someone who had been in the rave scene since the late eighties I should have already had a closet full of cool raver clothes. I knew where to buy records and electronics, but I'd never figured out where to buy clothes. Also, Kmart jeans were cheap, and I had decided that owning a $20 pair of jeans was more virtuous than owning an $80 pair. Every now and then somebody would give me some cool clothes, so I did have one reasonably good pair of raver pants, two Liquid Sky T-shirts, and one aging Fresh Jive T-shirt. And that was it. The rest of my wardrobe consisted of Kmart jeans and T-shirts, making me look like a roadie for a third-rate Midwestern indie band.

Now this would change. I would buy cool clothes and wear them with my cool blond hair, and I would not be consigned to the dust heap of unattractiveness. I would show Sarah that I could be just as attractive as demigod Matt, and that breaking up with me had been a mistake—even if I had broken up with her. Jenna and I grabbed some oversized rave trousers and some trendy shirts. I didn't try them on, as I had decided they were going to be perfect. I wanted to impress the cool cashier, so I added an Agnostic Front T-shirt to my pile of rave clothes.

My high school punk-rock band, Vatican Commandos, had exactly one claim to fame: in 1982, one of Agnostic Front's first-ever shows was opening up for us in Bridgeport, Connecticut. Agnostic Front went on to become New York punk-rock superstars. Vatican Commandos disbanded in the mideighties when everyone left for college. One member eventually started a media company and another became a brain surgeon (really).

I wanted the cashier to notice the T-shirt and fall in love with me, but she rang up my clothes, put them in two shopping bags, and sent me on my way. Clearly she was not my soul mate. Love had stood before her, openhearted, balding, and well intentioned, and she had ignored it, checking out a Cro-Mags poster on the wall.

Jenna and I walked through the rain to Angelica Kitchen, my favorite vegan restaurant. When I first went to Angelica in 1985 I didn't know the pronunciation of "vegan." My friend Eddie, who lived in New York and was cool, maintained it was "vee-gun." I, who lived in Connecticut and was not cool, believed it was "veh-jun." My logic was that it would follow the pronunciation of "vegetable" and "vegetarian."

I found out Eddie was right two years later at a different restaurant, when I asked if it was a "veh-jun" restaurant. The waiter sneered and said, "No, this is a vee-gun restaurant, not a veh-jun restaurant."

The rain beaded on Angelica's big windows; we stepped inside, past the racks of new-age magazines and Reiki advertisements. We ordered carrot-ginger juice and ate tempeh with mashed potatoes. "Thanks for helping me get cool," I said as we finished our food.

"You do know you're already kind of cool?" Jenna asked. "You make records and you go on tour. That's cool. Matt works part-time in a health-food store."

"Well, then thanks for making me cooler?"

"My pleasure. Thanks for the tempeh." She hesitated. "You know, Moby, lots of people find you attractive."

"Well, no, I don't think so. But thanks," I said awkwardly.

She looked at me and shook her head dispiritedly.

After lunch I said good-bye to Jenna and ran down Second Avenue with my blond hair and my pink-and-black shopping bags full of new raver clothes. I jumped over the big brown snowmelt puddles, waved to the nice lesbian couple in the used furniture store next to my apartment building, and ran up the old marble stairs to my apartment. I went straight to the mirror, and realized that with my new blond hair I looked like a nervous albino elf. Maybe in the right light at the right bar, I would look like a cool nervous albino elf. I wasn't sure if my new hair and clothes were an improvement, but at least they were a change.

To celebrate I put on an Iggy Pop record and jumped around my apartment to "The Passenger" and "Lust for Life."

That night I walked to meet Damian and get drunk in Tribeca. The rain had stopped, and I could feel the cold wind through my blond hair, caressing my scalp. At the corner of Broadway and Houston, on the way to the bar where Damian was waiting, I closed my eyes and smiled, listening to the sound of the city. There were ten million people surrounding me, and even through the winter rain everything felt clean and rife with new potential.

37

A MULLET THE SIZE OF A POODLE

was naked in the backseat of my friend Johnny Paisan's car. We were driving from Boston to New York; Johnny and Paul were in the front seat, listening to the Steve Miller Band on the radio.

"So, Paul, you know I've started drinking again," I said.

Paul was looking out the window. He didn't respond.

"Paul, I started drinking again," I said.

Paul kept looking out the window.

"Say, Moby," Johnny said casually from the driver's seat, "I hear you started drinking again?" Johnny had the deep voice of an old radio announcer and everything he said was delivered with an ironic formality.

"Why yes, Johnny, I did. Thanks for asking."

"And say, Moby?" he asked, his voice rumbling.

"Yes, Johnny?"

"Why are you naked in the back of my car?"

My first real album, *Everything Is Wrong*, had come out in May 1995, and it received enough good attention to get me booked on the second stage of the Lollapalooza tour that summer. At first being relegated to the second stage had made me feel like a techno stepchild—the legitimate musicians were on the main stage, while I was playing the second-stage ghetto. Then in Cincinnati I had gone to see Beck play his three p.m. set on the hallowed main stage. I loved Beck, but he was obviously suffering, playing for a thousand people scattered throughout an amphitheater with a capacity of nearly twenty thousand. He was doing his best, dancing and shaking his tambourine, but most of the Lollapalooza audience weren't arriving until six or seven p.m., and playing to a venue that was 5 percent full was dispiriting and grim.

I felt badly for him and Pavement and the other daytime main-stage bands, all playing for sparse and anemic audiences. But secretly, and shamefully, I was gloating. While the daytime main-stage Lollapalooza acts played to lackadaisical crowds, the second stage, which featured me and Built to Spill and Coolio, was getting thousands of kids moshing, stage-diving, and generally going crazy. Rumor had it that Beck had even asked if he could switch to the second stage—but no, he had signed up for the main stage, and that was where he was going to stay. So I gloated a little bit. Quietly.

It was summer, I was touring, I was booked for a tour with Flaming Lips and the Red Hot Chili Peppers in the autumn, people liked *Everything Is Wrong*, and I was drunk almost every night. Life glowed.

W hy am I naked in the back of your car, Johnny?" I said.

"If you don't mind my asking," he said formally.

"Not at all," I said, equally formally. "I'm naked in the back of your car because all of my clothes were disgusting and sweaty, so I threw them away at the rest stop near New London."

Johnny considered that answer. "That's a perfectly legitimate reason," he judged.

"Thank you. I thought so."

———

That day's Lollapalooza gig, just outside of Boston, had been a hot one. It was a scalding New England summer, the air swampy and heavy. I'd been wearing the same shorts and T-shirt for four days straight, and I stank.

Gene, our bus driver, greeted me as I got offstage, dripping and stinky: "Brother Pig-Pen!"

My band and crew all laughed. I had a nickname. "Hey, Brother Pig-Pen!" my monitor man Tim said. He was from Arkansas and had a blond mullet as big as a poodle.

"Seriously, Mo, you need to change your clothes. You stink," Ali said. Ali had been the bass player in Stiff Little Fingers and he'd been my tour manager and bass player for the last few years. He'd grown up in Belfast and still hadn't told me whether he was Protestant or Catholic.

"But I'm Brother Pig-Pen," I said.

Tim laughed. "Brother Pig-Pen, the world's stinkiest rock star."

Because of my years living in factories that didn't have showers, I'd long been far too comfortable with being unwashed. This summer I was taking it too far—I'd actually started to smell homeless again. My idea at the start of the tour had been simple: I'd go on tour with one pair of shorts and one pair of jeans, cadge free T-shirts from Lollapalooza, and jump in a pool every now and then. And now I was disgusting.

So now my clothes are in a garbage can near New London," I told Johnny as we drove through Bridgeport.

"You did smell pretty ripe today, Mo," Johnny said. "No offense."

"Oh, none taken," I said. "By the way, could you tell Paul that I've started drinking again?"

"I think he might have heard you," Johnny said as he pulled into a rest stop near Fairfield, Connecticut. "Hey, who wants coffee?"

"Will they let me in naked?"

"Probably not."

"Okay, I'll wear a towel." So we marched into McDonald's, Johnny and Paul clothed, and me wrapped in a towel I had swiped from my Lollapalooza trailer. Johnny got a Big Mac and a coffee. Paul got fries and a coffee. I got a coffee.

"Do you think there's beef in the coffee?" I asked Johnny.

"I don't believe so, no," he said.

"Okay, that's good," I said, sipping my black McDonald's coffee as we got back into Johnny's car.

We pulled back onto I-95 and I started talking to Paul from the backseat. "Paul, I know you don't want to hear this, but I started drinking again. I guess I'm not straight-edge anymore. I know I said I'd be straight-edge forever, so I guess I lied, and I'm sorry. But I like drinking. I won't drink around you and you won't see me drunk. I hope you can understand."

There was silence. Paul had never had a drink or a drug in his life, and for the last eight years, he and I had been straight-edge best friends together. He defined himself through his sobriety, and up until a few months ago, I'd been his only straight-edge friend. I was afraid that my drinking was going to end our friendship.

Paul sighed. "I just need some time to process this," he said.

"Okay," I said. "Did you hear that, Johnny? Paul knows that I'm drinking."

"He seems to," Johnny said. "Where does Lollapalooza go next?"

"Randall's Island tomorrow," I said, "then Trenton."

"How are Sonic Youth?"

"They're great, but it's heartbreaking. They're on last, after Hole, and while they're playing half the audience heads to the parking lot."

"But they're legends."

"To us. Not to the sixteen-year-old Cypress Hill fans."

"Have you seen Courtney Love?"

"A few days ago, she got out of a limo backstage with her baby. She was surrounded by security guards and nobody could get near her."

"So she's the rock star."

"Everyone else just kind of hangs out together," I said.

We sat quietly while we drove through Norwalk and Darien. "Hey, Paul," I said, "that's your exit."

"And that's where Pat Campbell killed his parents," Paul replied.

"Wait, what?" Johnny said.

Paul explained, "Pat used to beat me up in junior high school, and then he disappeared. One day he showed up at his parents' house to borrow money. They wouldn't give him any, so he killed them both with a hatchet and set their bodies on fire in the backyard. In good old Darien."

The next day was sunny and cloudless; fifty thousand people showed up for Lollapalooza on Randall's Island, just outside Manhattan. Patti Smith did a surprise performance on the second stage, and I was briefly annoyed, because that pushed back my set time. Then I remembered she was Patti Smith. I stood on the side of the stage with Perry Farrell and Jeff Buckley while she performed. Jeff was wearing a tight pink Kylie Minogue T-shirt and an oversized top hat. Perry was glassy eyed and beaming at everyone.

Patti finished her set and hugged Perry. The stagehands removed her equipment and set up mine. "Hey, Moby," Jeff said as I headed toward the stage, "Patti Smith was your opening act!"

"You're right, that's funny," I said. I jumped up and down in place, getting ready to perform.

"Oh, have you talked to Janet lately?" he asked.

"Not for a while," I said.

"Well, say hi to her, and have a good show!" He patted my back as I walked onstage.

We went on at six p.m., started with "Ah Ah," and then ran through an hour of rave and punk-rock songs. During the finale, "Feeling So Real," I dove headfirst into the crowd. The audience caught me and carried me while I screamed into the microphone. I climbed back onstage and stood on top of my keyboard, shirtless and filthy and yelling into the microphone. Then I walked offstage and Tim handed me a beer.

I smiled and said, non-ironically, "Rock and roll." I'd never actually said "rock and roll" to express enthusiasm before, but being handed a beer by a roadie with a mullet, it seemed appropriate.

"Rock and roll!" Tim agreed. We stood on the side of the stage and drank our Bud Lights as the sun set over Manhattan.

There was a Lollapalooza after-show party at Don Hill's, a degenerate rock club on Spring Street. By one a.m., I'd had seven or eight drinks and was dancing to Miss Guy's glam-rock band, the Toilet Boys. Miss Guy was the most beautiful drag queen in New York City, which was quite an accomplishment, given that the city had no shortage of beautiful drag queens. I had a can of Schaeffer in my hand and I was surrounded by a hundred sweaty drunks, all of us dancing to a Damned cover, when I felt someone kiss the back of my neck.

I turned around and saw a beautiful woman with short brown hair, wearing a pale blue sundress and smiling slyly at me.

"You kissed my neck!" I shouted over the music.

"I know!"

"Can I kiss your neck?"

She gave me a Gioconda smile and tilted her head, exposing her sweaty neck. I kissed her neck and then I kissed her mouth. The Toilet Boys started playing a New York Dolls cover while we kissed on the dance floor. "Let's go," she said.

Drinking had killed my father and Paul's mother and countless people I knew. Drinking was toxic and caused fights and deaths and infidelities and car crashes. But it also led me here, kissing a beautiful stranger and being led through the back door of Don Hill's, onto Spring Street, and into a taxi. Drinking led us to my apartment, where we went to the roof and kissed and talked and had sex while the sun came up over Manhattan.

I was single and in love. I was in love with dawn and drinking and New York and Lollapalooza and Jeff Buckley in his Kylie Minogue shirt and Perry Farrell with his Cheshire Cat smile and drag queens playing Damned covers and rooftop sex at dawn with beautiful strangers. Why would I ever choose straight-edge sobriety over sex on my roof at dawn with a beautiful woman in a pale blue sundress?

The sun rose in the sky over the East Village, and the world glowed.

38

NEON-GREEN MUPPET
MONSTER FUR

'm going to Nina Hagen's house in Laurel Canyon," Ali, my tour manager, said. "Do you want to come?"

Nina Hagen was a legendary punk priestess, so of course I wanted to go to her house, even if I was confused by the thought of her living in bucolic Laurel Canyon.

"Okay. Can Angela come?" I asked.

"The girl you met last night?" Ali asked.

"Yup."

He paused. "Um, sure."

The night before, Lollapalooza had played at Irvine Meadows, just south of Los Angeles. The second stage where I was playing was bathed in golden late-summer California light and surrounded by oak trees and kids in Soundgarden T-shirts. Backstage after the show I'd met Angela. She was wearing a floral-print 1960s Joni Mitchell dress and had shoulder-length light brown hair.

"Can I buy you a beer?" she asked.

"Okay, but they're free," I said.

"Even better," she said, smiling.

She got two beers and we sat at the picnic tables near the artists' trailers. We talked about Los Angeles: she had relocated from Minnesota three years before, and now she worked at a big talent agency.

"When I first came to LA in 1991 I thought I'd hate it, but I loved it," I said, drinking a can of Pabst.

"Me too," she said. "I thought it would be all plastic surgery and talent agents, but it's mainly coyotes and farmers' markets." She took a swig of her beer. "Do you think you could ever live here?"

"I don't know. I love LA, but I was born in New York and I'm pretty sure I'll live there forever."

When the sun set behind the oak trees she offered me a ride back to the Roosevelt, which at the time was a decrepit hotel in Hollywood where my band and I were staying.

"Do you want to have a drink by the pool?" I asked as she pulled into the parking lot.

"Sounds good," she said, and parked her pickup truck.

The rest of my band and crew were already by the pool, sitting under the banana palms and birds of paradise, getting drunk with three German tourists and two Australian women who identified themselves as aspiring porn stars. The German tourists were smiling naively and cradling their beers; the Australians were telling stories about trying to break into porn.

"Mo!" my drummer Scott said. "You made it!" Scott was a twenty-year-old musical prodigy from a steel town in Pennsylvania whom I'd hired to tour with me.

"You thought I'd kidnap him?" Angela joked.

"Don't kidnap the gravy train!" Scott yelled, already drunk. He stood up. "Who wants to swim? I want to swim! Come on, we're in LA, let's swim!" He jumped into the pool, alone.

"He seems happy," one of the aspiring porn stars said.

"This is his first tour," I said. "He's really excited." I saw Angela looking at the pool. "Did you know David Hockney painted the bottom of the pool?" I asked.

"Who's David Hockney?" the other aspiring porn star asked.

"He's the quintessential LA painter," I said, "even though he's British."

Scott pulled himself out of the pool. "Why won't anyone swim? It's LA! You should be swimming," he complained petulantly.

"Okay, settle down, Scooter," Ali said.

"I need a towel," he announced. "Why don't you come with me to my room and help me get dry?" he asked the aspiring porn stars.

"No," one of them said, "we're okay here."

Scott grabbed a beer and sulked off.

"How are the rooms here?" Angela asked.

"Do you want to see?" I replied. I led her to my room. It was $65 a night and looked like a decaying 1970s time capsule. The beige desk was chipped and crumbling, and the mattress was like a soft, thin canoe. As soon as we stepped inside the room, we started kissing.

"We just met, but I really want to take off my clothes with you," she said, smiling. "Is that okay?"

"I think that's okay," I said.

We had sex on the sagging canoe bed, and Angela was very loud. I hadn't known that anyone could be that loud. We had sex on the rickety chair, and then in the bathroom, with Angela sitting on the counter next to my Tom's of Maine toothpaste. And she got louder.

After thirty minutes, we fell back on the bed, sweaty.

"I think you broke me," I said.

She laughed. We lay there, holding hands on the squishy canoe mattress.

"It's still early," she said. "Do you want to go for a ride?"

I sat up. "I'd love to. Where?"

"Let's go up to Mulholland."

We pulled on her dress and I put on jeans and a Black Flag T-shirt.

"Black Flag?" she asked.

"When I was sixteen and seventeen, I was obsessed with Black Flag," I told her. "I saw them about twenty times in the early eighties. I even have three scars from Black Flag shows."

"You're so tough," she said, and kissed my nose.

We walked back out to the pool and everyone started applauding.

"That sounded *amazing*," one of the aspiring porn stars said.

"You are so loud!" Scott slurred. "Can I have sex with you?"

"Back off, Scooter," I said, putting my arm around Angela. "She's mine."

"Mo, you might want to shut your glass door next time," Ali said.

"You could hear us?" I said.

"Fucking hell," Ali said. "We heard everything. Everyone in the hotel heard everything. Everyone in Los Angeles heard everything."

"Well, I'm glad we entertained you," Angela said, smiling and coquettish. "Now we're going to have sex in my truck on Mulholland Drive." She took my hand and we walked away. We got into her pickup truck, a faded blue Dodge from 1972, and drove out of the Roosevelt parking lot.

She drove down Hollywood Boulevard, past the boarded-up storefronts and strip clubs. Apart from the homeless people sleeping on the sidewalks, Hollywood was deserted. All the legitimate businesses had left; the only things left were strip clubs and stores that sold shoes to strippers.

"When did Hollywood become so postapocalyptic?" I asked.

"I don't know," she said. "It's been this way as long as I've lived here."

We drove up Outpost Drive, and desolate Hollywood was replaced by Spanish mansions and tall trees. "It's like we're in the country, but it's a foot away from the crack addicts," I observed.

"Also, David Lynch lives here," she said.

"Really?" I asked, suddenly excited. David Lynch was my hero. "Where? Can we drive by his house?"

"I don't know exactly, somewhere near Mulholland."

I looked out the window of her pickup truck, trying to imagine David Lynch going for late-night walks underneath towering eucalyptus trees. "Are we still in the city?" I asked.

"Actually, we're in the middle of the city."

We came to a stop sign at Mulholland Drive. I saw some animals scurrying into the bushes. "Are those stray dogs?" I asked.

"No, those are coyotes."

"Coyotes? In the city?"

"They're everywhere."

Angela drove west on Mulholland and the city extended below us to the horizons, like a black sheet with a few million points of light. She took a cassette out from a box on the seat.

"What's that?" I asked.

"Led Zeppelin," she said. "Is that okay?"

"It's perfect."

We pulled off the road into a dirt parking lot. Angela turned off the engine. "Look," she said, pulling a six-pack from behind her seat, "I brought beer!"

"The way to a man's heart is through his liver," I said.

"Well, not anatomically."

She left the Led Zeppelin cassette playing. We walked to a picnic bench, sat down, and looked out at the endless lights of LA. I opened a beer for her and one for myself. I put my arm around her and we looked out at the lights. "I love it here," I said.

She took a breath. "This might sound odd because we just met, but I want to tell you something."

"You have a boyfriend?"

"No, not that." She took a sip of beer. "When I first started working in LA, I met a woman who asked me if I wanted to make money going out to dinner with rich older guys. She said I could make a thousand dollars a night, just going out to dinner with them."

"A thousand dollars a night?" I asked, stunned.

"Yup. I did it a few times. I got dressed up and went to the Beverly Hills Hotel or the Four Seasons, met rich guys, and had dinner with them. All I had to do was show up, look good, and be a good conversationalist. After I'd done this a few times my friend at the agency said, 'There's a guy you might like. It's a thousand dollars if you have dinner with him, but if you want to have sex with him, it'll be five thousand dollars.'"

"Five thousand dollars to have sex?"

"Well, she didn't really say sex, specifically, just that it'd be five thousand dollars to go back to his room. It was vague. She said, 'If you want to have sex with him you can, but there's no pressure.' So I went on the date and I really liked him. He was in his sixties and owned a company in Europe. After dinner, we went back to his room and had sex. And the next day my friend at the agency gave me five thousand dollars in cash."

I had no idea how to respond. A few years ago I'd been sober and teaching Bible study. Now I was drinking postcoital beer in Los Angeles with a woman telling me that she was a high-priced hooker. I'd never met a prostitute before, and I didn't know what to think. I was curious, and if I was being honest, I was even a little bit excited. I was also confused as to why she was telling me, since we'd known each other for all of five hours. It seemed like she was bragging and confessing at the same time.

"Do you still do it?" I asked.

"No, I stopped a while ago. I mean, I really liked it, but it started to feel too weird and it made it hard to date normally."

"What did you like about it?"

"These guys were so successful and smart, and they would go on and on about how beautiful and smart I was. Getting paid five thousand dollars a night to have sex with a charming billionaire in his suite at the Beverly Hills Hotel is pretty nice. I would've had sex with some of these guys even if I wasn't getting paid."

"Who arranged it?"

"My friend Heidi Fleiss. The funny thing is, most of these guys didn't want bimbos with huge fake tits. They liked me because I'd gone to Harvard and could hold my own." We sat silently for a moment, drinking our beers. "Does this freak you out?" Angela asked. "I know we just met, but I wanted to be honest with you."

"Yes, it freaks me out, but not in a bad way," I said. "Maybe it makes me feel a little inadequate. I'm not a billionaire with a suite at the Beverly Hills Hotel. I'm a musician with a cheap room at the Roosevelt."

She squeezed my hand. "I love that you're a musician with a cheap room at the Roosevelt."

I smiled. I could hear "Tangerine" playing in her truck. I gazed out on the clear lights of the valley. "There's no atmospheric disturbance," I observed.

"You are such a nerd," she said.

"So are you. A Harvard nerd who used to have sex for money."

She laughed and drank her beer.

The next day we woke up and the rain was falling hard, making a tiny lake on the concrete patio outside my sliding glass doors. Ali had rented a car and drove us up to Laurel Canyon to meet Nina Hagen. "Come as You Are" by Nirvana was playing on KROQ as he drove up the twisty turny roads.

"Ali, how do you know Nina Hagen?" Angela asked.

"She's friends with my ex-wife," Ali said. He rounded a curve and stopped the car. "Here we are!"

The rain was falling through the fragrant eucalyptus trees and there were muddy streams of rain coursing down each side of the street. We walked up a long, rickety wooden staircase to an old A-frame house hidden by bougainvillea and oak trees. The door opened, and there was Nina Hagen. She had bright pink hair and was wearing an orange and black kimono.

"Ali!" she said with a raspy German accent. "And this is Moby?"

"Hello," I said. "I'm Moby, and this is Angela."

"Come inside!" she said. "Do you want tea?"

She made tea and we all sat under a rain-covered skylight at her wooden kitchen table: pink-haired Nina Hagen, Ali my Northern Irish tour manager, Angela the former high-priced prostitute, and me, the erstwhile sober Christian.

"We need the rain so badly," Nina said. "This is from God." Then she remembered something. "Oh!" she yelled. "I need to get you something!" She jumped up and ran back to one of the bedrooms, her kimono streaming behind her. "Moby, I think you need this!" she called from down the hall.

She emerged from the bedroom carrying a huge green monster. "Here!" she said. "It's yours!" I took it. It was a furry neon-green jacket.

"Really?" I said. "Are you sure?"

"You take it! I never wear it and you should have it!"

I stood up and put it on.

"Wow," Angela said.

"It looks perfect!" Nina said. "Now you're an anointed rock star!"

I walked to a mirror and looked at myself. The jacket was about eight inches thick and made completely out of neon-green Muppet monster fur. "Are you sure?" I asked again.

"It's yours! You need to have it!"

I sat down in my giant green jacket and drank more tea. "Can you come to our show tonight?" I asked Nina.

"Oh, darling, no," she said. "I never go out."

"Like Greta Garbo?"

"Like Nina Hagen!" she said, laughing but serious.

Soon the rain was falling more heavily on the wooden roof.

"Mo, we should get going. We have sound check," Ali reminded me. We were playing Perry Farrell's Enit Fest at a theater in Hollywood. It was his underground electronic counterpoint to the behemoth he had created with Lollapalooza, and sound check was at three p.m.

"It was so nice to meet you, Nina," I said. "And I love my jacket."

"I love it on you! Your first rock-star jacket!"

We drove back to Hollywood in the rain. After sound check I met Angela at her apartment, tucked away on a side street near the theater. Her apartment had simple white walls, dark wooden floors, and second-hand Scandinavian furniture. I had imagined well-paid prostitutes living in apartments that were more, well, prostitutey, but her apartment seemed incredibly normal. Her kitchen had a blender and a full spice rack, which seemed surprising for some reason.

While Angela was getting dressed and doing her makeup, I spotted her bookshelf. "Can I look at your books?" I asked.

"Yes, but don't judge," she said.

I scanned the authors: Sylvia Plath, Albert Camus, Charles Bukowski, C. S. Lewis. "Why would I judge?" I asked. "I have all these books too."

"I'm almost ready," she told me. "Then we can talk books."

I moved on to her CD collection: Mazzy Star, Miles Davis, Nick Drake.

"I like your records," I said.

"Me too."

"Although a lot of these writers and musicians killed themselves," I pointed out. "Are you depressed?"

She laughed. "Not right now!"

I sat on her couch. "I really like having sex with you," I said. She sat on the edge of her bed, focused on pulling on a pair of stockings.

"I really like having sex with you too, Moby," I said in a high, fake voice. She laughed. "You're the best sex I ever had," I continued in my fake voice, "way better than those billionaires."

She emerged from the bedroom in a short black skirt, a white button-down shirt, and an old denim jacket. We walked out of her normal apartment to her pickup truck and drove through Hollywood in the rain.

The theater was hot and crowded when we arrived. Keoki was DJing; I hadn't seen him in a couple of years, so I walked over to the DJ booth and said hello. I'd known him since 1990—I'd always been better friends with his boyfriend, Michael Alig, but I liked Keoki. "How's Michael?" I asked.

A shadow passed over Keoki's face. "A lot's going on," he said. "I'll talk to you later."

Angela and I headed downstairs to my dressing room. "If you want to walk around, you should," I told her. "I'm going to get changed and get ready to play."

She kissed me. "Okay, see you after your show." I put on my black jeans and a black T-shirt. I jumped around backstage and banged on the couch with a couple of drumsticks. I left my dressing room and ran up and down the hallway, passing the dressing room of Traci Lords, who was DJing later. She was talking earnestly with some men in black button-down shirts. They looked like nightclub promoters or Eastern European pornographers. Traci and I had never met, but I waved to her. She waved back, a little confused.

Five minutes later I was running onstage, drumsticks in hand. We played a rave set, but before "Feeling So Real," I strapped my guitar back on and we played "Paranoid" by Black Sabbath. When we started playing "Feeling So Real," I looked at the side of the stage: Traci Lords and Perry Farrell were standing there with Charlie Sheen, who was dancing. Thousands of people in the theater were bathed in strobes and green lasers. It looked like an alien apocalypse.

As we walked offstage, the audience chanted my name and Tim handed me a beer. "I could get used to this!" I yelled at Scott and Ali. They smiled.

For the encore, I usually played "Thousand" by myself, standing alone on top of my keyboard. But I wanted tonight to be different, so I took off all my clothes.

"Mo, what are you doing?" Ali asked.

"Getting naked," I said.

"Um, your managers will kill me," he said.

I laughed and ran back onstage, nude. "Thousand" started and I climbed on top of my keyboard. As the strobes went faster I stood up, spreading my arms wide like I was trying to bless the ravers. Everyone in the crowd had their hands in the air, as if they were grabbing handfuls of light.

The song ended and I walked offstage, naked. Perry Farrell came over and hugged me—and then he grabbed my flaccid penis. "You're naked!" he yelled.

"Ha! I know!" I yelled back.

"Great show!" Charlie Sheen told me. "Go put some clothes on!"

Traci Lords started DJing. I watched her from the side of the stage and the irony struck me. The techno nerd was naked and the porn star was clothed. I went downstairs and got dressed. Angela came to the dressing room. "That was so great!" she said. "Everyone loved it."

"Can we go back to your house and listen to records?" I asked.

"You don't want to go out?" she asked.

"No, I just want to go back to your house and listen to John Coltrane while it rains outside."

"Okay, me too."

She helped me into my neon-green Muppet-fur jacket and we started to walk out the back door.

As we were leaving I laughed.

"What's so funny?" she asked.

"I just realized that now we've both taken off our clothes for work."

"So you're a hooker too?"

"Ha, I guess so," I said as we stepped outside into rainy Los Angeles.

39

ANTS AND THUMBNAILS

As I squatted on the sidewalk at the corner of Bleecker and La-fayette a bike messenger hovered over me.

"Yo, what are you doing?" he asked, peering down at me on the sidewalk.

"Looking at ants," I said.

He shook his head. "Fucked up," he said as he sped away down Bleecker.

It was two p.m. on a Wednesday afternoon. I'd been standing on the corner waiting for the light to change and I'd suddenly noticed the ants on the sidewalk: unseen to the rest of us, busy with whatever important work they were doing, speeding around in the crevices between the squares of pavement on the sidewalk. It was a normal autumn day—people were walking by with shopping bags, subways were rumbling underneath my feet—so I'd squatted on the sidewalk because I couldn't stop looking at these ants.

I could see thousands of them, and this was just one small piece of sidewalk in the middle of a huge city. I couldn't begin to count the number of ants on the whole block, and every one of these ants was made up of millions and millions of cells. Each ant had a tiny brain, and each brain was made up of countless more cells. They had lives and wills and preferences. They felt fear. They had eyes. And there were trillions of them on the planet, digging tunnels and eating bits of food that had been left on sidewalks.

I knew nothing about them. A single cell in one ant's eye was more complicated than anything I could even begin to comprehend. So if I knew nothing, then who was I to say who or what God was? I didn't understand even a single cell in a single ant, yet I'd claimed for years to know which God was the right God and which one was the wrong God, and how we should all worship and behave. I claimed to know who made the universe, why God had made it, and how and when.

But in truth, I knew nothing. I looked up from the ants and studied my fingers. At the end of my thumb was a gnarly, chewed-up thumbnail. I knew nothing about it other than how it appeared, and a few academic facts about cells. I remembered that each cell in my thumbnail had a nucleus and some mitochondria. I knew something vague about organelles from a biology textbook I'd read in eighth grade. But truly, I knew nothing.

And if I knew nothing about these basic things that were right in front of me, ants and thumbnails, then how could I make huge pronouncements about the architect of the universe? How could I say "I'm a Christian" and believe that I was right? I loved the teachings of Christ. I loved their emphasis on forgiveness and service. But I didn't know if I still believed that Christianity was the one true way of describing and worshipping a God I couldn't begin to understand.

I'd first embraced Christianity when I was thirteen and I had started masturbating. I assumed that masturbating was wrong, so every time I masturbated I prayed afterward and apologized to God. After a full year of adolescent masturbation I joined a Christian youth group as a way of appeasing God and keeping Him from dropping an anvil on my head. Eventually the masturbating started to seem normal, so I left the youth group and kept on masturbating.

I had been raised in a spiritually schizophrenic but nonjudgmental house. My mom had grown up Christian but became an open-minded spiritual pantheist in the sixties. She left behind her traditional Connecticut Christianity and started throwing the I Ching. She had a picture of Krishnamurti next to her bed; she went to tarot-card readers and the occasional Easter Sunday pancake breakfast. She never pressured me to believe anything, and I think she was disappointed when I became a fearful thirteen-year-old Christian.

After leaving the youth group and discovering punk rock I proclaimed myself an agnostic, because that seemed noncommittal and cool. My twentieth-century literary heroes, like Sartre and Camus, were atheists or agnostics, and I wanted to model my belief system on theirs. In college I majored in philosophy and read about Buddhism and skepticism and gnosticism and atheism and countless other isms, all designed to codify our place in the universe. So by the time I dropped out of college and moved in with my I Ching–throwing pantheist mom, I had become an agnostic/Taoist/existentialist/pantheist confused suburban skeptic.

And then in 1987 a friend got me to read the New Testament. Sitting on the couch in my mom's living room, I read the Gospel of Luke and immediately became a Christian. I traded in my agnosticism for faith, and spent the late eighties going to church and Christian retreats, happily proclaiming Christ as God of the whole universe. I found new, ostensibly Christian, heroes in Kierkegaard and Walker Percy and Flannery O'Connor.

So eight years later, on the sidewalk, contemplating these unknowably complicated ants and fingernails, how could I say that Christ was God? In the face of this unspeakably vast and complicated universe, how could I be so presumptuous as to make any claim to objective knowledge? I admitted, honestly, that I knew nothing. Which was liberating. And terrifying.

To arrive at my Christian faith I'd taken the Cartesian route to theosophy after college. I'd read the existentialists and I'd understood what they posited. They maintained that the universe was a cipher and that as humans we were inherently disconnected from any objective knowledge of anything. According to the existentialists the best we could hope for was some dim subjective inkling that there was something to be dimly and subjectively aware of.

Descartes had reached his conclusion centuries before. He'd doubted everything, but he couldn't doubt that he was doubting. So he'd said, *"Cogito ergo sum"*—*I think, therefore I am.* Or in his case, *I doubt, therefore I am.* The universe was unknowable, he'd realized, but he knew that he didn't know, and from that, he built his God-centered universe, as did I. If I doubt, I'd decided after college, then there must be a "me" who is doubting. So Descartes and I had decided that the world as we perceived it must be pretty close to how it objectively was, because God was clearly a benign anthropomorphized guy who wouldn't mislead us. Even Einstein seemed to take this view of God and the universe, assuming that to a large extent the universe as we perceived it was the universe as it actually was.

Now, in the presence of sidewalk ants and fingernail cells, my traditional Christianity with its certain knowledge fell away. I was seeing as clearly as I could, but suddenly the complexity of the world seemed vast and unknowable. I looked down at the ants. They were all so tiny, and that was just considering them with my naked eyes. They were made up of cells tinier than I could imagine, and in those cells were organelles that were even tinier. And in those organelles were even tinier things, and then even tinier things, leading to an ontological level of smallness that was beyond human comprehension. But that level of smallness was where the building blocks of the universe resided. If I couldn't, even for a second, comprehend the basic building blocks of the universe, then how could I claim true understanding of its creator?

My legs were getting tired, so I stood up. I felt like the universe had changed, although I was bathed in the same sunlight I'd been standing in ten minutes earlier. I was wearing the same jeans and the same Bad Brains T-shirt, but was anything the same?

I kept thinking of the Rimbaud quote I'd had taped to my mirror when I first moved to Manhattan, "I is another."

Thinking of the enormity and complexity of even a single cell made me want to evaporate. One cell in its unspeakable complexity would be worth the worship and awe of the entire universe. And cells were everywhere, their miraculousness diminished only by their ubiquity. I walked home, heading down Mulberry Street toward Houston. There was the same pool hall, the same bars, the same Italian restaurant. Everything was the same and nothing was the same, at least for me. I'd had a worldview, Christianity, and now I felt the weightlessness and freedom of my newly accepted ignorance. My professions of Christian belief had essentially been my whistling in the darkness of the Platonic cave, laboriously telling you that the shadows were real because the other Christians and I wanted them to be real.

Since I'd started drinking and gleefully hurling myself into the world of degeneracy and promiscuity, I'd already flirted with the idea that some Christian ethics seemed to be arbitrary. I understood applying ethical criteria to actions that affected other creatures, which was why I was a vegan, but I didn't understand applying ethics to sex and other actions that were consensual or self-directed. If I got drunk and had sex in a bathroom with a stripper, was I transgressing a universal ethical code? It felt thrilling to consider that most of the Judeo-Christian ethical codes I'd been raised with were arbitrary. But when I'd been having drunken sex in bathrooms and transgressing Christian ethics, I was still thinking of myself as a Christian. And now I didn't know if I still was.

I got back to Mott Street and looked at the church across the street. "I still love You, God, even if I have no idea who or what You are," I prayed. "And you too, Jesus. I know nothing, but I love you."

I was staring into the void, but I wasn't even sure that there was a void because I couldn't be sure of anything. When subjected to even a tiny bit of scrutiny the universe seemed to reveal itself as complicated beyond anything we as humans could ever possibly know. And there it was, the recurring thought: I knew nothing.

No. I realized that wasn't true. I knew that I really wanted pancakes.

I took the elevator up to the fifth floor, walked down the concrete hall, and opened my door. My loft was filled with perfect midafternoon light and the walls were glowing white. I looked up through the skylight and saw a lonely cloud sliding across the blue sky. I got out my old metal mixing bowl and took whole-wheat flour and vanilla soy milk out of the fridge. I turned on the stove and got a bag of frozen organic blueberries from the freezer.

Maybe this was the meaning of life: to live in the darkness of Plato's cave and stare endlessly into the void, but to make pancakes and watch Woody Allen movies and look at the sun coming through the skylights. Those were the comforts not of having true knowledge of the world, but of being a part of it and being amazed by it.

I made my pancakes and took them up to the roof, where I ate them under a vast canopy of blue sky. A mile away, I could see city hall and the Twin Towers. A few clouds blew across the sky, casting shadows on the towers. I couldn't profess my unwavering faith. I couldn't tell anyone what to believe. But I could sit under a beautiful Manhattan sky with a plate of pancakes.

40

PVC BODYSUIT

She was Jillian the aerobics teacher by day, and Mistress Dominika the dominatrix by night. At Crunch Fitness she pulled her blond hair into a ponytail and got on the StairMaster wearing a teal leotard. Behind closed doors she put on black vinyl and verbally abused businessmen while hitting them with riding crops.

We had met a few months earlier at a friend's karaoke party. I'd been drunk and attempting to sing "Rhinestone Cowboy." When I finished she bought me a Bud Light in a plastic cup and took me to her apartment on Seventh Street, where we had sex on her roof in a Mexican hammock. She was a dog lover too, so after sex we lay in the hammock and I told her about Walnut.

Walnut had survived parvo but had never gotten her effusive personality back. Eventually my disease-ravaged little pit bull went to live upstate with some friends of mine, and she seemed happier there than in the city.

Jillian and I never discussed being a couple, but we met up every two weeks to drink beer and have sex and talk about dogs.

One day Jillian sent me a fax. It read: "Call me—I want you to be a dominatrix."

So I called.

"I have a client who wants to dress up like a wig salesman," she told me. "He would be in my house pretending to sell me a wig. Then he'd put on the wig and my boyfriend would come home, get upset, and tell me to beat up the wig salesman. You would be the boyfriend. Will you do it?"

"Can you pay me a dollar?"

"Ha, sure. Why a dollar?"

"Because then I can say that I've been a professional dominatrix."

"Okay, I'll pay you a dollar. Oh, what's your dominatrix name?"

I thought. "Master Bobby?" I asked.

"Perfect. See you tonight at eight, Master Bobby."

At seven p.m. I looked in my closet to see what Master Bobby should wear. He needed to be tough, so I put on a sleeveless T-shirt, mirrored sunglasses, and an old jean jacket with a Def Leppard patch on the back. I looked at myself in the mirror: Master Bobby should have been menacing, but I looked like John Malkovich heading out for scones after a rough night. Maybe if I scowled at the businessman I would look tough. Or like a scowling John Malkovich.

I walked through the East Village to Jillian's building on Fifth Street. I went upstairs and took a deep breath. I wanted to respect her client and take this seriously. I was being paid a dollar; I wanted to be professional. I opened the door.

Jillian had turned herself into Mistress Dominika: She was standing by her Pottery Barn coffee table wearing a PVC bodysuit. She was holding a riding crop and looked tiny. Next to her was a morbidly obese businessman wearing fuchsia lingerie and a magenta wig. An Andrews Sisters cassette was playing, and he was dancing in circles on her sisal rug. Mistress Dominika looked at me. The obese businessman in the magenta wig looked at me.

"What the fuck!" I yelled menacingly and in character. "What the fuck is this guy doing in my house?"

"He came here to sell wigs and now he won't leave!" Dominika yelled back.

"Fuck that!" I yelled, warming to my role. "You should kick his fuckin' ass!"

"You think so?" she asked while the businessman in the magenta wig continued to dance to the Andrews Sisters.

"Fuck yes! Kick his fuckin' ass!"

"Get over here!" Dominika yelled at him. He stopped dancing and cowered by the sofa like a nineteenth-century pantomime actress. "Get over here now!" she yelled again. He walked over to her and she hit his arm with the riding crop. "Bend over that chair," she said quietly, pointing to her IKEA desk chair. He leaned over and she started hitting his enormous butt with the crop. "You like that?" she yelled. He just nodded.

"You think he needs more?" she asked me.

"Yeah, kick his ass!" I said, quickly running out of lines.

She took the long heel of her black boot and started poking it into his huge, pasty, lingerie-covered ass.

"Yeah, that's what he deserves!" I said, trying very hard not to laugh, as I really wanted to respect the obese businessman's wishes.

After a minute of grinding her heel into his gigantic ass, she told him, "Now get out of my sight! Get in the bathroom!"

"Yes, Mistress Dominika," he said demurely, and stepped into her tiny East Village tenement bathroom.

After he shut the door, I asked quietly, "Did I do okay?"

"You did great, Master Bobby," she said, smiling.

"When do I get my dollar?"

"Ssshh, after he leaves."

The door opened, and the businessman emerged, dressed in a gray pinstripe suit and black dress shoes, carrying a briefcase and wearing a Rolex. "Thank you, Mistress Dominika," he said. Then he turned to me and shook my hand. "And thank you, sir."

"My pleasure," I said.

"Have a good trip back to Jersey," Dominika said. "See you next week."

He left, pulling the door to her apartment closed. She walked across the apartment and turned off the Andrews Sisters. At that moment, I wasn't sure whether to think of her as Jillian or Dominika. "Want to get a drink?" Jillian/Dominika asked.

"Sure. You know, I tried so hard not to laugh."

"Well, I'm sure he appreciated that. Oh!" She reached into her purse. "Here's your dollar."

"I'm a professional dominatrix!" I crowed.

"You're a professional dominatrix, Master Bobby," she agreed, pulling off her stiletto boots and putting on her sneakers.

41

ROSE-COLORED LIGHTS

D amian and I were ordering drinks at the Nine Inch Nails after-show party when a perfume-drenched publicist in a leather jumpsuit came over and asked me, "Would you like to meet David Bowie?"

"Sure," I said calmly.

But I was not calm. Inside, I was doing backflips. I was going to meet my idol, David Bowie.

In 1978, when I was twelve years old, I'd worked as a caddy at Wee Burn Golf Course in Darien, just so I could save enough money to buy *"Heroes."* I was small and could barely carry a full bag of golf clubs, but I needed *"Heroes."* I spent most of my time playing cards in the caddy shack while I waited to carry old people's golf clubs, but after two weekends I'd made the $8 I needed to buy *"Heroes."* I rode my Schwinn ten-speed to Johnny's Records by the Darien train station, bought the cassette, and spent the rest of the summer in my stifling suburban bedroom poring over *"Heroes"* until it made sense to me. I memorized the lyrics. I memorized the liner notes. I memorized the artwork. Because I loved David Bowie.

And up until tonight I'd believed he could do no wrong. He and Nine Inch Nails had performed earlier in the evening at the Meadowlands Arena. I'd gone with my friend Mark Pellington, the biggest video director in the world, discussing the O. J. Simpson trial in the car down to New Jersey.

Nine Inch Nails went on first, and they were amazing. Their sound was huge and consuming, their visuals were dark and powerful, and Trent Reznor stalked the stage like a bitter demon, raging and screaming. The audience in the arena was his: young and suburban and angry. They knew all the words to all the songs and they received him like royalty.

Then David Bowie and his band came onstage. He opened with "Scary Monsters" and it was stunning. He seemed regal and dark. But then he started playing songs from his new album, and the energy visibly waned. The angsty nineteen-year-olds who'd been on their feet through the whole Nine Inch Nails show either slumped into their seats or walked out. After Bowie's fifth song the arena was two-thirds full, with a steady stream of goths in NIN shirts heading for the exits. This was heresy to me. Sure, his show was dull, but he was David Bowie.

He started to play "The Man Who Sold the World" and the teenager next to me said, "Cool, he's playing a Nirvana song." I said nothing and just sat there as the audience shuffled out of the arena.

After the show I'd ended up in a passenger van back to New York City with Trent Reznor, his girlfriend, and some people from his record company. I didn't know Trent very well and I was nervous, so I invited him and his girlfriend to the unheated two-bedroom cabin upstate I'd just bought.

"I just bought a cabin on a lake," I told him. "If you're free, you're welcome to come up and go hiking."

"Thanks, but I think we're touring for a pretty long time," he said politely as we drove through the Lincoln Tunnel.

"Okay. It's a pretty nice place. I even share canoes with some of my neighbors."

Someone from Trent's management company turned the conversation back to the O. J. Simpson trial and talk of my little cabin was forgotten. We got to the restaurant where the after-party was happening, and Trent was rushed through the entrance. I'd called Damian to come meet me, and now I was standing in line, waiting to meet David Bowie.

My whole life I'd imagined this moment. What would I say? Would I stand there, mouth agape, and just say over and over again, "You're David Bowie," until his security guards had to gently escort me away?

He and Trent were seated on an elevated dais, subtly hidden by a floral screen, and I was next in line. I wanted David Bowie to love me. I wanted him to say in his dark lizard voice, "Talking to you has been a revelation, Moby. I'm amazed by your wit and creativity. Let's be friends."

I drank the last dregs of my vodka and melted ice and put my glass on a table. "Okay, go on up," the perfumed publicist said, giving me a little push in the small of my back. I mounted the dais.

"Hi, Moby," Trent said.

I was jealous of Trent. In some ways, I felt like we were fraternal twins. We were both suburban punk rockers who'd fallen in love with electronic music in the eighties. He'd stuck with industrial goth and I'd embraced house music and techno. He stood for one thing, whereas over time I'd gone in a thousand different musical directions. My records sold in the thousands and I played concerts for hundreds of people. Trent had number-one albums that sold millions of copies, and he played concerts for tens of thousands of people. And he was a sex symbol. I wanted to be a sex symbol—or at least someone that women longed for. I wanted what Trent had, even though being solely aligned with one musical genre seemed arbitrary and limiting. But Trent was on the dais and I both liked and resented him.

"Oh, Moby," Trent said, "do you know David?"

I turned to meet David Bowie. "Moby," he said. "So nice to meet you."

David Bowie was sitting under rose-colored lights and wearing a dark blue suit with thin lapels. His hair was blond and silver and parted to the side, and he had just spoken to me in his voice that sounded like

Michael Caine crossed with a calm velociraptor. I knew that the rules of polite society involved my responding, but I just wanted to cry, hug him, and run away.

"Nice to meet you too," I said. "How are you feeling?" My opening line on meeting my favorite musician of all time: "How are you feeling?" I wondered if I'd crossed a line, like a commoner putting on airs and pretending to familiarity with royalty.

Bowie laughed. "I'm feeling fine, Moby. How are you?"

"Oh, I'm kind of drunk," I said, "but I'm okay."

He smiled, waiting for me to continue. I couldn't think of anything to say. "Where are you living these days?" I asked uncertainly.

"I'm in Switzerland," he said. "But I'm thinking of moving to New York for the art scene."

"Really? Where?"

"Probably somewhere in SoHo. Where do you live?"

"I live in Little Italy," I said, "just east of SoHo."

"In a loft?" he asked.

"Yes, I'm renovating a loft now." I was talking real estate with David Bowie? Maybe next we'd discuss our 401(k) plans and our dry-cleaning bills. I felt like I was blowing my audience with the king, but Bowie seemed calm and polite. He wasn't applauding my character and erudition, but he was smiling pleasantly and we were talking.

"That's exciting," he said. "I remember when I had one small apartment in New York. Things were so much simpler. Now I have all these houses everywhere. You should enjoy these times, Moby, when things are simple."

I couldn't think of anything to say and I felt anxious. I wanted to leave and drink more.

"Can I get you anything to drink?" I asked.

"No, I'm sober. But you should go and enjoy yourself."

I stood up, extending my hand. "It's a great pleasure to meet you, David."

He smiled and took my hand. "A great pleasure to meet you too, Moby."

I said good-bye to Trent and stepped down from the dais, back to my fellow commoners. The room was spinning and I was drained and delirious. I walked back to the bar, where Damian was drinking a gin and tonic. The DJ played "China Girl."

"Well?" he asked.

"Well," I said.

"What happened?"

"We talked about real estate. I need a drink." I ordered a vodka and soda with a slice of lime. There was a snaking line of people waiting to have an audience with David Bowie. I didn't know if meeting rock stars on a dais in a nightclub was common practice—I'd never heard of it before. But it seemed appropriate: he was David Bowie, in his chair, hidden by a screen, bathed in soft light.

"Did you talk to Trent?" Damian asked.

"I said hi, but I rode back from the Meadowlands with him. I invited him upstate."

"Really? What did he say?"

"He said thanks, but they were on tour."

"Trent could come upstate and sit in a canoe and drink Bud Light with you."

"Or I could introduce him to my neighbors and he could have a one-night stand with an eighty-five-year-old retired teacher."

Damian and I stood with our backs to the bar and stared at the line of people waiting to ascend onto David Bowie's dais.

"I met David Bowie," I said.

42

WET SWEATER

was spraying Keith Flint, the Prodigy singer with the horns, with a fire extinguisher. We had toured Germany together for the last two weeks and tonight had been our last show. He was laughing, but he was annoyed. "Fuck off, mate! Fuck off!" he yelled as I ran after him, spraying him. "That's not even fucking water!"

I chased him into the hotel room where the Prodigy and their road crew were drinking. I aimed the fire extinguisher at the people in the room and they all screamed and recoiled, some hiding behind the hotel bed. "Are you feeling lucky?" I yelled.

"No! Fuck off!" they cried, scurrying away from me and my fire extinguisher.

Ali, walking down the hallway, stuck his head in the door. "Everything okay?" he asked. I turned the fire extinguisher on him and pulled the trigger.

"Fuck, no!" he shouted, running away.

"You will all die!" I yelled as I chased him, quoting random movies I'd seen on the tour bus in the last couple of weeks. I chased Ali into the men's room, spraying him with whatever they put in German fire extinguishers.

"Stop it, Mo!"

"Okay. Sorry, Ali, but it's the last night."

He scowled at me and stormed down the hallway.

A Serbian woman who was dating Keith walked past me and into the women's room, so I followed her in. She went into the stall, pulled her yellow dress up, and started peeing with the door open. I stood in front of the stall. "How are you?" I asked. I'd had a bottle of Jack Daniel's after the show, and then a few beers in the van on the way back to the hotel, and I was swaying on my feet.

"I'm good," she said, smiling and peeing. "How are you?"

"Oh, I'm good. I guess I shouldn't have shot everyone with the fire extinguisher."

She laughed. "No, it was funny. Do you want to come into the stall?"

"Of course I do," I said, stepping into the stall.

"So, Moby, don't you have a girlfriend?"

"No," I said, thinking earnestly. "I don't think so."

"What about the girl from Berlin? Everyone said she's your girlfriend," she reminded me, still peeing.

"I think we're getting to know each other," I said. "But I don't know what will happen. And do you have a boyfriend?"

"Well, I'm sort of seeing Keith. But I know he has lots of girlfriends. It's not special." She stopped peeing but stayed seated on the toilet, with her yellow dress pulled up and her panties around her ankles.

"Can I kiss you?" I asked.

"In here?"

"Yes." And I sat on her lap and kissed her.

I heard the bathroom door open. "Hello?" It was Keith. I stood up.

"Fuck," she said, pulling up her panties and pulling down her dress.

Keith looked in the stall. "What the fuck are you doing?" he yelled, and stormed away.

She pushed past me. "Keith, wait! Keith!" She chased him down the hall.

I could hear him yelling. "What the fuck were you doing? With Moby! Fuck off!"

"No, don't leave!" she cried, her voice trailing down the hallway after him.

I walked down the hallway past the Prodigy room and into the room where my drummer, Scott, and the road crew were drinking, smoking weed, and doing lines of German cocaine. "I need a drink," I said.

Scott was sitting at the black, laminated hotel desk doing lines of coke. He had a bottle of wine and a bottle of Jack Daniel's in front of him. My soundman, J. P., and our British lighting designer, Tim, were both sitting on the bed, smoking weed. "Hey, Mo, what do you want?" J. P. asked.

"Beer, please," I said, grabbing one from a cooler at the foot of the bed.

"Do you want any coke?" Scott asked, wiping his nose.

I'd never done coke. I'd started drinking and doing drugs when I was ten, but coke had always seemed like the drug that ruined interesting people's lives. I believed alcohol was a force for good, but cocaine scared me. "No, just beer," I said.

"Do you want to listen to this Neil Peart drum solo?" Scott asked.

"Oh, no, please no," I said, clutching my beer and fleeing the room. I stumbled down the hall, giving a wide berth to the Prodigy room. I didn't really care if they were upset with me, but I didn't want to get punched in the face. Suddenly I had a good, drunken idea. I would take the stairs down to the lobby. That seemed much more exciting than taking the elevator. I pushed open the door to the stairwell. "They smell new!" I drunkenly announced to no one, my voice echoing.

I got to the ground floor and fell through the door. I picked myself up and turned the corner, and there was the bar. I decided to walk up to the bar like a distinguished gentleman so the bartender wouldn't know that I was very drunk. The two tour-bus drivers and the Prodigy's tour manager were at the bar. Keith's girlfriend was sitting with them in her yellow dress, sullenly drinking a vodka and tonic.

"Hi, everybody," I slurred. "Having a good night?"

They mumbled politely.

I staggered over to Keith's girlfriend. "Everything okay with Keith?" I asked.

"Eh, he's mad at me," she said. "What's his problem? He's on tour and he sleeps around. I don't care," she said, stoically if unconvincingly.

"Can I buy you a drink?" I asked, finishing the beer that I'd brought with me from Scott's room.

She smiled. "No, but I can buy you another drink." She ordered me another beer. "Where are you going next?" she asked.

"Back to New York tomorrow," I said, sucking on my beer and gazing at the well-lit liquor bottles behind the bar. "Don't you think liquor bottles are beautiful?" I asked.

She looked behind the bar. "They're okay."

"I think they're so beautiful," I said. "They're like beautiful glowing rocket ships, filled with god water."

She was confused. "God's water?"

"Or filled with love water. You know what I mean?"

"You okay, Moby?" my bus driver asked.

"I'm great!" I said. "I'm drunk and I'm with you guys and I'm great." I finished my beer. "Let's go outside," I said to Keith's now-former girl-friend.

"Why?"

"To look at the sky. It's night."

"I know it's night. Why do you want to go outside?"

"Come on! It'll be beautiful!"

She got off her stool. "Okay, for a minute."

Outside, the air was cold and clean. It was after midnight on Wednesday in Dortmund, the Cleveland of Germany, and everything was quiet. I threw my arms open wide and whispered, "Look at the sky! I can see stars!" She looked up. "Aren't they amazing?" I continued. "Did you know that we're looking at dead light? Most stars burned out thousands of years ago. We're just looking at their dead light, traveling through outer space."

"Really?" She laughed. "Are you always this lovely when you're drunk?"

I grabbed her. "Let's dance here," I said. I sang David Bowie's "Wild Is the Wind" and we slow-danced in front of the hotel.

"I had no idea you were such a romantic," she said.

"'Our love is like the wind,'" I sang, "'and wild is the wind.'"

I finished the song. We stood there, the stillness of the empty city pressing on us. "Let's go get another drink," she said. "I'm cold." We went back to the bar. The bus drivers and the tour manager were gone and the bartender was closing up. "*Ein vodka tonic und ein bier, bitte,*" she said.

The bartender shook his head. "No, closed."

"Please, I'm a guest in the hotel," I said. "Can we please have two drinks?"

He looked exasperated. "No, closed."

I searched in my pockets. "I have fifty deutschmarks. Can we please have two drinks?"

He crossed his arms. "No, closed."

She took my hand and led me to the elevators. "Come on," she said. "Let's get a drink in my room." We held hands in the elevator.

"Aren't you staying with Keith?" I asked as she opened her door.

"No. I get my own room always. What do you want to drink?"

I sat on her bed and concentrated on not slurring my words. "A beer, please." Her room was identical to mine: the polyester brown bedspread, the bright red German chair in the corner. "Do you want to be in love?" I asked her.

"Of course," she said. "Doesn't everyone?"

"I want to be in love," I said, "right now and here and then forever." And then I asked, "Do you have any music?"

"What time do you leave tomorrow?" she asked.

"You mean today," I said, thinking. "We get on the bus at seven a.m. and go to the airport."

She lit a cigarette. "I want to talk to you more, Moby, but not like this," she said. "I think I should go find Keith."

I looked in her eyes. "Okay," I said. "I hope we can slow-dance again. I like slow-dancing with you in front of hotels."

She smiled with her mouth but not her eyes and stubbed out her cigarette. "I hope so too." She leaned across the bed and kissed me sweetly. "You have a good soul, Moby."

I stumbled to the door, holding my beer. "You go find Keith and I'll go to my room. If Keith is mean to you, come find me. I'm in four nineteen." I walked down the hall and sat in the stairwell, drinking my beer.

"Ooh!" I said loudly, my voice reverberating in the empty stairwell. *I should record here*, I thought. *I'll make a great record in this stairwell.* I climbed up the stairs, saying, "Ooh!" and "Ahh!" and clapping my hands, listening to the echoes. When I got to my room I felt sick, so I finished my beer. Then I staggered to the bathroom and threw up in the bathtub. The bathroom floor was so clean, I thought that even the grout was germ-free, and I laughed. *What a funny name for a germ-free country. Germany. Many germs.* Then I threw up in the bathtub again.

I looked at myself in the mirror. My eyes were blank and red. I said, "Ooh!" again, but the acoustics in the stairwell had been much better. Time for bed. I lay down on the bed and immediately needed to throw up again. I didn't even make it off the bed. I leaned over, throwing up on myself, the bed, and the floor. My nice sweater was now wet with vomit. Susann from Berlin had given me this sweater. I had met her two weeks ago and I missed her. Why was I kissing other girls in bathroom stalls? I wanted Susann to be my love. I wanted to slow-dance with her instead of Keith's girlfriend. I sat up, and promptly threw up again.

The bus was supposed to leave in an hour, so I decided I'd go sleep on the tour bus. It was parked outside, and if I fell asleep there, I wouldn't have to wake up in an hour and get on the bus. I wandered around the room, vomited on the bed again, and packed up my things. I took my suitcase to the hall, hoping I had everything.

The lobby was dark and empty. I went outside to the bus but couldn't find my bus key in any of my pockets. I put my bag on the sidewalk and sat down on the ground. It was cold, but I had my sweater and my jacket on, so I could just sleep there. My pants and my sweater were wet with vomit, but I would be okay.

As I lay down I threw up again. I threw up on the sidewalk. I threw up on my luggage. Then I threw up on my jacket. Finally it seemed like I was done. My mouth tasted bitter and my throat burned. I had tears in my eyes from throwing up so much. I passed out on the sidewalk.

Mo!" I heard Ali's voice. "Mo! Wake up!" I opened my eyes. Ali was standing over me. "Are you all right?" he asked.

I looked around. It was a gloomy German morning and I was cold and wet. Why was I wet? Oh, vomit. My vomit.

"Are you all right?" Ali asked again.

I sat up and felt queasy. "I'm okay," I managed to say. "Can I get on the bus?"

"Okay," he said, annoyed. "I'll put your suitcase in the luggage bin."

I needed water. Or grapefruit juice. Or any liquid. My brain felt like a deflated and aching football, and my mouth was like a Dumpster. *Please, please let there be water on the bus.*

There was. I drank a bottle of water and then another and walked down the dark bus hallway to my bunk. I took off my vomit-soaked clothes and got into my bed. The bunk was cool and dark and felt like a safe coffin. All I needed was to stay in here, forever if possible. I felt the bus turn on, the deep rumble of the diesel engine underneath my bunk mattress. *Please just let me stay here, please.*

Today's itinerary included two hours in the Dortmund airport and then eight and a half hours in an economy seat on a flight back to New York. I just wanted to stay in the bus forever. We started moving, the bus bumping over uneven cobblestones. I closed my eyes and dreamed of the bus driving across the ocean to New York City, with me passed out in my cool coffin bunk the whole way.

43

SUGARCANE FIELDS

t had seemed like such a perfect idea. First I'd end the *Everything Is Wrong* tour and go back to New York to finish my next album, a guitar-fueled rock opus. Then I'd take a break and go to Barbados with some friends before beginning the promotion and touring that normal musicians did whenever they made records. *Wouldn't Bono and Trent Reznor do that?* I told myself. *They'd make a record, go to Barbados for a break, promote the record, go on tour, and be lauded and loved.*

There were some problems, though. The songs were written, but for some reason everything I'd recorded so far sounded terrible and was unusable. I'd bought my plane ticket and booked my hotel, so I was going to Barbados, but I was nowhere close to being done with my record, which I'd already named *Animal Rights*. And I was drinking almost nightly and experiencing constant panic attacks.

I'd first had panic attacks in 1984 when I was a philosophy major at UConn. They were debilitating, so I dropped out and moved home. At nineteen I found myself an unemployed college dropout sleeping on the couch in my mom's living room, battling constant panic. I drank and the panic persisted. I took Valium and it persisted. I drove my moped around Darien listening to Echo and the Bunnymen cassettes and it persisted. Over time I had made the panic attacks abate by leading a stable, albeit sad, life. And apart from some minor flare-ups, I'd had almost ten years of freedom from panic attacks.

Until a few months ago, when they'd returned. I'd been in a movie theater, watching *Happy Gilmore* with some friends, when the panic reappeared. I'd hoped it would be a minor flare-up, but as I worked on *Animal Rights* and realized that no one I worked with seemed to like it and I had no idea how to finish it, the panic had become a constant presence. Now I was hoping that a few days in a tropical paradise would help me to forget about my unloved and unfinished album and dispel the panic.

At the Barbados airport I got a taxi to take me to the hotel. I rolled down the window. The air was warm and it smelled like insects. "Are you a surfer?" the driver asked me.

"No," I said, inhaling as deeply as I could.

"Excuse me, sir, but then why are you staying at that hotel?"

"What do you mean?"

"It's a surfer beach. Only surfers stay there. That's all it is, just surfing."

My friend Ashley had booked the hotel, and he and his friends were all surfers. I'd known Ashley since the mideighties, when we'd taught Bible study together. He'd grown up blond and tan in Virginia Beach, next door to Jerry Falwell, and had become a born-again Christian and a surfer. After college he'd moved to New York and renounced his Christianity, but he still went on surfing trips with his born-again friends. They would all surf and his friends would try to get him to reject his newfound atheism.

At the hotel Ashley was in the lobby, wearing board shorts and flip-flops, drinking a Corona. "Moby!" he boomed. "Welcome to Barbados!"

"Ashley, the driver said this is a surfer beach?" I asked.

"Yup! It's awesome!"

"So what do you do if you don't surf?"

"Oh, I don't know, hang out?" he said, confused that anyone wouldn't be a surfer. "It's awesome here."

I stood there, worrying.

"Don't worry, Moby. It's Barbados. It's beautiful, relax!"

I walked through the lobby and got my key. When I opened the door to my room there was already someone there, sitting in the chair by the open window and drinking a Red Stripe. "Um, can I help you?" I asked.

"Hey, I'm Kit!" he said with a South African accent. He was wearing a Speedo and a Billabong shirt.

"Can I help you?" I said again.

"No, I'm good. You a friend of Ashley's?"

"Yeah. What are you doing here?"

"Barbados? Surfing, mate."

"No, here in this room."

"Oh, this is our room."

"Our room?" I asked, baffled.

"Yeah, we're going economy and sharing rooms."

I put down my luggage and walked back to the front desk. "Uh, I thought I had a private room?"

"No, you're sharing with Mr. Kit Walton," the desk clerk said.

"Do you have any private rooms?"

"Let me check." He stood there, clicking on his computer. "No, sir, no private rooms. I'm sorry."

My hands started sweating, my breathing became shallow, and my eyes flicked around the lobby as I looked for any way to flee the hotel. This was my vacation, and I had a twin bed in a small room with a Speedo-wearing South African surfer I'd never met. This might've been fine if I hadn't already been battling panic attacks. But panic is like a brushfire. It starts with the smallest irrational spark and then looks to feed itself on whatever it can find. Sharing a room with a stranger was an annoyance, but looked at rationally, not a tragedy. But panic doesn't look at things rationally. It discards the lens of reason and replaces it with a magnifying glass of distorted atavistic terror.

I headed back to the room—it was dark, so I turned on the lights.

"Oh, do you mind turning them off?" Kit asked cheerfully. "We're going surfing at five a.m., so I'm headed to bed."

I turned them off. It was nine fifteen p.m.

I left the room again, went outside, and tried some soothing self-talk: "Okay, so you can't actually hang out in your room unless you want to listen to Kit snoring in the dark. But tomorrow will be sunny and beautiful. You're in Barbados." I went back to the room, quietly brushed my teeth so as not to wake Kit, tucked myself into my twin bed that smelled like mildew, and tried to sleep through the panic.

In the morning I waited for the sun to come up, but the sky just turned lighter shades of gray. I got up and looked outside. It was raining and the ocean was flat and monochrome. I could see surfers in the distance, bobbing on the waveless sea.

I walked down to the restaurant and poked through the prosciutto and crabmeat in the buffet, looking for something vegan to eat.

"Are you Moby?" a woman asked me. "I'm Janine, Mark's wife, a friend of Ashley's." She had shoulder-length blond hair and was wearing a white Laura Ashley skirt and a teal T-shirt.

"Nice to meet you," I said.

"You're not surfing?" she asked.

"No, I don't know how."

"Then what are your plans today?"

"I don't know—I thought I'd go to the beach."

She laughed. "This beach? It's all rocks. It's only good for surfing—you can't even swim here."

"You can't swim at a beach?"

"No, it's all rocks and coral. There isn't any sand. But some of the other wives and I are taking the kids across the island to go to a kids' beach if you want to join us."

I paused. "Okay, thanks." I cobbled together some fruit and orange juice from the buffet, put on my bathing suit even though it was sixty-five degrees and raining, and met the wives and kids in front of the hotel. They had rented a minivan and were loading it up with towels and toys.

When we got in the minivan the wives and kids all bowed their heads and prayed: "God, please protect us on our trip today. Look after us and our families, in your name, amen."

A woman with short brown hair in the backseat of the minivan leaned forward and said, "Hi, I'm Annie. Are you a Christian, Moby?"

"Um, yes, I'm a Christian," I said, leaving out the part about my drunkenly dating strippers and dominatrixes and questioning the legitimacy of a belief system that presumptuously purported to comprehensively describe the architect of the entire universe.

"Oh, good. Are you born again?"

"Born again?" I asked back.

"Have you accepted Christ as your lord and savior? Have you been born again?"

I looked through the rain-streaked glass of the minivan. We were driving through muddy fields of sugarcane. The sky was even darker than it had been this morning, and the kids were singing Christian songs. I was in hell. "Yes," I said, to end the conversation. "I'm born again."

"Oh good!"

I was going to spend my vacation in a minivan with born-again Christians? I wanted to cry. We drove through endless sugarcane fields, sometimes passing shirtless men with machetes. "How long until we get there?" I asked after we had been driving for forty-five minutes.

Janine, the driver, said, "The map says we should already be there."

The kids had stopped singing—now they were fighting in the far back of the minivan. "Does Jesus like it when you fight?" Annie asked the kids, who promptly shut up, like animatronic Southern Baptists.

I borrowed the map and tried to figure out where we were. On our right were fields of sugarcane. On our left were fields of sugarcane. And in front of us was a sugarcane field. We were lost.

"What if we go left?" Annie said from the backseat.

"Shut up, Annie," Janine said.

Annie gasped. "I'm just trying to help!"

We drove for another thirty minutes and came to a store.

"We're saved!" I said.

"Through Jesus," Annie added.

We went inside. There were metal shelves filled with dish detergent and palm oil and some brown things that looked like coconuts. I picked up one of the not-coconuts and wondered if I could eat it. It was clearly vegan, but it possibly required a band saw or a James Bond laser to cut it open.

We went to the counter and asked for help: we'd given up on the kids' beach and just wanted to go back to the hotel. The man behind the counter looked at our map. "How'd you end up here?" he asked. "Your hotel is miles away."

Annie started crying.

"Don't worry. I'll get you back. It's easy—you just take these roads." He drew clear lines on our map, showing our route. We followed the new directions, and forty-five minutes later, we were back at the hotel. It was still raining. Panic was grinding through my synapses like gritty molasses.

Back in my room Kit had left his sandy bodysuit next to my bed and was showering with the door open. "That you, Moby?" he shouted from the shower.

"Yup! I'm going for a walk," I said, hating him and our shitty room and everything about Barbados.

I walked along the coast. I was in a rainy tropical hell with born-again Christian surfers. I was sharing a room with a stranger, and all I could eat was fruit and weird brown things that looked like coconuts but clearly were not. I walked for thirty minutes along the rocky shore and came to a little restaurant with a pay phone. An idea came to me: I could leave. I could leave the brown non-coconuts and the rocky non-beach and the born-again Christians and their minivan. I could call my managers and have them book me a flight home. I picked up the phone. There was a dial tone. I took out my AT&T calling card and pressed the numbers needed to make a call from Barbados to New York.

"Hello?" the receptionist at my management company said.

"Paula? It's Moby. I need to speak to Marci, urgently."

"Okay, Moby, here she is."

Marci picked up the phone. "Moby? I thought you were on vacation."

"I am. I hate it here. I need to come back. Can you book me a flight home? I don't care how much it costs."

"You sure? I thought this was your vacation."

"Marci, I'm sure. Please just book me a flight. I'll wait while you call the travel agent."

"Okay, hold on." She put me on hold, and I stood, waiting in the drizzle. A few minutes later she got back on the line. "There's a seven p.m. flight," she reported. "But they only have first class. The ticket's fifteen hundred dollars."

Aside from the free upgrade to business class on my flight to San Francisco a few years ago, I'd never flown business or first class; being small, I fit pretty easily in economy seats. I had also just bought a cabin in Garrison, New York, for $75,000 and a loft on Mott Street for $120,000. I had a few thousand dollars left in the bank, but not enough to casually spend $1,500 on a flight from Barbados to New York. But the panic had made me insane with the need to flee, and $1,500 seemed like a small price to pay to leave this loathsome rainy place.

"Okay, book it, please book it. Please."

She put me on hold again and I waited desperately. "Okay, it's booked. You need to be there by four p.m. It's on American."

"I love you, Marci. You've saved me. Thank you thank you thank you!" I said. I hung up and ran back along the path to the hotel. I was free. My panic lessened and suddenly the world seemed clear and full of potential. I'd fly back to New York and find a way to finish my record. I'd drink in bars and date strippers and never go on vacation again.

Back in my hotel room I checked the clock—it was two thirty p.m. I'd never unpacked, so I threw my toothbrush and toothpaste into my backpack and ran to the lobby. Kit was in the hallway, headed back to our room. "Kit, you have the room to yourself, I'm going back to New York," I said, running past him.

"But wait, what?"

"It's your room now!" I yelled, turning the corner to the lobby. I got in a taxi and arrived at the airport at exactly four p.m. I was giddy. I was going back to New York. Granted, I'd been gone for less than a day. But I was going home. My twenty-one-hour ordeal was coming to an end. When I picked up my ticket, I kissed it.

"Excited to go home?" the desk agent asked.

"Oh yes."

After the flight took off it broke through the clouds: I could see the sun setting behind towering pink clouds on the horizon. We landed at JFK, and I took a taxi to Mott Street, dropped my bags at my studio, and ran out the front door again. It was winter and freezing, but after Barbados, the New York City cold felt like a hug from God. I hurried through SoHo and got to Void, a degenerate two-room bar on the corner of Howard and Greene. The DJ was playing "I Wanna Be Your Dog" and my friend Fancy was sitting on the banquette, drinking a gimlet.

Fancy was a red-haired musician from Boston originally named Keith. A few years ago he'd moved to New York, dyed his hair black, and grown a John Waters mustache. He had named himself "Fancy" after his roommate's pet mouse. I hugged Fancy, not letting go.

"Moby? You're back?"

"I'm never leaving New York again," I said.

"Ha, who needs a vacation when you have sweet lady liquor?" he asked.

I sat down and I ordered a vodka and soda. Fancy did a magic trick involving a quarter coming out of a beer bottle and I kissed my friend Jen while the DJ played "Immigrant Song."

"I'm never leaving New York," I told Fancy again.

"Of course not," he said, sipping his gimlet.

44

ACOUSTIC FOAM

Okay, I get the point," Nancy Jeffries, my annoyed A & R person, said. She was sitting on a milk crate in my makeshift studio and clutching her Filofax.

I turned off the rough version of "Come On Baby" that I'd been playing for her. "Should I play the next song?" I asked meekly.

"No, I get it," she said, standing up and walking out the door without saying good-bye to me or Alan Moulder, the engineer who was helping me finish my album. Suddenly my studio felt very quiet.

"Do you think she liked it?" I asked Alan.

"Couldn't you tell?" he said. "She loved it."

"Oh, good, that's what I thought. I wasn't sure. But when she walked out without saying good-bye, that's when I knew she loved the music I'm working on."

"I'm pretty sure she's your biggest fan," Alan said from his own milk crate.

I had started working on *Animal Rights* six months earlier. In the summer of 1995 I'd been at a festival in Denmark, playing on the dance stage with Saint Etienne and Young American Primitive and Black Dog and Orbital. The audience in the dance tent were polite, but none of the Danes were dancing. The other performers made lovely music but were shy and standing still behind their keyboards. I left the rave tent and walked through a muddy field to the main stage, where Biohazard were playing. The band was energetic, the audience was going nuts, and there was a steady flow of people jumping off the stage. It was chaotic and exciting, and it felt more like a rave than the rave tent.

After touring I came home, took the Ibanez guitar I'd played with the Vatican Commandos in high school, and wrote twenty punk-rock songs. They sounded thin and raw and urgent. I fell in love with them and played them for my managers, Barry, Eric, and Marci.

"But you're an electronic musician," Barry said, confused.

"Why do you want to make a rock record?" Eric asked, dismayed.

"I don't know. It just feels right to me," I said.

They said nothing but were clearly thinking about the Prodigy and the Chemical Brothers and Fatboy Slim and all of my electronic-musician peers who were selling millions of albums and headlining festivals. They could see my success evaporating before their eyes. I imagined their internal monologue: *We're working with a techno musician at a time when techno is starting to gain mainstream acceptance. But rather than make a dance record that could sell millions of copies, he wants to make a dark, almost unlistenable punk-rock record. Why is he punishing us?* The more my managers encouraged me to make an electronic album, the more petulant and intransigent I became, determined to make a noisy rock record, even if no one apart from me liked the music.

I booked time in a studio with Scott Litt, who'd worked with R.E.M. and Nirvana, and called Earl from Bad Brains to see if he would play drums on the record. We spent a week of recording and doing rough mixes and I ended up with nothing but the flu and debilitating panic attacks.

Earl flew to Germany to visit his girlfriend, and Scott went off to make records with successful artists. I went back to my loft on Mott Street to hold my head and panic, with no idea how I'd ever finish this record. After going to Barbados for twenty-one hours I'd called Daniel Miller, the head of Mute records, hoping he'd have some good advice. He said, "Alan Moulder is a great engineer, and he's available. Maybe he could help you make the record?"

Alan Moulder had worked with U2 and Depeche Mode and P. J. Harvey. He was kind and successful and open to working with me. He showed up at my studio in April of 1996 wearing a corduroy jacket and looking like Nick Drake's long-lost brother.

Alan saw my studio and was taken aback: I had relocated to an even smaller space in the building on Mott Street while I renovated the loft that I'd bought on the fifth floor. My old plastic mixing desk was set up on a stack of brown milk crates I'd rescued from a Dumpster. Next to the mixing desk, on milk crates of their own, were some ADAT recorders and a few effects processors. There was also a chair, a guitar, some speakers, and a Roland Jupiter-6 synth—and that was it.

Alan had spent years in top-end studios with private chefs and full-time masseuses. And now he was in a small loft with fluorescent lights and some cheap equipment on milk crates. He took in the room and said, "Wow, punk rock."

"Do you know how to record guitars?" I asked him.

"Um, yes. Don't you?"

"Well, I've never really recorded guitars before," I confessed. "I just plug the guitar into the mixing desk and turn up the gain until it's distorted."

He nodded. "Well, there might be other ways of recording guitars," he said tactfully. "Although that is a novel approach."

The next day we took the subway to Manny's Music on Forty-Eighth Street to buy a little Mesa Boogie guitar amp. Then we went to the hardware store on the corner of Broome and Thompson and bought plywood and shipping blankets and acoustic foam. Back at my studio we took out a hammer and drill and built a plywood box for my amp so we could isolate the sound and record it more professionally. When the box was done, we lined it with blankets and foam and placed my amp snugly in its new home. We put a microphone up against the speaker and turned the amp on.

"Wow, it sounds like real guitars," I said, amazed.

Alan laughed. "Yes, that's the point. Now, what about drums?" I had recorded all of the demos with a cheap Yamaha drum machine, but I'd decided that if I was making a legitimate rock record I had to work with a live drummer. We booked a professional studio in Times Square and asked my friend Alexis from Girls Against Boys to come in and play drums. He played along with my cover of Mission of Burma's "That's When I Reach for My Revolver," and he sounded great.

After Alexis left, Alan did a rough mix. It sounded very good, but with the live drums, it was too conventional. I wanted to make a rock record that sounded energetic and desperate, but also like a strange apocalypse. Alexis's drumming made it sound like a well-made professional rock record. After Alan finished the rough mix we got lunch at a health-food store on Broadway and Spring Street. We sat with our hummus and carrot juice at a plastic picnic table at the back of the store.

"Alexis's playing was great," I said. "But maybe we want to use a drum machine instead."

"I completely agree," Alan said. "This album needs to feel kind of wrong, and the live drums just felt too right."

We agreed. In the time since I'd started working on *Animal Rights* it was the first time anyone had agreed with me. I wanted to hug Alan and start crying. But I was a grown-up, and I didn't know how well Alan would respond to a balding vegan crying in a health-food store.

"Should we do vocals today?" he asked.

"Okay," I said.

New York City was having a spring heat wave and my studio had no air-conditioning. It was eighty degrees outside, and with the equipment on and no ventilation it was ninety degrees in my studio. We opened the one window at the back of the studio, put on our headphones, plugged the microphone directly into the mixing desk, and I screamed the vocals to "Someone to Love."

When I finished my vocal take, sweaty and hoarse, an old Italian lady in the building across the street leaned out of her window and shouted, "You people shut up!"

Alan laughed. "Maybe we should shut the window for the next take?"

We worked eighteen-hour days recording guitars and bass and vocals, and after five days the songs were almost done. We had rough mixes that sounded wrong and dystopian and I loved them. And then Nancy Jeffries, my A & R person at Elektra, had invited herself over to my studio to sit on a milk crate and hear what we were doing. Then she walked out.

"Do we need to re-record anything?" I asked Alan, after we'd absorbed the situation.

Alan adjusted his lanky frame on his milk crate and thought. "No," he decided. "It's a difficult record, Moby, and it's going to have a hard life when it's released. But I think it's dark and special."

This was what I needed to hear. We didn't need to record cleaner guitars, conventional drums, or more palatable vocals. It was what it was: a flawed and desperate punk-rock record.

There was a knock on the door: it was Damian. "You guys look depressed," he said.

"Nancy Jeffries was just here," I said.

"Oh, your A & R person? What did she think?"

We said nothing.

"She loved it?" he said.

"She loved it so much she couldn't even stay to listen to it," Alan said.

None of the people whose opinions I valued and trusted thought that my making a rock record was a good idea. My managers gritted their teeth and winced whenever I played them these songs. My friends listened to the demos with patience and forbearance. My A & R person hated them so much she'd run out of the studio. And Daniel Miller was polite about the project, but he worked with satanic noise musicians, so he was accustomed to his artists making unlistenable records.

For some reason, though, making a rock record felt right to me. Not objectively or commercially right, but subjectively. And there was a chance that everyone around me was wrong. Maybe I'd finish *Animal Rights* and it would be loved and embraced critically and commercially.

"I think we need beer," I said to Alan.

"I think you're right," he said.

45

CHEETOS ON THE CASINO FLOOR

stole Cheryl's car," Vanessa said.

"You mean you borrowed her car without her knowing about it?" I asked.

"Yes, I stole her car," Vanessa said, as if explaining something to a dim child. "So where should we go?"

"Atlantic City?" I suggested.

A month ago I had met Vanessa at the Baby Doll Lounge in Tribeca, where she worked as a stripper. Damian and I had been walking by the Baby Doll on a humid Wednesday night and realized that neither one of us had ever been to a strip club.

"Should we go in?" I asked Damian.

"I don't know, can we?" he said.

The bored doorman on the bar stool by the door checked our IDs and we went inside. The Baby Doll was a tiny run-down strip club with a bar on the left and two small stages on the right. When we walked in a DJ was playing an Alex Chilton record while two topless blond women danced on the stages. We sat at the bar and ordered beers, trying to look nonchalant, pretending that this wasn't the first time we'd been in a strip club.

The women left their stages, put on thin T-shirts, and sat a few feet away from us. Damian and I worked up our courage and bought them drinks. We soon admitted to them that we'd never been to a strip club. They thought we were cuter than the methadone addicts and homeless guys who normally hung out at the Baby Doll, and now we were both dating them.

Vanessa had moved to New York from Indiana in 1991 to go to fashion school. She had ended up living in a windowless room on the Bowery and doing too many recreational drugs. She had thick, bleached-blond hair. When she wasn't working she tried to dress conservatively and cover her tattoos.

"Have you ever been to Atlantic City?" I asked her.

"I worked there a few years ago. It's a shithole. Let's go."

"What do you want to do there?" I asked as she drove west on Canal Street toward the Holland Tunnel and New Jersey.

"Get a hotel room, have sex, get drunk, go to a strip club, have sex again," she said.

"Sure," I agreed, spinning the radio dial. We sat in traffic on I-95 and the Garden State Parkway, passing the exit in Westfield, New Jersey, where my paternal grandmother had lived. When I was in elementary school and junior high one of the highlights of my year had been the annual trip to New Jersey to spend a few days at my grandmother's retirement home. My mom and I would drive to New Jersey in the Chevy Vega my grandfather had bought her, singing along to the Eagles and Donna Summer and the Bee Gees on the radio, while my mom smoked Winstons with the windows rolled down.

My grandmother's brick retirement condo had been built in the sixties and had air-conditioning, and the residents of the retirement community shared a pool. I loved my grandmother, but I would've made the trip to New Jersey just to sleep in air-conditioning and swim in a pool, as we didn't have either at home. My father had been an only child, and I was my grandmother's only grandson. She loved me and spoiled me when we visited her, buying me all the food my mom and I couldn't afford to have at home. During the day I'd swim in the retirement community pool from when it opened at eight a.m. until it closed at six p.m., stopping only to drink Coke and eat Popsicles and the fancy cookies that my grandmother bought for me. Most of the people at the retirement home were too old to swim, so for ten hours a day, I'd be in the pool by myself.

My grandmother died when I was twenty-two. With the small amount of money she left me I bought the samplers and keyboards I'd used to make my first records. She had also been a Christian Scientist and had never had a drink or a drug.

"I'm still hungover," Vanessa said with a Florida-panhandle twang. "Enter Sandman" came on the radio, so we drove past my grandmother's exit singing along with Metallica.

We got to the Atlantic City Expressway and I read the billboards as we passed them, wondering if we'd be able to see a show. "Crystal Gayle!" I yelled. "With Eddie Rabbitt!"

"September sixteen," Vanessa noted.

"What's today?" I asked.

"August something, I think."

"Lionel Richie! REO Speedwagon!" I shouted.

"Neil Diamond!" we yelled together.

"I love Neil Diamond," I said. "When's he playing?"

"September twentieth," she said.

"Fuck."

Eventually the Atlantic City billboards turned into Atlantic City itself. "You're right," I said as we passed a pawnshop next to a vacant lot, "it's a shithole."

"Where should we stay?" Vanessa asked.

"I don't care."

"There's a Days Inn. How about there?" We parked and locked the stolen car and walked into the lobby.

"Do you have anything available?" I asked the lady at the reception desk.

"Yup. You want a room?"

"Yes, please," I said.

"He's so polite," Vanessa said to the receptionist. "He's a Christian."

The receptionist shook her head dismissively and handed me the key to our room. "Elevator's through the lobby," she told us. "Have a good night."

The lobby was beige with a few tartan-covered couches. Next to the elevator was a metal stand filled with pamphlets from the local casinos and pawnshops. "I wish there was alligator wrestling," Vanessa said.

"We're not in Florida," I reminded her.

We found the elevator and went up to the fourth floor. "Is this like being on tour?" Vanessa asked as we walked down the maroon-carpeted hallway.

"Minus the tour manager and the nicer hotels, yup," I said.

In our room, we turned on the air conditioner, got undressed, and had sex on the stiff, green bedspread.

"That bedspread just gave us hepatitis for sure," Vanessa said when we were done.

"What should we do now?" I asked. "It's only midnight."

"Let's go to a casino and get drunk."

We left the Days Inn and walked past the empty parking lots with grass sprouting through the cracks, the strip clubs with hip-hop and country blaring out of their open doors, the new Trump hotels, the shuttered pawnshops, and ended up at Merv Griffin's Resorts International Hotel and Casino.

The bar was blue and silver and empty. An elderly bartender sat by a cash register, reading the *New York Post*. He made a Stoli and soda with a slice of lime for me and a martini with two olives for Vanessa.

We sat at our table and within a minute had finished our drinks. "I'll get more," Vanessa said. She came back and put four drinks on the table. "I got us each two drinks so we wouldn't have to fight the crowd," Vanessa said, pointing at the empty blue and silver room. I drank my second vodka and soda, and then my third, and looked around. This was all an experiment for me, or so I'd decided. I was a former Bible-study teacher getting drunk with my stripper girlfriend in a casino at one a.m. on a Sunday night. I told myself I was a drunk anthropologist, not a frightened alcoholic with attachment disorder.

"I have to pee," I said.

"Come back," Vanessa said.

I walked through the empty room and stopped at the side entrance to the casino. There were two kids, around four and six, picking up spilled Cheetos off the casino floor and eating them. Squatting next to them was their obese dad, wearing a Dallas Cowboys jersey, denim shorts, and sandals. He smiled and winked at me, as if to say, "Kids, am I right?"

I thought, *God came and took His chosen people a long time ago and this is what's left. Before heading to heaven with His chosen few, God looked at the Earth and its remaining millions and thought,* Well, I could smite the rest of them, but what if I leave them alone for a while and see what happens? *Now the chosen ones are in heaven playing cloud croquet and we're left to watch kids eating Cheetos off the floor of a casino after midnight on a school night.*

I walked to the bathroom. At the urinal I studied my distorted reflection in the polished chrome plumbing. When I got back to the table, Vanessa asked, "Where did you go?"

"I stopped to watch the apocalypse," I said. I told her about the large man and his tiny children and how they were harbingers of the apocalypse. Maybe they were at the rear of the apocalypse parade, just behind the pale horse and the pale rider. The last horse of the apocalypse was bright orange, like a giant Cheeto, and it was ridden by a chubby guy in a Cowboys jersey.

"Let's get another drink," Vanessa said.

I beamed at her. "I love it here," I told her. "Let's move to the Merv Griffin hotel and casino. We can watch the apocalypse, get drunk, and see Neil Diamond."

"First I have to give Cheryl back her car," she said.

"Let's never get sober," I said, and kissed her hand as a John Denver song came on the stereo.

46

ORANGE JACKET

E ven before *Animal Rights* was released it had failed.

Pre-release it had received a slew of egregiously bad reviews, and my American record label, Elektra, had stopped returning my managers' phone calls. Nevertheless we had scheduled an album release party for the week it came out. Before leaving my loft I put on *Roots* by Sepultura, took out my clippers, and tried to give myself a Mohawk. Halfway through I gave up, realizing that my receding hairline had become a receded hairline. I shaved the last bits of hair that were clinging to my head and walked to Don Hill's, the bar we'd rented for the party, with the cold rain falling on my newly bald head.

At the party I got drunk and played a short live set, managing to alienate the members of Blur, who for some reason were in the audience, as well as the handful of Elektra employees who'd shown up. The next morning I woke up hungover and flew to New Orleans to play in a small bar for a collection of radio programmers at a national convention. Trent Reznor came to the show, and before we performed he came to the beer-storage room we were using as a backstage area to say hello. He had just finished another sold-out arena tour and was home in New Orleans for a few weeks. He stood in the doorway of the beer-storage room for a couple of minutes, said a few nice things about *Animal Rights*, and then went to sit in a booth with his bodyguard and some friends.

Earlier that day I'd gotten a voice mail message from Axl Rose, who said that he loved *Animal Rights* and was listening to the song "Alone" on repeat as he drove around LA at three a.m. He even said that he'd be interested in working together. So Trent Reznor and Axl Rose liked *Animal Rights*. If only they wrote reviews for *Spin* or the *NME*.

During my show the radio programmers were focused on the free liquor and the presence of Trent Reznor, and most of them had their backs to the stage as I played.

The next day I flew to London; Soundgarden had asked me to open up for them in Europe. I tried to ignore the terrible reception *Animal Rights* was getting in America and pinned my hopes on touring with Soundgarden. The tour started and Soundgarden were unfailingly kind and supportive toward me, even if their audience was uninterested in me and the music I was playing.

I was playing a very loud, fast punk-rock and heavy-metal set, but in the eyes of most Europeans I was a techno musician, even when I wasn't playing techno. Night after night I'd play to Soundgarden's European fans, who sat or stood, dismissive and bored. They were there to see the last Seattle rock gods standing, not a newly bald techno guy who'd decided to make a lo-fi punk-rock record with a drum machine.

Sometimes during my show Chris Cornell or Kim Thayil or Ben the bass player would stand on the side of the stage, watching and nodding their heads, trying to be supportive. The audience would cheer, and for a second I thought they were finally responding to what I was doing. But then I'd realize the audience was cheering for the actual rock stars on the side of the stage.

My original plan had been simple: Make *Animal Rights*, go on vacation in Barbados, release *Animal Rights*, enjoy some good reviews, be embraced by modern-rock radio and MTV, go on tour with Soundgarden and be received lovingly by their audience, go on a victory-lap tour of my own to cement the album's success. Unfortunately none of that had worked out as planned, and *Animal Rights* was seen as an abject failure.

The Soundgarden tour ended and my solo tour began. My managers and I had opted for small European clubs, imagining them to be crowded and raucous and overflowing with punk-rock energy and mayhem. Most nights, though, we had a hard time selling even 20 percent of the tickets in what were already tiny venues. In Paris we played a legendary punk-rock club, L'Arapaho. The Damned had played there. The Clash had played there. And then I played there. It held two hundred people and we sold ninety tickets. By the end of my show, over half the ninety people had walked out and there were forty people in the venue.

The second-to-last show of the tour, in Greece, had been a bright spot, as we'd sold almost 60 percent of the tickets. To celebrate one good night out of three months of failures I put on my favorite Pantera T-shirt after the show and got very drunk, stumbling around Athens with Bubba, my guitar player. We ended up at a house in the Athens suburbs at five a.m., where I threw up in someone's garden while trying to convince Bubba to start a new band with me.

The next day was the final show of the tour, in an Eastern European country I'd never been to before. On the plane I held my head in my hands and lamented to Ali, "I'm so hungover."

"Serves you right, eejit," he said in an exaggerated Northern Irish Ian Paisley accent.

My hangover only got worse as we flew over the Aegean Sea, and as we landed I realized I wasn't just hungover, I had the flu. We drove to the InterContinental Hotel and I fell into bed, feverish and delirious and sweating, and promptly fell asleep.

Five minutes later, the phone rang. "Hello?" I croaked.

"Mo, it's Ali. The promoter's at the hotel and he wants to talk to you."

"Ali, I'm really sick. I just need to sleep."

"I know. He's worried about the show. He's in the lobby and insisting that he talk to you."

"Okay." I sat up. The air was cold and burning on my fevered skin. I stood up, shivering, and pulled on my Pantera shirt and black jeans from the night before. I looked at myself in the tall hotel mirror on the back of the closet door. I wanted to feel glamorous, a rock star at the end of a tour, vaguely dissipated in a nineteenth-century hotel. But I looked sick and bald. I wasn't dissipated, I was wrung out like an old bar towel.

When I stepped out of the elevator in the lobby I saw four large men in suits standing with Ali by the reception desk. One of them walked over to me and extended his hand. "Moby, nice to meet you. I am Constantin, your promoter."

I shook his hand and said, "Hi."

Constantin was tall and well dressed, with black hair slicked back over his ears, just touching the collar of his perfectly pressed dress shirt. Standing stoically behind him were the other three tall and well-dressed men, also with black hair slicked back over their ears. I noticed they all had gun bulges under their jackets. I had never seen gun bulges under jackets in real life, but I knew from TV what they looked like.

"So, sit down." Constantin gestured to a couch. "Ali tells me you're not well?"

I wanted to tell him all my problems: the record had failed, the tour had failed, I was battling panic attacks, I'd lost my hair. But I simply said, "Yes, I have the flu."

"I'm so sorry. But we have good show planned tonight, no?" he asked.

I had a fever of 103 or 104. I could barely stand or think. But my promoter was clearly Eastern European Mafia, and even in my fevered brain I knew that I couldn't cancel the show and expect to leave with all of my fingers. "I'm very sick, but hopefully I can do the show," I said weakly.

"Oh, good. You do show. Good," he said, patting his legs. "Also, you do promo for album?" he asked, almost contritely.

"What sort of promo?" I asked.

"I own record label," he said, "so onstage you throw cassettes into audience?"

I laughed. "You want me to throw cassettes into the audience?"

"Yes, for promotions," he said with black-eyed earnestness. "Also, MTV are filming show."

"Okay." I looked over at Ali, who was standing quietly at a distance. "Ali, is that okay?"

"It's okay, no problem," Constantin answered for Ali. He stood up and his bodyguards looked around, checking the windows and corners of the room. "Nice to meet you, Moby," he said, patting me on the shoulder. He walked away through the hotel lobby with his bodyguards.

Ali and I watched him go. "Still want to cancel the show?" Ali said.

"I'd rather not die here," I said. "I'm going back to bed."

"Lobby call in ninety minutes," Ali said, thoroughly enjoying himself at my expense.

"Good night," I said, heading back to my room and an hour of fevered daytime sleep.

I was woken up by a ringing telephone. "Hello?" I croaked again.

"Wakey wakey, Mo, time to go throw cassettes into the crowd," Ali said.

"I'm dying," I complained.

"Well, you will be if you don't do the show," he said, laughing.

I pulled on my stage clothes, which were basically identical to my nonstage clothes: jeans and a T-shirt and a warm orange jacket that I thought looked like something Flea would wear. I looked at myself in the long mirror again. No, I didn't look like Flea. I looked like a sick man with a receding hairline and a ridiculous orange jacket.

Ali and the band were in the lobby.

"How are you feeling, Moby?" Bubba asked.

"I want to go home," I said.

"Tomorrow, nine a.m.," Ali said.

A minivan took us to the venue, which turned out to be a hockey arena. "Are we playing on the ice?" Bubba asked.

"No, they put plywood on the ice," Ali said.

The venue was cold and the floor was covered in damp wood. I went backstage, wrapped myself in my absurd orange jacket, lay down on a bench by the hockey players' lockers, and fell asleep.

I was woken up by Ali. "Mo, Constantin is here," he told me. I sat up.

"Hey, Moby! How you feel?" Constantin asked as he entered the locker room.

"Still sick," I said.

"Ha, you be fine. Here are cassettes for promo."

He handed me a box of cassettes. I opened them. "These are cassette singles of 'Feeling So Real,'" I said.

"Yes, is song people know," Constantin said.

I was too tired and scared to protest. It was the last night of a terrible tour and I was being asked by the local Mafia boss to throw cassette singles into the crowd. Cassette singles of a song that had been on my previous album.

"Okay, I throw them in during 'Feeling So Real,' is encore," I said in suddenly broken English.

"Great!" he boomed, and his security guards sort of smiled. "Oh, this is my stadium, you like?"

"It's great."

"Also, I own MTV here, so do good show for them," he instructed me. "And this my girlfriend," he said, gesturing to an absurdly tall and bored model. "She wanna be Miss Bulgaria. She don't know you music but tonight she will." Constantin, the aspiring Miss Bulgaria, and his bodyguards left the locker room. I lay back down on the bench and passed out.

At nine p.m. Ali woke me up again. "Get your throwing arm ready," he said. "The kids want their free cassette singles."

I walked onstage, my eyeballs hot with fever. The arena was almost half-full, and the audience was excited. We were mainly going to play older dance songs, as clearly the audience didn't want to hear anything from *Animal Rights*. During the first song I felt my flu abating a little bit. By the third song I was banging on my Octapad and yelling into the microphone. Was this the cure for the flu? Being compelled by mob bosses to play old rave anthems?

As the set was ending, Ali brought the box of "Feeling So Real" cassette singles onto the stage. He mimed throwing one into the crowd and said in his best Eastern European accent, "Is promotion," and I laughed.

"Thank you for a great night!" I yelled, and the crowd even yelled back. "This next song is 'Feeling So Real,'" and the three thousand people in the arena yelled even more, as "Feeling So Real" had been a hit throughout Eastern Europe. As the song started I took a handful of cassette singles and hurled them into the crowd. The people in the audience scurried to pick them up as if I were throwing millet into a UN refugee camp.

I looked over at the side of the stage. Constantin had taken his jacket off. He and his bodyguards and his girlfriend were smiling and dancing like little kids. I smiled, happy that I was going back to New York with all of my fingers.

47

CONDENSATION ON
FREEZING GLASS

An older man in a white suit was screaming in a freight elevator. "Fuck this! I'm leaving! Fuck you! I will not be treated like this!"

Damian and I and everybody else in the elevator on their way to a Diesel party stared at the floor. Who was this man and why was he screaming?

"They've already apologized for the car," a woman standing next to the screaming man was saying. "It was supposed to be a limo. They're really sorry."

"Fuck them! Tell them there's no fucking way I'm going on! Fuck this shit!" He kept screaming, looking more like an angry rooster than a human.

It was an old industrial elevator with walls covered in sheets of metal, lifting us up to a party in a loft nearby Penn Station. I had finished the *Animal Rights* tour a month ago and returned to New York. The album had been a failure. The tour had been a failure. My relationship with Vanessa had been a failure. And so, by authorship and association, I was a failure. Now all I wanted to do was go out, drink vodka, and salve my wounds.

As we got closer to the top, the *oomph-oomph-oomph* of a disco kick drum came down the elevator shaft. We all silently willed the elevator to go faster so we wouldn't have to spend any more time in a metal box with this crazy screaming person who didn't get his limousine. "Press 'stop'! I'm going back to the hotel! Fuck this! I'm leaving! Blaaargh!" He was becoming feral; the end of his last scream wasn't even language.

Finally the doors opened. We all fled the claustrophobic metal box for the safety and sanity of a loft full of people on drugs. "Who the fuck was that?" asked Damian, traumatized.

"I have no idea," I said. "A singer?"

"Whoa," Damian said. Not "Whoa, who was the crazy person?" but "Whoa, look at this." We had entered a huge loft filled with soft red and pink lights, beautiful women, vodka being poured down ice sculptures, throbbing disco music, and vast panoramic views of the Hudson River and lower Manhattan. Damian turned to me and smiled. "This is amazing," he said.

"I need a drink," I said. We walked past hundreds of beautiful men and women and got to the bar. "Two Stolis and soda with a slice of lime, please," I said. The bartender poured our drinks while we gazed upon the party in all its majesty and potential.

"You know we're still not going to talk to anyone here," Damian said. We had both dated attractive women, but deep down, Damian and I were still Connecticut nerds, too shy to talk to anyone not wearing a *Star Trek* shirt or a Devo hat.

"Oh, there's Chloë," I said to Damian. "She'll talk to us." We took our drinks and walked over to her. "Chloë!" I said.

"Hey, Moby," she said. "Hi, Damian."

She paused.

"Oh, this is my boyfriend, Harmony."

"Hi, Harmony. I used to see you at NASA, right?"

Harmony and I reminisced about the glory days of rave culture and NASA. "Weren't you sober back then?" he asked.

"I was," I said, looking down and noticing that my drink was empty. "I'm going to get another drink. Do you want one?"

"No thanks."

I wandered through the crush of beautiful women and stood at the bar, trying to get the bartender's attention. The woman standing next to me was trying to flag him down too. "If he picks me can you order me a drink? And if he picks you I'll order you a drink?" I suggested.

"Okay," she said. "What are you drinking?"

"Stoli and soda with a slice of lime. And you?"

"Stoli cosmo."

"What's your name?"

"Anna. What's yours?"

"Moby."

Her eyes lit up. "Oh, Moby!"

I smiled. "That's me," I said.

"I used to see you play back in Rochester," she said.

"So you're an old raver?"

She paused, not sure whether she should be offended. "Well, I'm not old, but I used to be a raver." The bartender approached her first; she ordered our drinks.

"So what do you do now?" I asked.

"I'm getting my MFA at Parsons." Our drinks arrived. Mine was perfect and strong. "I always thought you were sober," she said.

"Well, I was back in the rave days."

"Well, nice to meet you, Moby. Hopefully see you later," Anna said, and walked away.

"Nice to meet you too. Thanks for the vodka!" I walked back to Damian, who was still nursing his first drink. "Damian, why haven't you finished your drink?" I demanded.

"Unlike you, I'm not an alcoholic," he said.

"I'm not an alcoholic, I'm an alcohol enthusiast," I said. I was saying that more frequently lately.

"Chloë and Harmony left," he said. "I wasn't cool enough for them to talk to." As we drank, he pointed out a girl he had his eye on: a beautiful model standing with her friends by the dance floor.

"She's too skinny," I said.

"You're crazy," he said.

"No, I'm a chubby chaser."

He laughed. The model he was staring at came over. "Hi," she said to Damian.

"Hi," he said, startled.

"My name's Petra. Who are you?" she asked in accented English.

"I'm Damian. Do you want a drink?"

"Yes!" she exclaimed, taking his hand and walking him to the bar. He looked back at me, his eyes wide and filled with terror and joy. I laughed, and noticed that my drink was finished. I needed another vodka, but I also wanted to walk around. I was in paradise and I needed to see everything. I walked past the beautiful women doing vodka shots from ice sculptures. I walked down a hallway and found another room, even bigger than the first. The crazy screaming man from the elevator was onstage here, singing a disco hit from the early eighties. He was wearing a white suit and he was smiling and sweating. Now he looked like the happiest person at the party.

I found another bar and ordered another Stoli with soda and a slice of lime. It wasn't as strong as my last drink, which was probably for the best, since I wanted this night to last forever. I wanted to find the perfect point of drunkenness and stay there for hours. Or ideally, years.

I walked over to the windows and drank my vodka while gazing on the panorama of New York City at night. The Hudson River and lower Manhattan were spread in front of me; the air was clear, and each light was twinkling. I put my hand on the window glass. It was a cold night, and I left little prints of condensation on the freezing glass. I stared at the cold night sky and thought about cancer.

Earlier in the day I'd been on the phone with my mom. She'd told me that she'd been to the doctors and they'd diagnosed her with lung cancer. "Is it treatable?" I asked.

"I'm starting my first round of chemotherapy next week," she said.

"And what do the doctors think?"

"They're optimistic," she said cautiously.

"How are you feeling?" I asked.

"I feel okay. Mobes, don't worry. I'm sure it'll be fine."

I realized I should be reassuring her, not the other way around. "It's 1996, they cure cancer all the time," I told her.

"You're right. Don't worry."

"I'm not worried," I said. "Are you worried?"

"A little bit," she said, her voice breaking. "Okay, I love you."

"I love you too, Mom." And we'd hung up.

My mom had been a smoker for most of her life. And now she had lung cancer. She had started smoking in 1958, when she was fifteen, and had smoked two or three packs of cigarettes a day, up until a few years ago, when her doctor had finally gotten her to quit. When she was growing up, smoking had been normal. Cigarette companies had advertised the health benefits of smoking in magazines and on TV. My mom even told me that when she was pregnant with me she'd been anxious, and her doctor had advised her to smoke more to battle anxiety. And now she had lung cancer.

I finished my drink and touched the cold window again. I wouldn't worry. It was the twentieth century. Nobody died of cancer anymore.

"Moby?"

Anna was standing next to me at the window, with some of her friends. She introduced us: Kendra, who worked for Marc Jacobs, and Elanna, who was accompanied by her tall model boyfriend. We headed for the bar as the DJ played "More, More, More" by Andrea True Connection.

"I need to find a soul mate!" I yelled to Elanna's boyfriend as the porn-themed disco boomed in our ears. "What about Anna?"

"Boyfriend!" he yelled back. Ah.

I saw Michael Musto, wearing dark glasses and standing by a pillar. He had been the nightlife writer for the *Village Voice* for decades, and he was at the tippy-top of the New York nightlife pantheon. "Hi, Michael!" I yelled. "You look great!"

"Hi, Moby," he said quietly. "You look drunk."

"I'm so happy," I said, pointing to the stage. "Look, there's Lady Bunny!" He just smiled.

Damian walked over to me with Petra. "Mo, we want to go. Where should we go?"

"Let's go back to your house!" I found Anna and her friends. "Anna!" I yelled. "Let's all go back to Damian's loft! Come on!"

"Well, let me ask my friends," she said.

"Here, let me. Friends! We're all going back to Damian's loft! Let's go!" I led Damian and Petra and Anna and her friends across the dance floor, feeling like the Pied Piper of Vodkaland. We got into the elevator with a bunch of other drunks and gangly models. "We're going to Damian's house!" I announced to everyone in the elevator. "You can come too!"

The doors opened and we spilled out into the street. It was a cold night. "Look, I can see my breath!" I yelled. "I'm a smoker!" I got in the back of a taxi with Kendra and Petra while Damian got in the front. "One twenty-four Broadway at Church," he told the cabbie. I looked at Kendra as we headed south. She had long dark hair and was wearing an old Billy Idol shirt and tight white jeans. "You are gorgeous," I told her as the cab slowed down on lower Broadway.

She laughed. "Are we here?" We stopped in front of Damian's building. I got out of the cab and fell on the sidewalk. Kendra leaned over me. "Are you okay?" she asked.

"Kiss me!" I said. She bent down and kissed me. I grabbed her so she lost her balance and fell on top of me, giggling. "Kiss me!" I yelled.

Damian and Petra were standing next to us, uncomfortable, while Kendra and I kissed on the cold sidewalk. "Come on, Moby," Damian said. "Let's go inside." As we got up we were joined by Anna, Elanna, Elanna's boyfriend, and three people we didn't know. We all squeezed into the elevator and went up to Damian's studio on the tenth floor.

"Damian!" I said like a drunk, excited child. "We're at your house!"

He rolled his eyes. "Yes, Mo, we are."

"Is he always such drunk?" Petra asked, in adorable broken English.

Damian's apartment was an old, small loft at the end of a long, green hallway. All of his neighbors were small businesses or artists, and nobody was there after dark except for Damian. "Turn on your stereo!" I shouted. "Put on Mötley Crüe!" The opening of *Shout at the Devil* came on as everyone made drinks and sat on Damian's futons. I took Kendra's hand and a bottle of vodka. "I want to show you Damian's paintings," I said.

We walked around the corner to Damian's painting studio and sat on the floor. I started kissing Kendra. She put her hands in my lap and started unbuttoning my jeans. Her friend Elanna walked around the corner. "Kendra, where'd you—" Then she saw us groping each other. "Oh, sorry!" Elanna said, and backed away.

I put my hand up the back of Kendra's vintage Billy Idol shirt and undid her bra.

"I just had breast reduction surgery," Kendra said. "Do you want to see the scars?"

"Of course," I said. "I love scars." She took off her shirt. She had two of the most beautiful breasts I'd ever seen, and under each breast was a perfect upside-down capital-T scar. "They're beautiful," I said. "And you're beautiful."

"Thanks," she said. She paused. "I have to tell you something." And she paused again. "I still live with my boyfriend, but we're about to break up."

"I understand," I said, taking a swig from the bottle of vodka.

"So I can't sleep with you."

"Okay."

"But I can do this." She leaned down and took me in her mouth.

"Oh," I said. "Oh."

Elanna walked around the corner again. "Kendra, I'm going!" she called. She saw Kendra going down on me, said, "Okay!" and turned around.

We finished as "Too Young to Fall in Love" came on the stereo.

"Come here," I said, pulling her up to me and handing her the vodka bottle. She drank from it and handed it back. "That was amazing," I said, kissing her. "What a perfect night."

"A perfect night," she agreed.

"Can I see you when you break up with your boyfriend?" I asked. "Can I take you on a real date?"

"Let's see. I hope so."

Somebody in the other room stopped the Mötley Crüe CD and put on the Pixies. "I love the Pixies!" Kendra said. And she started singing along with "Debaser."

I took another pull from the vodka bottle and looked at the painting Damian had just finished. It was an image of a female terrorist standing in front of a burning forest. The terrorist looked defiant and beautiful. The flames were destroying the forest and reaching far up into the sky. The terrorist had her back to the destruction she'd caused.

"Kendra!" Elanna said from around the corner. "Are you guys done?"

Kendra laughed. "We're done!"

"Let's go!" Elanna said.

"Moby, I have to go," Kendra said. "Thank you for an amazing night." She pulled on her clothes, kissed me sweetly, and left. I zipped up my pants and walked out of the studio. Damian was sitting by himself on a futon.

"Did you just have sex?" Damian asked.

"No, she has a boyfriend. She just went down on me."

"That part I saw."

"Oh. Where's your Petra?"

"She left."

"Will you see her again?"

"No, she has a boyfriend."

"Everyone has a boyfriend," I said. "I hate boyfriends."

"It's the ugliest word in the English language," he said.

"Oh, your new painting is amazing, Damian," I said. "I was looking at it while I was getting blown."

He laughed.

"No, really. It's amazing. I want it."

"Well, make me an offer."

I took another drink of vodka. I could hear a siren passing by on Broadway. "So my mom has lung cancer," I said.

"What?"

"My mom has lung cancer."

"Wait, what? Why didn't you tell me earlier?" he asked.

"I don't know," I said. "I don't know."

48

DARK WATER

was in Connecticut, walking across the concrete bridge where I used to go in high school to listen to Joy Division and think about killing myself. I used to stand on the bridge and listen to *Closer* while watching the cars below on Interstate 95; I'd imagine jumping but always walked home instead. It had been a few months since my mom had been diagnosed with cancer, and she had called me yesterday to say that she'd gotten the test results after her last round of chemotherapy. She wouldn't talk about them over the phone and asked me to take the train to Darien so we could go for a walk on the beach and talk in person. She also warned me that due to the chemotherapy she'd finally lost her hair.

I walked over I-95, down the hill on the other side, and passed Walmsley Road, where my mom had lived when she was growing up. Through my childhood I'd heard my mom and my aunts and my grandmother talking about the time my mom was five years old and saw some meat on the counter and ate it, only to find out it was dog food. Or the time she was six and pulled the legs off a daddy longlegs and ate the middle, thinking it was candy.

This happened to her for the rest of her life, thinking that a bad thing was something benign. Thinking that the sociopath Hells Angel who worked at the gas station was a good catch and would be a loving boyfriend. Thinking the pedal-steel guitar player who stole her car and her money was still a good guy. Thinking that her has-been son was still a successful musician. All her mistakes were fueled by naïve hope. If only the world had been kind and given her hamburger instead of dog food, a successful son instead of a drunk failure.

I got to her house and collected myself on the doorstep. I hadn't seen her since she lost her hair and I didn't want to look upset by her being bald. "Hello!" I called brightly as I opened the door.

"We're in the kitchen," her husband, Richard, said. I walked back. My mom and Richard were sitting at the kitchen table with glossy pamphlets in front of them. I gave my mom a kiss and Richard an awkward hug. My mom was wearing gray sweatpants and a dark blue sweatshirt; there was a homemade magenta wool hat on her head.

"Let's see," I said, gesturing at her cap. She took it off and put it on the kitchen table. "You're bald!" I said. "We're twins!"

She laughed. "I feel like Sinéad O'Connor," she said, delicately touching her head.

"I think you look great," I said.

"Narcissist," she said.

I made a cup of tea and sat down at the kitchen table with them. The pamphlets they were looking at came from funeral homes.

"You sure you want to go for a walk on the beach?" I asked.

"I haven't been outside all day," my mom said. "Let's go to Pear Tree Point." I'd spent my summers at Pear Tree Point Beach, eating hot dogs covered in sand and avoiding the water, which was brackish and smelled like motor oil. "One condition," she added as she finished her coffee. "I'm driving."

I looked at Richard, who rolled his eyes.

"I have cancer but I can still drive," my mom said insistently. We stood up and got our coats.

"Richard, you're not coming?" I asked.

"No, you and your mom should have some time together," he said.

"I see him all the time," my mom said, gesturing to Richard. "We're sick of each other."

Richard laughed.

In the summer the parking lot at Pear Tree Point would be filled with cars, but on a cold day in early spring it was empty. My mom parked her Saturn under a leafless tree at the back of the beach and we walked by the shoreline. The back part of the beach was more interesting than the front: it was where all the dead things washed up. When I was in elementary school I'd wandered around here all the time, finding dead horseshoe crabs, rotting flounder, and once, a tiny dead shark. "Did you know this is where you first went in the water?" my mom asked, wiping a sheen of drizzle off her bald head.

"No," I said. "Where?"

"Here," she said, pointing into the dark water.

"I went swimming here? How old was I?"

"About a year old. Your grandfather had brought his boat up and we were loading things on. Someone handed you to Grandma and she dropped you in the water. You were wearing a life preserver. We were all yelling and trying to get you out of the water, but you were floating and happy."

I laughed. We stood by the dark water, looking at the small oil slick gleaming on its surface.

"So I got the results back from my last chemo treatment," she said.

I swallowed. "And?"

"And the cancer has spread. At first it was just lung cancer, but now it's spread almost everywhere."

"What can they do?"

"They could try more radiation and chemo, but Richard and I have talked about it and I've decided not to do more treatment."

"What does that mean?"

"It means that as the cancer gets worse I'll go into hospice care. They won't try to keep me alive, they'll just try to make me comfortable."

I looked at the docked sailboats, bobbing in the brown water and wrapped up for winter. "So you're going to die?" I asked.

"We're all going to die, Mobes," she said. "I'm just probably going to die sooner than the rest of you."

"Is there a chance you'll get better?" I said, trying to keep my voice steady.

"There's a chance. The doctor said that some people actually recover when they stop doing chemo. They'll know in a month or two if the cancer's still spreading or not. But most likely I'll have a few months before I go into hospice."

"I'm sorry, Mom," I said, and I hugged her. The sun went behind the clouds and the air got colder. I expected one of us to start crying, but we stopped hugging and just stood there.

"There's one other thing I have to tell you," she said.

"More? Apart from you dying?"

"When I was in high school, I got pregnant," she said. "I ended up having the baby and putting it up for adoption," she said.

I waited.

"So I wanted you to know that you have a brother."

"A brother?"

She nodded. "You have a brother."

"Um, do you know anything about him?" I asked.

"No. Once I put him up for adoption, I stopped thinking about him. In my mind, you're my only son."

My mom was dying, I had a brother, and I didn't know what to feel. Why wasn't I crying? Or feeling angry or excited to learn at age thirty-two that I had a brother? I was just numb and confused. And I felt badly for my mom. My eighteen-year-old mom in 1961, pregnant and scared and forced to give up her child. And my mom now, with cancer spreading and leaving her with no choice but to die. I didn't feel badly for myself; I didn't even know if that was allowed.

"How are you feeling?" I asked my mom.

"Cold," she said. "Let's go back to the car." She was fading before my eyes: walking slower, her neck bent, her bald head hanging forward.

"Did you ever want to find your other son?" I asked.

"No. I just wanted to have another. And I did. You." When we got to the car, she handed me the keys. "Can you drive?"

"Last time I drove your car I wrecked it in a parking lot," I said.

"I remember," she said, smiling. "I just want to close my eyes for a while."

I drove us home. She was small, and sitting in the passenger seat with her eyes closed and her bald head, she looked like a baby bird. When I pulled into her driveway, she opened her eyes.

"This is going to be hard, Mobes," she said gently. "But remember, I love you."

"I love you too, Mom."

"Can you stay for dinner?"

"Yes, as long as we have deep-fried veal."

"Okay, you can have veal with extra bacon," she said. "And maybe some fried cheese for dessert."

I laughed and wondered when the disease would make her stop being funny. We walked inside. The sun had set behind the clouds, silhouetting the suburban houses across the street and the dormant winter trees that looked like tired hands.

Richard made brown rice and vegetables for me and chicken cutlets for him and my mom. Before eating we cleared the funeral-home pamphlets off the table.

After dinner Richard offered to drive me to the train.

"No thanks, I like to walk," I said. "It makes me feel like I'm in high school again."

"Except you're not wearing a black jumpsuit and gold boots," my mom said.

"What?" Richard asked.

"It's what he wore to high school," she said. "Like a weird pirate."

We walked to the door. I hugged Richard. "Good-bye, Richard. Thank you," I said. I hugged my mom. "Good-bye, baldy. I love you," I said.

"Good-bye, Moby. I love you too." My mom was smiling, but her eyes were wet. I didn't want to cry here. Once I started, I didn't know if I could stop.

"I have to go," I said, and I walked to the station. I stood on the platform and waited for the train to take me away from Darien, away from slow death.

I found a pay phone and called Damian. "You're in Connecticut?" he asked. "How is it?"

"Interesting," I said. "I found out I have a brother I've never met, and also my mom has decided to die."

He said nothing.

"But in other news, I need to go out tonight," I said.

"Are you sure?"

"In my entire life, I've never been more sure of anything. I want to get drunk and wake up dead."

49

EIGHTEEN INCHES OF MUD

was looking out the bus window at a sea of mud. "Tell me again what you're doing now?" I asked my friend Julie, who was six thousand miles away, in Detroit.

"We're in the sun drinking cocktails," she said. "It's ninety-two degrees and there isn't a cloud in the sky."

Julie had directed two of the videos for *Everything Is Wrong*. The "Feeling So Real" video had been shot next to a homeless shelter in LA and was memorable because of the hordes of homeless teens stealing the crew's equipment while we shot. The "Everytime You Touch Me" video was supposed to be sexy, involving people eating food off each other. We'd used vegan chocolate pudding for a bunch of the scenes and later realized that vegan chocolate pudding just looked like poo on film. So we had to reshoot with vegan foods that didn't look like I was licking poo off of the models' stomachs.

Now Julie and her friends were sitting by the pool at her parents' house, getting ready for her wedding, and I was at Glastonbury, cowering from the elements in my tour bus. Glastonbury was supposed to be the biggest and most celebrated festival in Europe, but right now the rain was falling steadily and there was a foot and a half of mud outside. Although it was July it was fifty-two degrees Fahrenheit at

Glastonbury. "It's too bad you're not here!" Julie said from sunny Michigan.

My tour bus floor was wet and muddy. My bandmates and managers were wearing raincoats and had mud-covered garbage bags over their shoes. The rain on the roof of the bus sounded like a million metal insects. "You're right," I said. "It's too bad I'm not there."

"We're going inside now," Julie said. "It's too hot by the pool."

Ali interrupted me. "Moby, you have an interview now in the media tent."

"Okay, Julie, I have to go now. Have a good wedding!" We hung up and I walked to the door of the tour bus. I donned my raincoat and tied garbage bags to my feet. Stepping out of the bus was like walking onto the deck of a North Sea oil derrick. The wind blew the rain into my face and I was plodding through eighteen inches of mud.

"Ali!" I yelled.

"Yes, Mo?"

"This sucks!"

"Yes, Mo."

We came to a small ridge and looked down at a flooded campsite. Glastonbury was centered around a river, which had overflowed its banks. Now all you could see were the tops of tents sticking out of the brown water. Ali pointed to his left: somebody had stripped naked and was swimming to his tent, presumably hoping to recover his possessions. His friends were standing by the brown water, cheering him on. "Stu! Stu! Stu!" they chanted.

"Fuck! Fuck! Fuck!" the aforementioned Stu was yelling from the water.

Ali and I kept walking, the mud sucking at our feet with industrial force. Finally, we came to the media trailer and went inside. "Moby, hi!" the media rep said. "You made it!"

"Is Glastonbury always like this?" I asked, removing my coat and garbage bags.

"Ha! It's the Glastonbury vibe!" the rep said.

"The vibe?" I asked.

"Ha! Yes, the mud! It's the Glasto vibe!" He checked his clipboard. "Ah, right, you were scheduled for a six p.m. interview with the *NME* but the journo isn't here."

"Do you know when he'll be back?" Ali asked.

"No, sorry. Do you have a mobile? I could call you." He copied down Ali's mobile number.

"Are any other journalists here?" I asked sadly.

"We've got the BBC and *Q* here, but they're interviewing Blur." He checked his clipboard again, didn't find anything, and gave me a big grin. "But I'll call you if anyone else shows up. Sorry you walked all the way over here!"

"No worries," I said. I put on my green raincoat again and we headed back into the rain. Ali went to inspect the stage where we were playing and I returned to the bus.

"How was the interview?" my manager Marci asked me as I stripped off my muddy rain gear again.

"The journalist wasn't there," I said.

"Oh," she said. Glastonbury was the most important festival in the world, and it was surprising given the failure of *Animal Rights* that I'd been asked to perform, so my management team of Eric, Barry, and Marci were all with me. We sat in the bus and said nothing, listening to the rain hammering on the roof. I ate a cookie.

Ali returned. "I have good news and bad news," he said, and paused dramatically. We waited. "The tent where we were going to play flooded, so they brought a sewage truck in to suck out the mud and water," he said. "And the genius operating the sewage truck hit the wrong button. Instead of sucking up the mud in front of the stage he expelled all the raw sewage that was in the truck. So there is now a huge lake of raw sewage in front of the stage. The health department has shut down the tent and there are barriers by the entrances and security guards making sure nobody goes in."

"There's a giant lake of shit in front of the stage?" Marci asked.

"There's a giant lake of shit in front of the stage," Ali confirmed.

"Is that the good news or the bad news?" I asked.

"That's the bad news. The good news is they've moved us to a bigger stage in a bigger tent. But now we go on at seven."

"Seven?" Marci said. "That's in sixty minutes."

"Yup," Ali agreed. "I'm getting the gear moved over now." He headed back into the rain.

"A bigger stage!" Marci crowed. "That's great!"

"Better than playing in shit," Eric observed.

"Oh, seeing as we're all here, I wanted to tell you I have an idea for my next record," I said. "I really want to make a dark and slow heavy-metal album."

My managers looked at me, trying to figure out if I was kidding. After the abject failure of *Animal Rights* they had assumed that I was done with making guitar albums that nobody liked or wanted to listen to. When he realized I was serious, Barry said carefully, "You know, you're good at making rock records and some people like your rock songs. But people really love your electronic music. It makes them happy."

Barry had said similar things before, but for some reason this time I listened. I loved playing punk rock and speed metal, and I loved screaming at the top of my lungs. But I realized that he was right: the electronic dance music I had done in the past made people happy. And if I had the ability to make music that gave people some happiness, then that was what I should do. I could still play punk rock and speed metal, but maybe in my spare time, or drunkenly with friends in shitty bars. My own records should be melodic and emotional, and I should do my best to make music that could give people happiness, or at least a beautiful sadness that offered consolation.

If Barry had said, "We really think you should make dance music because it sells well," I would have petulantly resisted. Told that my dance music made a lot of money, I would have clenched my jaw and made an album of twenty-minute death-metal dirges with detuned guitars. But he had told me that my electronic music made people happy.

"You're right, Barry," I said. "Let me think about it."

We all gathered by the door, wrapping our feet with garbage bags and wrapping our bodies with rain gear. When we opened the door, a huge gust of rain and wind filled the bus. "Fuck!" I yelled.

"Yes, fuck," Barry agreed.

The four of us trudged through the mud and wind and rain, past the campground that had become a lake, past the sewage-filled dance tent, arriving at our new stage, covered by a yellow and blue circus tent. It also had a lake in front of the stage, albeit a small one made of mud, not human excrement. A few ravers were standing at the edge of the muddy lake, gamely attempting to dance while a Dutch DJ played minimal techno. The tent, which could hold ten thousand people, was one-third filled. Most of the ravers were too exhausted and defeated by the elements to do anything other than stare vacantly at the DJ.

Ali came over to me. "We're on in fifteen minutes," he said.

"Is there a trailer or a dressing room?" I asked.

He smiled sadly and shook his head. I walked backstage to find my band sitting on a giant black flight case. Scott was hungover and not saying anything. Bubba was hungover and not saying anything. For once I wasn't hungover, but I sat next to them, not saying anything. The *oomph-oomph-oomph* of the minimal Dutch techno sounded wet, like elephants methodically stomping their feet in the mud.

"We should play a punk-rock set," Scott said. Bubba and I looked at him. "I mean, we're in a freezing dance tent in Glastonbury. It's cold and wet and who cares what we do? We should just play Black Sabbath covers."

"I don't know," I said. "If I were at a festival in the mud, I think I'd want to hear some happy techno."

Scott looked dejected.

"Maybe one Sabbath cover?" Bubba suggested.

"Okay, just one," I said, and we walked onstage.

50

STAGNANT GREEN WATER

was staring out of my motel window at a half-empty swimming pool. The water was dark green, sitting at the bottom of the pool, undisturbed by swimmers or wind or attention. It was early September 1997; I was in Portland, Oregon, on the last night of a tour that Elektra had asked me to do. They had released a compilation album of my film music, *I Like to Score*, and had asked me to go on tour in America to support it, and then as the tour started had told me they would most likely be dropping me from the label.

The tour had been especially rough. Most of the shows were barely attended. Some nights we'd sold around 20 percent of the tickets and played to small, almost-empty venues. In Cleveland we played outdoors and sold less than 5 percent of the tickets, accidentally reenacting the scene in *This Is Spinal Tap* when they played at an amusement park and opened up for a puppet show. Tonight in Portland might be better, though, as we'd sold almost half the tickets in advance.

I was sitting by the window of my motel room because I was on the phone, talking to my stepfather, Richard. I'd called to talk to my mother, but she was too sick to come to the phone. "It's good you're coming home tomorrow," Richard said, his voice breaking. "Your mom's really not doing well."

I talked about my travel logistics to avoid discussing the fact that my mom would probably die in the next few days: "Well, I get in tomorrow night and I can probably be in Darien by noon on Tuesday."

"That sounds good. Hurry home, Moby."

"Okay, Richard, I'll see you soon."

I hung up the heavy beige hotel phone and thought about the pool. It was the end of summer—why hadn't they ever cleaned the pool and filled it with water? Shouldn't motels, even run-down motels for has-been musicians, be able to maintain a swimming pool with clean water? In the late-afternoon light, the tint of the stagnant water was beautiful, the same color as old jade.

I grabbed the plastic-fobbed motel key and walked out the door. I passed the ice machine and the RC Cola machine and went downstairs to the pool. It was surrounded by a chain-link fence that somebody had locked, so I hopped over and sat on a moldy white pool chair. I still couldn't believe my mother was dying. When she was diagnosed ten months earlier I had hoped it would be something that we laughed about at Christmas, along with the time Grampa fell through the ice at Tilley Pond: brushes with adversity that became holiday anecdotes. When Richard said she wasn't doing well, what did he mean? That she was tired? That she felt nauseous? No. He meant something more ominous. "She's not doing well" meant that she'd gone from being a healthy person battling an illness to a sick person who was about to die. She had lost.

I sat on the moldy chair in the sun. The pool and the parking lot were still, and huge white clouds were being pushed slowly around the sky above the motel. The distant sound of the freeway was a quiet hum, more quiet than actual noiselessness. It made me think of the white-noise generators they used at therapists' offices. The clunky white noise masked the sound of people as they cried and grieved and tried to reconcile the disappointing facts of living with the assumptions they'd always made about their lives.

Ali was walking across the parking lot to the bus. I called to him: "Ali! What time are we leaving?"

"Hey, Mo! Fifteen minutes!" He looked at the empty pool with the green water at the bottom. "Going for a swim?"

I returned to my room and put on my rock-and-roll stage clothes: unwashed jeans and a T-shirt. I looked out the window again at the green water. It was swarming with life. The pool had been taken over by organisms that were inimical to us, and now it was a world unto itself, silent and hostile. Life had won, even if it wasn't the life we wanted and needed.

I got on the bus and sat in the back lounge with Steve, my new roadie, and Scott. They were watching *Shakes the Clown with Bobcat Golthwaite* for the four hundredth time.

"Hey," I said. "*Shakes the Clown* again?"

"Yup," Steve said. "It never gets old."

After sound check I walked to a vegan deli near the venue and bought a fake chicken sandwich and a cherry cola. I walked back, sat in my small dressing room, and ate my dinner while reading the layers of graffiti. The yellow walls were covered with black ink: "Lee Ving's cock is a destroyer," "Sluts try harder," "The Wallflowers," "Free beer tomorrow." After dinner I read the local alternative newspaper to see if they'd mentioned me or tonight's show.

In the nightlife section, there was a short article: "Moby, the Great White Wail": "As the Chemical Brothers and Fatboy Slim and the Prodigy have risen to rock-star status, Moby has become the techno stepchild, left behind to play small bars while his peers fill arenas." I couldn't complain—it was honest.

At eight p.m. the doors opened and the audience started drifting in. I remembered opening up for the Red Hot Chili Peppers and the Flaming Lips in Europe in 1995, when hordes of people would rush into huge venues, running to stake out their spots by the front of the stage. The few hundred people tonight entered tentatively, avoiding the area by the stage in favor of standing at the bar and buying drinks.

I was in the dressing room, drinking my cherry cola and reading an article about Portland's bookstores, when Steve came in with two girls. "Moby, this is Lorena and Michelle," he said.

"Hi, how did you all meet?" I asked.

"Oh, Steve was in Portland with Tommy Lee and we all met at the Lusty Lady," Lorena said.

So they were strippers. In most cities the strippers carried themselves with a slight air of shame and defeat, but in Portland, the strippers were proud. Some of them had even unionized and opened their own club. These were proud strippers, and I loved them for it.

I looked at Lorena, and she looked at me. The slow, time-honored look backstage between a stripper and a musician. "When do you go on?" Lorena asked.

"What time is it now?" I asked, and looked at the clock. "Oh, in fifteen minutes."

"Okay," she said. "See you onstage." And she walked out with her friend.

It was the end of another failed tour, playing to a couple of hundred people in a run-down rock club. In the morning I was going home to my dying mother. But at that moment, after locking eyes with Lorena, I felt alive again.

The show started: I screamed and banged on my Octapad and tore at my guitar and ran around the stage. I wanted to be a rock star. I wanted the sound to be perfect and for the lights to hit me just right, so that Lorena would long for me and stay with me in my motel room before I flew back to Connecticut. After each song the audience applauded, reserved and polite. This was supposed to be a bacchanal. Why weren't people having sex on the dance floor and bleeding from the rafters? It felt tepid, so I screamed more and I flailed more. I thrashed as hard as I could, playing both rave anthems and punk-rock songs.

"Please make this okay," I wanted to say to the audience. "Please love me. Please keep my mother from dying. Please get Lorena the stripper to think that I'm attractive. Please." The audience warmed up toward the end of the set, and by "Feeling So Real," they were almost excited. We played the last song and I walked offstage, shirtless and sweaty. Steve met me at the side of the stage and handed me a dirty old black cowboy hat.

"I found this on the street," he said. "I thought you'd want it."

"You're right. I do want it." I put on my filthy cowboy hat, picked up a bottle of Jack Daniel's, and walked to the dressing room. A few minutes later, Michelle and Lorena came in. "Did you like the show?" I asked them.

"Oh, yeah!" Lorena said. "We loved it."

I got them beers and poured Jack Daniel's into little Dixie cups for each of us. "Cheers!" Michelle said, and we downed our drinks.

"Let's go find Steve and see when he's done working," I said. I exited my dressing room, still shirtless, with a cowboy hat, a bottle of Jack Daniel's, and two proud strippers. My mom might die tomorrow, but tonight was one big crucible of alcoholic promise. As we walked to the side of the stage, I heard a small voice behind me.

"Moby?"

I turned around. Standing by the backstage door was a young teenage boy. He had brown hair and was shorter than I was. He was wearing creased jeans and a U2 T-shirt. "Moby?" he said. "I know you're a Christian. Will you sign my Bible?"

Oh God. I handed the Jack Daniel's bottle to Lorena and took the boy's Bible and his pen. "You know I didn't write this?" I joked. He didn't laugh. "What's your name?" I asked.

"Greg. I just really wanted to have you sign my Bible," he said earnestly.

Suddenly everything was very still. I felt foolish standing shirtless in my cowboy hat in front of this boy. What should I sign? I held the pen, hovering over the first page of his Bible. He and Lorena and Michelle were looking at me, waiting. All I wanted was to disappear into a cheap motel room with Lorena with enough alcohol to make sure I didn't live very long.

"dear greg," I wrote, "god loves you. i'm not sure if he loves me. but he loves you. thanks, moby." And I drew a picture of an alien standing on a lonely moon.

Greg took his Bible. "Thank you, Moby."

"No, Greg," I said, looking him in the eye, and trying to seem like an earnest Christian and not a drunk lover of strippers, "thank you."

He looked at me for a second, looking like he was about to ask a question, but then he walked away. I took the bottle of Jack Daniel's back from Lorena.

"Does that happen a lot?" Michelle asked.

"What, signing autographs?" I asked blithely.

"No, signing Bibles."

Inside, I sighed, ashamed. "I've signed T-shirts and breasts and drum machines and wheelchairs and asses. But no, I've never signed a Bible before."

Lorena asked, "Are you a Christian?"

"Well, it's complicated. Do you want to talk about it later?"

"Sure," she said. "I used to be a Christian. I grew up in the church."

Then Steve came around the corner and rescued me from an impromptu backstage discussion of theology and hermeneutics with Portland strippers.

"Does anyone know what time it is?" he shouted.

"Eleven p.m.?" Michelle guessed.

"No!" he bellowed, opening a longneck Budweiser. "It's beer o'clock!"

"You're right!" I exclaimed. "We need beer!" We went back to the dressing room, where Scott and Ali were already quietly drinking. "Ali, ye idjit!" I yelled, my terrible fake Northern Irish accent making me sound like a Jamaican leprechaun. "We need beer!" We opened beers and did shots of Jack Daniel's, and then we did some more. After an hour of drinking, I said, "Let's get on the bus and go drink at the motel!"

We grabbed all the beer and the vodka and the Jack Daniel's, and piled onto the bus with Michelle and Lorena. I put *Shout at the Devil* on the CD player and sat next to Lorena, one hand on her thigh and the other hand holding a beer. I was still shirtless and still wearing my filthy cowboy hat. But now I was drunk.

Steve and Michelle started making out. Scott asked Lorena, "Do you have any friends you can call?" Lorena laughed and put her hand on my hand. She was warm and I was in drunk-love. Not just with Lorena the proud stripper, but with this bus and my band and our morbidly obese bus driver. I was in love with Mötley Crüe on the stereo and the Jack Daniel's bottle on the floor. I was in love with not being alone in my motel room, preparing to get on a plane in the morning that would take me to Connecticut and my dying mother.

Then I remembered that I'd signed a Bible. What did God think of me? Was I too far gone, the prodigal son who would never come home? I wanted to have sex with Lorena on the moldy white pool chair and then have her take a knife and lovingly stab me until I died. I wanted her to push my body into the swimming pool and let me sink beneath the sick green water. Let the water eat me the way the cancer was eating my mother. Let me die. Let me die.

Lorena opened another beer and asked, "Does the motel have a pool? Can we go swimming?"

THE RAVE'S PROGRESS, 1997–1999

51

OAK TREES

I flew back from Oregon and arrived at my mom's hospice room two days before she died. Most of the time I spent with her she'd been medicated and sleeping under her favorite quilt, but for one moment she woke up and I took her hand. The rest of my family had left to get lunch, so she and I were alone in her room. The sun was coming through the blinds on the window and touching her fragile skin. She looked up at me and smiled. She couldn't speak, but I held her hand and we looked in each other's eyes. We stayed that way for a few minutes. I smiled at her and said, "It's okay, it's okay." The sun lit her pale skin, she closed her eyes, and she died.

Now it was seven thirty a.m. on the morning of her funeral and my phone was ringing. Again. *I'll sleep for another thirty minutes*, I thought, *then get up and see who's been calling.* I started to fall back asleep, and the phone rang again. I got out of bed and picked it up, annoyed at whoever was calling at seven thirty a.m. on the day of my mother's funeral.

"Moby! Where are you?" Paul said.

"I'm home," I said—obviously, since he'd called me on my home phone.

"Why aren't you here?"

"Here where?"

"Your mom's funeral."

"It's seven thirty in the morning. Her funeral starts at eleven. I've got three and a half hours. Why are you calling so early?"

"It's ten thirty, you idiot! Her funeral starts in thirty minutes!"

"What? No, it's seven thirty," I said, but looking at my downstairs clock. My bedroom clock said seven thirty, but the downstairs clock clearly said ten thirty a.m. Now I was confused.

"It's ten thirty!" he yelled.

"Shit. Fuck. My alarm clock broke. I'm rushing out the door. I'll see you as soon as I can."

"You know you're going to miss your mom's funeral?"

"I know. I'll see you later."

"Okay. Hurry."

I checked the alarm clock in my bedroom again: It said 7:35 a.m. even though it was 10:35 a.m. I was baffled as to why it was off by three hours. My clock wasn't broken. I hadn't been keeping it on West Coast time. It wasn't unplugged. The only possible, bizarre truth was that my subconscious had woken me up in the middle of the night and reset the time. It didn't want me to go to the funeral, and changing the time on my clock forward twenty-one hours was the only thing that my subconscious could think to do.

It was a given that children attended their parents' funerals, and it was an extra given that the only children of single parents attended their parents' funerals. I lived forty miles away from the church where my mom's funeral was going to be happening, and I didn't have a real job, so I had no excuses for missing my mom's funeral other than an overprotective subconscious.

I rushed to my closet, grabbed a black suit, and got dressed. I tied my tie, put on my shoes, and grabbed my wallet and keys. I put the wallet in the inside pocket of my suit jacket, but there was something there already: a matchbook from the Harmony Burlesque Theater. I opened it to read "CRYSTAL XXX," written above her phone number. The suit I was wearing to my mother's funeral had last been worn to the Harmony Burlesque in Tribeca, the dirtiest and most debauched strip club in New York City. There was probably still perfume and glitter in the crotch. I was, simply, a terrible person.

I rushed out the door and hailed a cab. "Can you take me to Norwalk, Connecticut?" I asked the driver.

"That's about two hundred dollars," he said.

"Okay, let's go."

We sped down Houston and up the FDR toward I-95 and Connecticut. I looked at my watch. It was 11:05; I assumed the funeral was just starting. By keeping me from the funeral, my subconscious could pretend that it wasn't happening. And it could pretend that my relationship with my mother had been simple and fine.

I loved my mom. She was one of the smartest and funniest and most interesting people I'd ever known. But growing up with her had never been normal. My first memory in life was flying with her to San Francisco in 1968. My father was dead, I was almost three years old, and my mom had just become a hippie. It was the Summer of Love and she had let her blond, preppy shoulder-length hair grow long and wild. She wanted to visit friends in California, take LSD, and lose herself in Haight-Ashbury.

We landed in San Francisco and my mom's friends met us at the airport. These were kids she'd grown up with in Darien. A few years earlier, they'd been preppy college students drinking gin and tonics on their parents' sailboats on the Long Island Sound. Now they had long hair and beards and David Crosby fringe jackets with pockets full of drugs. They put me in the back of their VW bug and headed to their apartment in the Haight. The car filled with pot smoke and laughter and the sound of Jefferson Airplane on the radio. I tried to sit up so I could peer out the window. I knew not to complain—if I complained, I would probably get yelled at.

Growing up, I never knew who I'd get, my smart-and-funny mom, or my sullen-and-vitriolic mom. When she was angry I sat quietly and waited until my warm mother returned, wondering the whole time what I had done to make her so mad. Now in the back of the car I discovered I had another mom: absent mom, a twenty-four-year-old aspiring hippie caught up in drugs and men and the 1968 counterculture. I sat in the backseat of her friend's VW, breathing the secondhand pot smoke.

That night after dinner she and her friends took LSD and snuck me into an X-rated movie, *Myra Breckinridge.* I was almost three years old, so they hid me under a coat and walked into the theater.

I'd been in San Francisco during the Summer of Love and seen an X-rated movie two years before I started kindergarten, so maybe it wasn't a surprise that I had a matchbook in my pocket signed "CRYS-TAL XXX" with her phone number.

Now I was thirty-three years old and stuck in traffic somewhere in Westchester County. I knew I should feel sad—I'd lost my only mom. But I just felt vague and confused and guilty. Where was my outpouring of grief? My whole life I'd had a parent, and now I was an orphan. I felt unmoored, less tethered to Connecticut, to childhood, to Darien, to the small house we'd lived in by the train station. The woman who'd birthed me and raised me and taken me to dentists' offices and fed me and loved me was now, simply, gone. The woman who'd paid for my guitar lessons and listened while my punk-rock bands had practiced in her basement was gone. She was dead, but "dead" just described the body. "Gone" described the person.

The traffic on I-95 had broken up and we were moving again. We passed through Stamford, then Darien, going by the exit for the house where I'd grown up. I looked at the meter: $180. That money could be spent buying beer and lap dances and OxyContins, or it could be spent on a taxi ride to lunch at my grandmother's house after missing my mom's funeral. "This exit," I said to the driver. He grunted, put on his signal, and pulled into the exit lane.

We got to my grandmother's house and I paid the taxi driver. Now I had to explain to my grandmother and my aunts and uncles and friends why I'd slept through my only mom's only funeral. I walked across the lawn, stopped short, and started laughing. Paul was waiting for me by the front door, standing next to Lee.

Paul and Lee loved my mom, and it would've been odd for them to have missed her funeral. Not as odd as my missing my mom's funeral.

But still odd. For the past few years Paul had been shaving the front half of his head and letting the back half grow, giving him a clown nimbus of hair on the back of his head. Normally he wore dresses and punk-rock T-shirts and had his remaining hair dyed bright orange. But for the funeral he'd borrowed a dark blue suit that was about four sizes too big for him, and he was wearing a jet-black wig that looked like it had been stolen from an Eastern European mannequin in 1975.

"You look amazing!" I said, laughing hysterically.

"I wanted to look respectable," Paul said, a little wounded.

"You look very respectable," I said, still laughing. "Did they let you inside the church?"

Lee said, "Moby, everyone's inside. You just missed your mom's funeral—you might want to stop laughing."

"You're right," I agreed, and stopped laughing. I looked at Paul and started laughing again. "Ha ha ha! You look like a clown!"

"I am a clown," Paul conceded, almost laughing.

I stifled my laughter. "Okay, I'll be serious," I said, and walked inside. My family was in the living room, eating little sandwiches and quietly grieving. When they saw me they all stood up and started lobbing questions at me. I explained, sort of. I said, "My alarm clock broke—I didn't wake up until Paul called me from the church." I left out the part where my subconscious reset the time on the clock, ensuring I'd miss the funeral.

"Your alarm clock broke? On today of all days? I'm so sorry," my uncle Dave said.

My subconscious was congratulating itself. *See?* it said. *They're not mad, they're not going to yell at you. They're sorry for you that you missed the funeral!* But I felt low and guilty. I loved my family, and by missing my mom's funeral, I'd created terrible and unnecessary stress for them. She was my mom, but she was also their daughter and sister and aunt.

"How was the funeral?" I asked. Then, sheepishly, "Is that something you ask?"

They told me about the funeral. It had been lovely, the sun coming in through the windows of the same Presbyterian church in Darien where my mom had been married, where my grandfather had taught Sunday school, where my grandmother volunteered, where I'd been baptized, and where we'd all spent Christmas Eves and Easters.

"Was there music?" I asked.

"Your mom wanted 'Morning Has Broken' by Cat Stevens played at her funeral, so we played that," Richard said. He started choking up, so I hugged him.

We went to the backyard and stood around with sandwiches and beers. I looked at Paul in his wig and started laughing again. "Where did you get that wig?" my aunt Anne asked, trying to suppress her giggles.

"You look like a Russian hit man," my uncle Joseph said. And soon we were all laughing, even my grandmother.

"Paul," my grandmother said, "we know what your hair looks like. You don't need to wear your wig." Paul pulled off his jet-black mannequin wig.

"Your hair's pink!" my astonished eight-year-old cousin Noah said.

"I dyed it last night," Paul said.

We were smiling in the backyard, holding beers and sandwiches, standing underneath the autumn sun. I looked at my aunts and uncles and grandmother and cousins and realized how much I loved my smart, funny, kind family. I imagined my mom watching us under the trees, laughing happily with Paul about his ludicrous hair. Maybe she was there, incorporeal, in the oak trees, watching her family, her husband, her child, her mother, her friends, all laughing, and for a moment at least, happy. And maybe then she said good-bye, going back through the leaves and the sky to God.

52

WEDDING RECEPTION

My mother had been dead for a week and I needed to go out.

It was Wednesday night, and on Wednesdays I went to Windows on the World at the top of the World Trade Center. Windows on the World was a bar and restaurant that was a time capsule from the 1980s, with post-disco furniture and wall-to-wall orange and brown carpets. It had been designed to impress tourists, so when my grandmother came to visit me in New York City, I would take her there, to the top of the Twin Towers, for lunch. She would get a chicken salad and an iced tea, and we'd walk over to the windows and look at the Woolworth Building, where my grandfather, her husband, had worked for decades. The windows came right down to the floor, so you could stand one inch away from the glass and float thirteen hundred feet above the world, with all of New York City and New Jersey laid out before you.

A year ago a club promoter had talked the owner of Windows on the World into letting him host parties on Wednesday nights. The DJs played Herb Alpert and Nancy Sinatra and Fatboy Slim. People drank and danced and stared out the window at New York and all its rivers and bridges.

At nine p.m. I was in my loft getting ready to go out. I put on a

Clash record, mixed myself a vodka and soda, and decided which of my polyester suits to wear. For the last few years I'd been going to the Goodwill on Prince Street and buying old polyester suits. Whenever I wore an old suit I got compliments, so I kept buying and wearing old $20 suits. Choice one was my beige three-piece polyester suit. I was getting chubby from drinking too much, so the suit was too tight and made me look and feel like a Southern insurance broker who produced amateur porn on weekends. Choice two was my light blue three-piece polyester suit. This one made me feel like an alcoholic doorman at a singles bar in Palm Beach in 1975. Choice three was my white three-piece suit. I had worn it too often and now it was stained brown at the cuffs and on the butt. The final choice was an old black tuxedo. I thought it made me look like an out-of-work caterer, but it got the most compliments of any of them, so it won out over the other polyester suits.

The Clash CD ended. I put on a Roxy Music album and mixed myself another drink. I made a pocket square out of some folded toilet paper—something I'd started doing because I didn't have any actual handkerchiefs—finished my second drink, and left my apartment. It had rained earlier, but now the wind was blowing. Clouds were being broken up and pushed out to sea. The streets were wet and empty.

I walked through SoHo, thinking about how it was changing. The galleries were leaving, the recording studios were leaving, the artists were leaving. Change in New York was exciting, even when it was awful. Even music was changing: hip-hop was transforming from being a voice of protest to a celebration of bottle service and expensive watches. Cities change, careers end, parents die.

I reached the Hudson River. A few years earlier, the riverfront had been abandoned and covered with transsexuals and homeless teenagers looking to sell sex and buy drugs. Now it was a sprawling construction site, with paths and playgrounds and picnic areas all being built next to the filthy water. I walked by the office buildings of lower Manhattan, all lit up with cleaning crews or Ritalin-fueled commodities traders. Eventually I came to the Twin Towers: these sentinels, stoically anchoring Manhattan like the bottom of a compass. The greatest, most subtle thing about the Twin Towers was when you could see the shadows of clouds on their faces. They were always taller than I expected. I got to the base of the south tower and stared up. I had done that a hundred times, and every time, it made me feel like gravity was inverted and I was falling upward.

The lobby of the south tower was full of drunk hipsters, waiting for the elevator to take them up 106 stories to Windows on the World. My friend Marcus was there, talking to the promoter. I'd known Marcus for a few years, and we had become steady drinking buddies, going out together five nights a week. He dressed like a skinny 1950s gigolo in old black suits, and he always carried an old leather briefcase with his flask tucked inside. When he saw me, he waved me over and we got on the elevator.

On the 106th floor we walked out of the elevators, taking in the long glowing bar on the left, the tables and booths on our right, and the dance floor in front of us. The DJ was playing a mash-up of the Chemical Brothers and the Velvet Underground. Marcus and I headed to the bar for cocktails.

We ordered four drinks, two each for both of us, and looked at the women gathered around the bar. I was a bald has-been musician and Marcus looked like a shorter, homeless David Lynch, but somehow we both kept dating beautiful women. We wore old suits that smelled like the Salvation Army. We got drunk and danced badly. We told terrible jokes. And by the end of the night, we usually found drunk women who were temporarily charmed by us.

We took our cocktails past the dance floor, greeting the DJ, who was now playing a track with a sitar and a breakbeat. We sat down in a booth next to our friends Florence and Beth. Florence was a Scottish writer with dark brown hair who wore Eisenhower-era dresses and horn-rim glasses. Beth was a pretty Irish book editor with long red hair who lived with her green-card husband in a tiny studio in Tribeca. Marcus put down his drink and said, "Florence, let's go make out in the bathroom!" They'd dated on and off for a few months, so she said, "Let's!" and they ran off.

I sat and drank, watching people dance and drink and flirt. By day we battled the human condition and went to therapists and lamented failed relationships and dead parents. But here, people were happy and drunk, bathed in soft lights and Ravi Shankar remixes. The consequences of drinking six nights a week hadn't found their way up to the 106th floor of the World Trade Center.

I finished my second drink and ordered another one. Marcus came back with Florence and they sat down, looking sweaty and bashful. "What happened?" I asked.

"Um, we made out in the bathroom," Marcus said. Florence laughed, jumped up, and headed to the bar.

"You made out? That's all you did?" I asked.

Marcus conceded, "And we had anal sex."

"In the bathroom? Just now?" I looked over at Florence, who was standing by the bar. She looked at me, laughed, and turned away. Beth put her drink down on the table. "Okay," she announced, "Moby and I are going to have anal sex in the bathroom, too."

"We are?" I asked. Beth and I had gone on a few dates and had sex on my roof late at night a couple of times before she had to go home to her green-card husband, but this was uncharted territory.

"Yes, we are."

There was a line at the bathrooms, since everyone was drunk and needed to pee or do cocaine in the privacy of their own toilet stall. "Wait," I said, pointing down a hallway leading away from Windows on the World, "there are bathrooms down there." We walked down the hall to a private event space that had been rented for a wedding party. A Jewish husband and a Korean bride, with their families and friends, all dancing to ABBA and looking out at Manhattan and enjoying their little slice of the future.

Beth and I snuck into the ladies' bathrooms off the event space, found a stall, stepped inside, and locked the door. We started making out, and then she pulled up her dress and stepped out of her underpants. I pulled down my tuxedo pants and my underwear, and we started having sex. Beth was loud, but we were drunk and a quarter-mile over New York City, so neither one of us cared. We could hear women coming in and out of the bathroom, and somebody saying, "Is someone having sex in there?"

I whispered to Beth, "Should we have anal sex?"

"Of course we should," she said.

Someone started banging on the door. "Finish up!"

"We will!" Beth shouted, and I started laughing. We finished, Beth pressed against the side of the stall, and me leaning on her. We pulled our clothes back on and tried to leave the stall casually, walking out under the harsh bathroom lights and the baleful glares of the waiting women.

An older woman smoking a cigarette and doing her makeup looked at me and said, casually, "You missed a spot."

I looked down and saw that I had semen drying on the front of my Salvation Army tuxedo trousers.

When we got back to our booths Marcus and Florence were sitting there with some of our friends. They all turned to us, silent and expectant. "Okay, yes, we just had anal sex in the bathroom," Beth said.

They all shouted, "Hooray!" as if she'd just gotten a promotion at work.

I stopped the waitress. "A Stoli and soda and a slice of lime for me, and a vodka gimlet for my lady friend, please."

She smiled. "Good choices."

The DJ played "I Feel Love" and our drinks arrived. I couldn't sit down because I loved the song, but I wanted to drink. So I tried to do both, moving around the dance floor with my vodka and soda as Donna Summer sang to me. The world was an empty cipher, falling into structure or chaos, and we responded with bathroom sex and Russian vodka and old disco.

I took my drink and walked to the windows, where I rested my head against the glass. I drank my vodka and stared down. The storm clouds were still being dispersed, and we were above them. I could see the delicate lights of the Brooklyn Bridge glowing through the clouds like a soft landing strip. I saw the Statue of Liberty in the harbor. And in the distance, I saw the ocean, black and cold. It was beautiful and unfathomable.

With my forehead pressed against the glass, I realized I was crying. I blamed the vodka and the beauty of New York City seen from the top of the Twin Towers. The DJ played Petula Clark's "Downtown." I finished my drink and turned my back on the world.

53

RAIN ON THE SKYLIGHTS

On a cold and rainy Sunday night everyone I knew was home nursing hangovers and watching bad TV. I wanted to go out and drink. I wanted to be invited to the best party I'd ever been to and to meet my unimpeachable soul mate. But I checked my e-mail and my answering machine, and then I checked them again. It was a cold, rainy Sunday night; there was nothing happening.

So I decided to order Chinese food and work on music. I picked up the phone and called my favorite vegan Chinese restaurant, Tsien Garden on Allen Street, and ordered what I always ordered: seitan with carrots and potatoes, carrot juice, brown rice, and a small salad. I knew that when the delivery boy showed up I'd be gripped by guilt. I'd stand at the elevator, warm and dry and wearing fuzzy slippers, and he'd be cold and wet and wearing a poncho, trying not to shiver as he handed me my wet bag of Chinese food.

Aside from the impending guilt, I felt cozy. The rain falling on my skylights and the wind whistling as it tried to find its way through the edges of my windows were two of my favorite sounds. I pretended that I was in a lonely castle tower, surveying Tolkien-map mountains, rather than in a loft building on the Lower East Side that used to be a slaughterhouse.

While I waited for my food I padded in my slippers down the hallway to my studio and turned on the equipment. First the power strips, then the synths and samplers. Then I loaded the discs into my Akai samplers, listening to them whir and click quietly as they took code from the discs and loaded it into their Japanese sampler brains. I climbed under a table and turned on my Soundcraft twenty-four-channel mixing desk, and finally I turned on the power amplifier for the speakers. My studio was up and running and making the calm hum that is the quiet background noise of a studio, like distant traffic or a beach at night.

I didn't know what I was going to work on, so I loaded up some old gospel samples I'd had for years but never figured out how to use. Years ago I'd written a fast euro track called "Why Does My Heart?" that used these samples. Luckily I'd never released it, as it was pretty bad. But I'd always loved the vocals and I wanted to write a song that would do them justice. For years I'd been collecting vanity-pressing gospel records from the 1940s and 1950s, and these samples had come from one of these old, dusty, home-produced records. I programmed a slow drumbeat, as it seemed more in keeping with the quality of these beautiful old samples than a 130-beats-per-minute techno drum pattern. These were plaintive, heartfelt voices—they didn't need to be shoehorned into a generic techno track. The samples fit well against this new, slow drum pattern. And then the doorbell rang.

I was hungry, and I did want my seitan and potatoes, but I had been getting into the obsessive hypnotic workflow that was better than liquor or drugs or sex or science-fiction books. I put my fuzzy slippers back on, grabbed my wallet, and let the delivery boy into the building. The elevator doors opened and it was just as I had feared. The delivery boy stood there, about five feet five inches tall, wearing a soaking-wet poncho. He even had plastic bags tied around his feet. He handed me the brown paper delivery bag, which was also dripping wet. *I'm the worst person on the planet*, I thought, *asking this poor man to ride his bike to my apartment so I can sit inside, warm, dry, self-obsessed, and well fed.*

"How much?" I asked.

He gave me a huge smile from underneath his waterlogged poncho hood. "Fourteen dollars, sir!"

I started to give him a $20 bill, then felt bad and gave him an extra $5 for a total of $25.

"Oh, thank you, sir! Good night!"

I opened the bag and unpacked my seitan and carrots and potatoes, putting them on an actual plate so I wouldn't feel too much like a sad vegan bachelor by himself on a rainy Sunday night. I sat down at my stainless-steel table with my plate of food, my box of salad, and my glass of carrot juice, and read *The Once and Future King*. I loved this book, and I'd read it over and over again, starting at the age of twelve. It never got old, and the parts toward the end always made me cry, even though I knew they were coming. In *The Once and Future King*, King Arthur is innocent and hapless and incapable of holding guilt or grudges. There's even a scene where's he sitting by himself, quietly mending his own socks. This was my literary hero when I was growing up: a guileless king who mended his own socks.

I finished my dinner and put my plate and glass in the sink. When I renovated my apartment I found most of what I needed in junk shops or in the garbage. The discarded sink came from the trash on Bond Street. The metal dish drainer I bought for five dollars on the Bowery. I found the $10 lampshades at a secondhand store in Chinatown. This was my little kitchen: it was simple and functional and it made me happy.

After washing my plate and glass and putting them in the drying rack I returned to my studio. The equipment was still on, gently sipping electricity. The work I'd been doing was paused exactly where I'd stopped, waiting patiently for me to return. I sat in front of my computer screen, hit "play," and listened to the track as I'd left it. The drums were rudimentary, but they sounded good with the vocal samples.

I chopped up the vocal samples so that they almost felt like a verse:

Why does my heart
Feel so bad?

Why does my soul
Feel so bad?

The vocals were in C major, but I wanted the track to have a mournful beginning, so I started with an A-minor piano chord. The sad A-minor chord felt so good against the first vocal sample that I went to the even darker and sadder E minor for the second sample. Then I went to G major for the third vocal line, creating an unresolved hope or optimism. I finished the verse with D major, ending on a light note. As the rain pattered against the skylights I lowered the room lights and sat in my chair, listening to the drums and the vocals and the chords looping over and over again.

I turned on an old digital synth from the late eighties that had a nice piano/string combination and played a descending melody over the chords and the vocals. It sounded nice, but it needed a chorus. The last chord of the verse was D major, so I went down a whole step for the chorus, starting with C major. It felt like a good, if obvious, start. Then from C major back to A minor, which sounded plaintive but hopeful over the vocal "He's opened doors." The I went from A minor to F major, and the chorus felt like a celebration. After that, back to C major, the expected resolution, anchoring the hope and joy of the chorus.

I sat back and felt that buzz I got only when I'd written something that might be good: a sense of space and expansion in and around my head, as if time were slowing and becoming richer. I needed to add orchestral strings, maybe just in the chorus. I wrote some simple string arrangements for the chorus, and they worked really well with the chord changes. The chorus started to soar, so I added a second string part of root notes and fifths and sevenths.

I wondered what else the song needed. I added some subtle cymbal crashes in the choruses and delicate ride cymbals in the verses. And after two hours, the song was done. Wait—did it need a bass part? The verses felt so resigned and the choruses felt so expansive and hopeful. I wondered if a bass part would make the song better, or if it would drag it down and make it too conventional and leaden. I tried playing a *basso ostinato* part over the verse and it sounded terrible—plodding and stiff.

Then I thought, *Maybe it doesn't need a bass part as much as it needs a bass sound.* I turned on my Roland Juno-106 synth and created a very simple and understated bass sound. All low end, no attack, no high end. Just simple, anchoring bass. I played it over the chords and it worked. Most people wouldn't even notice the bass; it just sat there underneath the song, holding it together.

I gave the song an uncomplicated structure, going from intro to verse to chorus to verse to minimal outro. And I then it was really done. I didn't know whether it was good; I didn't know whether anyone else would like it. But sitting cloistered in my tiny studio, sheltered from the cold rain, I thought it was complete and beautiful.

54

WINDOWLESS BEDROOM

Damian and I walked into Spy Bar in SoHo and saw Vanessa with her porn-star friend, Heidi. Vanessa was trying to look normal, so she was wearing a short skirt and a gray business jacket that almost covered her tattoos. "Oh, fuck," she said, putting down her drink, "you two."

I hadn't seen Vanessa since we split up, about a year before. When we broke up she threw the giant green Muppet-fur coat that Nina Hagen had given me in the garbage and tried to burn me with a candle. "Hi, Vanessa," Damian said.

"Hi, Damian," Vanessa said.

"Hi, Vanessa," I said. "My mom is dead."

She paused and her rage abated. "Okay, do you want a drink?"

"I've already had five drinks, but yes."

"Oh, this is my friend Heidi," Vanessa said, even though she'd introduced me to Heidi once before when we'd been dating. Heidi had a nest of bleached-blond hair and gigantic fake breasts underneath a tiny white T-shirt and a leather vest.

Heidi sized me up, clearly not remembering having met me before. "So you're the one who broke Vanessa's heart," she said.

"Well," I told her, "I like to think that we broke each other's hearts."

She laughed and looked at Damian. "Whoa," she said. "You're cute. I'd totally fuck you." Damian stood there, looking nervous.

I walked up to the bar and ordered tequila shots—eight of them, so we each had two. "Let's go," I said, and we all did our first tequila shot. "And again," I said, and I did my second shot while they all held theirs. "Come on," I said. "Don't be pussies. Drink your tequila." Heidi and Vanessa did theirs; Vanessa looked like she might throw up. I took Damian's second shot and did his, as well.

Vanessa had started to ask me, "So what happened to your—" when Heidi punched a stockbroker in the mouth.

"He grabbed my ass!" she yelled. "Motherfucker!" Black-clad security guards grabbed all of us, including the ass-fondling stockbroker, and threw us out on the street.

"What happened?" I asked once we were out on the sidewalk.

"That motherfucker grabbed my ass so I punched his fucking mouth!" Heidi said, straining against the security guard who was holding her back.

"You fucking whore!" the stockbroker with a bloody lip yelled at her.

"Whoa, asshole, shut the fuck up," a security guard said.

"She fucking punched me! Arrest her!" he demanded.

The security guards laughed. "Everyone just walk away and don't come back," the first guard said, like a stern elementary-school teacher. The bloody stockbroker was already walking north, toward Prince Street, and yelling, "Fucking whore!" over and over.

The security guard pointed south and told us, "Go that way." Then he went back inside. Vanessa and Heidi and Damian and I started walking south on Mercer Street.

"Do you want to go to Night of a Thousand Stevies?" Vanessa asked. Night of a Thousand Stevies was a party thrown by Johnny Dynell and Chi Chi Valenti where drag queens dressed up as their favorite incarnation of Stevie Nicks. Some dressed up as Fleetwood Mac–era Stevie Nicks. Some dressed up as mideighties Stevie Nicks. And the larger drag queens dressed up as midnineties Stevie Nicks.

We got into a cab in SoHo and went up West Street to the Meatpacking District. My mom was dead, but who cared? I didn't. Or I didn't want to. Why would I care about anything that didn't involve being drunk in this cab en route to a party full of drag queens dressed like Stevie Nicks? The outside world of dying parents and failing careers was sad and confusing. Alcohol didn't numb the pain, but it did turn it into an interesting place full of distorted mirrors. I wanted to choose what I felt and not spend any more time having my feelings foisted upon me. The world outside of lower Manhattan was loathsome and needed to be exorcised.

We pulled up to the club, at Fourteenth Street and the West Side Highway. "Damian!" I shouted as we got out of the taxi. "Let's go to Mars!"

"What's Mars?" Heidi asked.

Damian explained, "Mars was a club ten feet from here, where Moby used to DJ when he was sober. Now it's an empty lot."

We walked into the club. The DJ was playing "Edge of Seventeen" and the drag queens were all singing along underneath a forest of disco balls. "This is amazing!" I yelled. "I want to be Stevie!" I went to the bar and ordered another eight tequila shots, two for each of us. I drank my first shot, and then my second shot. Damian was holding his first shot, and his second was untouched. I picked it up and drank it.

"Moby," he said, "you need to slow down."

"And you need to drink more!" I said.

Vanessa and Heidi gave their shots to a tall transsexual vaguely dressed like Mick Fleetwood. "Let's dance!" Heidi said, and we walked onto the dance floor. Everywhere we looked, there were beautiful men dressed like Stevie Nicks. After a few minutes of dancing, I went back to the bar and ordered more tequila for myself. I did two more shots under a disco ball, hugged Johnny Dynell and told him I loved him, and returned to the dance floor.

The DJ played "Rhiannon" and Vanessa and I started kissing. I put my hand between her legs. "Oh man," she said, "come here." She walked me to a dark corner and stepped out of her panties. She undid the button on my pants and pulled down the zipper. The DJ played "Go Your Own Way" as Vanessa put me inside her. A drag queen named Stevie saw us and said, "Oh my God, the straight people are fucking!"

His friend said, "Ew, that is so gross!"

The DJ played a Stevie Nicks song I didn't know as a few more Stevies gathered around to watch Vanessa and me having sex in a corner of the dance floor. "Woo!" they were yelling. "You girls go!"

I felt taken care of by Vanessa and the beautiful Stevie trannies. This cloistered degeneracy felt like kindness, a buffer between me and all the sharp things I hated. We all lived in a place where things didn't work. Our lives weren't working, our parents were dying, our careers were falling apart, the city barely functioned. But at that moment Vanessa and I were having drunken sex on the dance floor surrounded by drag queens dressed like Stevie Nicks, and we had simply chosen not to care.

The DJ started playing "Edge of Seventeen" again. I pulled out and came on the dance floor. I leaned against Vanessa, drunk and sweaty and holding on to her. The Stevies clapped and went back to dancing.

"Where are my panties?" Vanessa asked. I looked around. The dance floor was filled with dancing Stevies.

"I think they're gone," I said.

"I'm going to find Heidi," she said.

I stood there, staggering and dancing in my own semen, surrounded by hundreds of incarnations of Stevie Nicks. I tried not to bump into them, but I couldn't help myself. I needed this, being surrounded and supported by all these beautiful Stevies. I closed my eyes and danced, feeling the bodies around me, hearing another Fleetwood Mac song playing while the transsexual Stevies sang along.

My mom was dead, but at that moment, it seemed remote and universal, like a badly named comet passing far away from Earth. Vanessa found me and we danced some more. I bought us more tequila, and after hearing "Edge of Seventeen" for the fourth time we stumbled outside and took a taxi back to her apartment. As we headed down Fifth Avenue, she leaned across the seat and started going down on me.

The taxi driver said, "Hey! Not in my cab!"

Vanessa stopped for a second, said, "Oh, relax," and kept going down on me. I laughed.

The cab driver kept mumbling, "Stupid fucking Americans, I hate this country."

Vanessa stopped again, said, "Then leave," and kept blowing me. The driver became even angrier, yelling in Arabic at his steering wheel and the coconut-scented pine tree hanging from his rearview mirror. He pulled up in front of Vanessa's door on the Bowery and slammed on the brakes. I gave him $20 and got out.

"I'm sorry, sir," I slurred, "she's a racist." And I shut the door.

In Vanessa's apartment her roommate was up, doing coke at the kitchen table. "Moby? What are you doing here?" he asked.

"Shut up, Jeremy," Vanessa said. "We're not getting back together. His mom died and we're having sex."

"Okay," he said. "Hi, Moby, nice to see you."

"Hi, Jeremy," I said. "Good night."

We walked into Vanessa's room and fell onto her bed. She said quietly, "I'm really sorry about your mom, Moby."

I kissed her forehead. "Thanks, Vanessa."

She fell asleep, snoring quietly on my shoulder. Her tiny room in this loft on the Bowery was a womb: no windows, pitch black, and quiet. I was drunk and the bed was spinning. Connecticut was forty miles away, but I knew it couldn't find me in New York City in this windowless closet at the back of a low-ceilinged loft.

The door was shut and Vanessa and Jeremy were my degenerate guardians, even if Vanessa was passed out and Jeremy was in the middle of a two-day coke bender. Vanessa's tiny, windowless bedroom was soundproofed, so all I could hear was Vanessa snoring next to me. In the morning the world would look for me, but for now, I was protected.

CHAIR WITH CIGARETTE BURNS

t was three a.m. in Switzerland and I had insomnia. I had flown to Zurich to play "Feeling So Real" and some other older songs at a local radio concert and I was heading back to New York in the morning. Most European cities at three a.m. are as still as empty theaters, but as a New Yorker the idea of a sleeping city was baffling to me. Even at five a.m. New York was alive with stumbling drunks and garbage trucks and crazy people screaming at fire hydrants.

I had finished my fifteen-minute oldies set for the radio station at nine p.m. and gone back to my budget hotel room. It was small and had a twin bed with stiff sheets, a desk chair with red foam rubber cushions, and a small black desk facing a window that looked out on a half-lit office building. I sat on the bed and ate a bowl of muesli and soy milk, trying to watch *Bonanza* in German.

At midnight I turned off the TV, put on my army jacket, put a Joy Division CD in my Discman, and left the hotel to wander around quiet, empty Zurich. The air coming down from the mountains and across the lake was cold; the only businesses open were an Arab grocery and a brothel called Sex USA. I'd been to Arab groceries, but even though I'd dated sex workers I'd never been to a brothel.

The city felt so empty that I would've been willing to pay $100 to spend time with a hooker just to know that there were other people awake and alive. I stood outside the brothel for a minute with "Insight" playing on my headphones before I accepted that I was too scared to walk into a brothel. I stopped at the Arab grocery and bought a bottle of fizzy water before walking to the train station, where junkies slept on the sidewalk swaddled in blankets and leather jackets. After making sure they were breathing, I walked back to the hotel.

I got back to my room at two a.m. I spent a few minutes reading a Nelson DeMille paperback I'd bought in the airport but ended up sitting in the desk chair with the cigarette burns on the red cushions and staring at the empty office building across the street. It had been two months since my mom had died, and I still hadn't grieved conventionally, the way that I thought a son should grieve for his mother. Immediately after she died I went into the bathroom of her hospice room and sobbed in darkness for five minutes. But apart from a few drunken sniffles I hadn't really cried since.

So many people had died in my life—maybe death had just become a normal part of being alive. My grandfathers were dead, my father was dead, my father's mother was dead, three of my friends from high school were dead, and I couldn't count the people I knew from New York nightclubs who had been killed by AIDS or gunshots. And now my mom was on the list of people I'd known who had at one point been alive.

I was supposed to grieve, but grief was a function of missing someone and lamenting the abrupt end of their life. I missed talking to my mom and visiting her. But I couldn't say that her life had been cut short or ended abruptly. She had quit smoking three years before she died, but it was hard to shake my fist at God and curse the cruelty and unfairness of the death of a former smoker in her late fifties who'd died of lung cancer after an illness of many months.

It was hard to accept that the woman I'd known since I was a two-celled zygote no longer existed. Sometimes I'd pick up the phone to call her and realize that no, she was gone. I didn't grieve when that happened, but I did miss her and think about the emptiness left when someone died, as if they'd simply been removed from the world. Their clothes still sat on hangers in closets. Their shampoo still sat on a shelf in the shower. The things that marked their presence in the world were still there, but the person was gone.

I took out a sheet of hotel stationery and sat at the scratched desk to write a journal entry about my lack of grief and how confusing it was. I held the plastic hotel pen over the paper and thought about my mother's life. All of her ambitions. All of her disappointments. All of her sadness. I remembered how when I was growing up she would stand on our back porch at night, smoking and crying.

Thinking of her standing underneath a twenty-five-watt bulb and crying as she longed for a life that she didn't have, I put down the pen and started to cry. I lay down on the bed, buried my face in the cheap foam-rubber pillow, and sobbed. I wasn't grieving my loss, I was grieving hers.

She had been so smart, so creative, so funny, and had ended up with a life that had disappointed her. She had loving friends and family, but I knew in her heart of hearts she had disappointed herself. She'd wanted to live in a city, paint and make music, and be around other artists. She wanted to have art shows and hang out in galleries, but her shyness prevented her from showing her remarkable paintings to anyone. So she ended up in the suburb where she'd grown up—a place she hated, but a place that was safe and familiar.

The more I thought about her sadness and disappointment, the more I sobbed into the pillow. That was the unfairness. Not that she'd died relatively young of lung cancer. But that she'd bitterly blamed herself for not creating the life that she'd longed for. That was the tragedy: that she had let her fear and caution keep her from having the life that she'd wanted. The cigarettes and the junk food helped the cancer grow, but deep down I knew that her frustration and sadness had killed her.

I cried for an hour into the stiff pillowcase, mourning not her death but her compromised life. I cried because I missed her insights and her intelligence and the sound of her voice. But mainly I cried for the life she'd wanted but didn't have.

56

MELTING POOLS OF SNOW

February and March in New York are like twin bullies. One trips you into the mud while the other kicks you in the stomach when you're down. Now and then they give you the tiniest glimmer of hope that winter won't last forever—but then they take your hope and cover it in piles of filthy snow.

It was the end of February 1999 and I was hungover. Since I'd started drinking again I'd developed an odd love for hangovers. They seemed like a nauseous lifeline between me and my drunken literary heroes. When I was walking down Houston Street, hungover in the freezing rain, I would think to myself, *I wonder if Dylan Thomas was ever hungover in the rain on Houston Street?* If geniuses like Thomas and Faulkner and Bukowski had chosen a life of drunkenness, then clearly I was right to be following in their dissipated footsteps.

The night before had started at ten p.m. in an old Mafia bar on Mulberry Street, then moved to a party on Crosby Street and another bar on Broome Street, and had ended with beer and vodka and a four-some at five a.m. in my apartment with Marcus and Jillian and Jillian's friend Dahlia.

Now it was two p.m. and I was hungover, sitting on a wet bench in a park on the south side of Houston Street, between Chrystie and Forsyth. My lawyer had faxed me this morning to let me know that he'd just received the termination agreement: I'd officially been dropped by Elektra Records. I had hoped my contract with Elektra would weather the failure of *Animal Rights*, but it hadn't. I had been expecting this termination agreement for almost a year, ever since my manager, Barry, had been on the phone to the president of Elektra.

"So how are things going with Moby?" Barry asked.

"Well, we're having a hard time with all our British bands right now," the president said.

Barry paused politely. "Um, you do know that Moby is neither British nor a band?"

So it wasn't surprising that I'd been dropped. I was still signed to my European label, Mute records, because they had never dropped anyone. I was grateful to still have a European label, but it was hard to feel terribly special when you remained undropped on a label that had never dropped a single artist.

The bench I was sitting on was missing a few of its slats. I was wearing a gray Salvation Army overcoat and listening to some of my new songs on a MiniDisc player.

One song in particular, "Porcelain," didn't make sense to me. I had been working on it for a month and I just couldn't finish it. I liked some of its elements but the mix was soft and mushy, and it didn't really have a chorus. It felt more like a B-side than an album track. Of course, that was assuming that anyone would allow me to release another album.

While I hadn't been dropped by Mute there was no guarantee that they would like my new music enough to release it. My managers had known for months that I was going to be dropped from Elektra, so they had been meeting with different labels in the States to pursue a new American record deal. Chris Blackwell, who'd started Island Records, had expressed some polite interest. Apart from him, every label who'd heard my new music had said either no or nothing at all.

Some A & R people had been kind, returning my managers' phone calls and letting them know that they didn't think that I was a good fit for their labels. Some A & R people had been hostile, calling my managers just to tell them how much they disliked me as a person or as a musician or both. And some A & R people simply never returned my managers' calls.

I turned off my MiniDisc player and admitted to myself that my career as a musician was probably over. My last record had failed and the songs I was working on were inadequate and poorly mixed. I kept the headphones on my ears to keep them warm. Sad and defeated, I conceded that if this album were actually released it would disappear into obscurity. Maybe I was at the end of Elisabeth Kübler-Ross's stages of grief: acceptance. I accepted that my ten-year run as a professional musician had come to an ignominious end. I accepted that my mother was dead.

From my bench I could see homeless men standing in the line at the soup kitchen on Forsyth. In a nearby playground a four-year-old and his parents tried to have urban winter playtime in the slush. The buses and taxis were sitting in traffic up the street and honking pointlessly.

My heart leaped as I saw a couple of rats run out of the public toilets and into the bushes. To be clear, my heart leaped with happiness, because I loved rats. When I was a baby in Harlem my parents had a menagerie of two cats, three lab rats, and one dog in our basement apartment. The first picture taken of me as an infant was me in my baby bath while the dog, cats, and rats all watched me. My parents fought constantly in that basement apartment before my dad died, when I was two. I don't remember anything before I was two and a half years old, but since my parents were screaming at each other I assume the only calm and reassuring things in our basement apartment in Harlem were the dog, the cats, and the rats. Now when I saw rats on the street my limbic system woke up and told me I had seen friends.

I thought about listening to "Porcelain" again to see if I could think of anything that would fix it. But I'd listened to it a hundred times and it wasn't getting better, so instead I thought about what other jobs I could do. I had studied philosophy; maybe I could teach philosophy at a community college somewhere in New England. I loved architecture; maybe I could go back to school and become an architect.

I watched a few more rats running out of the public toilets and thought that maybe I was wrong. Maybe "Porcelain" and the rest of my new songs weren't as mediocre as I imagined them to be. I turned on my MiniDisc player and listened to "Porcelain" again with fresh ears. No. It was just as inadequate and badly produced and badly mixed as I'd thought. I knew that the same song might actually be good in a hands of a better engineer, or better mixer, or better songwriter.

My friend Ysabel was a graphic designer, and in a fit of optimism she'd helped me mock up some fake art in case Mute let me release another album. I even had an album title I liked, *Play.* There was a playground on the corner of Mulberry and Spring, and one hungover morning I'd walked by it and seen the word PLAY! painted in giant letters on the wall by the basketball court. It seemed like a good choice for an album title, and maybe a reminder to me that I shouldn't be such a worrywart.

But now I assumed that the songs and the title and the fake artwork would be put on a shelf, maybe to be dusted off in ten years and looked at wistfully when I was back in Connecticut, living in a studio apartment by a 7-Eleven. Luckily even if I taught philosophy at a community college or became an architect I'd still be able to work on music in my spare time. And, I thought, I should be grateful.

All I'd hoped for ten years earlier was to be able to live in New York City, to get a few DJing jobs, and maybe to release a couple of dance singles. All that and more had happened, and I *was* grateful. I'd traveled the world and made records and stood onstage in front of thousands of people. Careers end, I told myself. That was the way of things. If this was the end of my career, that was okay. I'd had a remarkable and unexpected run. I took my MiniDisc player; stood up from the cold, broken bench; and walked home through the melting pools of snow.

57

BEIGE CAMRY

My friend Gregor and I needed to get to Boston to help Paul with his student film about a sex shop being taken over by aliens. Gregor was a kindhearted Russian from Brighton Beach; he and I had been friends since the early nineties, when he'd been an NYU film student living in my neighborhood. After film school he'd moved to LA to produce obscure indie films but had ended up making his living producing hard-core porn in the San Fernando Valley.

The irony in his being a porn producer was that he was a sober Christian who only dated other Christians. One time, an actress on one of his films had asked him out on a date after she'd finished shooting a scene. She stood before him, naked and covered with semen, and asked him if he wanted to get a cup of coffee.

"No thanks," he'd said. "I don't like to mix work and pleasure."

"Well, that's ironic," she said, and went to wipe the semen off her body.

Gregor couldn't drive: he'd been working nonstop in LA and hadn't slept in two days, so he couldn't keep his eyes open. He asked me to drive his car. I agreed, with two caveats. The first was that I didn't have a driver's license. The second was that while I drove I wanted to listen to a cassette of the music I was working on for my next album. He ac-

cepted both conditions—he just wanted to curl up in the backseat of his
1990 beige Toyota Camry and sleep for a few hours.

I started the car and tried to remember how to drive. My license had
expired in 1993 and I hadn't driven in almost five years. In high school
I'd mindlessly driven my mom's red Chevy Chevette down I-95, eating
Cheetos and listening to Bad Brains cassettes. "I'm a member of the
right brigade," I'd scream with a mouthful of Cheetos, ignoring the cars
around me and secretly hoping to crash into a truck, incinerating in a
romantic suburban Chevette fireball. Now, driving east on Houston
Street at eleven p.m. on a cold Sunday night, I was trying to be the best
and least conspicuous driver on the planet, so I wouldn't get pulled over
and arrested.

"Let me know if the music's too loud, Gregor," I said. "Gregor?" I
looked in the backseat. Gregor had a gray T-shirt wrapped around his
face and was already asleep, dead to the world.

While I was happy to spend two days in a sex shop to help Paul
make his alien-invasion movie, I was also glad to have the opportunity
to hear how the music for my new album sounded in a car.

Daniel Miller at Mute had heard some of the music I was working
on and had politely agreed to release it on his label. I still assumed my
career as a musician was over, but maybe *Play* would be my obscure
swan song before I disappeared into the bowels of New England to
teach community college and die on a futon.

I pulled onto the FDR Drive, drove north, and pressed "play" on the
tape deck. I smiled, realizing that whenever anyone pressed "play" on a
tape deck or a CD player, I'd get a tenth of a second of free advertising.
The first song on the cassette, "Honey," sounded okay, largely because
I hadn't mixed it. Mario Caldato Jr. had mixed it—he had also mixed
most of the Beastie Boys' albums and he was very good.

I pulled off the FDR to take the secret toll-free route out of Manhattan that my grandfather had taught me: over the Third Avenue Bridge,
through the South Bronx and Hunts Point, past the Golden Lady strip
club and the fish markets, and up the entrance ramp to 687 and I-95.
This was the way my grandfather had always taken us out of the city,

and following the route made me feel connected to him. When I was a little boy he would let me sit in the front seat of his Toronado, the fanciest car I'd ever been in, as we drove out of the city after visiting his office at the Woolworth Building and headed back to Connecticut. His car smelled like cigarettes and aftershave, and he always had 1010 WINS news on the radio.

As a seven-year-old in 1972 riding through Harlem and the South Bronx, I'd look out the car window at the empty lots and burned-out buildings, then at my grandfather in his perfect suit and his carefully cropped steel-gray hair. He radiated stability, like a war veteran super-hero. The world outside the car windows was horrifying. The world I had at home with my mom and her Hells Angels boyfriend was chaotic. But here in his car I was wrapped in a cocoon of my grandfather's aftershave and ex-Marine competence. If he had said in his deep voice, "So, Moby, how about we drive for the next ten years, stopping only when it's time for you to go to college?" I would have desperately and happily said, "Yes, please."

Now it was 1998 and I was illegally driving an old Camry through the Bronx with a passed-out pornographer in the backseat. I stopped at the traffic light by Hunts Point Market in the Bronx. Even by jaded New York criteria, Hunts Point Produce Market was an unspeakably terrible place. It was where crack-addicted and diseased hookers went to give $10 blow jobs to truckers and psychopaths. As we waited at the light I could see the emaciated prostitutes standing on five-inch heels in the recesses of the underpass. This was a lifeless place, the concrete stained black with decades of truck and car exhaust.

I drove up the entrance ramp to route 687 as the next song, an in-strumental without a name, began. In my rearview mirror I could see the jagged towers of Manhattan. The pianos and strings kicked in. To my right were abandoned warehouses and tall flames from natural-gas storage tanks. Contrasted with this blasted urban blight populated by dying hookers the music sounded sad and hopeful.

On I-95, "Bodyrock" came on. It wasn't as good as a well-mixed song by the Chemical Brothers or the Prodigy, but with its brittle guitars it had a nice punk-rock quality. When it ended I fast-forwarded the cassette past a few generic techno tracks I'd written. They weren't bad, but they weren't very special and didn't make sense on this primarily down-tempo album.

When we reached Port Chester, "Natural Blues" came on the tape. The contrast between the plaintive vocals and the digital strings and drums sounded surprisingly good late at night.

I'd driven this empty stretch of freeway a few thousand times in the eighties. After dropping out of UConn in 1984 I'd lived at my mom's house in Darien and gotten a job DJing at a small run-down bar in Port Chester called the Beat. It held forty-five people and was dark and filthy, but it was the only counterculture hangout in the area, and I was thrilled to be paid $25 a night to DJ from ten p.m. until five a.m. I was nineteen and my girlfriend was in high school and living with her billionaire mother in a twelve-bedroom waterfront mansion in Greenwich, which was a few miles away from where I worked in Port Chester. I'd borrow my mom's car, try to have sex with my girlfriend in the third-floor bedroom of her mother's mansion, and then go to the Beat and drink vodka and play New Order and Johnny Cash records for seven hours to unemployed artists and methadone addicts. At six a.m. I'd drive back to my mom's house and sleep until two p.m. on the same sheets and in the same twin bed I'd had since junior high school.

"Natural Blues" ended and we drove through Greenwich as "South Side" came on. I'd mixed most of the songs on *Play* in my bedroom, but I'd rented a real recording studio to mix "South Side" and it almost sounded professional. My vocals sounded kind of thin in the choruses and I wondered if I could find a female singer to sing the song with me, almost as a duet. Compared to the other songs on the record, "South Side" was perhaps too straight and conventional. Then again, nobody was going to hear the music on this album, so why did I care?

A dozen people might listen to this, my last album, and then I'd move to a condo by the freeway in Connecticut. When I moved back to

Connecticut I'd probably end up sitting on my futon, drinking Bud Light, and watching *Wheel of Fortune* until I died of whatever disease would be merciful enough to kill me.

I drove through Darien, where I had lived for decades. For twenty years I had driven my bike or moped or borrowed car down every road in Darien. For twenty years I'd longed for every unattainable preppy girl in Darien. I'd started my first punk-rock and new-wave bands here and lost my virginity here—and while living in this small, pretty town I'd quietly learned to fear everyone and everything.

"Run On" started with an ostinato piano part, and I passed the exit for the Holiday Inn where Robert Downey Jr. and his family had lived when they were moving out of Darien. Robert Downey Jr. had been my best friend in third grade. We'd bonded because we were both neurotic eight-year-olds, and his parents and my mom were the only adults in Darien who smoked pot. In the autumn of 1973, Robert, his sister, and I made a short movie with the Super 8 camera belonging to his dad, Robert Downey Sr. We reenacted a scene from the TV show *Ironside*, with Robert playing a wounded cop and his sister and I playing his grieving wife and partner. Robert's mom developed the film, and we sat in the Downeys' kitchen on Mansfield Avenue and watched our three-minute movie projected against the back of their basement door.

Then on a sad day in 1974 Robert's parents decided to move to Essex, an hour up the Connecticut coast. Robert and his mom and sister had moved into the Holiday Inn before moving to Essex; I'd visited them with my mom to say good-bye and swim in the hotel pool. As we got off the elevator Robert and his sister ran barefoot out of their room to meet us and ran through a pile of broken glass in front of the ice machine. The trip to visit my best friend involved all of us in the bathroom cleaning glass and blood out of the feet of Robert Downey Jr. and his sister while his mom and my mom smoked pot.

The Holiday Inn was also where I'd gone in 1993 for my ten-year high school reunion. There had been a picture of me on a table by the entrance with a sign that said DHS CLASS OF 1983 IN THE NEWS! Set esc tr 60The reunion organizers had found a short *People* magazine piece on me, blown it up, and put it on a stand next to pictures of some other '83 alumni. I'd hovered around the picture, thinking that one of the girls I'd had a crush on in high school would deign to notice me now that they were aging and I was almost famous. I hoped that in the ten years since we'd graduated their standards had dropped to the point where falling in love with a balding musician wasn't inconceivable. But by ten p.m. I was still unsuccessfully hovering, so I left the reunion and took a taxi back to my mom's house to sleep on her couch.

I drove through Westport at exactly the speed limit and fast-forwarded the cassette through some new punk-rock songs that I knew wouldn't make it onto the album. We came into Bridgeport as an instrumental I'd tentatively named "Inside" started playing. Bridgeport was a city of empty warehouses, drug dens, and giant factories rusting by the water. At one a.m., "Inside" made the squalor look stoic and beautiful. Everything outside the car felt slower and emptier. The highway lights strobed by and the strings of industrial lights around the power plant looked delicate, like Christmas Eve on the moon.

After Bridgeport came Stratford. My mom and I had lived in Stratford for two years in the midseventies when we had been really, really poor. We'd always been poor, but when my mom and I lived in Stratford we hit new lows of poverty. My mom was out of work, so we'd gotten by on welfare and food stamps and money borrowed from her friends and parents. One time in 1974 my mom had given me $20 in food stamps to buy groceries at the supermarket near the house where we rented two rooms. After he rang up the groceries, the old man working the cash register shook his head and said, "Keep your food stamps, son, this is on me." I took the small bag of groceries. He smiled sadly and said, "Good luck, little guy."

I was scared the whole two years I spent in Stratford. Scared of being poor, scared of the gangs who hung around outside of my elementary school, scared of all the kids who were bigger than me. Just scared.

I passed the gas station in Stratford where I'd ended up lost when I was nine years old. I'd been walking home from a friend's public-housing apartment and had ended up at the gas station after walking through empty streets and housing projects for two hours. I started crying: "I'm lost, can you call my mom?" They found her number in the phone book, called her, and said, "You've got a lost little boy here, ma'am." She picked me up and drove me home. I sat in the front seat of her Chevy Vega and couldn't stop crying.

With Gregor snoring in the backseat, I drove by the exit for the Stratford sporting goods store. When I was ten I'd saved five dollars from doing odd jobs for our neighbor and gone there to buy a trophy with my name on it. I wasn't very good at sports, but I really wanted a trophy with my name on it. The man behind the counter knew me: I'd been coming in once a week to look at the blank trophies. I took out my five crumpled dollar bills from the pocket of my blue windbreaker and asked about buying a small gold-cup trophy. "I'm sorry," he said, "we can only sell trophies to schools and teams." Then he tried to encourage me: "One day you'll be a great athlete and have lots of trophies!" I walked home with my five dollars to watch *Star Trek* on our black-and-white TV with a clothes hanger for an antenna.

As we left Stratford and drove over the Housatonic River, "Down Slow" came on. I checked the backseat. Gregor was still asleep. Or passed out. Or dead. I fast-forwarded through a few songs, and "My Weakness" started playing. Gregor woke up and pulled himself up to a seated position. "Where are we?" he asked.

"New Haven," I said. "You've been asleep for a while."

"Oh. What is this music?"

"Something I'm working on."

"Hmm. I like it." Then he lay down and went back to sleep. At least now I knew he wasn't dead.

The strings in "My Weakness" built and crescendoed as I drove out of New Haven. In the early seventies, my mom and I spent our weekends going to communes near New Haven, or sometimes visiting hippies she knew in Old Saybrook or Old Lyme.

When we visited communes I'd wonder if I'd be sharing a bed with hippies or if I'd get my own sleeping bag. Or if in the morning I'd be wandering around trying to find someone who wasn't passed out, so I could get help making breakfast. I never asked my mom where we were going—I knew it wasn't my place. I could ask about songs on the radio, though.

"Is this song about a bald woman?" eight-year-old me asked my mom.

"This song?" she asked, exhaling cigarette smoke.

"Yes, the chorus, 'bald-headed woman'?" I asked.

She started laughing and laughing, so I started laughing. Then she started singing along with the Bee Gees: "Bald-headed woman to me!" I sang along too.

"What are they really saying?" I asked during the bridge.

She laughed some more. "'More than a woman,'" she explained. "But 'bald-headed woman' is better."

"My Weakness" ended and "Guitar Flute and String" played as we sped further east through Connecticut on the way to Boston. The road became even darker and emptier.

"The Sky Is Broken" came on. I liked this song. I could write romantic songs, but I couldn't battle my panic attacks long enough to actually have relationships. "The Sky Is Broken" was about a relationship I'd never had, with vulnerability and closeness and trust. My relationships were desperate and fueled by panic. Before we'd broken up Sarah had told me that I was like a scared, beaten dog who lived under a porch. And I agreed. I wanted to finally move out from under the porch and live in the daylight, but I couldn't.

Under the porch was lonely and dark. But it was familiar, and nothing could really hurt me there. If I came out from under the porch and ran around in the light I would be seen for who I really was: the inadequate eight-year-old boy with food stamps in his pocket. If I enjoyed life or opened up to anyone I would be ridiculed and hurt. Then I'd slink back under the porch, remonstrating with myself for ever leaving in the first place. Better to stay under the porch and be safe than to leave and be hurt.

I was single and lonely and wanted to end this cycle of giving in to panic and running away from love. At some point soon I needed to find a woman who would love me for who I was and let me know that I was okay. I didn't actually want to spend my life having drunken one-night stands. I wanted to sleep next to someone and feel safe. "Speak to me in the middle of the night," my voice said on the cassette as I drove through the darkness. I would trade all the parties and vodka and threesomes and foursomes and sevensomes for one moment of safety and comfort, speaking quietly to someone I loved in the middle of the night.

"The Sky Is Broken" ended. I turned off the cassette and drove down the highway in silence.

AFTERWORD

When I first talked to a literary agent about writing a memoir I mentioned that it would be really fun to hire a writer and get them to write this book for me. Lots of people hire other people to write their books, sometimes with great results. *The Dirt* by Mötley Crüe, for example. They, Mötley Crüe, told Neil Strauss their amazing stories and he crafted them into an amazing book. So, I wondered, why couldn't I do something similar?

It seemed so seductive and appealing to spend a few hours a week telling my stories to a professional writer and letting them craft something wonderful for which I could take most of the credit. Then my literary agent said, "You're descended from Herman Melville. You need to at least try to write the book on your own."

With regret, I agreed. To be descended from Herman Melville and not try to write my own memoir would seem like a bit of a hereditary affront. After accepting that no one was going to write my memoir for me, I opened up my laptop and started writing.

And, happily, it turned out that I love to write. Sitting down and spending hours, and ultimately months, reinhabiting my past and writing about it is like heaven to me. It's narcissistic time travel.

An author authoring their own book shouldn't be surprising or something for which they deserve a pat on the back. It's akin to the time I saw Alicia Keys perform at an MTV awards show. She played piano. And after her performance the people around me were amazed. "She plays piano!" they crowed. Which made me wonder when it became surprising for a musician to know how to play an instrument. Or for a writer to write their own book.

If my book is bad it's bad because of me. I can't blame anyone. Of course if it's good I will give justified credit to Daniel Greenberg and Scott Moyers and Gavin Edwards, who helped me to push my life through the winnowing filter of editing and rewriting.

Thanks.

MOBY

P.S. I've changed some names and identifying characteristics out of respect to other people and have modified some sequences and details of events, but all the stories in this book actually happened.

IMAGE CREDITS TK